EX LIBRIS
BPP-03743 © 1994 Antioch Publishing
T3-BNU-883

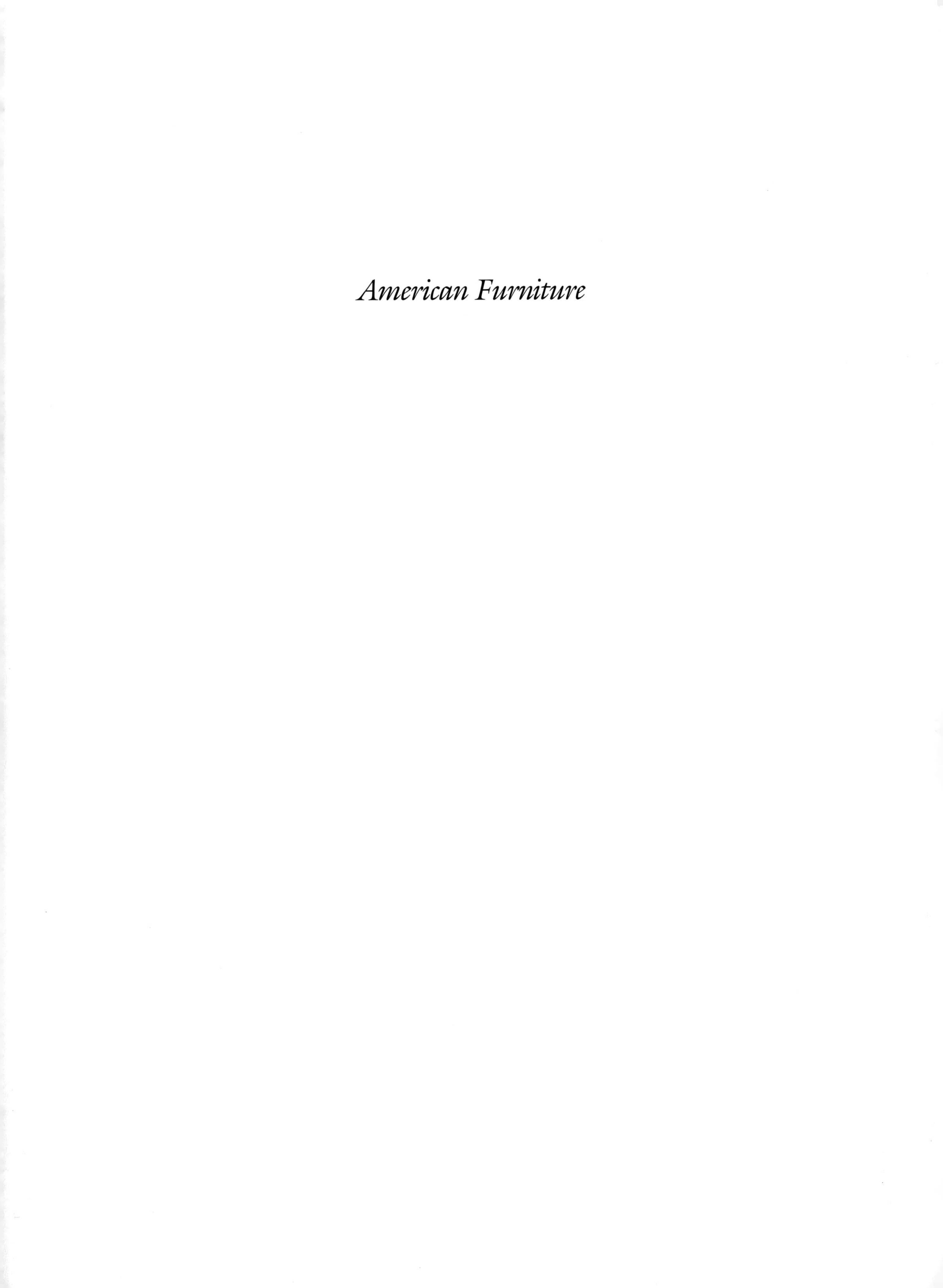

American Furniture

AMERICAN FURNITURE 1995

Edited by Luke Beckerdite
and William N. Hosley

Published by the CHIPSTONE FOUNDATION

Distributed by University Press of New England

Hanover and London

Cover Illustration: Detail of a chest with drawers, probably Hadley, Massachusetts, 1695–1700. (Courtesy, Wadsworth Atheneum.)

Design: Wynne Patterson
Photography: Gavin Ashworth, New York, New York

Published by the Chipstone Foundation
Distributed by University Press of New England, Hanover, NH 03755

Printed in the United States of America 5 4 3 2 1
ISSN 1069-4188
ISBN 0-87451-727-3

Contents

Editorial Statement

American Furniture is an interdisciplinary journal dedicated to advancing knowledge of furniture made or used in the Americas from the seventeenth century to the present. Authors are encouraged to submit articles on any aspect of furniture history, essays on conservation and historic technology, reproductions of transcripts of such documents as account books and inventories, annotated photographs of new furniture discoveries, and book and exhibition reviews. References for compiling an annual bibliography also are welcome.

Manuscripts must be typed, double-spaced, illustrated with 8" × 10" black-and-white prints or transparencies, and prepared in accordance with the *Chicago Manual of Style*. Computer disk copy is requested but not required. The Chipstone Foundation will offer significant honoraria for manuscripts accepted for publication and reimburse authors for all photography approved in writing by the editor.

Luke Beckerdite

Preface

The Chipstone Foundation was organized in 1965 by Stanley Stone and Polly Mariner Stone of Fox Point, Wisconsin. Representing the culmination of their shared experiences in collecting American furniture, American historical prints, and early English pottery, the foundation was created with the dual purpose of preserving and interpreting their collection and stimulating research and education in the decorative arts.

The Stones began collecting American decorative arts in 1946, and by 1964 it became apparent to them that provisions should be made to deal with their collection. With the counsel of their friend Charles Montgomery, the Stones decided that their collection should be published and exhibited.

Following Stanley Stone's death in 1987, the foundation was activated by an initial endowment provided by Mrs. Stone. This generous donation allowed the foundation to institute its research and grant programs, begin work on three collection catalogues, and launch an important new journal, *American Furniture*.

Mrs. Stone passed away in May of this year, but the foundation and its educational endeavors survive as a testament to her and Mr. Stone's vision and commitment to the decorative arts field.

Allen M. Taylor

Introduction

Luke Beckerdite

The 1995 volume of *American Furniture* is largely comprised of papers presented at "Diversity and Innovation in American Regional Furniture," a 1993 symposium in Hartford, Connecticut, sponsored by the Wadsworth Atheneum, Trinity College, and the Chipstone Foundation. As William Hosley notes in "Regional Furniture/Regional Life," the program sought to answer a variety of questions central to regional furniture studies by assembling a group of scholars whose backgrounds, interests, and analytical methods are as diverse as the objects they discussed. In fact, the symposium could have been titled "Material Culture and the Study of American Life" or "Perspectives on American Furniture"—the same names chosen for two important Winterthur Conferences and their published proceedings.[1]

Material Culture and the Study of American Life (1975) began with the assumption that "the study of artifacts has altered our perception of American history," a point that was both challenged and qualified by several of its contributors. Social historian Cary Carson, for example, maintained that although material culture had contributed little "to developing the *main themes* of American history" objects had enormous potential for the study of people, family roles and work routines, household, regional, and interregional economies, and a broad range of social and cultural issues.[2] Several of the articles in this volume of *American Furniture* support that assertion. In "Furniture as Social History: Gender, Property, and Memory in the Decorative Arts," Laurel Ulrich's brilliant analysis of the social construction of gender in furniture and female ownership and inheritance greatly enhances our understanding of the inequalities that attended female life during the late seventeenth and eighteenth centuries. Edward S. Cooke's "Social Economy of the Preindustrial Joiner in Western Connecticut, 1750–1800" demonstrates how the products of tradesmen "emanated from and responded to a specific set of social relationships" and how craft traditions are useful in charting the movement and convergence of people, ideas, and cultures. In a somewhat different vein, Neil Kamil's "Hidden in Plain Sight: Disappearance and Material Life in Colonial New York" explores the relationship among artisanry, ethnic identity, and the mastery of cultural space by examining the transatlantic context of the Boston leather chair and its New York derivatives. Either directly or indirectly, these essays reveal that material culture studies *are* altering our perception of American history and that they may eventually influence our interpretations of major historical themes.

Perspectives on American Furniture (1989) evaluated traditional methodologies for furniture studies and suggested a range of new ones.[3] The same is true of *American Furniture* 1995. Arguing for a more contextual approach to the study of American furniture, Philip Zea's "Diversity and Regionalism in Rural New England Furniture" dispels numerous misconceptions about vernacular furniture by showing how diversity and choice are the products of "rural culture, economy, technique, and design." Kevin Sweeney's "Regions and the Study of Material Culture: Explorations Along the Connecticut River" uses furniture and other artifacts to illustrate problems inherent in the concept of regionalism and to emphasize the translocal qualities of communities and craft traditions that are often simplistically termed "traditional" or "folk." In "Definition and Diaspora of Regional Style: The Worcester County Model," Donna Baron points out the intimate relationship between the development and diffusion of regional style and new technologies, transportation systems, communication systems, and marketing strategies. Finally, William Hosley's article shows how current regional scholarship has emerged from an "ideological battle between historicism and modernism, regionalism and aesthetics." His sensitive and skillful analysis of furniture, architecture, gravestones, and other objects leaves little doubt that a "sense of place" has been and remains an integral component of American life.

Clearly, the concept of diversity is central to both the theme and the message of this issue of *American Furniture*. The insightful interpretations found in these articles reflect diverse points of view by individuals whose methods collectively traverse the boundaries of social, cultural, and economic history and theory, sociology, anthropology, art history, and traditional connoisseurship. More importantly, they signal the need for a "new connoisseurship"—one that acknowledges that *all* artifacts are potentially significant historical documents, even those that fail to meet the shifting, subjective, aesthetic requirements of "art."[4]

To continue this dialogue, the Chipstone Foundation and the Colonial Williamsburg Foundation will cosponsor a symposium in November 1997 entitled "A Region of Regions: Cultural Diversity and the Furniture Trade in the Early South." The papers presented at the symposium will appear in that year's volume of *American Furniture*. For information on registration, please contact: Deborah Chapman, Office of Special Events, Colonial Williamsburg Foundation, P.O. Box 1776, Williamsburg, Virginia 23187-1776.

1. The conferences were held at the Winterthur Museum in 1975 and 1985 respectively.

2. Ian M. G. Quimby, ed., *Material Culture and the Study of American Life* (New York: W. W. Norton for the Winterthur Museum, 1978). Cary Carson, "Doing History with Material Culture," in Ibid., pp. 41-64.

3. Gerald W. R. Ward, ed., *Perspectives on American Furniture* (New York: W. W. Norton for the Winterthur Museum, 1988).

4. One of the most forceful arguments along these lines is "New Connoisseurship," a lecture presented at the 1995 Williamsburg Antiques Forum by Jon Prown, Assistant Curator of Furniture at Colonial Williamsburg.

American Furniture

William N. Hosley

Regional Furniture/ Regional Life

▼ IN PREPARING FOR the tour of Brock Jobe's exhibition, *Portsmouth Furniture*, organized by the Society for the Preservation of New England Antiquities and the Currier Gallery of Art, the Wadsworth Atheneum faced the problem of finding a way to position a regional subject outside the subject region. The curators, educators, media, and marketing people who ponder such things asked the obvious question, "Why should Connecticut care about New Hampshire furniture?" Said another way, Why should one part of the country care about a different part of the country, especially where there is no obvious connection between them? Most of the time, the basic answer—it's art, it's beautiful, it's important—works. But playing the regional card always seems to throw the pundits off balance and usually results in a subject being diminished and reclassified as of "local significance." Clearly, however, *Portsmouth Furniture* contained not only splendid "works of art" but a message that is universal in its appeal, transcending the peculiarities of place. Is that a surprise?

We struggled with the problem and in the end decided to enmesh *Portsmouth Furniture* in a program that included a Connecticut component and a Massachusetts component—a three-ring circus of regional furniture with Portsmouth in the center ring. The now-clichéd quest for a "sense of place" was the overarching theme. "A Sense of Place: Furniture from New England Towns," and the conference that gave rise to this collection of articles, was our way of addressing the problem of moving a regional subject outside its subject region. The solution worked (good attendance, lots of publicity, and a sold-out conference), but it should not have been necessary. Why is contemporary life so poorly connected with the extraordinary language of regional life? How has a quality once so totally enveloping and pervasive (the violation of states rights and regional self-determination was one of the causes of the Civil War) become so mysterious and inaccessible? Is this loss of regionalism a result of the global village?

History shows that regional identity has not always been so hard to embrace. The national media, "global" corporations, and command-and-control government bureaucracies, however, have spent the past half century evangelizing national culture and globalism. The regional dimension of culture has been stigmatized. To be "provincial" or "parochial" is to be dismissed. History, as it is taught where it matters most—at the elementary and secondary level—is about "the national experience." Granted, it is difficult to customize texts and curricula to reflect state and local conditions.[1] Although regional and (more often) ethnic diversions provide anecdotal seasoning, the "main storyline" rarely accounts for the extraordinary texture and diversity of cultures and culture regions that is and has long been a powerful but elusive feature of the United States, a nation much of the rest of the world regards as hopelessly and frighteningly expansive.

It is perhaps sensible to tread lightly in citing literature with an imprint date of 1972, but, in a short essay titled "The Regional Motive," Wendell Berry—the poet laureate of American regional life—had much of current relevance to say on this subject. Berry, whose writings emanate from a sense of his Kentucky surroundings, describes the word "regional" as often "either an embarrassment or an obstruction," "sloppily defined in its usage," and "casually understood." Dismissing "'regionalism' based upon pride" as well as that which "tends to generalize and stereotype" by imposing "false literary or cultural generalizations upon false geographical generalizations," Berry, instead, defines regionalism as "*local life aware of itself.*" One might, to good effect, engrave the frieze of a public building with Berry's words: "By memory and association men are made fit to inhabit the land." He concludes, "Without a complex knowledge of one's place, and without the faithfulness to one's place on which such knowledge depends, it is inevitable that the place will be used carelessly, and eventually destroyed." According to Berry, only through such "knowledge and faithfulness" does a culture (or antique furniture, for that matter) avoid being reduced to the merely "superficial and decorative." The regional dimension thus matters much, and it is almost certainly the quality that gives antique furniture such enduring power, not only in museums and collections but especially in those places of "memory and association."[2]

Because art museums often serve as proxy for museums in general, and because they are so dominant in the museum economy, it is interesting to ponder the ways in which "the regional motive" plays out in these institutions renowned for their commitment to globalism and cosmopolitanism. My director, an Anglo-Australian, has marveled from time to time at the almost fetish-like way American museums collect and display furniture, to a degree apparently unmatched elsewhere in the world. I suspect he would regard Winterthur and Historic Deerfield as uniquely American sorts of institutions, and I would argue that it is the "regional motive" that makes them special. Also, until about 1975, the "field" of paintings was so dominated by Eurocentrists that the decorative arts was about the only avenue for American art in American art museums. American painting, then mostly looked after by curators of antiques who preferred "pots and pans" and curators of paintings who preferred Europe, never quite got out of the bag. Today, American paintings are very much out in front, having marched rapidly from obscurity to prominence, leaving to furniture and "antiques" an ever-more iconoclastic role.

Is American furniture art, or is it history? The fact that historians in the field are notoriously and almost uniquely equivocal on this point is proof of the intractability of an ideology rooted in regionalism and antiquarianism, areas of study strikingly incompatible with "modernism" and traditional art history. I prefer to characterize modernism as "the 'art-for-art's sake,' one-world point of view" that *willfully* drains art of the context that gives it meaning. Antiquarianism, on the other hand, is an extension of love for one's surroundings, or even love of the earth. It is potent stuff, and it is ancient in its practice. The Japanese have a long tradition of antiquarianism that elevates reverence for objects (partly a spiritual quest for knowledge, not unlike what the West calls connoisseurship) to an art. Antiquarianism is inevitably centered in the study of place, and it is no accident that the greatest antiquarians have also been regionalists or, at least, persons who practiced the kind of "complex knowledge" and "faithfulness to one's place" that Wendell Berry describes so artfully. Antiquarianism thus survives—albeit barely—in art museums in the guise of furniture studies, period rooms, and exhibitions like *Portsmouth Furniture*, and in other manifestations of "civic mission."[3]

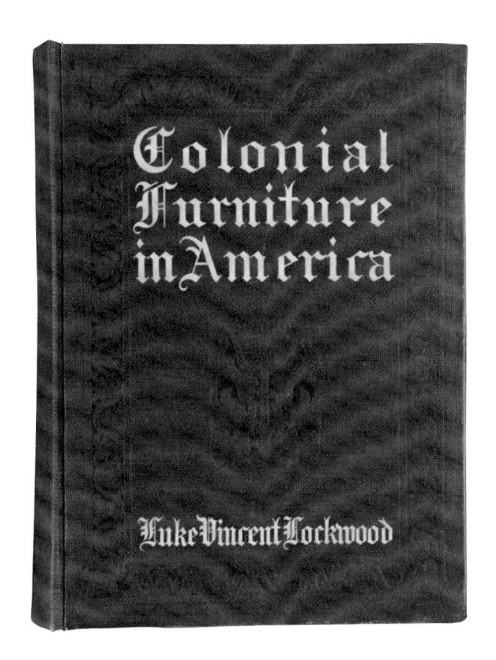

Figure 1 Cover of Luke Vincent Lockwood's *Colonial Furniture in America* (New York: Charles Scribner's Sons, 1901; photo, Gavin Ashworth). The first edition of this milestone publication featured cover art derived from the "Hartford chests" Lockwood so admired. A "Hadley chest" illustrates the title page, and the frontis features a highly stylized "Portsmouth" blockfront. Although the text is far from exclusive in its emphasis on regional styles, there has never been an American furniture survey that balanced the regional and the cosmopolitan more equally.

American furniture studies is not monolithic and, over the years, has been unmistakably committed to exploring aspects of aesthetic pluralism and regional diversity. As early as a century ago, pioneers like Irving Lyon and Luke Vincent Lockwood hinted that the regional character of early American craftsmanship was the primary source of its appeal (fig. 1). Many of the pioneer collectors who built the great public collections were antiquarians and regionalists who sought the convergence of art, history, and place.[4]

Figure 2 Portrait of Homer Eaton Keyes, ca. 1925. (Courtesy, *Antiques*.)

The eclipse of the antiquarian tradition in American furniture studies began in the 1920s with the quest to annoint cabinetmaking's canonized saints. The first issue of the magazine *Antiques* embraced both modernist and anti-modernist sentiments. In spite of feature articles such as "A Cabinet-Maker's Cabinet-Maker, Notes on Thomas Sheraton," founding editor Homer Eaton Keyes (fig. 2) was able to write a mission statement for the magazine that skewered modernism as "purposely disdainful of tradition, sublimely certain of its own ability to invent, devise, design in and for the future, . . . without recourse to an obviously . . . incompetent past." Playing on Daniel Webster's famous claim about Dartmouth College,

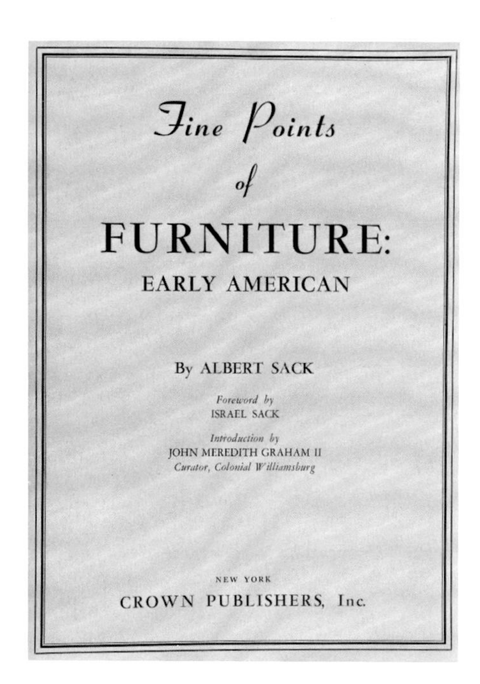

Figure 3 Frontis of Albert Sack's *Fine Points of Furniture: Early American* (New York: Crown Publishers, 1950). (Courtesy, Israel Sack, Inc., N.Y.C.; photo, Gavin Ashworth.)

Keyes acknowledged that "the past is, indeed, sorely disprised; yet there are those who love it." Furthermore, in a passage worthy of Edmund Burke, Keyes outlined the essential conservatism of the antiquarian tradition, claiming that among the "defenders of the past are some who realize . . . things *have* been done as well as human inventiveness . . . can do them; far better . . . than they are likely ever to be done again." The "industrial arts and crafts," Keyes concluded, are the perfect antidote to "novelty for novelty's sake," providing a "humane acquaintance" with the past.[5]

Regionalism and antiquarianism were never eclipsed entirely, and throughout the Depression, studies of Hadley chests, Connecticut furniture, and Sandwich glass, among other things, show the persistence of regional scholarship in the field of American "industrial arts and crafts." The middle half of the twentieth century marked the triumph of aesthetics over antiquarianism, epitomized in Albert Sack's *Fine Points of Furniture* (1950), which coined the term and gave rise to the "good, better, best" school of furniture appreciation (fig. 3). Although antiques evangelists like Wallace Nutting (*Furniture of the Pilgrim Century* [1924] and *Furniture Treasury* [1928]) were basically aiming for the same target, Nutting was either unwilling or unable to advance a fully developed hierarchy of quality amidst the messy jumble of facts, images, and anecdotes that characterize his work. Nutting remained to the end as much minister as man of commerce. He was never very facile at manipulating the commercial side of his passion for antiques, and he never fully embraced the property of art that now makes it such a powerful vehicle for articulating prestige. Nutting was a transitional figure between the antiquarians and regionalists and their modern (and modernist) counterparts in the auction houses and museums.[6]

The ideological battle between historicism and modernism, regionalism and aesthetics, recently played itself out in a very public and tangible way at the flagship museum of Americana, Colonial Williamsburg. Curators there spent much of the 1970s and 1980s "restoring" regional context and socio-economic authenticity (not to mention regionally appropriate furniture) to houses that had served primarily as architectural settings for "tasteful" assemblages of great collections (figs. 4, 5). It is ironic that Williamsburg's legendary curator, the late John Graham, wrote the introduction to *Fine Points*, where he rightly claimed for Colonial Williamsburg an important influence "toward improving the general taste of the country." Apparently there are *still* legions of admirers who regret that Colonial Williamsburg abandoned its use of historic houses as models of good taste and interior design. In the midst of its campaign of reinterpretation, Colonial Williamsburg created the DeWitt Wallace Decorative Arts Gallery (1985) (fig. 6), a museum-within-the-museum that not only provides for thoughtful temporary exhibitions but is especially devoted to the display of furniture and related decorative arts as art.[7] Colonial Williamsburg and its visitors are richer for the diversity of its new and improved programs of interpretation that, in addition to aesthetics and period verisimilitude, also feature craft demonstration and "living history." With Williamsburg, Virginia has a museum of international significance that has struck a skillful balance of art and history.

Figure 4 Governor's Palace dining room as furnished ca. 1950. (Courtesy, Colonial Williamsburg Foundation.)

Figure 5 Governor's Palace dining room as furnished ca. 1980. (Courtesy, Colonial Williamsburg Foundation.)

After a long exile, regionalism and antiquarianism are back and, for the first time since the 1920s, rival "good, better, best" as an ideology in American furniture studies. Neo-regionalism, if I may call it that, began thirty years ago with John Kirk's pathbreaking article on "Sources of Some American Regional Furniture." This piece not only invoked the concept of "regional furniture" but grappled with the central argument that inspired this collection of articles by asking, "How much originality is to be attributed to American furniture makers?"[8] Not surprisingly, the search for answers to this important question has not always interested furniture historians, and I would argue that differing attitudes about dependence versus independence is at the heart of the ideological tension that makes American furniture studies so interesting.

Figure 6 Furniture exhibit in the DeWitt Wallace Decorative Arts Gallery, ca. 1988. (Courtesy, Colonial Williamsburg Foundation.)

Like Colonial Williamsburg, John Kirk has also straddled both sides of the fence in ways that have given his work tremendous durability and importance. After reopening the door to regionalism in 1965, Kirk organized a landmark exhibition, *Connecticut Furniture: Seventeenth and Eighteenth Centuries* (1967) (fig. 7), and eventually provided a cogent analysis of regional diversity and regional culture in *American Chairs: Queen Anne and Chippendale*. Yet, fifteen and twenty years later in an essay on "dependence and independence" in his *American Furniture and the British Tradition to 1830* and in a subsequent article on "American Furniture in an International Context," Kirk chided regionalism for its excesses, noting that "until recently parochialness and chauvinism made it nearly anti-American to think of our culture and its expressions as extensions of Europe." Kirk warned against "this myopic view of our art," noting that the "recent acceptance of the integration of American and European art" was threatened by what he dubbed "the new chauvinism." The search for regional style, Kirk argued, was a false quest that overlooked the persistent indebtedness of American artisans and their clients—even those in "provincial" settings—to British influence. Without directly repudiating regionalism, Kirk undermined one of its traditional assumptions, the notion of American inventiveness and originality. With hundreds of case studies and comparisons, Kirk showed how even obscure furniture-making traditions were closely related and probably derived from British and European sources. Again, globalism scores.[9]

Does Kirk's proof that American furniture makers often depended on European ideas disprove the occasional act of inventiveness? That much American furniture was based on European models is hardly as surprising as the fact that some was *not*. To reduce interpretation to an argument

Figure 7 *Connecticut Furniture*, Wadsworth Atheneum, 1967. In addition to its role as a catalyst for the study of regional furniture, this exhibition was also the first to display furniture on high pedestals as "art." John Kirk designed the installation.

Figure 8 Portrait of Alice Winchester, ca. 1970. (Courtesy, *Antiques*.)

between regionalists and aesthetes trivializes the depth and mutual indebtedness both points of view have to each other and to other areas of study. Nonetheless, American furniture studies remains polarized in its view on originality and innovation. Regionalists and antiquarians generally champion the notion of an indigenous American craft tradition of distinction *and* originality, while the aesthetes prefer to dwell on the continuity of Anglo-American culture, anxious to avoid looking "provincial" by ignoring stylistic dependence on "the mother culture." The truth, such as it is, however, is mostly a matter of degree. Originality varies depending on *where* you look, hence, once again, the importance of place. It is thus the relationship between innovation, diversity, and place that the regional furniture symposium and these papers explore.

Call it what you will—neo-regionalism, "the new chauvinism," or the new antiquarianism—beginning in 1965, regional furniture began its slow march back to respectability as art and as a point of view. On the heels of *Connecticut Furniture*, Alice Winchester (fig. 8), the editor of *Antiques*, dedicated a theme issue to the subject of "country furniture." She convened a "symposium" during which leading authorities, such as Charles Hummel and Charles Montgomery of Winterthur, the late antiquarian/collector Nina Fletcher Little, Frank Horton of the Museum of Early Southern Decorative Arts, and Connecticut antiquarian, William Warren, were asked to "define country furniture."[10] Its purpose was to honor and recognize the importance of rural work, much neglected after years of emphasis on Boston, Newport, and Philadelphia; on Frothingham, Seymour, Goodard-Townsend, Affleck, and Savery. It also served to revisit the question of American inventiveness that the panelists widely and almost unanimously associated with rural work.

Charles Montgomery characterized country furniture by its "bold statement of city elements," perpetuation of tradition, use of native woods, and, perhaps most importantly, by the tendency of makers to borrow from whatever sources were handy. He concluded by asserting that the act of making an object that "shrieks its countryness" is "highly creative." In *Connecticut Furniture* and "American Regional Furniture," John Kirk said essentially the same thing, noting that "small individual style centers developed an originality of interpretation which is characteristic of rural furniture in all countries," and that, "while they did not create something wholly new, they drew upon their heritage to create something distinctive and to that extent original."[11]

In March of the following year, the reawakening of interest in rural, regional, and vernacular art continued with Winterthur's conference, corresponding "rotunda exhibition," and conference report titled *Country Cabinetwork and Simple City Furniture*. The conference aimed to "define country furniture" (their term for the tendencies Kirk, myself, and others describe as "regional"), describe the contacts between rural and urban craftsmen, analyze the relationship between central and regional style centers, and ultimately address "those who assail museum collections as not representing the objects owned by a cross section of earlier Americans." Ironically, it was Winterthur's concern about this last point that shifted the discussion from an emphasis on the inherently "elitist" notion of innovation to the anti-elitism of "less sophisticated furniture." Winterthur's contribution to the study of "country furniture" had the effect of linking the subject with a campaign to, as one conference participant put it, become "involved in the history of the working classes; . . . history from the 'bottom up.'"[12] The subtext of the conference, which conjoined "country cabinetwork" with "simple city furniture," submerged country furniture into a grab-bag of underrepresented, nonelitist "goods," now presumably as worthy of study as "the best." It is hardly a surprise, given the mood of the 1960s, that museums were anxious to refute charges of "elitism." By associating "country" with other forms of "non-high-style" furniture, Winterthur helped transform the study of regional furniture into a program aimed at establishing parity for, or at least the viability of studying, *all* furniture-making regions. Unfortunately, doing so diverted the discussion from more reliable issues, and it certainly left many questions—questions that speak directly to the subject of American cultural identity and the social uses of furniture—unanswered. When examining the Dunlaps, Hadley chests, or even Vermont painted furniture, anti-elitism is hardly the first thing that springs to mind in a first encounter.

Since Winterthur helped pry open the door to the study of furniture regions everywhere, the flurry of scholarship and activity has been almost too much to keep up with. Whether or not audiences are large for monographs such as *Furniture of the Georgia Piedmont Before 1830*, *New London County Joined Chairs, 1720–1790*, *North Carolina Furniture, 1700–1900* (1977), *Raised-Panel Furniture 1730–1830* (of the Eastern Shore, Virginia), or for studies of furniture from the Upper St. John Valley (in Maine), Ohio, or even Long Island, these books and articles, not to mention the proliferation of scholarship out of institutions like the Museum of Early Southern Decorative Arts, prove the vitality of regional scholarship, a pursuit once

Figure 9 *Arts of the Pennsylvania Germans*, Philadelphia Museum of Art and Winterthur Museum, 1983. (Courtesy, Philadelphia Museum of Art.)

nearly given up for dead. Add to this plethora the related scholarship on ethno-regional art and history, notably, *The Arts of the Pennsylvania Germans* (fig. 9) and *Remembrance of Patria: Dutch Arts and Culture in Colonial America*, and the impression of a stampede is complete.[13] Knowledge about rural craft, the relationship between "rural" and "urban" places, relations among ethnic subcultures, and the issue of inventiveness in furniture design has finally reached the point where it was worth revisiting the subject with the goal of drawing some new conclusions and, perhaps, resolving some of the questions first raised by Kirk and the symposium participants at *Antiques*, almost thirty years ago.

Where does the renaissance in regional scholarship leave the aesthetic tradition? Alive and well. Is it not a healthy sign that "furniture studies" admits multiple points of view? Indeed, some of the best work in American furniture studies is unabashedly aesthetic in perspective, striving, as always, to document, define, and qualify aesthetic excellence. That it is not always reliable in its historical interpretation is no surprise. Authors of the recent exhibition catalogue *American Rococo, 1750–1775: Elegance in Ornament* stated their purpose in selecting "the best examples of domestic creativity," which they defined as objects of "exceptional workmanship and aesthetic merit."[14] Actually, as masterful as the work may be, American furniture of "exceptional workmanship and aesthetic merit" may well be the least expressive of "*domestic* creativity."

Pejorative notions of provincialism oversimplify and undermine one of the most interesting processes in American art, the formation of high-style work that actively resists conforming to cosmopolitan design standards. In condemning the "new chauvinism," John Kirk talked about the "recent acceptance" of internationalism as if there was resistance. Since the late 1970s, however, no topic in furniture studies has been nearly so prominent as the debunking of American originality, the effort to prove that virtually

Figure 10 *American Rococo*, Metropolitan Museum of Art, 1992. (Courtesy, Metropolitan Museum of Art.)

none of our American furniture—especially the symbolically charged "furniture of the pilgrim century"—failed to exhibit British influence.[15]

In hindsight, the clamoring for British acceptance, implicit in the late Charles Montgomery's *American Art: 1750–1800, Towards Independence* (1976), an exhibition that celebrated our bicentennial by attacking the notion of American independence, strikes me as ironic. Similarly, John Kirk's *American Furniture and the British Tradition* provided a breathtaking panorama of American *dependence* by illustrating hundreds of styles, forms, and regional craft traditions that link America to British design. Mutual respect and understanding between the ideological poles has not always been generously forthcoming. Most recently, in *The American Craftsman and the European Tradition* (1988), Michael Conforti announced that "in time, the sentimental patriotism on which the study of American decorative arts was founded will be *completely erased* from the institutional and museological programs it fostered." The introduction to this recent exhibition and catalogue dismissed the quest for a romantic vision of the heroic past as "patriotic antiquarianism" while positing an internationalist view emphasizing webs of influence and dependence. Certainly, such intolerance is unintended and based on an incomplete reading of the antiquarian tradition, which, as I have suggested, was always more than the sum of its caricature, a caricature peopled with provincial regionalists, "sentimental patriots," bigots, and Anglophiles.[16]

American Rococo, the last major furniture exhibition before *Portsmouth Furniture*, appealing as it was, is a topic that could not fail to underscore the notion of American dependence on British and European tradition. Who can recall a more impressive assemblage of impeccibly crafted and intricately designed American furniture (fig. 10)? It must have been especially com-

Figure 11 *The Great River*, Wadsworth Atheneum, 1985. (Courtesy, Wadsworth Atheneum.)

Figure 12 China table attributed to Robert Harrold (fl. 1765-1792), Portsmouth, 1765–1775. Mahogany and mahogany veneer with maple and white pine. H. 28 5/8", W. 36 1/4", D. 22 7/16". (Courtesy, Carnegie Museum of Art; museum purchase, Richard King Mellon Foundation grant, acc. 72.55.2.)

forting to those fond of the idea of Americans communing with European art and culture. No style in the history of American furniture was ever more elitist in its practice and origin. In the hierarchy of "good, better, best," American rococo is generally perceived as the best of the best. When authors talk about engraved designs, print sources, pattern books, imported objects, and immigrant artisans as vehicles for the transmission of the rococo style, they are looking at a context that was almost exclusively urban and not especially representative or "inclusive." So what? American rococo-style furniture is some of the best American art, even if it is often American with a small "a." But it is a different kind of art than I see from my perch in Connecticut country. Some years ago, when we were preparing *The Great River: Art and Society of the Connecticut Valley, 1635–1820* (1985) (fig. 11), I was amused to discover no evidence of furniture or architectural pattern book ownership anywhere in the Connecticut Valley before the Revolution. Probably, few practiced cabinetmaking as a specialty then, let alone carving, upholstery, or chairmaking. It was a different world. Regional versus cosmopolitan habits were thus mostly a matter of degree and vary depending on *where* you look.

The aesthetic and regional approaches are both useful, and each contributes significantly to making American furniture studies vital and interesting. In addition to its luscious sensuality, efforts like *American Rococo* dispel provincial anxiety by emphasizing international networks of style and the formation of artisan skill. Antiquarians and regionalists mostly agree that aesthetic quality matters. Noting Israel Sack's criticism (preface to *Fine Points of Furniture*) of people who value antiques "merely because of their age," regionalists do not value furniture only because of *its place* of origin. Skillfulness at craft and inventive design vary between places and within them. The fact that something was made in Portsmouth, for example, does not mean that Portsmouth antiquarians will necessarily prize it. Antiquarians and aesthetes alike can share admiration for an aesthetic tri-

Figure 13 East Windsor and Philadelphia compared: *Left:* Side chair, attributed to Eliphalet Chapin, East Windsor, Connecticut, ca. 1780. Cherry with pine. H. 38", W. 22 3/4", D. 18". *Right:* Side chair, Philadelphia, ca. 1755. Mahogany with pine. H. 40 1/4", W. 23 1/2", D. 18 1/2". (Courtesy, Wadsworth Atheneum; Hartford. Gift of Mrs. Gordon W. Russell *[left]*. Gift of Samuel P. Avery *[right]*.) Eliphalet Chapin made "Philadelphia chairs" for a Connecticut market. They were related in proportions, construction, and form, but different in materials and decorative details.

umph like the great Portsmouth-made rococo china table (fig. 12) while acknowledging that its design was conceived three thousand miles away in Britain. In *The Great River,* we were just as interested in documenting Boston, New York, and Philadelphia objects and influences (fig. 13; see Philip Zea's article in this volume, fig. 32) as in showing the peculiarities of our subject region. Of course, devotees to Philadelphia and Boston would be correct in identifying a regional dimension in that furniture as well. English pattern books were not used much anywhere, so again, the rivaling perspectives quibble mostly over matters of degree.

It is not surprising to find the "Hadley chest" (fig. 14) in the crossfire on this issue of dependence and independence and as a symbol of an indigenous American art. In addition to *Portsmouth Furniture*, our program—"A Sense of Place: Furniture from New England Towns"—included a special gallery tour of the Wadsworth Atheneum's "Furniture Treasures from Connecticut Towns," and a splendid exhibition, *Hadley Chests,* organized by Suzanne Flynt and the staff at Memorial Hall in Deerfield. Admired by collectors for more than a century, the Hadley chest seems inherently intriguing, and its power acts in strange ways. Efforts to deny this iconic example of American originality have, I think, failed.[17] Instead, their study has led to demands that we reopen the question Kirk and the participants

Figure 14 Chest with drawers, probably Hadley, Massachusetts, 1695–1700. Maple with pine. H. 45 1/8", W. 43 1/2", D. 19 3/4". (Courtesy, Wadsworth Atheneum; Evelyn Bonar Storrs Trust Fund and gift of J. Pierpont Morgan, by exchange, acc. 1991.18.) This chest is presumed to be the earliest of several variants of the "Hadley chest" produced in the mid-Connecticut Valley between about 1685 and 1730. This example is the most similar to carved chests from the Wethersfield, Hartford, and Windsor vicinity and is believed to have been adapted by joiners from that area.

in *Antiques*' "country furniture" symposium sought to answer in the first place: "How much originality *is* to be attributed to American furniture makers?" What defines originality? Where should we look for it? Is the legend of Yankee ingenuity a reality or a myth? Might regional diversity be the root of innovation?

To address these and other pertinent questions, a group of prominent academics and museum curators gathered in Hartford, Connecticut, on March 26, 1993, for a one-day program entitled "Diversity and Innovation in American Regional Furniture." This meeting was the intellectual centerpiece of a program called "A Sense of Place." Beginning in the spring of 1992, assistant curator Karen Blanchfield, museum educator Cynthia Cormier, and I planned the program, solicited papers, lined up sponsorship from the Connecticut Humanities Council, and collaborated with "Connecticut Antiques Show" manager, Linda Turner, and Trinity College's American Studies department chair, James Miller, in concept development and promotion. Best of all, the Chipstone Foundation kindly agreed to adopt the theme of the conference for this special issue of *American Furniture*, thus enabling us to attract and publish new work by leading experts: Donna K. Baron, curator at Old Sturbridge Village, Edward S. Cooke, professor of art history at Yale University, Neil D. Kamil, professor of history at the University of Texas at Austin, Kevin M. Sweeney, professor of history and American studies at Amherst College, and Philip Zea, curator at Historic Deerfield. We were especially fortunate in Laurel

Thatcher Ulrich's willingness to provide a keynote address. Now a professor of history at Harvard University, Ulrich at the time was riding a wave of acclaim for her widely touted, *A Midwife's Tale: The Life of Martha Ballard, Based on Her Diary, 1785–1812*, a social biography that captures the essence of daily life, place, and personality with alluring power.

Citing precedent from John Kirk's writings and from the *Antiques* and Winterthur programs twenty-five years earlier, conference participants were asked to consider "how regional cultures interface with each other and with 'parent' cultures"; if a "buy local" policy may have affected consumer choice; the relationship between art, ethnicity, and place; the "impact of industrialization and mass communications on regional art during the 1810s–1830s"; the relationship between furniture studies and other "non-traditional modes of scholarship"; and, most importantly, the role of cultural diversity in fostering innovation.

In "Furniture as Social History: Gender, Property, and Memory in the Decorative Arts," Laurel Ulrich sets the tone with a call for furniture historians to reconnect objects with social context and by asking the surprising question: "If tables and chairs have arms, legs, and toes, do they also have sex?" Ulrich's essay reminds us that beyond fashion and place are men and women with personal needs, making personal choices. Her study of the social economy of women's work has greatly enhanced awareness of the intractable and unquantifiable factors that shape the lives of individuals and communities. Nowhere is the effectiveness of her approach more apparent than in her pathbreaking analysis of Hannah Barnard's cupboard, one of the most richly symbolic and totemic pieces of early Connecticut Valley furniture. By shifting the emphasis from furniture makers to furniture owners, Ulrich helps us personalize and humanize matters of style and innovation. By providing a perspective on women's roles in the consumer culture of colonial America, Ulrich has broadened the notion of diversity and made it easier to grasp how peculiarities of gender may have affected the use and appearance of furniture.

With "Hidden in Plain Sight: Disappearance and Material Life in Colonial New York ," Neil Kamil has produced a crisply articulated analysis of ethnic subcultures that shared space and shaped civic culture together. Skillfully deploying furniture and artifacts as powerful and convincing documentary evidence, Kamil takes aim at the Knickerbocker myth and reveals how the "real story of New York's material culture was . . . ethnic and cultural diversity." Almost as an aside he makes the most convincing case yet for the role of "Boston chairs" as a "medium of intercolonial communication" and as icons of cosmopolitanism. Kamil's mysterious Huguenot artisans emerge as deft cultural arbitrators greasing the wheels by which diverse European joinery traditions and cultures converge in a new world environment.

In "Regions and the Study of Material Culture: Explorations Along the Connecticut River," Kevin Sweeney, eminent Connecticut Valley historian and the primary collaborator on *The Great River* exhibition, offers valuable historiographical insights into the uses and abuse of "regionalism" and a thoughtful selection of case studies exploring aspects of design, innovation, and cultural accommodation through regional furniture. Sweeney distinguishes between regional history and "regionalism," a concept that too often devolved into a search for the "the essence of America and a yearning for community stability." In a meticulously reasoned case study on Wethersfield, Connecticut's famed "sunflower" chests, Sweeney brings closure to a long-standing debate about the source of this renowned and iconic "American" design. Although indebted to several imported joinery traditions, including one from the north of England and another rooted in the Low Countries or the Channel Islands, the unusual configuration of carved flowers, geometric panels, and applied turnings was invented in Wethersfield, the result of diverging subcultures and the quest for consensus among competing artisans.

Philip Zea, Historic Deerfield's resident regionalist and a noted evangelist for rural material culture, broadened the discussion with a series of multiregional case studies spanning almost two centuries, entitled "Diversity and Regionalism in Rural New England Furniture." Zea surveys New England's material landscape, selecting regional objects with a seasoned eye and demonstrating aesthetic complexity with case studies that point out how situational and irreducible the creative process can be. Connecticut inventors Benjamin and Timothy Cheney adapt an inheritance of woodworking knowledge to come up with the first American timekeeping mechanism made of wood, an achievement largely overlooked by aesthetes because the cases that house their clocks do not conform to high-style paradigms. Seasoned by the old rythmns of the agricultural year, improvisation was natural for first-generation "urban" cabinetmakers like William Lloyd of Springfield, who answered the need for new forms by reshaping and adapting components of the old. Zea illustrates the process of hybridizing fashion and treats the diversity of regional furniture as metaphor for the dynamic complexity of regional life.

"The Social Economy of the Preindustrial Joiner in Western Connecticut, 1750–1800" is Ned Cooke's contribution to the problem of explaining the extraordinary stylistic diversity of rural work, especially in Connecticut, the least centralized of the thirteen colonies and one with incredibly diverse furniture styles. Zeroing in on the critical last half of the eighteenth century, Cooke provides a new reading of the "social contract" within the apprenticeship system as a basis for exploring the "social economy of joinery." The foundation of "Yankee ingenuity" must lie somewhere near Cooke's image of the rural joiner who, if not a jack-of-all-trades, was often a master of design, workmanship, decoration, and marketing—furniture and buildings—bundled together before the "era of specialization." Cooke's declaration that "part time does not mean part skilled" reveals the rural joiner as the quintessential inventive mind at work.

Finally, Donna Baron takes us into the nineteenth century with "Definition and Diaspora of Regional Style: The Worcester County Model." However one defines regional art, at some point furniture apparently ceases to be a powerful medium of regional culture. Baron's study of Worcester

County's remarkable and under-reported role as a precedent-setting incubator for industrial technology and marketing illustrates the forces that reduce "our chair" to a universal, mass-produced, mass-marketed product I like to call "McChair." Worcester County chairmakers intentionally hybridized stylistic sources to create *the* chair that would test the waters of mass production and mass marketing. Baron's description of Worcester County chairs as "undistinguished but typical," unappetizing as it sounds, explains an important process at work. Do we expect more of a homogeneous, one-size-fits-all style?

This collection of essays opens some new doors while answering questions raised both now and thirty years ago. In addition to the material assembled here, I share below a portfolio of illustrations and some interpretations in hopes of stimulating further inquiry into regional furniture and joinery, work that testifies to the power of regional life in early America.

Interlocking Trades and Parallelism of Style

Regional furniture represents a conversation between theory and practice, patron and maker, tradition and fashion. It might be understood as a bottom-up solution to a top-down problem. Sources of influence are not easily pinned down because, in the life of the multi-skilled, multi-occupational country joiner, sources were everywhere and anywhere. One of the most conspicuous features of regional work is what Jules Prown and others have described as the parallelism of style. Objects linked in place, time, and sensibility are illustrated by four Connecticut Valley items in the rural baroque style of the 1765–1780 period, objects that epitomize the quality Wendell Garrett once described as "artisan mannerism."[18] The Hampshire County desk-and-bookcase illustrated in figure 15, the scroll-topped "Connecticut Valley doorway" from the Daniel Fowler house in Westfield, Massachusetts (fig. 16), the gravestone of Samuel Pease in Enfield, Connecticut (fig. 17), and the corner cupboard from the Alexander King house in Suffield, Connecticut (fig. 18), are each striking examples of what Kevin Sweeney, Scott Swank, and others have described as "rural bourgeois art." Artisan mannerism describes a craftsman pushing the boundaries of skill through what Phil Zea describes as purposely hybridized mixing and matching of elements, with details not infrequently carried out in multiples. Here, however, the impression is not just of craftsmen drawing on a common language of ornament but of actually looking over each other's shoulders—perhaps even working together—to create a fusion art of totemic significance to their place in time.

This kind of animated dialogue turns up over and over in the Connecticut Valley and also among the Pennsylvania Germans, where, in addition to furniture, architecture, and gravestones, a lively tradition of ornamental painting and ornamental cast and wrought iron reveals an astonishing level of aesthetic integration between craft media. Instances of parallelism abound in the Connecticut Valley: a gravestone (fig. 19) ornamented with the signature feature of the valley's much-admired "scalloped-top tables," other gravestones in which the "Connecticut Valley doorway" is mimicked, and,

Figure 15 Desk-and-bookcase, Hampshire County, Massachusetts, ca. 1775. Cherry with pine. H. 82 3/4", W. 35 1/2", D. 19 3/4". (From the collections of the Henry Ford Museum and Greenfield Village.)

Figure 16 Door from the Daniel Fowler house, Westfield, Massachusetts, ca. 1765. (Courtesy, Metropolitan Museum of Art; photo, Gavin Ashworth.)

Figure 17 Gravestone of Samuel Pease, possibly made by Ezra Stiles, Enfield, Connecticut, 1770. (Photo, William Hosley.)

the most suggestive of all, the gravestone for Mehetabel Smith (1770) (fig. 20), whose husband Eliakim is credited with introducing a stylized variant of Boston block-front furniture to the mid-Connecticut Valley.[19] The latter's signature-flowered pilasters (fig. 21; see also Zea, fig. 35) are the same as the border design on his first wife's gravestone, one he undoubtedly bought and that might have been the inspiration behind his use of the motif in furniture, or the other way around. In the social economy of face-to-face relationships and custom work, anything is possible.

Figure 18 Cupboard in the Dr. Alexander King House, attributed to Eliphalet King, Suffield, Connecticut, ca. 1764. (Courtesy, Suffield Historical Society.)

Figure 19 Gravestone of John Thrall, carved by Phineas Newton, East Granby, Connecticut, 1791. (Photo, William Hosley.)

Figure 20 Gravestone of Mehetabel Smith, Hadley, Massachusetts, 1770. (Photo, William Hosley.)

Figure 21 Detail of the pilaster of a high chest of drawers attributed to Eliakim Smith, Hadley, Massachusetts, ca. 1770. Cherry with white pine. H. 89 3/4", W. 39 15/16", D. 20 3/8". (Courtesy, Historic Deerfield, Inc.; photo, Amanda Merullo.)

Adapt and Improvise

The late Charles Montgomery characterized "country furniture" by its "bold statement of city elements," perpetuation of tradition, and use of native woods. Of rural joiners, Montgomery noted: "As Jacks-of-all trades, he may have been master of none but he was not timid."[20] Indeed, the rural joiner was a master of appropriation whose mantra was "adapt and improvise," "adapt and improvise." At its best, regional furniture is like jazz. Philip Zea shows how this process unfolded in the creation of japanned furniture in East Windsor Hill, Connecticut (see Zea, fig. 23). Other examples

Figure 22 Chest-on-chest, southern New Hampshire, ca. 1780. Maple with pine. H. 89", W. 40 5/8", D. 19 7/8". (Courtesy, Currier Gallery of Art; photo, Frank Kelly).

Figure 23 Chest-on-chest on frame by Samuel Loomis, Colchester, Connecticut, ca. 1775. Mahogany with pine. H. 88", W. 45", D. 26". (Courtesy, Wadsworth Atheneum; gift of Mr. and Mrs. Arthur L. Shipman, acc.1967.140.)

abound. A chest-on-chest from southern New Hampshire (fig. 22) shows how an unidentified regional joiner, probably in answer to a patron's demand for a Boston-type, block-front chest, translated that city's style into a regional idiom. Instead of mahogany, he used stained maple; instead of a classical, evenly lobed fan, he carved a highly idiomatic, peacock-like motif with outward sweeping lobes; and where Boston work is structurally refined—the work of a new brand of specialist called "cabinetmakers"—this chest is a joiner's work, the product of a hand (and tool chest) as accustomed to running cornice moldings on houses and laying floors as making finely dovetailed drawers. Massive, bulky, and sculptural, it owes as much to the logic of house joinery as to that of fine cabinetwork. The drawer sides are made of thick, local pine stock, finished with a fat beaded molding on the upper edge. The drawer bottoms are also much thicker than in comparable Boston work, finished with deep chamfering where the edges fit into the drawer sides. Most emblematic of all, the drawer bottoms are fastened at the rear, not with nails as invariably found in city work, but with trunnels (wooden pegs).

Another remarkable example of regional adaptation is the work of Samuel Loomis (1748–1814) of Colchester, Connecticut. Loomis is one of the key figures in the "Colchester School." The chest illustrated in figure 23, possibly the heaviest and bulkiest American example of this form, is architectural and yet represents a skillful adaptation of the widely exported and eminently cosmopolitan work of Newport's Goddards and Townsends.[21] The incised vine tracery of its upper drawers suggests a kind of traditional medievalism filtered through the sensibility of the rural bourgeoisie, and where the Newport chests achieve a kind of fussy, repetitive perfection in their finials, Loomis and his New London County peers transform the finial into a virtuoso piece, subject of relentless variety and experimentation.

The Social Economy of Joinery

The "social economy" that Ulrich and Cooke describe so well functions in furniture making by way of customwork and the commitment to "buy local" among community elites. Remember the custom tailors and shoemakers of old? Until the nineteenth century, most regional furniture was produced the same way. An interpersonal dimension thus becomes inherent in the actual product, with occasionally extraordinary results. Laurel Ulrich explores this aspect in the remarkable Hannah Barnard cupboard (see Ulrich, fig. 16) that, in addition to its identity as a product of gender-based familial relations, is also a remarkably inventive demonstration of the expansibility of the Hadley chest.

One of the most memorable examples of the social economy of joinery is the image of Jonathan Smith of Conway, Massachusetts working through a mound of indebtedness to Simon DeWolf and Lydia Batchelder by making one of the most obvious examples of "artisan mannerism" ever produced in the Connecticut Valley (fig. 24). Naturally, two pediments would have to be twice as good as one, especially if they are the only way you are ever likely to see the money this poor but inventive joiner owed you. In

Figure 24 Chest-on-chest by Jonathan Smith Jr., Conway, Massachusetts, 1803. Cherry with white pine. H. 83 1/4", W. 37 1/2", D. 23 1/4". (Courtesy, Historic Deerfield, Inc.; photo, Amanda Merullo.)

addition to providing a means to work off debts, the community elite who commissioned the joiner's most expensive work were anxious to promote harmony by keeping the home team at work and on the field of play.[22]

Shaker furniture provides another notable instance of a social economy in operation. Although widely recognized for their role in adopting ma-

Figure 25 Cupboard and case of drawers, Mount Lebanon, New York, ca. 1820. Painted pine with fruitwood knobs. H. 96", W. 54", D. 14". (Courtesy, Mount Lebanon Shaker Collection. Circulated by Art Services International, Alexandria, Virginia.)

chine technology and for mass producing certain standardized furniture forms, the Shakers also produced a bewildering array of work customized for a domestic economy of obsessive orderliness.[23] Is there another class of American furniture that exhibits more variety than the ubiquitous Shaker cupboards (fig. 25) with their seemingly infinite door and drawer arrangements and built-in and free-standing forms? Symmetry yes, but repetition, almost never. "A place for everything and everything in its place," but also *every place* customized to the requirements of the Shakers' unique social dynamic. That the Shakers were mostly situated in rural locations, inhabited by refugees from a foundering rural economy, only partly explains the inventiveness of Shaker cupboards.

Hyper-Regionalism and Mass Communications

Donna Baron's discussion of the standardization and mass marketing of furniture during the early nineteenth century calls for an examination of a kind of hyper-regional response that coincided with its development. Specifically, we are led to a discussion of the mannered and conspicuously stylized furniture that was produced in places that may have felt threatened by the onslaught of urbanization, mass communications, and, eventually, the mass marketed furniture that put country joiners out of business. This phenomenon has been neglected in the past, but some tentative interpretations may be suggested from a reading of the furniture itself.

In traveling the back roads of New England and New York, it is imme-

Figure 26 Gibson House, Canandaigua, New York, ca. 1820. (Courtesy, Ontario County Historical Society.)

Figure 27 George West house, Irasburg, Vermont, 1824–1834. (Courtesy, Middlebury College and Erik Borg.) This is one of a group of houses built in the upper Connecticut Valley from the mid-1820s until about 1850. The earliest examples appear to have originated in the northern part of the state and may have roots in French Canadian building practices.

diately apparent that the early architecture and furniture in places like Canandaigua (fig. 26), Utica, and Painted Post, New York, and Castleton, Irasburg (fig. 27), Middlebury, and Chester, Vermont, displayed a pronounced local peculiarity. The impression of worldly and ambitious people marking their turf with an art of their own is overwhelming, especially when traveling from one region to the next. These mostly new communities, founded by educated lawyers, doctors, and entrepreneurs, published their own newspapers and were relentlessly expansionist;[24] nevertheless, at the very moment when these country towns, villages, and regional centers were becoming connected via turnpikes and mass communications, the need to articulate or preserve differences apparently intensified. At a time when pat-

Figure 28 Desk-and-bookcase, Middlebury, Vermont, ca. 1820, Maple and cherry with pine. (Courtesy, Sheldon Museum.) Although the contrasting veneers of this desk-and-bookcase are stylistically related to cabinetwork from Portsmouth, New Hampshire, it is part of a group of western Vermont furniture distinguished by brilliantly figured curley and bird's-eye maple panels and veneers.

Figure 29 Desk-and-bookcase by John Shearer, Martinsburg, West Virginia, 1801 (desk) and 1806 (bookcase). Walnut, cherry, and mulberry with yellow pine and oak. H. 106", W. 45", D. 24 1/2". (Collection of the Museum of Early Southern Decorative Arts, Winston-Salem, North Carolina.)

tern books, urban design sources, and other modes of transmitting cosmopolitan culture were finally more widely available, a sort of hyper-regionalism kicked in.

A recent *Wall Street Journal* article described a "global paradox," noting that in spite of "the growth of the global economy and of more powerful transnational institutions, . . . nationalism is flourishing. . . . big corporations and institutions shaping the world economy seem so remote that many people turn to local ethnic groups and obscure languages for their identity." Eventually, it noted, "the world may fracture into 500 states from the current 200, . . . with the central government little more than a shell and power residing in the regions." Surely, the revolution in transportation and communications that swept America between 1790 and 1830 had as much impact on their time as the technological changes of today are having on ours. In Portsmouth and Haverhill, New Hampshire (see Zea, fig. 9), in Shaftsbury (see Zea, fig. 5) and Middlebury, Vermont (fig. 28), through western New York and Ohio,[25] and south into West Virginia (fig. 29), cabinetmakers and clients did a last tango around woodwork that was flamboyant and distinctive. If not a gesture of defiance to the homogenizing waves of progress, the items were at least a celebration of cultural control through art. Work that might have been labeled folk art twenty years ago as often as not belonged to well-traveled and educated regional professionals, movers and shakers fully aware of the choices they were making.

Ethnicity and Region

At a time when "cultural diversity" is widely equated with differences in ethnicity, perhaps there is value in demonstrating that regional diversity also has a long history in the United States. Indeed, ethnic differences are so conspicuous that they are nearly taken for granted. Dutch (fig. 30), French,

Figure 30 Gravestone of Cornelius C. Van Wyck, Fishkill, New York, 1767. (Photo, William Hosley.)

Figure 31 Gravestone of Catherina Elserin, Adamstown, Pennsylvania, 1793. (Photo, William Hosley.)

Figure 32 German Palatine Church, Stone Arabia, New York, 1770 with tower about 1805. (Photo, William Hosley.)

Germans (fig. 31), Swedes, and Scotch-Irish have long been recognized as a significant presence in early America.[26] The discussion of ethnic subcultures is usually confined to the specific regions where their numbers were greatest; still, without leaving the Northeast one can find abundant evidence of ethnic diversity.

Philip Zea interprets the style of the Dunlaps—New Hampshire's most renowned country joiners—as a product of their Scotch ancestry (see Zea, figs. 14, 27). Kevin Sweeney and Susan Prendergast explore the French Huguenot roots of the Wethersfield "sunflower" chests.[27] Neil Kamil shows how New York's Huguenots positioned themselves at the center of a cosmopolitan cultural triangle involving New York, Boston, and London. But what of the German Palatines (fig. 32) in upstate New York, or the linger-

Figure 33 Gravestone of Cuffe Gibbs by Pompe Stevens, Common Burying Ground, Newport, Rhode Island, 1768. (Photo, William Hosley.) The several dozen stones marking the graves of African slaves in Newport's largest colonial burying ground is the largest concentration in New England. This stone is signed by an African American stonecutter, Pompe Stevens, who probably worked in the shop of John Stevens, Newport's most skilled and prolific stonecutter.

Figure 34 Gravestone of Dr. John Henry Burchsted, Lynn, Massachusetts, 1721. (Photo, William Hosley.) This prominent physician was from Silesia, and his gravestone is one of the most expensive from its time.

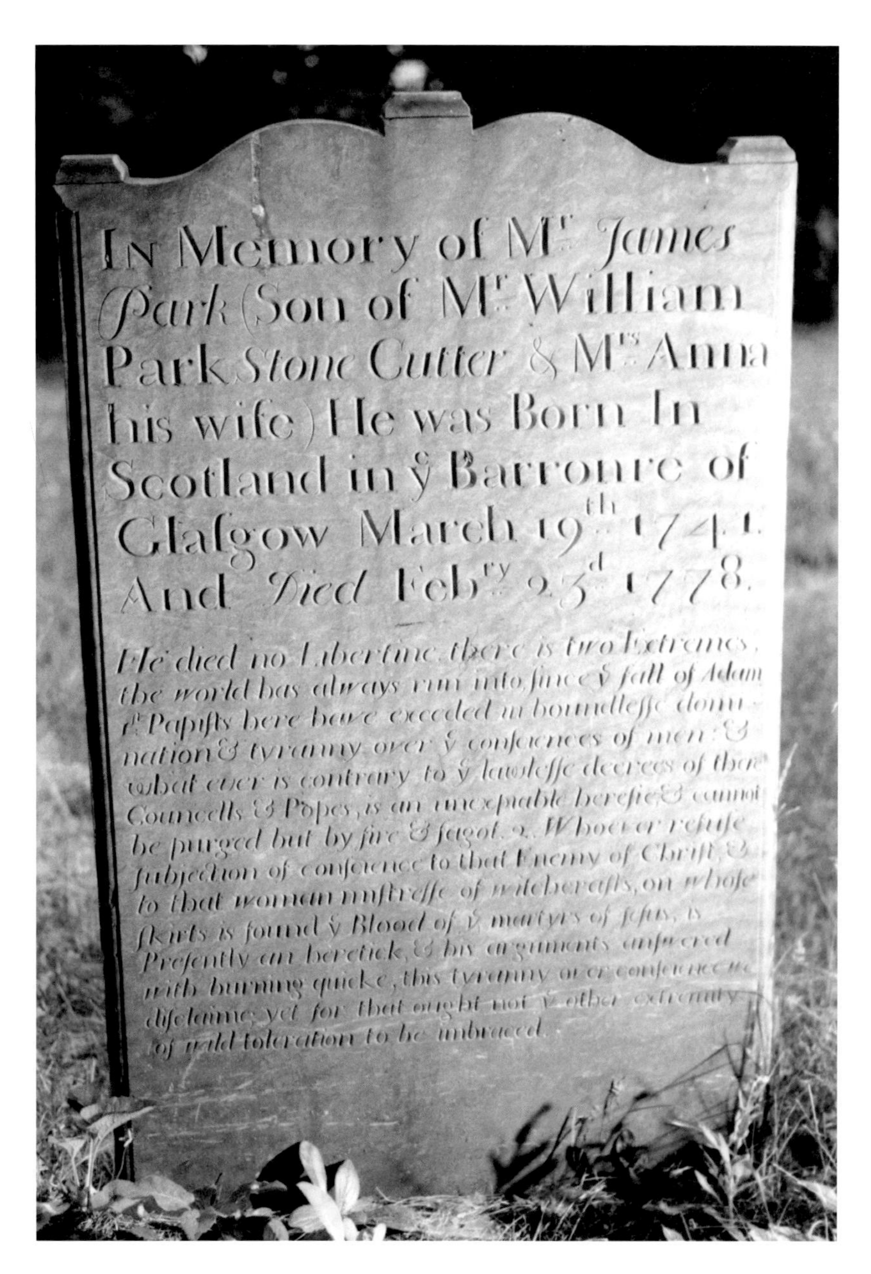

Figure 35 Gravestone of James Park, Groton, Massachusetts, 1778. (Photo, William Hosley.) The Park family of Groton were a multigenerational dynasty of Scotch stonemasons.

ing influence of the French in Vermont and the Champlain Valley, or the continuing presence of Native Americans throughout the Northeast and the large concentrations of African slaves in places like Newport, Rhode Island (fig. 33)? There were "strangers" everywhere, and, often enough, they had wealth, connections, and new ideas (figs. 34, 35). How might their presence have affected the art and material culture of the various regions? A good road-trip survey or a walk through almost any old burying ground offers much evidence and more than a hint at new directions for research.

Several purposes were in mind when we set out to revisit the subject of regional furniture. As much as anything, we believe it worthwhile to create an American furniture history that more closely resembles the history of the people who lived here. In the usual chronologies of "style," too much gets left by the wayside.[28] Given the abundance of high-style urban furniture, it is certainly possible to form dozens of public collections in which each period is represented by urban "examples" of the various "style periods"—nice and tidy, but redundantly bland. To be sure, it is more difficult to be inclusive and impossible to be comprehensive. Unfortunately, too much of what ends up on the cutting floor is the art that tells the richest story.

Implicit in the prospectus for the conference that lead to this collection of articles was the notion that diversity and innovation are somehow related. It is no accident that the industrial era in American history is brimming with the kind of inventors who gave rise to the myth of "Yankee ingenuity." More often than not, these inventors—men like Samuel Colt, Eli Whitney, Charles Cheney—had roots in the trades. Without leaving the Connecticut Valley one can find numerous examples of legendary inventors who were both the lineal and spiritual descendants of rural artisans. The quality of inventiveness is partly a consequence of circumstances and partly temperament. Artisans working in the "out-and-beyond" inevitably learn to adapt. The capacity for self-teaching and the ability to strip problems to their absolute essentials, coupled with persistence, tenacity, and unusual curiosity, are characteristics of inventive minds, and these, more than a skill at marketing, management, or capital formation, are what distinguished many of the best rural artisans.[29] Their furniture solved problems inherent in bridging the gap between fashion and tradition, worldliness and a sense of place. The rules by which we measure their success should be not only aesthetic but situational.

The issues of art versus history, dependence versus independence, and international versus regional define the two-party politics of American furniture studies. Although one point of view may hold sway over the other, is it not good that both remain intact? Although we bunk, debunk, rebunk, and bunk again, in the end we share a purpose in seeking new ways of seeing old things. Furniture is art, but it is also a manifestation of the character and quality of place. With place-markers getting harder and harder to find, it is no small wonder that we can stare a chair in the splat and say, "I know you from whence you came."

1. State and local history is almost never available in the schools and, when available, usually reflects the initiative of individual teachers with a keen interest and a willingness to try something different. When recently contacted about the status of state and local history in secondary school curriculums, Luanne Sneddon of the American Association for State and Local History cited, "Junior Historical Society" programs run by the Indiana Historical Society and the New York Historical Association. The Texas Historical Commission recently produced *A Teacher's Companion, Activities and Resource Book* (Austin, Tex.: Texas Historical Commission, 1994) to accompany its popular *A Shared Experience,* a published survey of the history, architecture, and historic sites between Laredo and Brownsville on the Rio Grand.

2. Wendell Berry, *A Continuous Harmony* (New York: Harcourt Brace, 1972), pp. 63–70.

3. Early Western art critics and travel writers marveled at Japan's sense of history and reverence for craft. Art reform critic and aesthetic designer Christopher Dresser described the importance of Shinto, the traditional state religion, in keeping "alive a sense of gratitude" in *Japan: Its Architecture, Art and Art Manufacturers* (1882; reprint, New York: Garland Publishing, 1977), p. 230. Legendary Japanophile, antiquarian, and collector Edward S. Morse of Salem, Massachusetts, wrote of the importance of collecting among Japanese nobility, citing centuries-old family collections of pottery, swords, brocade, and "roofing tiles" passed down with reverence, generation after generation, in *Japan, Day by Day* (1917; reprint, Dunwoodly, Ga.: Norman S. Berg, 1978), pp. 106–7; Morse further described a renowned

Japanese antiquarian who "held it to be a solemn duty to learn any art or accomplishment that might be going out of the world, and then describe it so fully, that it might be preserved to posterity" in *Japanese Homes and Their Surroundings* (1886; reprint, Rutland, Vt.: Charles E. Tuttle, 1972), p. xxxi. In Japan, antiquarianism is connected with the ancient rituals of the tea ceremony and "tea culture" (Richard L. Wilson, "Tea Taste in the Era of Japonisme: A Debate," *Chanoyo Quarterly* 50 [1988]: 23–39). State and local historical societies were the pioneer institutional antiques collectors. The Massachusetts Historical Society has collected paintings and antiques since the time of its founding in 1791 (see *Witness to America's Past: Two Centuries of Collecting by the Massachusetts Historical Society* [Hanover, N.H.: University Press of New England, 1991]). The oldest continuously operated museum in the United States, Pilgrim Hall (founded 1820) has always concentrated on art and antiques. Elizabeth Stillinger's *The Antiquers* (New York: Alfred A. Knopf, 1980), gave less attention to the earliest collectors and failed to mention legendary figures like George Sheldon of Deerfield (see Suzanne L. Flynt, Susan McGowan, and Amelia F. Miller, *Gathered and Preserved* [Deerfield, Mass.: Pocumtuck Valley Memorial Association, 1991]) and Thomas Robbins of Hartford (see Robert F. Trent, "Thomas Robbins and Early Antiquarianism in New England," lecture at the 1994 Winterthur Conference on "Perceptions of the Past: Private Collections/Public Collections," [publication forthcoming]). These men—staunch regionalists all—were giants who layed the foundation for the work that followed. Stillinger profiled a few pioneer antiquarians such as the Rev. William Bentley (1759–1819) of Salem, "who collected a variety of things related to the history of Essex County"; John Fanning Watson (1779–1860) of Philadelphia, whose "study of colonial customs in his area" involved pioneering efforts at oral history, collecting antiques, and designing "relic furniture"; and Cummings Davis (1816–1896) of Concord, Massachusetts, whose "extraordinarily rich collection of the antiques of Concord" is the core of the Concord Antiquarian Museum (recently renamed The Concord Museum) (Stillinger, *The Antiquers*, pp. 17, 19, 22). The notion of "civic mission" is used by urban museums to describe service programs for and about the city or region where the museum is located. Although the *priority* given to the museums' "global artistic mission" is typically undeclared, it plays out in the quest to be artistically correct and typically involves buying and exhibiting artists, both living and dead but never local, who have been vetted by the professional (and predominately commercial) networks devoted to such things. In 1993, I delivered a paper for the closing ceremony of Historic Deerfield's Summer Fellowship Program on "The Role of Museums in Creating and Fostering Civic Identity." I argued the importance of the role museums have to play in preserving "authenticity of experience" and "a sense of place in the face of an astonishing assault by our nation's commercial popular culture." What is indigenous or distinctive—a locale's history, industries, and art, for example—is the only thing most places can still claim as their own. Although regional knowledge is not based entirely on indigenous stories and things, a place without them is unlikely to maintain or develop a strong or very durable identity or economy.

4. Stillinger, *The Antiquers*, pp. 69–81, 88–94, 133–41, 155–70, 174–75. Although Stillinger's story downplays the importance of the early antiquarians and overlooks entirely the regional motive behind their work, the generation that followed also included regionalists. These "pioneer museum men" included Irving W. Lyon (1840–1896) and Henry Wood Erving (1851–1941) of Hartford, best remembered for "discovering" and naming the "Hadley chest"; A. T. Clearwater (1848–1933), the man most responsible for discovering the importance of New York silver; George Dudley Seymour (1859–1945), renowned for building the first collection of Connecticut furniture and as a relentless champion for Connecticut patriot Nathan Hale; Henry Watson Kent (1866–1948), who arrived at the Metropolitan Museum of Art via Norwich, Connecticut, the place he credited with solidifying "his love of the American past"; and Albert Hastings Pitkin (1852–1917), best known for his studies of regional pottery.

5. "A Cabinet-Maker's Cabinet-Maker: Notes on Thomas Sheraton, 1751–1806," *Antiques* 1, no. 1 (January 1922): 25–30. Homer Eaton Keyes, "*Antiques* Speaks for Itself," ibid., p. 7.

6. Clair Franklin Luther, *The Hadley Chest* (Hartford, Conn.: Case, Lockwood & Brainard Co., 1935). Luther was minister of the Second Congregational Church in Amherst, Massachusetts, a daughter town to Hadley. *Three Centuries of Connecticut Furniture* (Hartford, Conn.: Morgan Memorial, Wadsworth Atheneum, 1935). This exhibition was conceived and carried out by Hartford's legendary antiquarian-collectors—notably, William B. Goodwin, William Putnam, Morgan Bulkeley, Morgan Brainard, and Henry W. Erving—and the catalogue was written by New York attorney, Luke Vincent Lockwood, whose lifelong love of

antiques was inspired by Henry Erving while Lockwood attended Trinity College in Hartford. Kirk J. Nelson's "Foreward" in Raymond E. Barlow and Joan E. Kaiser, *The Glass Industry in Sandwich* (Windham, N.H.: Barlow-Kaiser Publishing Co., 1993), pp. vii–ix, explains how Sandwich glass was initially used to promote Cape Cod tourism. Albert Sack, *Fine Points of Furniture* (New York: Crown Publishers, 1950). In his preface, legendary antiques dealer Israel Sack wrote: "The idea which some people have—that antiques are valuable merely because of their age—is wrong. No matter how old a piece may be, it has no value unless it is of good quality. . . . Of prime consideration are the quality of the article, the design and the maker, the fineness and durability of the woods, and the mellowness imparted to them by a hundred or more years of natural wear."

7. In an April 3, 1979, lecture at Winterthur, Brock Jobe, who was curator of Exhibition Buildings at Colonial Williamsburg, described John Graham as "a decorator" who set out to "acquire great objects and didn't care if documentation got in the way." The earliest attempt to furnish accurately a period room was Ivor Noël Hume's "traveler's" room in the Anderson House (Conversation with Graham Hood, January 1, 1995), but it was not until Hood's arrival in early 1971 that the "old decorator tradition" began to give way to historic documentation. The Brush-Everard House, Raleigh Tavern, and Geddy House were the first properties to undergo major refurnishing; however, the greatest challenge involved refurnishing the Governor's Palace—a veritable cultural icon. The Governor's Palace is the signature building in the restoration and the most popular destination for museum visitors. Efforts to introduce historical accuracy in a building that epitomized Williamsburg's role as tastemaker were amply chronicled in a special edition of *Colonial Williamsburg Today* 3, no. 3 (spring 1981) and in Michael Olmert, "The New, No-Frills Williamsburg," *Historic Preservation* 37, no. 5 (October 1985): 27–33. Response was not always supportive. One long-time supporter described the restored buildings as "gloomy," and at one point the administration received several letters of complaint per week. The Foundation responded with a candid, polite letter explaining the value of change and how John D. Rockefeller Jr.'s original intent was for Colonial Williamsburg to remain the leader in research pertaining to the town. As curator John Sands explains it (interview December 22, 1994), Colonial Williamsburg recognized that it was tampering with an icon cherished for reasons unrelated to the staff's quest for historical authenticity and that some people would never accept the change. C. Knight, "Elegance Underground: The DeWitt Wallace Decorative Arts Gallery, Williamsburg, Virginia," *Architecture* 75, no. 1 (January 1986): 52–55. "The New DeWitt Wallace Decorative Arts Gallery at Colonial Williamsburg," *Antiques* 128, no. 4 (October 1985): 266–69.

8. Jane C. Nylander, *Our Own Snug Fireside: Images of the New England Fireside, 1760–1860* (New York: Alfred A. Knopf, 1993), is arguably the best recent example of what I call the "new antiquarianism." Simply put, I believe that "material culture," the banner under which revisionists attempted to unseat "the decorative arts" as the reigning ideology behind object study, failed to evolve into a program that followers could grasp or care for. The conflict at the heart of material culture and the decorative arts is, perhaps, best summarized by Michael J. Ettema's controversial article, "History, Nostalgia, and American Furniture," *Winterthur Portfolio* 17, nos. 2/3 (summer/autumn 1982), 135–44, and by the unprecedented outpouring of commentary from colleagues and professionals (see *Winterthur Portfolio* 17, no. 4 (winter 1982): 259–67. Ettema had little good to say about furniture studies or the decorative arts, and he was also critical of what he called "scientific antiquarianism" and the "antiquarian tradition." He was searching for a program where objects are "used to enhance our understanding of history" rather than the other way around. I like to think of what I do as "object-based history," not "art history," recalling years ago a conversation with an art historian who preferred to be called a "professor of the history of art." It is an important distinction. The merging of object study (involving connoisseurship) with social history is what "new antiquarians" do and, I believe, what antiquarians have always done to the limits of their ability and resources. Imagine Darret B. and Anita H. Rutman's brilliant but visually challenged *A Place in Time: Middlesex County, Virginia 1650–1750* (New York: W.W. Norton, 1984) with a dollop of object knowledge, or imagine an illustrated version of Laurel Thatcher Ulrich's *A Midwife's Tale: The Life of Martha Ballard, Based on Her Diary, 1785–1812* (New York: Vintage Books, 1990), and you begin to see visually rich, human narrative the equal or better of film in communicative power. In addition to Jane Nylander's work, Richard Bushman's *The Refinement of America* (New York: Alfred A. Knopf, 1992); Elisabeth D. Garrett's *At Home: The American Family, 1750–1870* (New York: Harry Abrams, 1990); and several of the marvelous and underexposed exhibition catalogues

produced by the staff at the Margaret Woodbury Strong Museum in Rochester, New York, show what is possible when object knowledge and documentary resources are deftly deployed with the aim of *rendering the past*. Ultimately, this work is either that of gifted generalists or teams of collaborating specialists, hence it flourishes outside the academy where the tradition of scrupulously segregated fields of study continues to suppress the kind of multidisciplinary work that I regard as essential to the task of rendering the past or even rendering American furniture as more than "superficial and decorative." John T, Kirk, "Source of Some American Regional Furniture," *Antiques* 88, no. 6 (December 1965): 790–97.

9. John T. Kirk with Henry Maynard, *Connecticut Furniture: Seventeenth and Eighteenth Centuries* (Hartford, Conn.: Wadsworth Atheneum, 1967); John T. Kirk, *American Chairs: Queen Anne and Chippendale* (New York: Alfred A. Knopf, 1972). In *American Chairs,* Kirk broke new ground by abstracting the writings of pioneer American linguist, Hans Kurath (see his *Handbook of the Linguistic Geography of New England* [Providence, R.I.: Brown University, 1939]). Kurath's analysis of linguistic subregions was thought to parallel the material culture regions of New England. Basically, the notion that culture is fluid, not always respecting political boundaries and certainly neither monolithic or "derivative," was ably conveyed by Kurath's pathbreaking research. The possibilities inherent in Kirk's analogy with object study still merit further investigation. John T. Kirk, *American Furniture and the British Tradition to 1830* (New York: Alfred A. Knopf, 1982), pp. 3–6; John T. Kirk, "American Furniture in an International Context," in *Perspectives on American Furniture*, edited by Gerald W. R. Ward (New York: W.W. Norton for the Winterthur Museum, 1988), pp. 39–62.

10. "Country Furniture: A Symposium," *Antiques* 62, no. 4 (March 1968): 333–71.

11. Charles F. Montgomery, "Country Furniture," *Antiques* 62, no. 4 (March 1968): 355-59. Kirk with Maynard, *Connecticut Furniture*, p. xiv; Kirk, "American Regional Furniture," p. 798.

12. The passages cited are from E. McClung Fleming, "Foreward," and Charles F. Hummel, "The Dominys of East Hampton, Long Island, and Their Furniture," both in *Country Cabinetwork and Simple City Furniture,* edited by John D. Morse (Charlottesville, Va.: University Press of Virginia for the Winterthur Museum, 1970), pp. xi, 67. The conference took place March 27–29, 1969, a year after the *Antiques* issue on "country furniture" and after the tumultuous Democratic National Convention in Chicago. *Country Cabinetwork* was originally billed as a conference on "less sophisticated furniture." *Winterthur Newsletter* 15, no. 3 (March/April 1969): 5. Wendell D. Garrett, "The Matter of Consumer's Taste," *Winterthur Newsletter* 15, no. 3 (March/April 1969): 210. To me and to several of the conference participants (cited in the transcription of the post-lecture roundtable discussions, p. 281), the most intriguing idea in Garrett's essay was the notion of "artisan mannerism," a phenomenon not fully developed in the essay or in the other associated papers. Garrett's emphasis on social context and labor history, witnessed in the citing of then *au courant* revisionist literature, such as Barton J. Bernstein's, *Towards a New Past: Dissenting Essays in American History* (New York: Pantheon Books, 1968), helped move the emphasis from issues of place to issues of politics and class.

13. Henry D. Green, *Furniture of the Georgian Piedmont Before 1830* (Atlanta: High Museum of Art, 1976); Robert E. Winters Jr., ed., *North Carolina Furniture 1700–1900* (Raleigh: North Carolina Museum of History, 1977); Robert F. Trent with Nancy Lee Nelson, "New London County Joined Chairs, 1720–1790," *Connecticut Historical Society Bulletin* 50, no. 4 (fall 1985); James R. Melchor, N. Gordon Lohr, and Marilyn S. Melchor, *Raised-Panel Cupboards of the Eastern Shore of Virginia* (Norfolk, Va.: Chrysler Museum, 1982); Dean F. Failey, *Long Island Is My Nation: The Decorative Arts and Craftsmen, 1640–1830* (Setauket, N.Y.: Society for the Preservation of Long Island Antiquities, 1976); E. Jane Connell and Charles R. Muller, "Ohio Furniture 1788–1888," *Antiques* 125, no. 2 (February 1984): 462–68; Edwin A. Churchill and Sheila McDonald, "Reflections of Their World: The Furniture of the Upper St. John Valley, 1820–1930," in Ward, ed., *Perspectives on American Furniture*, pp. 63–92. Since 1975, the Museum of Early Southern Decorative Arts's *Journal of Early Southern Decorative Arts* has been the leading forum for scholarship on southern antiquities. Scott T. Swank et al., *Arts of the Pennsylvania Germans* (New York: W.W. Norton for the Winterthur Museum, 1983); and Roderic H. Blackburn and Ruth Piwonka, *Remembrance of Patria: Dutch Arts and Culture in Colonial America, 1609–1776* (Albany, N.Y.: Albany Institute of History and Art, 1988).

14. Morrison H. Heckscher and Leslie Greene Bowman, *American Rococo, 1750–1775: Elegance in Ornament* (New York: Harry N. Abrams, 1992), p. xiii.

15. Robert Blair St. George, *The Wrought Covenant: Source Materials for the Study of Craftsmen and Community in Southeastern New England, 1620–1700* (Brockton, Mass.: Brockton Art Center, 1979); and David Grayson Allen, *In English Ways: The Movement of Societies and the Transferral of English Local Law and Custom to Massachusetts Bay in the Seventeenth Century* (Chapel Hill, N.C.: University of North Carolina Press, 1981). Jonathan L. Fairbanks and Robert F. Trent, eds., *New England Begins: The Seventeenth Century*, 3 vols. (Boston: Museum of Fine Arts, 1982). Among the many valuable contributions made by this milestone exhibition, the idea that seventeenth-century New England was peopled by settlers who "transferred their entire culture to the New World, maintained strong ties with England, . . . and enjoyed a complex geometric, artificial, and colorful artistic style now called Mannerism" (p. xvii) now seems somewhat reductionist. Layering example upon example of "transferral" and dependence, *New England Begins* virtually ignored the possibility of invention. The one chapter that focused on furniture (Robert F. Trent, "New England Joinery and Turning before 1700," pp. 501–50), although a brilliant analysis of craft and style, mostly illustrates objects that are emphatically derivative. Where Hadley chests are discussed (p. 529), the narrative trails off with a disclaimer that "it is impossible to suggest any exact origin for them" but that tracing "Connecticut River Valley craftsman to England's North Country may someday provide a valuable clue."

16. Francis J. Puig and Michael Conforti, eds., *The American Craftsman and the European Tradition, 1620–1820* (Hanover, N.H.: University Press of New England, 1989), p. xiii. The most blistering attack on antiquarianism and "sentimental patriotism" is Wendy Kaplan, "R. T. H. Halsey: An Ideology of Collecting American Decorative Arts," *Winterthur Portfolio* 17, no. 1 (spring 1982): 43–53. This article, and its corresponding historiographical trend, made a cottage industry of trashing antiquarianism by caricaturing the efforts of pioneer museum men like R. T. H. Halsey, the creative spirit behind the Metropolitan Museum of Art's 1924 American wing. Halsey's "hymn to individual achievement," with its mission to (among other things) help immigrants "attempting to become good Americans," is ridiculed by innuendo and association. The problem is not Kaplan's analysis but its intentional implications. Associating Halsey—a visionary by any measure—with "intense Anglophilia" and identifying the campaign of "Americanization" (see William B. Rhoads, "The Colonial Revival and the Americanization of Immigrants,"in *The Colonial Revival in America*, edited by Alan Axelrod [New York: W.W. Norton, 1985], pp. 341–61) with nativism and the Ku Klux Klan is unjustified. Although paradoxically both inclusive and exclusive, the Americanization campaign looks, in hindsight, like a responsible and refreshingly gentle attempt at social engineering. Today, with confidence in the public sector at an all-time low and given the searingly divisive role of "multiculturalism," victim group "rights," and bilingualism (to name only three of the obvious targets), antiquarians like Halsey are no longer viable targets for ridicule. Indeed, the image of museums with so strong a sense of purpose and so engaged with issues in the world around them is inspiring.

17. Philip Zea and Suzanne L. Flynt, *Hadley Chests* (Deerfield, Mass.: Pocumtuk Valley Memorial Association, 1992); this exhibition was sponsored by Israel Sack, Inc., and opened in their New York gallery several months before joining the tour of *Portsmouth Furniture* in Hartford. Kirk, *British Tradition*, pp. 95–118. Both Kirk and Philip Zea have labored to prove that Hadley chests were the result of some still-undocumented migration of craftsmen from the Lancaster Lakes region of England. Although comparisons between the Hadley tradition and the work of British North Country artisans is noteworthy, Kevin Sweeney's analysis of adaptation among converging styles by seventeenth-century Wethersfield, Connecticut, joiners is far more convincing (see his article in this volume). In any event, the Hadley chest is different enough from any of the joinery traditions with which it has been compared that the quality of invention is unmistakable. Just as there is no such thing as an entirely original design, there is also no such thing as one that is entirely derivative. Even the work of Thomas Dennis of Ipswich, Massachusetts, contemporaneous with the invention of the Hadley chest and widely touted for its similarity to the joinery tradition of the region (Exeter, West Country, England) where he was trained, exhibits some features of adaptation and change. "Innovation," such as it is, is inevitably a matter of degree. The unidentified joiners who "invented" the Hadley chest exercised a significant degree of adaptation and inventiveness. Even after its invention, the style continued to change and "evolve" in practice.

18. Jules David Prown, "Style as Evidence," *Winterthur Portfolio* 15, no. 3 (autumn 1980): 197–210. Garret, "Consumer's Taste," pp. 206–7.

19. Swank, et al., *Pennsylvania Germans*. William N. Hosley and Gerald W. R. Ward, eds., *The Great River: Art and Society of the Connecticut Valley, 1635–1820* (Hartford, Conn.: Wadsworth Atheneum, 1985), pp. 226–27.

20. Montgomery, "Country Furniture," pp. 355–59.

21. Houghton Bulkeley, "The 'Aaron Roberts' Attributions," *Contributions to Connecticut Cabinetmaking* (Hartford, Conn.: Connecticut Historical Society, 1967), pp. 11–14; Robert F. Trent, "The Colchester School of Cabinetmaking, 1750–1800," in Puig and Conforti, eds., *The American Craftsman and the European Tradition*, pp. 112–35. Margaretta M. Lovell, "Such Furniture as Will be Most Profitable: The Business of Cabinetmaking in Eighteenth-Century Newport," *Winterthur Portfolio* 26, no. 1 (spring 1991): 27–62.

22. Philip Zea, "The Emergence of Neoclassical Furniture Making in Rural Western Massachusetts," *Antiques* 142, no. 6 (December 1992): 842–51. Robert Blair St. George, "Artifacts of Regional Consciousness in the Connecticut River Valley, 1700–1780," in Hosley and Ward, eds., *The Great River*, p. 34. St. George's discussion of the "ideology of community" chronicles the various ways in which the Connecticut Valley's elite "managed" the social dynamics of class in an agrarian society. Among other things, they "actively patronized local artisans and relied upon their skills rather than importing urban craftsman whose understanding of . . . theory may have been more 'correct.'"

23. Timothy D. Rieman and Jean M. Burks, *The Complete Book of Shaker Furniture* (New York: Harry Abrams, 1993), pp. 66–77.

24. William N. Hosley Jr., "Architecture and Society of the Urban Frontier: Windsor, Vermont in 1800," in *The Bay and the River: 1600–1900. The Dublin Seminar for New England Folklife: Annual Proceedings 1981*, edited by Peter Benes (Boston: Boston University, 1982), pp. 73–86.

25. Bob Davis, "Growth of Trade Binds Nations, but It Also Can Spur Separatism," *Wall Street Journal* (New York), June 20, 1994. Brock Jobe, ed., *Portsmouth Furniture: Masterworks from the New Hampshire Seacoast* (Hanover, N.H.: University Press of New England for the Society for the Preservation of New England Antiquities, 1993), pp. 114–23, 176–81. Of all the furniture produced in Portsmouth, the most distinctive is work by Judkins & Senter (fl. 1808–1826) and their competitors, who were the last generation of Portsmouth furniture makers to enjoy a solid market for high-style cabinetwork. Portsmouth's furniture industry was largely swept away by competition from Boston, New York, and elsewhere after 1830. Connel and Muller, "Ohio Furniture," p. 466; a sideboard made by Jacob S. Ware (1802–1860) about 1830 in Frankfort, Ohio, is typical of the over-reach and flamboyance characteristic of furniture made by the last generation of regional cabinetmakers to enjoy local patronage for high-style furniture.

26. David Hackett Fischer, *Albion's Seed: Four British Folkways in America* (New York: Oxford University Press, 1989). With essays on "The Revolution as a Rising of Regional Cultures" (pp. 827–28), "The Friends' Migration: Ethnic Origins" (pp. 429–39), and "Ethnic Origins: 'We Are a Mixed People'" (pp. 618–21) about the Scotch and other "back country" settlers of West Virginia, this book is bursting with insight about the diverse subcultures that shaped political and social history in early America.

27. Susan Prendergast Schoelwer, "Connecticut Sunflower Furniture: A Familiar Form Reconsidered," *Yale University Art Gallery Bulletin* (spring 1989): 20–37.

28. Elizabeth Bidwell Bates and Jonathan L. Fairbanks, *American Furniture, 1620 to the Present* (New York: Richard Marek, 1981). This is the only survey of American furniture that has attempted to be culturally inclusive by featuring not only the usual high-style urban work but also the regional vernacular, ethnic subcultures and "cheap" furniture intended for other purposes than parlor use and display.

29. The origins of the idea of "Yankee ingenuity" are not clear. It may have originated, and was certainly stimulated, by the success of New England manufactured products (notably the firearms manufactured by Robbins & Lawrence in Windsor, Vermont, and the revolvers manufactured by Samuel Colt in Hartford, Connecticut) at the 1851 Crystal Palace Exhibition (see Brooke Hindle and Steven Lubar, *Engines of Change: The American Industrial Revolution, 1790–1860* [Washington, D.C.: Smithsonian Institution Press, 1986]; Nathan Rosenberg, "Why in America?" in *Yankee Enterprise: The Rise of the American System of Manufacturers*, edited by Otto Mayr and Robert C. Post [Washington, D.C.: Smithsonian Institution Press, 1981], pp. 49–62). As early as 1851, a Hartford newspaper described New England's "laying claim . . . to extraordinary ingenuity and inventive power," as if it were then already a part of the mythol-

ogy of the region (*Hartford Daily Times*, August 1, 1851). An 1855 article on "Connecticut Manufacturers" claimed that the nation's "largest axe factory," "largest clockmaking establishments," "most numerous and extensive paper mills," and "largest silk factory" were in Connecticut and noted how glass bottles, silverware, guns, clothespins, pianos, scythes, oars, coffee mills, steam engines, pewter ware, "and a hundred other things, are made in Connecticut, whose sons are famous for ingenuity and honest industry"(*Hartford Times*, July 12, 1855). Hank Morgan, Mark Twain's fictional "Yankee inventor" in *A Connecticut Yankee in King Arthur's Court* (1889), describes a personal history that could as easily have been that of the regional joiners and blacksmiths: "My father was a blacksmith, my uncle was a horse doctor, and I was both. . . . Then I went over to the great arms factory and learned my real trade; learned all there was to it; learned to make everything; guns, revolvers, cannon, boilers, engines, all sorts of labor-saving machinery. Why I could make anything a body wanted—anything in the world . . . and if there wasn't any quick new-fangled way to make a thing, I could invent one—and do it as easy as rolling off a log." Daniel V. DeSimone, "The Innovator," *The Engineer* 8, nos. 1, 2 (1967), in *Dartmouth Readings in the History and Philosophy of Technological Development: The Invention and Development Phases*, edited by Joseph J. Ermenc (Hanover, N.H.: unpublished manuscript, Thayer School of Engineering, Dartmouth College, 1977), pp. 267–71. Tom D. Crouch, "Why Wilbur and Orville? Some Thoughts on the Wright Brothers and the Process of Invention," in *Inventive Minds: Creativity in Technology,* edited by Robert J. Weber and David N. Perkins (New York: Oxford University Press, 1992), pp. 80–81. The Wright brothers were noted for their "relentless drive and will, their ability to look skeptics and rivals in the eye without blinking," and for their "hard-edged and uncompromising personalities."

Laurel Thatcher Ulrich

Furniture as Social History: Gender, Property, and Memory in the Decorative Arts

▼ I AM NOT a furniture historian. I am a social historian who in a moment of whimsy (or hubris) agreed to keynote a furniture symposium. I must admit that my initial forays into the literature were daunting. References to "stop-fluted pilasters," "pendant drops," and "double-arched beads" sent me scrambling back to more conventional history.[1] But as I persisted, I recognized beneath the technicalities a passionate enterprise of discovery. Material objects literally carry the print of their maker's hand, but only those who are willing to narrow their gaze will find that evidence.

As the essays in this volume show, however, objects are not enough for historical discovery. The best furniture studies take us full circle from objects to documents and back again, showing how chests and chairs reveal societies and events as they derive new meaning from changing economic and social contexts. Ned Cooke's marvelous phrase "part-time is not part-skilled" could only have been created by a person comfortable both in the archives and the gallery. Ned examined furniture, but he also used account books, probate records, and tax lists—the routine sources of social history—to reconstruct the rhythms of work among Connecticut furniture makers.[2] As I began my own research, I hoped to follow that example, but I also wanted to broaden the canvas of furniture scholarship by suggesting new ways of connecting it to social history.

Fifteen years ago, Robert Blair St. George urged his fellow scholars to recover the lives of the men who made furniture. "While studies of material life must begin with the artifact," he wrote, "too frequently is the maker miraculously forgotten, obliterated by the supra personal creep of diffusion patterns or reduced to a finite set of oppositions that profess to capture his mind without capturing his feelings."[3] The makers of early American furniture have begun to emerge from the shadows. We know far too little, however, about the auxiliary crafts related to furniture construction. Where are the upholsterers, stainers, painters, and chair caners who completed the work of cabinetmakers, joiners, and chairmakers? We also know too little about the ordinary patrons, including the female patrons, who made this work possible. Nor has enough been written about the relationship between furniture and other consumer goods, including ceramics and textiles. To focus on furniture without considering the broader consumption patterns of ordinary households is to leave out a vital part of the story; to think about consumption without considering the social context in which tables, chairs, chests, blankets, petticoats, and pots were acquired is to divorce objects from the human relations that gave them value. From my own position as a historian of early American women, I would argue that an essential step in broadening furniture scholarship is to begin thinking about gender.

Gender is the social construction of sexual difference. It is present symbolically in language, gesture, and costume; structurally in the organization of law and politics; and practically in the ordering of daily life. Yet it is often invisible. As Mary Douglas has written, "A . . . social order generates its pattern of values, commits the hearts of its members, and creates a myopia which certainly seems to be inevitable."[4] For those with eyes to see, however, the social construction of gender can be found everywhere—even in furniture. To begin with, the visual and tactile qualities of furniture suggest new ways of thinking about the body and its reconfiguration over time. In the first half of my paper, I will pursue that theme, relating furniture to recent scholarship on clothing. The second half of the paper raises a more concrete issue—the question of female ownership and inheritance. My objective is not to give a definitive statement either about gender or furniture but to raise questions for further analysis. The methods I have suggested can be applied to other themes in social history, particularly to race and ethnicity, but since gender cuts across many human boundaries, it is an appropriate place to begin.

When I attended the Portsmouth furniture exhibit at the Currier Gallery in the winter of 1992, I was struck by the anthropomorphic (as well as zoomorphic) qualities of the artifacts. The notion that tables and chairs were somehow alive was reinforced by many of the period terms used to describe furniture and its components: head (pediment), legs, heel, feet, toes, arms, elbow, ears, cheeks (wings of an upholstered chair). Certain twentieth-century terms, such as bonnet (a closed head), are also anthropomorphic and gender based.[5] The fact that furniture forms are related to human forms is hardly surprising. We spread our bodies on and around furniture, extending our own trunks and limbs by appropriating the trunks and limbs of trees. A table is a kind of lap, an enlarged pair of knees for working or eating. A chair, too, offers supporting thighs for sitting on and a spine (or cushioned breast) to lean on. Clearly, the human body shapes furniture just as furniture constrains and sustains the human body.

I wanted to push that insight one step further. If tables and chairs have arms, legs, and toes, do they also have sex? That question forces us to define sexual difference. We could take a Freudian approach, looking for projecting appendages or inner and outer space. I chose a more historically grounded method derived from costume history. Since clothing almost always differentiates adult males from females, it is a perfect vehicle for understanding the ways in which gender changes over time. As Valerie Steele has written,

> An article of clothing has no inherent meaning. Trousers do not have the idea of masculinity built into them, nor does a skirt automatically signify that the wearer is either female or feminine. The meaning of clothing is culturally defined. . . . It is the history of clothes and the context in which they are worn that determine the meanings that we ascribe to them.[6]

Figure 1 *Elizabeth Paddy Wensley,* artist unknown, 1670–1680. Oil on canvas. 41 1/2" × 33 1/4". (Courtesy, Pilgrim Society, Plymouth, Mass.)

A search for the aesthetics of gender in furniture might begin, then, with a series of comparisons between furniture forms and human forms—or, more precisely, *elite* human forms as defined by fashionable clothing.

To explore some of the possibilities of this form of analysis, I compared a series of well-known New England portraits with furniture from the same period. I was surprised and delighted to see how in each period clothing rhymed with furniture. The lace, ribbon, lawn, and silk on Elizabeth Wensley's sleeves (fig. 1), like the carving, paint, and moldings on a contemporary New England joined chest (fig. 2), form a series of clearly defined bands, each embellished with surface ornament. In both the painting and the chest, variety is the dominant aesthetic principle, as though each artist tried to see how many different colors and textures could be layered on one form. These late-seventeenth-century objects contrast with two eighteenth-century artifacts, a Connecticut high chest attributed to Eliphalet Chapin (1741–1807) (fig. 3) and John Singleton Copley's portrait of Dorothy Wendell Skinner (1733–1822) (fig. 4). The eighteenth-century forms are

Figure 2 Chest attributed to the shop of Thomas Dennis (w. 1659–d.1706), Ipswich, Massachusetts, 1676. Red and white oak. H. 31 11/16", W. 49 5/8", D. 22 5/8". (Courtesy, Winterthur Museum.)

sculptural, light, and playful. Height, rather than width, gives dignity to Chapin's chest. The chest's "head" is crowned with an open, scrolled ornament, whereas Dorothy Skinner's is crowned with a delicate, lacy cap. Gilded looking glasses from the period also employ architectural elements and ornaments such as those on Chapin's chest. An eighteenth-century lady, her hair dressed in the latest fashion, might see a double reflection of herself in such a mirror.

Costume historians warn against the tendency to abstract gendered meanings from broad stylistic changes that affect both sexes. Claudia Kidwell offers a particularly compelling example:

> In 1840 an individual strolled through the city park cutting a fashionable figure in bottle green cloth and yellow brocaded silk. The figure was shaped like an hourglass. The fashionable silhouette had sloping shoulders, a padded chest, and a narrow, cinched waist. The clothing was seamed to fit snugly over the waist and flared over the hips into a full skirt. This could have been a skirt of a woman's dress or the skirt of a man's coat.[7]

An "hourglass" figure, then, is not an eternally feminine symbol, nor do ruffles, flowered fabrics, or satins belong exclusively to women. The first task in any study is to distinguish between design motifs that unite men and women in a given period and those that distinguish one sex from another. Although the contrast between the seventeenth and eighteenth centuries is more easily illustrated with women's portraits than with men's, the basic differences do in fact cross gender lines. Thomas Smith's portrait of an unknown gentleman, circa 1680 (fig. 5), is every bit as fussy with surface details as that of Elizabeth Wensley, whereas in portraits by Blackburn or Copley, men as well as women, shimmer with light.

Careful reading of male and female clothing within the same period can, however, yield gender distinctions. The paintings of John Singleton Copley provide a rich field for such an analysis. Because Copley was interested in

Figure 3 High chest attributed to Eliphalet Chapin, East Windsor, Connecticut, 1771–1795. Cherry with white pine. H. 87", W. 39 1/2", D. 18". (Courtesy, Wadsworth Atheneum, Wallace Nutting Collection. Gift of J. Pierpont Morgan, by exchange and The Evelyn Bonar Storrs Trust Fund.)

furniture, his paintings also help us connect chairs and tables with gender. In the eighteenth century, bare forearms were strongly associated with women, shapely legs with men. Significantly, in Copley's paintings wom-

Figure 4 John Singleton Copley, *Dorothy Wendell Skinner*, Boston, 1772. Oil on canvas. 39 3/4" × 30 3/4". (Courtesy, Museum of Fine Arts, Boston; bequest of Mrs. Martin Brimmer.)

en's arms were often displayed against polished wood, as in the painting of Dorothy Skinner (fig. 4). Although men's hands (though never their arms) are sometimes reflected in polished tables, men usually grasp some object (fig. 6)— a paper, book, tool, or in one case a squirrel. Only with women does Copley emphasize the flesh alone. Here he is employing an aesthetic principle enunciated by the eighteenth-century philosopher Edmund Burke:

> I do not now recollect any thing beautiful that is not smooth. In trees and flowers, smooth leaves are beautiful; smooth slopes of earth in gardens; smooth steams in the landscape; smooth coats of birds and beasts in animal beauties; in fine women, smooth skins; and in several sorts of ornamental furniture, smooth and polished surfaces.[8]

Copley reflects one kind of smoothness in the other.

Artists in other times and places might enjoy the play of light and shadow on a sun-freckled or mosquito-bitten arm or a fruit-stained or grease-splattered table. The gestures of Copley's sitters—women resting on the surfaces

Figure 5 *Portrait of a Gentleman* (possibly Elisha Hutchinson or George Downing), attributed to Thomas Smith, Boston, ca. 1680–1690. Oil on canvas. 43½" × 35⅞". (Courtesy, Harvard University Portrait Collection.)

of their polished tables, men fluttering their important papers—capture gender codes that might not be visible in other ways. In most of the female portraits, the tables are purely ornamental, dazzling mirrors for displaying female arms. In the portraits of men (and in the single case of Mrs. Thomas Mifflin who is working at a table loom), tables are settings for displaying if not for doing work. If one cannot imagine Paul Revere actually engraving a tea pot on the table pictured in Copley's portrait, the surface nevertheless made a fine place for displaying his work and tools. More commonly, Copley's gentlemen use tables for writing.[9] There is no difference in form between the pedestal table used by one of Copley's scholars (fig. 7) and the table portrayed in a contemporary cartoon of an old maid at tea (fig. 8). The polished table in Dorothy Skinner's portrait is neither a woman's table nor a man's table, neither a tea table nor a writing table, but an all-purpose surface for sustaining and displaying beautiful things—smooth arms, polished tools, sleek animals, and perhaps silken prose (fig. 4).

In Copley's iconography, pen and paper are simultaneously marks of gentility and of industry—but only for males. Although nearly a quarter of his men are portrayed with loose papers, or account books, fewer than 2 percent of his women are shown with any kind of paper, including loose pages

Figure 6 John Singleton Copley, *Paul Revere*, 1768–1770. Oil on canvas. 35" × 28 ½". (Courtesy, Museum of Fine Arts, Boston. Gift of Joseph W., William B., and Edward H. R. Revere.)

Figure 7 John Singleton Copley, *Thomas Hollis*, 1766. Oil on canvas. 94" × 58". (Courtesy, Harvard University Portrait Collection.)

that might be letters. None of his women is pictured with a pen. This omission is surprising given the importance of letter-writing in the education of eighteenth-century women. Copley frequently pictured women with books, but apparently even among his elite clientele, quill and ink were still too closely associated with masculinity to fit comfortably into a female portrait, even into a portrait of a woman as literate and literary as Sarah Prince. Sarah holds her book in a vaporous landscape, while her husband, Moses Gill, receipt in hand, leans one elbow on what appears to be a merchant's desk.[10] In comparison with Copley's paintings, the contemporary engraving of Phillis Wheatley, quill in hand, seems even more revolutionary. Modestly (but tastefully) dressed in the garb of a gentlewoman's maid, Phillis sits in a late baroque side chair, papers spread on what appears to be a pillar-and-claw tea table (judging from the shape of the top), about to compose her next line of poetry (fig. 9).

A table became a man's or a woman's table by virtue of its use. For the women in Copley's portraits, a table was a place for quiet reflection and perhaps conversation. In a few paintings, female sitters finger fruit or flowers,

Figure 8 *The Old Maid*, London, 1777. Engraving on paper. 10 3/16" × 8 3/16". (Courtesy, Library of Congress.)

Figure 9 *Phillis Wheatley, Negro Servant to Mr. John Wheatley, of Boston*, London, 1773. Engraving on paper. 6 1/2" × 4 3/8". (Courtesy, New York Public Library.)

traditional emblems of beauty and fertility, though in some of Copley's paintings fruit may represent horticultural achievement as well. Mrs. Ezekiel Goldthwait, for example, rests one plump hand on a bowl of fruit while the other rests quietly on the polished surface of her table. Her bare arm is central to the composition, its reflection completing a circle of light from fruit to wood (fig. 10). In contrast, Mr. Goldthwait turns away from the table, his arms covered by his austere coat, his hands leading the eye downward from the stile of his chair to his smoothly stockinged leg (fig. 11). For Copley, men's legs were as important as the bare arms of women.

To a twentieth-century eye, the graceful curves of a cabriole chair leg might appear "feminine," a massive chest with stubby bracket feet, "masculine." In the colonial world, the gender attributions were probably reversed. In both the seventeenth and eighteenth centuries, a well-formed leg was one of the defining attributes of an upper-class male. Working men and sailors might disguise their calves in pantaloons, women in skirts, but elite males exposed and embellished their lower limbs. Here, too, furniture and fashion changed together. The decorative pulls on a baroque high chest (fig. 12) mirror the knobby ruffles and bows on the legs of a late-seventeenth-cen-

Figure 10 John Singleton Copley, *Mrs. Ezekiel Goldthwait*, 1770–1771. Oil on canvas. 50" × 39 ½". (Courtesy, Museum of Fine Arts, Boston. Bequest of John T. Bowen in memory of Eliza M. Bowen.)

tury male (fig. 13), whereas the smooth silk stockings and tightly fitting shoes of eighteenth-century gentlemen reflect furniture styles of that time. In his rather awkward, full-length portrait of Thomas Hancock, Copley acknowledged that relationship (fig. 14). Here the white-stockinged legs of the sober merchant are flanked by the wood and gilt legs of high-style furniture, the velvet-covered armchair appealingly empty, the gentleman's outstretched arm inviting a real-life lady to take her place beside the fanciful nymph who grows, mermaid-like, out of the curving legs of the table. The same table—and the same rhyme with a man's leg—reappears in Copley's better-known portrait of Jeremiah Lee of Marblehead.

For a commercially successful artist like Copley, men's legs were a bit of a problem. Few Boston patrons were willing to commission full-length portraits. In three-quarter-length poses, particularly when the subject was seated, men's appendages could appear awkwardly cut-off at the ankles. In dozens of portraits painted between 1758 and 1774, Copley experimented with various devises to integrate silk-stockinged calves—*sans* feet—into his images of aspiring males. The Ezekiel Goldthwait portrait represents two of his most commonly used solutions. In the Goldthwait painting, as in

Figure 11 John Singleton Copley, *Ezekiel Goldthwait*, 1770–1771. Oil on canvas. 50" × 40". (Courtesy, Museum of Fine Arts, Boston: Bequest of John T. Bowen in memory of Eliza M. Bowen.)

those of John Gardiner, Daniel Rogers, and Isaac Royall, the man's leg, highlighted in white silk, outlines the shape of the chair.[11] The Daniel Rogers portrait is particularly striking in this regard. Copley must have experimented for some time to achieve the marvelous blending of the subject and the chair. Rogers is seated at cross-angles to the chair, his right leg obscured by drapery, his left extending and completing both the back support and the rear leg (fig. 15).

The Ezekiel Goldthwait painting also exemplifies Copley's use of quill pens as a rhyme for men's legs. Goldthwait grasps his quill firmly between his thumb and index finger, establishing a vertical line that parallels the fold of his wig, the buttoned flap of his waistcoat, and the barely glimpsed stile of his chair. The point of the pen leads the eye ever so subtly to the bended row of brass nails that completes the edge of the chair. In his portraits of Issac Smith, John Erving, and Thomas Boylston, Copley used quills in similar ways.[12] In the Isaac Smith portrait, for example, the quill remains in its stand, tilted at the exact angle of Smith's leg; the brass buttons of the man's breeches and the brass nails of his chair bend in opposite directions.

Copley's eye captured some of the gestures that distinguished women

Figure 12 High chest possibly decorated by Charles Gillam, Saybrook or Guilford, Connecticut, 1703–1725. Pine, tulip poplar, and ash. H. 54 5/8", W. 40 1/8", D. 21 1/8". (Courtesy, Wintherthur Museum.)

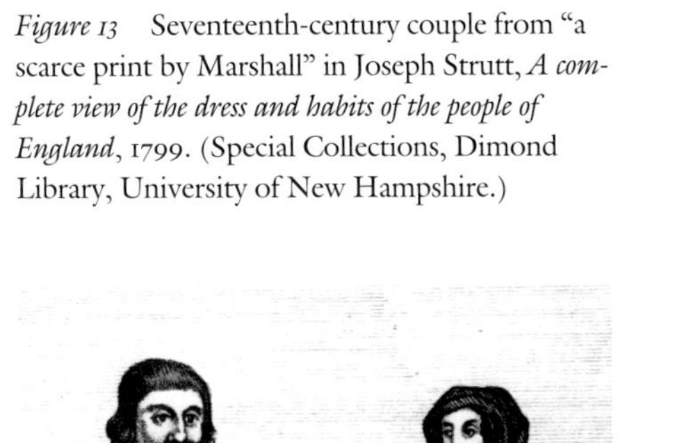

Figure 13 Seventeenth-century couple from "a scarce print by Marshall" in Joseph Strutt, *A complete view of the dress and habits of the people of England*, 1799. (Special Collections, Dimond Library, University of New Hampshire.)

from men in eighteenth-century Boston, but gender codes are best conveyed in action. Portraits freeze people in time and space. If we could see more motion, actually observe these dignified gentlemen and ladies bowing, dancing, eating, working, or laughing, our conclusions about the period might change. Did the presence of high-style furniture inhibit or structure motion? Did a polished table presume an arm in repose? Did a lady reveal some part of her leg as she lifted her skirt to ascend a stair, perform a minuet, or cross a muddy street? Did a gentleman—or for that matter a prosperous mechanic like Paul Revere—ever roll his sleeves to the

Figure 14 John Singleton Copley, *Thomas Hancock*, 1764–1766. Oil on canvas. 95 1/2" × 59 1/2". (Courtesy, Harvard University Portrait Collection.)

Figure 15 John Singleton Copley, *Daniel Rogers* [?], 1767. Oil on canvas. 50" × 40½". (Courtesy, Museum of Fine Arts, Boston. Bequest of Dr. Morrill Wyman.)

elbow? It seems inconceivable that men worked with their loose shirts falling to the wrists, yet engravings of street riots, like genteel portraits, show men's forearms covered and their legs revealed. Legs are so thoroughly male in the visual grammar of the era that it is difficult not to see the carefully turned legs of period furniture as a celebration, if only subliminally, of the male human form.

If the Portsmouth furniture show provoked me to meditate on the symbolic meanings of arms and legs, the Hadley chest exhibition returned me to the material base of social life in eighteenth-century New England. Again the issue of gender rose to the forefront. I was not the only person intrigued by the remarkable Hannah Barnard cupboard (fig. 16). The curator of the exhibit purposefully "set up the other chests like so many little pews leading up to the cupboard, which sat there like a kind of throne or altar." One observer saw a "proto-feminist statement" in Hannah's cupboard. In this "rigidly patriarchal age," he reasoned, only a rebellious woman would

Figure 16 Cupboard, inscribed "Hannah Barnard," Hadley, Massachusetts area, ca. 1715. Oak and yellow pine. H. 61 1/8", W. 50", D. 21 1/4". (From the collection of the Henry Ford Museum and Greenfield Village; photo Amanda Merullo.)

emblazon her name on a cupboard. Another suggested, more mildly, that Hannah's cupboard must have been a gift from her future husband, "a valentine in furniture."[13] As the only specialist in women's history represented on the program, I felt compelled to explain Hannah's cupboard. I began by asking furniture scholars how unusual it was for names—particularly women's names—to appear on furniture. I soon learned that Hannah's cupboard was closely associated with a large group of chests made in the Connecticut River Valley between the 1680s and about 1730.

The more than sixteen variants of the so-called "Hadley chest" share certain design elements—undulating vines, tulip and leaf motifs, pinwheels, and letters with curling tendrils. Most are marked with initials; at least six have complete names, all of women.[14] The floral ornamentation on the Hadley cupboards and chests reinforces the notion that they were "dower" or "marriage" furniture. Most are exuberantly carved or painted, though the motifs they employ vary widely. The so-called "SH" chest (fig. 17), for example, employs design elements present in a seventeenth-century bed hanging at the Wadsworth Atheneum (fig. 18). The very different style of the "MS" chest with drawers (fig. 19), made about the same time as the Hannah Barnard cupboard, echoes design elements widely used in samplers (figs. 20, 21).

Figure 17 Chest with drawers, initialed "SH," Hadley, Massachusetts area, ca. 1710. Oak with white pine. H. 45¼", W. 44½", D. 18½". (Courtesy, Pocumtuck Valley Memorial Association, Memorial Hall Museum, Deerfield, Massachusetts.)

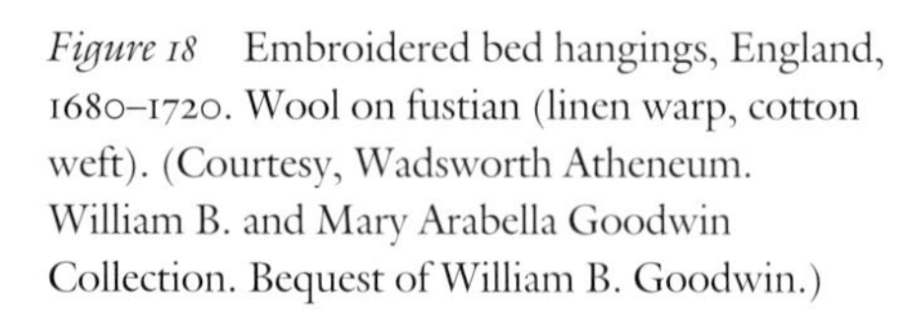

Figure 18 Embroidered bed hangings, England, 1680–1720. Wool on fustian (linen warp, cotton weft). (Courtesy, Wadsworth Atheneum. William B. and Mary Arabella Goodwin Collection. Bequest of William B. Goodwin.)

Figure 19 Chest with drawers, initialed "MS," Hadley, Massachusetts area, ca. 1715. (Courtesy, Wadsworth Atheneum.)

The association with embroideries is hardly surprising. We have already noted common elements in furniture and clothing within a given period. This connection is merely another example of the well-known unity of decorative arts. Furniture reflects architecture, gravestones, silver, and even pie crust vents from the same period (fig. 22). Seen in isolation, no motif would mark a piece of furniture as a "woman's" cupboard or chest. It is the combination of decoration and form with the presence of women's names that leads to that conclusion. Though almost all of the identified initials on Hadley chests (and all of the full names) belonged to women, plainer board chests from the same time and place were owned by men.[15] The terms "marriage cupboard" or "dower chest" are modern, but they point in the right direction. The Hannah Barnard cupboard marks a transition point in a woman's life, the stage at which she left one household to join another.

Cupboards and chests, like the textiles, ceramics, and silver they were designed to store, belonged to that category of property known as "moveables." Moveables were associated both with the marriage portions of daughters and with bequests granted to widows. In the Connecticut River Valley, as in most of the western world, "real" property or land followed the male line of inheritance. Women typically inherited portable forms of property—cooking equipment, animals, bed linens, and furniture. In such a system, women themselves became "moveables." When Hannah Barnard married John Marsh in 1715, she changed her name, shifting her allegiance from one male-headed household to another; but her cupboard, like the marked

Figure 20 Sampler by Mary Holingworth, Salem, Massachusetts, ca. 1665. Silk on linen. 24¾" × 7½". (Courtesy, Peabody Essex Museum, Salem, Mass. Bequest of George Rea Curwen, 1900, 4234.39.)

Figure 21 Sampler by Abigail Pinniger, Rhode Island, 1730. Silk on linen. 16" × 9¾". (Courtesy, Museum of Art, Rhode Island School of Design, gift of Miss Susan B. Thurston, 14.60.)

sheets, pillow beers, and silver spoons she brought to the marriage, carried her maiden name.[16]

Although initials were more commonly used than full names, household goods preserved a woman's birth name even as she lost it in marriage. The eighteenth-century meaning of such a practice is suggested in the memoir of a Vermont woman, Mary Palmer Tyler. Shortly after she and Royall Tyler were married, he purchased a dozen small and three large spoons and had them marked with her maiden initials "MP." Since they were already married, it is surprising that he did not have the spoons marked "MT" for Mary

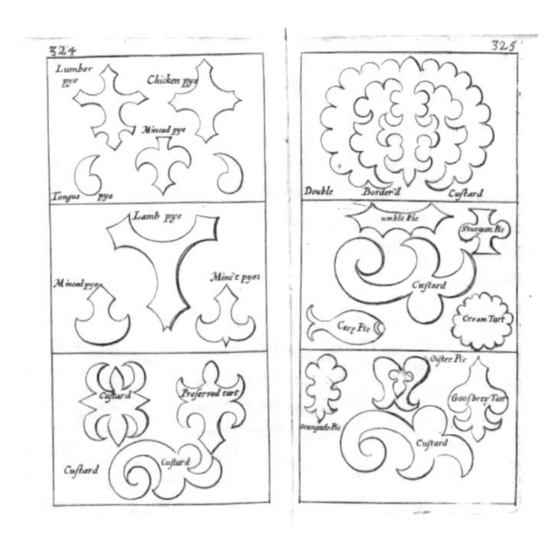

Figure 22 Pie crust vents from a seventeenth-century English cookbook. (Courtesy, Bodleian Library, Oxford University.)

Palmer Tyler or even "R T M" for Royall and Mary Tyler, as was sometimes done on linen, silver, pottery, and occasionally even furniture. To Mary, his selection of her maiden initials demonstrated his sensitivity to her parent's precarious circumstances. "[H]e knew I could not purchase them," she wrote, "and he wished to make it appear that my parents did so." Hannah Barnard's flamboyant cupboard not only preserved her personal identity, it ratified her connection with her family of origin. Significantly, a mammoth table stone in Hadley cemetery lists Hannah with her father rather than with her husband. Although this circumstance was probably a consequence both of Hannah's early death and the remarriage and subsequent death of her spouse, there seems to be no question that she continued to be identified as a "Barnard" even after she became a "Marsh."[17]

Still, the visibility of Hannah's name on her cupboard speaks of more than family pride. Many women preserved their maiden identities by embroidering their initials onto linens or bed coverings. Few women emblazoned their full names on so visible a household object as a cupboard. In fact, the Barnard family seems to have nourished female independence as well as family pride. Hannah was named for her grandmother and for her paternal aunt, Hannah Barnard Westcar Beamon, a childless woman, twice married and twice widowed, who appears several times in Hadley and Deerfield records. In 1673 the aunt was acquitted of wearing silk contrary to law. In January 1677 she was again presented "for wearing silk in a flaunting garb to the great offence of several sober persons in Hadley." Her first husband had died two years before, leaving an estate of £431. In 1694, now remarried and a schoolmistress in Deerfield, she rescued the town's children from a French and Indian attack by rushing them to the fort. She died in Deerfield in 1725 in sober respectability, leaving her considerable estate to the town for the support of schools. It is not hard to imagine the niece of such a woman emblazoning her name on a cupboard. In fact, something about the arrangement of letters on the cupboard suggests a primer or a slate. Could Hannah also have been a teacher, like her aunt? If her recorded birthdate is correct, she was thirty-one years old when she married John Marsh, a widower five years her senior. (Hannah's older sister had married at eighteen.)[18]

Hannah died in 1716, leaving an infant daughter, Abigail. Her husband married a third time, fathered several more children, then died in 1725. His will makes clear what the cupboard only suggests, that certain objects in the household were marked, literally or figuratively, with female lineages. Marsh promised his only son, a child of his third marriage, all of his real estate, reserving moveable property for his daughters. Hannah's child was to receive £120, "to be paid in what was her own Mothers," plus "her Mothers Wearing Cloaths . . . to be given her free." The inventory contains separate lists for each of the wives. Although Marsh, as head of the household, controlled all this property, he understood its origins. The moveables each wife brought to the marriage formed the core of her own daughters' inheritance. Hannah's daughter Abigail grew up in Hadley, married Waitstill Hastings in 1736, and in 1742 had a daughter whom she named, not

Figure 23 Settee, Portsmouth, New Hampshire, 1800–1810. Mahogany and birch with maple and white pine. H. 34¾", W. 84⅛", D. 16¼" (seat). (Courtesy, Winterthur Museum.)

just *Hannah*, but *Hannah Barnard* Hastings.[19] Not surprisingly, this fourth Hannah Barnard eventually inherited the cupboard.

In the Marsh family, demographic accidents—the early deaths of two wives, the husband's own premature demise—exposed female lineages. More commonly, the formulaic dispersal of moveables, as in "one-third of my household goods," concealed the female labor that created and maintained those goods and the social customs, if not the female voices, that directed their disposal. Because daughters customarily received their portions at marriage rather than at the death of their father, wills and inventories actually mask much of what moved from one generation to another. Land can be traced in deeds, but moveables, by definition, flowed outside the constraints of law. For this reason, object-centered research is most useful. Probate records can tell us what sorts of objects people possessed at any one time and what kinds of things decedents willed to their children, but only detailed histories of surviving objects can tell us how certain moveables were transmitted—or lost—over time.

Establishing provenance is so basic to decorative arts scholarship that researchers may have overlooked its potential as social history. The range of possibilities—as well as the difficulties—are suggested in catalogues and books such as Brock Jobe's *Portsmouth Furniture: Masterworks from the New Hampshire Seacoast*. Provenances range from a despairing "early history unknown" to complete genealogies stretching through centuries. Many of these document lineal descent from mother to daughter, even though, until the middle of the nineteenth century, husbands legally owned and controlled all of the property their wives brought to marriage. Thus, a secretary-and-bookcase by Langly Boardman, stamped on the bottom of every drawer with the name "Dr Dwight," actually came to Susannah Dwight as part of her inheritance from her father, Thomas Thompson. It then descended to Susannah's daughter, Martha Rundlet, who in turn gave it to her daughter, who gave it to a sister. Dwight's stamp survives as an ironic commentary on male ownership of what was in fact female property.[20]

From the standpoint of social history, the most frustrating entries simply say, "Descended in the ______ Family." Since families survive only by integrating new blood in each generation, one can never be certain what such an entry means. After all, Hannah Barnard's cupboard descended through the Marsh family and the Hastings family while retaining the Barnard name. Because of the male bias of western naming practices, unbroken descent from father to son is easily traced, particularly when "moveables" become attached to houses. Thus, the magnificent neoclassical settee illustrated in figure 23 passed from father to son through three generations while remaining in the entry hall of the Pierce mansion. In contrast, the impressive *Sherburne* high chest passed by a circuitous route to the *Penhallow* and *Swan* families, eventually returning to the *Warner* house (figs. 24, 25).[21]

The history of the Sherburne chest reinforces a point made earlier in this paper about the importance in conducting research of moving between documents and objects. Until research began for the Portsmouth furniture book, the former owner of the chest did not know the meaning of the initials "I*S" on the tympanum (fig. 26). Three years later, he stumbled across an answer in an antiquarian bookstore. A 1902 furniture book identified "I*S" as John Sherburne, a Portsmouth mariner who died at sea in 1735. Genealogical research sustained the attribution. Sherburne was indeed a direct ancestor of the Penhallows, who owned both the Warner house and the chest in 1902. In the intervening century, however, John Sherburne's marvelous highboy suffered a peculiar fate. As the 1902 history explained, "The legs of the chest were ruthlessly sawed off many years ago, in order that it might stand in a low-ceilinged room." (The current owner had the feet restored in the early 1950s.)[22]

The last private owner believes that Elizabeth Warner Sherburne moved the highboy to the Warner house when she inherited it from her uncle in 1814. If so, it must have left the house again, because the 1902 history says,

Figure 24 High chest of drawers, Portsmouth, New Hampshire, 1733. Walnut and maple and walnut veneers with white pine. H. 86¼", W. 40½", D. 22¼". (Courtesy, Warner House Association, gift of Mr. and Mrs. Thaxter Swan; photo, David Bohl.)

Figure 25 Provenance of the high chest illustrated in fig. 24: Mendum–Sherburne–Warner–Penhallow connections.

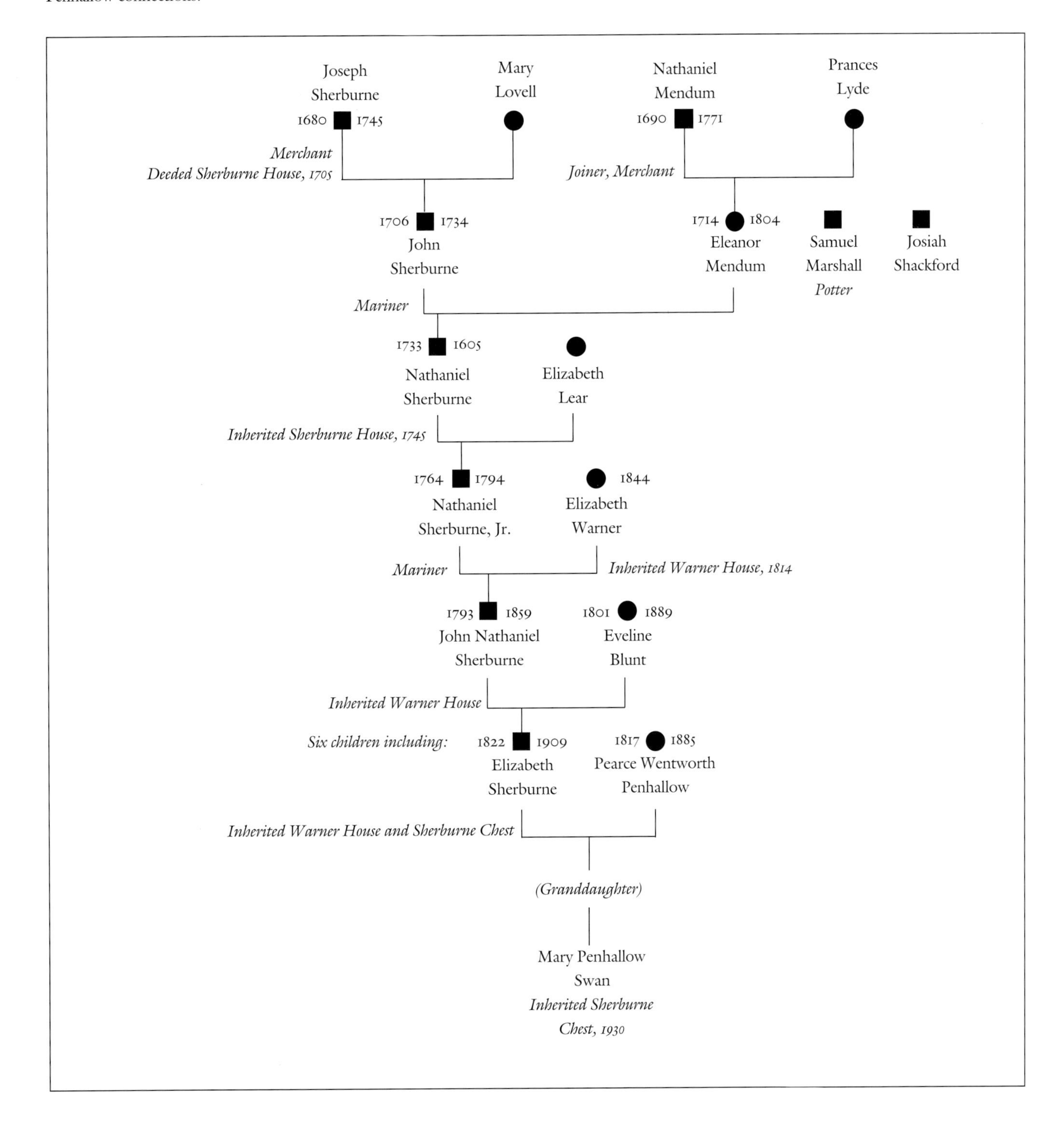

Figure 26 Detail of the initials and date on the inlaid heart of the chest illustrated in fig. 24. (Photo, Brock Jobe.)

Figure 27 Detail of the inlay on the upper drawer of the high chest illustrated in fig. 24. (Photo, David Bohl.)

Figure 28 Detail of compass star inlaid on the case sides of the chest illustrated in fig. 24. (Photo, David Bohl.)

"it is only in comparatively recent years that it has belonged to the branch of the family now owning the Warner house." Again the phrase "the family" is confusing. Was the author referring to Sherburnes, Penhallows, or both? Did one of Elizabeth Warner Sherburne's grandchildren (there were six) take the chest after her death in 1844, cutting off the feet to accommodate a smaller house? If so, the chest with its outraged limbs returned to the Warner house during the tenure of Elizabeth Warner Pitts Sherburne Penhallow, who died in 1909 and who must have been the informant for the 1902 history. The mystery of the missing feet is of more than antiquarian interest. It is evidence not only of the shifting value of "old time" furniture as it passed from old to old-fashioned, to antique, but of the economic imperatives that shape history and memory. A high chest required a high-ceilinged room. At least one of John Sherburne's descendants must have experienced downward mobility.[23]

The eighteenth-century history of the chest is obscure, though there are tantalizing hints in the family history and on the chest itself. The date on the tympanum below the center finial has puzzled researchers, since it doesn't seem to refer to any known life event. The heart suggests a marriage, but according to local records, John Sherburne and Eleanor Mendum were married in 1731, not 1733.[24] Perhaps the baroque shell inlay on the large top drawer (fig. 27) signifies another, now lost, event in the life of its first owner—the birth of a first child named John (the couple's only recorded child is Nathaniel, born just before or after his father's death) or even the completion of a successful voyage or an ascendancy from "mariner' to "captain." There is nothing particularly personal about the imagery, however. The whimsical cherubs and Doric columns flanking the shell and the compass stars with faces on the case sides are distinctive interpretations of relatively generic, eighteenth-century ornaments, though the imagery is appropriate to an aspiring provincial class (figs. 26–28). The materials from which the chest is constructed—pine, walnut, burled maple—demonstrate the material base of Portsmouth's rising gentility. Surveyors' compasses as well as mariners' compasses did indeed lay the foundations of Portsmouth—and Sherburne—wealth.

As James Garvin has written, "The period from 1725 to 1750 witnessed a dramatic mercantile expansion that bore fruit by mid century in a new generation of grand houses, in a notable increase in the display of personal wealth among the oligarchy, and in social stratification which strengthened the status of those few families that had seized wealth earlier in the century."

Figure 29 Prudence Punderson, "First, Second, and Last Scenes of Mortality." (Courtesy, Connecticut Historical Society, Hartford.)

John and Eleanor Sherburne's kin were among those families. Eleanor's father, Nathaniel Mendum, rose from "joiner" to "shopkeeper" to "Esquire" during this era. John's father, Joseph Sherburne, became a member of the King's Council in 1734 and a justice of the Supreme Court in 1739. About 1730 he added a room (possibly a shop) to the Puddle Dock house he had accepted from his mother as part of the settlement of his father's estate. Before the decade was out, he had completely gutted the old house, adding a proper Georgian stairway in the space once held by the old chimney and creating neoclassical orders from the then-outmoded windows and doors.[25]

The spate of building that began in 1729 with the purchase of an additional strip of land adjoining the back garden may indeed have been motivated by the coming-of-age of the Sherburne children. John's marriage in 1731 and Joseph's in 1734 marked a new stage in the family life cycle as one generation aged and the other prepared to take its place. John's death in 1735 interrupted but did not halt this process. His wife soon married Samuel Marshall, who operated a pottery just across Horse Lane from 1736 until his death in 1745. (In fact, waste pieces from the Marshall pottery were found in the trench under the Sherburne addition when it was excavated in the 1980s.)

There is no way of knowing where young Nathaniel Sherburne or his father's chest spent the 1730s and 1740s. Presumably the child and the chest were both cared for in the Marshall house or the neighboring Sherburne house. Joseph Sherburne's 1745 inventory does, in fact, list a "Chest of Draws" that may have been a high chest.[26] It is conceivable that young Nathaniel, the oldest son of an oldest son, was raised in his grandfather's house. By 1759, Nathaniel had inherited that house, receiving his father's double portion as oldest son. He lived there until his death in 1805—with or without the Sherburne high chest. The family genealogist believes the chest passed from Eleanor Mendum to her son Nathaniel at her death. Perhaps it did, but since Nathaniel outlived his mother by only a year, it is also possible the chest bypassed him entirely, going directly from one John Sherburne, via his widow, to another.

Eleanor Mendum Sherburne Marshall Shackford, having survived three husbands, died in Portsmouth on February 4, 1804, at the age of ninety. Ten years before, she had witnessed what must have been a striking replay of her own life history. Her grandson, Nathaniel Sherburne Jr., a mariner, died of yellow fever a year after his marriage to Elizabeth Warner, leaving a son. Like Hannah Barnard Hastings, this little boy seems to have inherited both a chest and a name. He was christened John Nathaniel Sherburne. Perhaps he received the chest from his grandfather. It is just as likely that his great-grandmother bequeathed it directly to his mother—or to him (he was ten years old when she died). He became the father of the Elizabeth Sherburne who married Pearce Penhallow in 1845, connecting the Sherburne chest with the Penhallow family. By the twentieth century, the Sherburne association might have been lost entirely if it hadn't been for that mysterious, heart-shaped inscription on the chest. The Sherburne high chest, like the Barnard cupboard, helps us understand how objects preserve lineages through time.[27]

Furniture scholars have adopted part of the vocabulary of social history. They now write of "ethnicity" as well as "taste," "social economy" as well as "aesthetics." Inspired by colleagues in other fields, they are likely to speak of networks as well as masterworks. But there is more to be done. To place furniture in a larger context requires the recovery of the unspoken assumptions that animated ordinary life. Furniture speaks about gender, family, literacy, gentility, and even mortality. It teaches us to look at the way objects are used, reused, inherited, and remembered, as well as at how they are made. Prudence Punderson's tiny silk embroidery, "The First, Second, and Last Scenes of Mortality" (fig. 29), brings together many of these themes.

Prudence Punderson was born in Preston, Connecticut, on July 28, 1758, the oldest of eight children born to Prudence Geer and Ebenezer Punderson. Her father was a merchant and (later) a Loyalist. Her mother, too, had a genteel upbringing, as evidenced by Prudence Greer's fine crewelwork embroidery now at the Connecticut Historical Society.[28] Prudence Punderson's own medium was silk. Unlike most eighteenth-century embroiderers, she seems to have worked from life rather than from English models. Her remarkable embroidery, one of the few surviving representations of a prosperous New England drawing room, is filled with little-known details about eighteenth-century households, from the fringed rug on the floor to the slave child rocking the cradle. And it has a great deal to say about furniture.

Prudence's embroideries of a falling leaf table, a pillar-and-claw tea table, a crested looking glass, and a rococo chair are punctiliously specific. Her family, in fact, owned and preserved the very items commemorated in the picture, which is, on the one hand, a remarkably realistic portrayal of an actual room and a stylized representation of the waxing and waning of human life. While the diminutive slave rocks a child not much smaller than herself, a young lady seated at a polished table works at her embroidery, a pewter or silver ink stand beside her. To her right is a shrouded mirror marking the passage of the "P.P.," whose initials mark the coffin. Significantly, the tea table holds implements for writing as well as for needlework. Pewter ink stands, like those on the table, survive in Connecticut collections.

In Prudence's picture, the tea table sustains work; the long table displays death; but it is the empty chair that signifies loss. If the child, the young woman, and the coffined corpse represent Prudence in the first, second, and last scenes of her life, the chair represents the male partner who might have arrived had death not cut short the journey. One scholar believes that the embroidered picture-within-a-picture above the slave child's head represents Mary Queen of Scots summoned by the executioner. If so, this was probably not a random choice. In November 1778, Prudence Punderson fled Connecticut with her mother and sisters. Her father, Ebenezer Punderson, was already in exile on Long Island, serving as commissary for the King's Troops. An undated manuscript in Prudence's hands suggests that she had an offer of marriage at the time but chose instead to join her family. As she told her unnamed friend, "from the tumultuous jarring times of Civil War I think may be raised many objections against settling for Life & my Ill state of Health which look but too probably to end only with my Breath makes me unwilling to bestow on my Friend or go to my Paren[t]s under their present situation such a helpless Burthen."[29]

Her embroidery is undated, but if it was created during this period, the meaning is less generic than has commonly been supposed. Prudence had reason to be thinking both about death and politics. The furniture was gathered, the young lady was educated in all the arts of gentility, but death and war, not a lover, knocked at her door.[30] The fine furniture in the embroidery adds poignancy to the representation. Furniture, embroidered textiles, and sometimes slaves were part of the "moveables" prosperous young gentlewomen brought to marriage. The empty chair represents, then, not only the accouterments of a genteel household but the missing "friend" who might give purpose to her accumulated goods and gifts. The Prudence Punderson of the picture will never change her name. Her goods will never form the core of a new household because her life is about to be interrupted by death.

Punderson did in fact die young, though not before marrying her cousin, Timothy Rossiter, and giving birth to a daughter, Sophia. Sophia's birth transformed the linear narrative into a circular tale. As Prudence died, her infant picked up the story again, the narrative moving from the coffin back to the cradle as well as from cradle to coffin. Superimposed on the ancient theme of mutability was a new motif. Things—tables, chairs, cradles, curtains, mirrors, rugs, and embroidered pictures, the dross of the world that moralists condemned and that the dying can never take with them—conferred their own immortality. Prudence's needle celebrates the material objects that were eventually passed on to her child, to her sibling's children, and to their children's children, coming in time to the Connecticut Historical Society as monuments to her own short life.

Prudence Punderson's realism preserved another detail too often overlooked in New England social history as well as in decorative arts scholarship. Slaves were frequently part of the households that generated the magnificent furniture celebrated in publications like this one. Hannah Barnard's husband, John Marsh, owned an "Indian [perhaps West Indian] Boy Sippey about 14 Years Old" at the time of his death in 1725. Joseph Sherburne owned "1 Negro Man" valued at £200 and "1 Ditto Woman" valued at £50 when his inventory was taken in 1745. The child rocking the cradle may be the "wench Jenny" mentioned in Ebenezer Punderson's will. Seldom do these persons appear in eighteenth-century portraits, but Jenny, Sippey, and their kin were part of a social order that made high-style furniture, damask dressing gowns, and gilded mirrors possible.

Prudence Punderson's embroidery is an imperfect mirror of her world, but in its focus on the female life cycle, its integration of furniture and textiles, and its acknowledgment of the inequality that underlay genteel households, it is more complete than much of what has been written since. By placing eighteenth-century furniture in context, it highlights new directions in social history.

1. This essay could not have been written without the help of Bill Hosley, Brock Jobe, Philip Zea, and Suzanne Flynt who generously offered time, insights, photographs, sources, and encouragement. For a helpful introduction to the vocabulary, see the catalogue entries in Brock Jobe and Myrna Kaye, *New England Furniture: The Colonial Era* (Boston: Houghton Mifflin, 1984), pp. xiii–xviii.

2. See the essay by Edward S. Cooke, Jr., in this volume.

3. Robert B. St. George, *The Wrought Covenant: Source Material for the Study of Craftsmen and Community in Southeastern New England 1620–1700* (Brockton, Mass.: Brockton Art Center, 1797), p. 16.

4. Quoted in Cynthia Fuchs Epstein, *Deceptive Distinctions: Sex, Gender, and the Social Order* (New Haven, Conn.: Yale University Press, 1988), p. 9. Epstein's summary of recent literature is a good beginning point for understanding contemporary scholarship.

5. Most of the anatomical terms are from Martin Eli Weil, "A Cabinetmaker's Price Book," in *American Furniture and Its Makers Winterthur Portfolio,* vol. 13, edited by Ian M. G. Quimby (Chicago and London: University of Chicago Press, 1979), pp. 80–192; "Thomas Elfe Day Book, 1768–1775," bound compilation of transcripts published in *The South Carolina Historical and Genealogical Magazine*, photocopies at the Museum of Early Southern Decorative Arts, Winston-Salem, N.C.; Brock Jobe, ed., *Portsmouth Furniture: Masterworks from the New Hampshire Seacoast* (Boston: Society for the Preservation of New England Antiquities, 1992); Brock Jobe, "An Introduction to Portsmouth Furniture of the Mid-Eighteenth Century," in *New England Furniture, Essays in Memory of Benno Forman*, edited by Brock Jobe (Boston: Society for the Preservation of New England Antiquities, 1987), pp. 163–195.

6. Valerie Steele, "Appearance and Identity," in *Men and Women: Dressing the Part* , edited by Claudia Brush Kidwell and Valerie Steele (Washington, D.C.: Smithsonian Institution Press, 1989), p. 6.

7. Claudia Brush Kidwell, "Gender Symbols or Fashionable Details?" in Kidwell and Steele, eds., *Men and Women*, p. 126.

8. Jules David Prown, *John Singleton Copley*, 2 vols. (Cambridge, Mass.: Harvard University Press, 1966), 1:figs. 158 (Thomas Hollis, 1766), 163 (Henry Pelham, 1765), 172 (Paul Revere,

1768–1770), 288 (Rev. John Oglivie, 1771), 219 (John Erving, 1772). Copley uses draped tables or pedestals more frequently than polished surfaces, especially in earlier portraits. Ibid., 1:figs. 161 (Mrs. Samuel Waldo, 1764–1765), 162 (Mrs. Theodore Atkinson [with squirrel], 1785), 273 (Mrs. Ezekiel Goldthwait, 1770–1771), 283 (Mrs. Humphrey Devereux [with mitts], 1770–1771), 315 (Mrs. Richard Skinner, 1772), 327 (Mrs. John Winthrop, 1773), 332 (Mr. and Mrs. Issac Winslow, 1774). An exception for women is fig. 331 (Mr. and Mrs. Thomas Mifflin, 1773), which shows Mrs. Mifflin with a tape loom. Burke is quoted in Richard Bushman, *The Refinement of America: Persons, Houses, Cities* (New York: Alfred A. Knopf, 1992), p. 72.

9. Prown, *Copley*, 1:figs. 80, 141, 158, 272. Although Copley places books and papers on many kinds of surfaces, more of his male subjects sit at tables than at desks.

10. On Sarah Prince as correspondent, see Carol Karlsen and Laurie Crumpacker, "Introduction," *The Journal of Esther Edwards Burr* (New Haven, Conn.: Yale University Press, 1984).

11. Prown, *Copley*, 1:figs. 193, 217, 254.

12. Ibid., 1:figs. 183, 255, 319.

13. Owen McNally, "Window to the Past," *Hartford Courant*, February 6, 1993, p. B8.

14. Clair Franklin Luther, *The Hadley Chest* (Hartford, Conn.: Case, Lockwood, and Brainard Company, 1935); Philip Zea, "The Fruits of Oligarchy: Patronage and the Hadley Chest Tradition in Western Massachusetts," in Jobe, ed., *Early New England Furniture*, pp. 1–65; Philip Zea and Suzanne L. Flynt, *Hadley Chests* (Deerfield, Mass.: Memorial Hall Museum, 1992).

15. Suzanne Flynt alerted me to the similarities between certain Hadley chest elements and the pie crust vents I had published as an illustration in *Good Wives: Image and Reality in the Lives of Women in Northern New England, 1650–1750* (New York: Alfred A. Knopf, 1982). William N. Hosley Jr. and Philip Zea, "Decorated Board Chests of the Connecticut River Valley," *Antiques* 119, no. 5 (May 1981): 1148–51.

16. Toby Ditz, *Property and Kinship: Inheritance in Early Connecticut, 1750–1820* (Princeton, N.J.: Princeton University Press, 1986), p. 65. When daughters received real estate, it was because personalty was lacking, and the value of the land was always significantly less than that inherited by sons. By custom and law, fathers "could simply exclude all daughters and members of daughters' families from heritable rights in land and confine their share of property to personalty." In the case of daughters, Ditz argues, bequests of land were substitutes for personal property. She notes, however, that wills undervalue bequests to daughters since most probably received all or part of their portions of moveable goods at marriage (ibid., pp. 69–70). Hannah had a silver cup, three silver spoons, eighteen sheets, and thirteen pillow beers. John Marsh Inventory, Hampshire County Probate Records, 4:138–140.

17. Quoted in Jane Nylander, *Our Own Snug Fireside: Images of the New England Home, 1760–1860* (New York: Alfred A. Knopf, 1993), pp. 59–60. The author thanks Bill Hosley for bringing this gravestone to her attention.

18. Hannah may have become her father's housekeeper after her mother's death in 1709, but responsibility for younger children cannot explain her late date at marriage. Her youngest sibling, a girl, was already eighteen. Lucius M. Boltwood, "Family Genealogies," in *History of Hadley*, edited by Sylvester Judd (Springfield, Mass.: H.R. Huntting, 1905), pp. 8, 91.

19. John Marsh Will, June 5, 1725, Hampshire County Probate Records, 4:134, Microfilm, LDS Family History Library, Film Number 0879184. As it turned out, little John never did come of age. He died July 3, 1726, age three. Boltwood, "Family Genealogies," p. 92, 8, 64, 91–92. I can find only three girls in colonial Hadley given a surname for a middle name. Hannah Barnard Hastings may be the only child in eighteenth-century New England named for a cupboard.

20. Jobe, ed., *Portsmouth Furniture*, pp. 164–65.

21. Ibid., pp. 343, 127; Thaxter ("Tack") Swan, "Just the Facts: A Slice of Swan History," typescript, Portsmouth Athenaeum, Portsmouth, N.H.

22. Frances Clary Morse, *Furniture of the Olden Time* (New York: Macmillan, 1902), p. 26, photocopy in Swan, "Just the Facts."

23. Swan, "Just the Facts," chapter 14, p. 2. The catalogue entry in Jobe, ed., *Portsmouth Furniture* says that the feet were cut off "during the late eighteenth century" (p. 127) but doesn't explain why then and not later.

24. *New England Historical Genealogical Register*, 15: 118.

25. James L. Garvin, "That Little World Portsmouth," in Jobe, ed., *Portsmouth Furniture*,

p. 19. Faith Harrington, "The Emergent Elite in Early 18th Century Portsmouth Society: The Archaeology of the Joseph Sherburne Houselot," *Historical Archaeology* 23 (1989): 2–12. My discussion of the Sherburne family and the Sherburne house is also based on unpublished research reports by Richard Candee, Mary Dupry, and Claire Dempsey, undertaken as part of a NEH Planning Grant to Strawbery Banke Museum. Dempsey's compilations and summaries of primary sources were especially helpful.

26. Jobe, ed., *Portsmouth Furniture*, pp. 124–27.

27. This reconstruction has no more or less support in surviving documents than any other. I suggest it as a way of expanding the notion of provenance to include broader readings of "inheritance." There is abundant evidence of the use of objects to reinforce family connections and to tell family stories. There is no reason to assume that objects passed in lock-step from one generation to another or that they moved only at death or marriage. In fact, one of the unexplored themes in the Sherburne chest history is its possible relation to the Mendum as well as the Sherburne family. Eleanor Mendum's father Nathaniel is listed as a "joiner" in Portsmouth records of the 1720s, though he, like Joseph Sherburne, soon ascended to "shop-keeper" and then to "Esquire." I wonder if he made or commissioned the Sherburne chest as a gift to his oldest daughter and her husband. If the chest came two years after marriage, the initials of the husband, rather than the wife, are appropriate. Interestingly, Nathaniel Mendum's estate inventory of 1774 is filled with "curly maple" furniture (Nathaniel Mendum, Craftsmen's Files, Portsmouth Athenaeum).

28. Cora Ginsburg, "Textiles in the Connecticut Historical Society," *Antiques* 107, no. 4 (April 1975): 712–16

29. William Warren, "The Prudence Mourning Picture," typescript, used by permission, Connecticut Historical Society, Hartford. Prudence Punderson Journal, MS79240, Connecticut Historical Society.

30. On October 18, 1783, she married Timothy Rossiter. She gave birth to a daughter, Sophia, on July 18, 1784, and died less than a month later. Marriage Certificate, Punderson Papers, folder 2, Connecticut Historical Society.

Philip Zea

Diversity and Regionalism in Rural New England Furniture

▼ THIS ESSAY EXPLORES diversity in the marketplace by examining New England furniture as an extension of rural culture, economy, technique, and design. Generations ago, rural style did not evolve in a vacuum.[1] Diversity was a fact of life. Household objects came from near and far and were always the products of personal attitudes about the right way to build something based on training and cultural preference. Today, choice is an illusion in the marketplace. The car bought in California is like the one purchased in Vermont. This homogeneity of material culture results from specialized labor and from interchangeable parts stocked on endless shelves. The product itself plays second fiddle to market share, labor cost, and corporate monopoly. Some will lament the loss of old-time standards of quality or distinctiveness, while others thrive on change. In either case, the modern manufacture and use of goods has created false assumptions about the context of objects created years ago.

Mapping provincial design is more complicated than simply drawing dissemination on the model of a wagon wheel. The original concept may well reside at the urban hub, with consumers and their ideas ranged along the spokes. The vernacular, nonacademic, naive furnishings are then usually placed at the distant rim. But the perception of distance to a point and its relevance depends upon location. If you are living well at the rim, the hub seems vague, superfluous, and distant. Furthermore, the end of each spoke is linked to other spokes by the rim, giving another avenue for the exchange of ideas and for strengthening cultural expression.

The nature of New England cabinetwork is clarified by acknowledging modern perceptions of antique furniture and by coupling them with valid hypotheses about rural society. We must recognize that the upland towns, while distant, were not isolated, and that craftsmen were businessmen eager to expand their patronage in order to make a living. Despite die-hard assumptions about isolation and homogeneity, these conditions were not uniform throughout the land. Most American subcultures were neither isolated nor homogeneous in their tastes. Separate traditions coexisted. Although the basic elements of language, law, government, economics, land use, religion, and family structure were shared, personal belongings usually demonstrate cultural pluralism. Trade was valley oriented and could not have flourished in isolation. Fashion rode easily on the back of commerce.

If the theory of isolated regionalism is tossed aside, the usual questions become more complex. Does rural design reflect only ignorance and eccen-

Figure 1 Chest-on-chest-on-frame attributed to Elisha DeWolf Jr. (1772–1855), inscribed for "L.[ucy] D.[eWolf] Allis," Conway or Ashfield, Massachusetts, ca. 1800. Cherry with white pine. H. 85", W. 40", D. 22½". (Courtesy, Historic Deerfield, Inc.; photo, Amanda Merullo.) The style of furniture made in New York during the last quarter of the eighteenth century was fashionable in the Connecticut River Valley, where this cabinetmaker reoriented the concept of a gadrooned base molding to serve as a mid-molding between the two cases.

Figure 2 Chest-on-chest attributed to Daniel Clay (1770–1848), Greenfield, Massachusetts, 1792–1800. Cherry with yellow poplar. H. 74", W. 45", D. 18¾". (Courtesy, Historic Deerfield, Inc., bequest of Rowena Russell Potter; photo, Helga Studio.)

tricity? Does it confound classification and analysis? How can objects so provincial have been high style and expensive? What was the impact of a confidence born from a prosperous agricultural economy on the selection of ornament and the creation of form in rural cabinet shops?

Although a lot of good design was fashioned in the countryside, as elsewhere, inventiveness is often tagged as eccentric and confused with ignorance. The "folksy" flowering of native motifs never grew in isolation nor without inspiration. Wonderful hybrids of design created in "the back of beyond" document the cosmopolitan influences that shaped rural culture and the expectations of its people (fig. 1). Other furniture made simultaneously nearby (fig. 2) is devoid of ornament and illustrates the "neat and plain." Although the absence of ornament may seem an odd statement of popular design (and a good excuse for saving the expense of hiring specialists), the clean appearance of some eighteenth-century furniture was purposeful, with deep roots in Enlightenment thinking. As noted by John Witherspoon (1723–1794), president of the College of New Jersey: "It may also appear from . . . those compositions which have most simplicity and such excellencies as are most solid, with fewest of the casual ornaments of fashion. . . . The same thing holds with pieces of furniture that are elegant but plain."[2]

Figure 3 Chest of drawers inscribed "Made in the Year 1800, By Mr. John Cardwill for Mr. Willis Griswold of Middletown In Vermont." Cherry with white pine. H. 38½", W. 38½", D. 19". (Courtesy, Shelburne Museum.)

The American romance with independence has created a place for regionalism in the national ethos. The passage of time and improvements in technology and transportation have resulted in a selective memory that fuels clichés about rural isolation, regional distinction, and simpler times.[3] Consequently, furniture with heavy doses of imitation or innovation is invariably defined according to rural stereotypes and to economic conditions assumed to be prevalent at distant points. We like to think of brigadoons safe from the homogenization of culture. These sanctuaries are usually fortified, in the mind's eye, by mountains or water and are places like Vermont, the Smokies, the Bayou country, New Mexico, the Rockies, and Quebec Province. They are often places with distinctive food, or at least beer, and some of them are ethnically distinct, or used to be. In these places, regionalism may exist, if a little contrived, through the sheer vigor of myth and marketing.

Vermont is a good example. Despite the myth of isolation, at least four distinct types of furniture were made there before 1840.[4] First was generic, eighteenth-century-style furniture, some made after the year 1800. It is

Figure 4 Card table, probably Rutland, Vermont, 1805–1815. Cherry and mahogany veneer with white pine, yellow poplar, and yellow birch. H. 27⅞", W. 36⁵⁄₁₆", D. 17³⁄₁₆" [closed]. (Courtesy, Bennington Museum; photo, Ken Burris.) Card tables with five legs were especially popular in New York City and the Hudson Valley, and they influenced design in western Vermont.

Figure 5 Chest with two drawers, Shaftsbury, Vermont, ca. 1825. Painted white pine. H. 41", W. 41⅛", D. 19¼". (Courtesy, Bennington Museum; photo, Blake Gardner.) The Matteson family of carpenters and ornamental painters have been credited with producing this type of furniture, which was made throughout northern New England.

Figure 6 Secretary made by Anthony Van Doorn (1792–1871), Brattleboro, Vermont, 1836–1847. Mahogany and mahogany veneer with yellow poplar, basswood, and white pine. H. 55⅜", W. 45", D. 22¾". (Courtesy, Historic Deerfield, Inc., gift of Dr. and Mrs. Gary Russolillo; photo, Amanda Merullo.)

invariably misattributed to elsewhere in New England, because that is where first-generation Vermont artisans learned their trade (fig. 3). Next, some wealthy patrons developed an appetite for stylish furniture that hybridized urban styles made in the large seaports along the New England coast and in New York City (fig. 4). A third and cheaper type of furniture was made fashionable by ornamental paint that imitates and exaggerates expensive materials (fig. 5). This furniture is associated with Vermont but was often factory made, especially chairs. Last, generic, high-style furniture of imported designs and materials indistinguishable from elsewhere in the Northeast was available to patrons of small factories (fig. 6).

Creation and consumption are seldom strictly local phenomena, at least in rural furniture. A healthy economy is built on openness and assimilation, not isolation and independence. Some of the most notable "regional" furniture is the product of a single, dominant craft tradition with links far beyond local boundaries. The Gaines family of turners in coastal Ipswich, Massachusetts—John II (1677–1748) and Thomas I (1712–1761)—emulated popular Boston designs when making thousands of chairs, far more than their neighbors could use (fig. 7).[5] The Gaineses shipped these chairs in the coastal trade. Volume permitted them to perfect their skills, designs, and production methods and to create a memorable form mistakenly regarded as a local rather than as a commercial and cosmopolitan occurrence.

Figure 7 Side chair attributed to John Gaines II or Thomas Gaines I, Ipswich, Massachusetts, 1720–1745. Maple and white pine. H. 46", W. 18¼". (Courtesy, John Whipple House, Ipswich Historical Society; photo, Richard Cheek.) The chair descended in the Appleton family of Ipswich.

Figure 8 Chest of drawers inscribed "Alden Spooner Athol," Athol, Massachusetts, ca. 1810. Cherry and mahogany, birch, and maple veneers with white pine. H. 42½", W. 40", D. 21¼". (Courtesy, Historic Deerfield, Inc., photo, Amanda Merullo.)

Sometimes, rural craftsmanship is so true to urban prototypes that its design, proportion, and materials lead to confusion with coastal cabinetwork, like the furniture of Alden Spooner (1784–1877) of Athol in western Massachusetts (fig. 8). Other times, clear urban antecedents were adapted to local conditions. Michael Carleton (1793–1876) made the sideboard illustrated in figure 9 at Haverhill, New Hampshire, using templates for a chest of drawers. Apparently built for a patron with a small house, the half sideboard (the period term) incorporates the trappings of modern design with the astragal corners and drop panel popular in Portsmouth, a hundred miles away. Himself a native of the lower Merrimack Valley, Carleton provided his customers with current, coastal styles.[6]

Later in the nineteenth century, manufacturing accelerated the homogenization of furniture design throughout New England. Divergent forms could be made quickly under the same roof in order to expand business through the offer of one-stop shopping. In western New Hampshire in about 1830, Willard Harris (1782–1848) of Newport employed up to fifteen workers, including Horace Ellis (b. 1807) and Martin Bullock (1810–1876), and simultaneously sold fashionable mahogany Empire bureaus and fancy painted dressing tables, signed by these craftsmen (figs. 10, 11).[7]

From childhood, we are trained to categorize things by their appearance. Consequently, the questions often heard in the analysis of artifacts are: What characterizes the object? And, what characteristics are shared with

Figure 9 Sideboard made by Michael Carleton, Haverhill, New Hampshire, ca. 1815. Cherry; cherry, maple, mahogany, and birch veneers; and whitewood inlay with white pine. H. 38½", W. 43", D. 20½". (Courtesy, New Hampshire Historical Society; photo, Bill Finney.)

Figure 10 Chest of drawers made by Horace Ellis, Newport, New Hampshire, 1832. Mahogany and mahogany veneer with white pine and basswood. H. 57⅛", W. 47⅛", D. 22½". (Courtesy, New Hampshire Historical Society; photo, Bill Finney.)

Figure 11 Dressing table made by Martin Bullock, Newport, New Hampshire, ca. 1835. Painted white pine and maple. H. 38¾", W. 32⅜", D. 16½". (Courtesy, New Hampshire Historical Society; photo, Bill Finney.)

other objects? Many people scrutinize antiques by "regional characteristics," which help to organize visual information, like arranging books alphabetically or by subject matter. The irony is that "regional characteristics" paint an incomplete picture of regional life and the conditions reflected in people's possessions. The evolution of distinctive regional traits, and the reasons behind them, vary dramatically over time. The quality of life in a first-generation, seventeenth-century town was quite different in 1850. Furthermore, so-called style regions usually supported several craftsmen working in the same medium. They might make different styles to suit the pocketbook or cultural preferences of various buyers in the American melting pot. Indeed, the purchaser controls economic exchange and determines the appearance or style of artifacts. If the customer cannot or will not pay for it, no craftsman is foolish enough to make it.

The relationships exposed by categorization are important, but they do not tackle the most essential question in the study of three-dimensional, material culture: Why do things look as they do? We can examine history through the study of material culture if we learn its language.[8] Artifacts or antiques, depending on your viewpoint, inspire speculation about what life was like at a given point in time. Consequently, they are sources of ideas and information when closely read. The conditions of life, just like the characteristics of a chair or chest, are rarely beautiful, but they are invariably revealing if one moves beyond the patina of age or the scars of use. Although this approach may seem too history based for some connoisseurs, studying the environment and economy invested in the appearance of each wonderful thing leads to understanding artifacts better.

Although teacups and tables force us by their inanimate nature to ask what they are, we are most interested in who stood behind them as makers and owners. This is where the romance and sinew of history lie. It is the human condition surrounding the object that holds the most relevant information. After the physical characteristics of the bureau illustrated in figure 12 are defined, the real question jumps out: *Why* did the owner commission, and the craftsman make, this large cherry and yellow poplar chest, inlaid

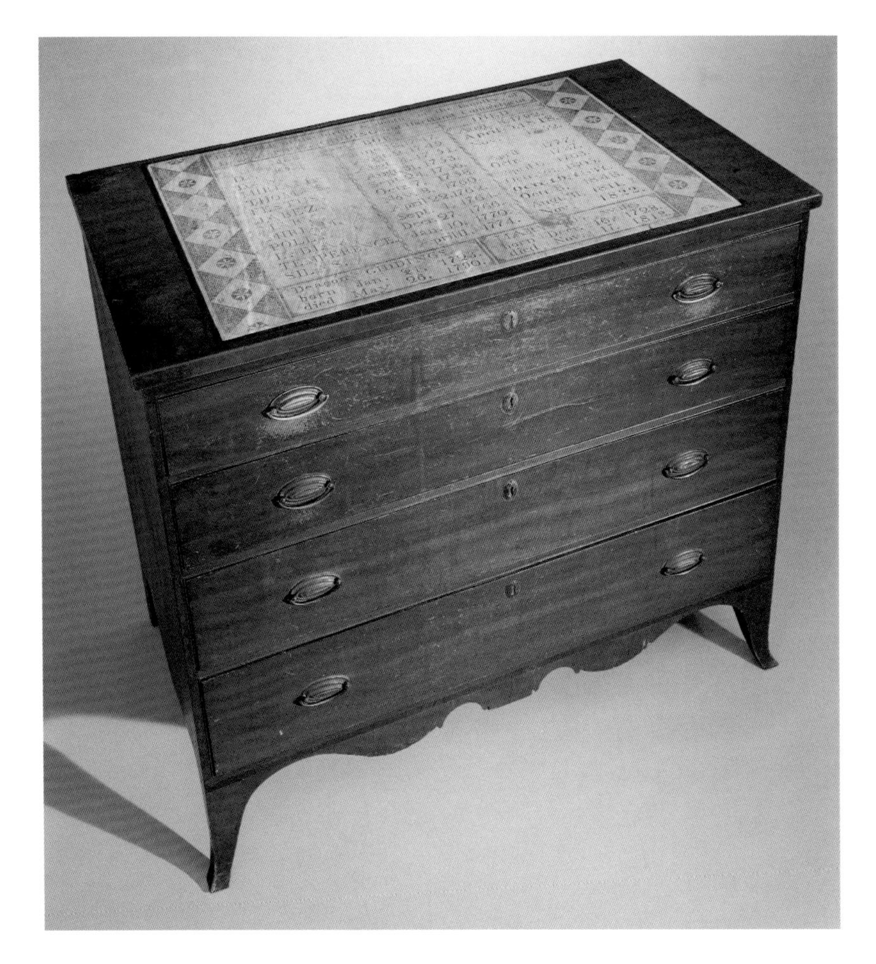

Figure 12 Chest of drawers with Thomas Giddings family register engraved in marble, Hartland, Connecticut area, 1812–1818. Cherry and marble with yellow poplar. H. 39", W. 43 3/8", D. 24 1/8". (Courtesy, Shelburne Museum; photo, Ken Burris.)

with an inscribed marble family register? We can only hypothesize about the conditions that led to its manufacture, the merger of skills involved, and the strong statement of ownership and commemoration. Although the exact reasons are lost, few Anglo-American items bear such a totem-like presence.

Some objects offer clear proofs in the historical analysis of a time and place. Their vocabulary, although unspoken, can be quite detailed. Westfield, Massachusetts, cabinetmaker Erastus Grant (1774–1865) signed the serpentine chest of drawers illustrated in figure 13 on October 11 and

Figure 13 Chest of drawers made by Erastus Grant, Westfield, Massachusetts, 1799; inscribed "E Grant/Oct 11 1799," "Grant/Novr 2, 1799," and "E Grant Cabinet Maker." Cherry, cherry veneer, and whitewood stringing with yellow poplar and white pine. H. 35", W. 43¼", D. 23½". (Courtesy, Historic Deerfield, Inc., Mr. and Mrs. Hugh B. Vanderbilt Fund for Curatorial Acquisitions; photo, Amanda Merullo.)

November 2, 1799. The date range says something about the time spent in constructing such a chest. Grant used new-fangled, cut nails to fasten the drawer bottoms and backboards, which tells us that the economy and technology surrounding nail production had modernized in western Massachusetts before the autumn of 1799. Simultaneously, Grant's addition of an inlaid patera on the top and quarter-round fans on the drawer facades makes this chest the earliest documented piece of furniture with neoclassical detail made in western Massachusetts. His use of a dustboard between the second and third drawers is similar to the workmanship of Eliphalet (1741–1807) and Aaron Chapin (1753–1838), with whom he probably trained in Hartford, Connecticut. This construction detail is common on Philadelphia case furniture and may have been learned by Eliphalet when he worked there as a journeyman between 1767 and 1771.[9]

The analysis of objects is improved by grappling with them on their terms and by discarding as many modern preconceptions and conditions of our own culture as possible. One example is the search for folk art in the texture and ornament applied by anonymous people to simple, useful objects. Art-by-guess-and-by-gosh is rarely simple. A grain-painted chest or clock case executed by a specialized ornamental painter to simulate more costly materials entails complex expectations and procedures. As for the simple way of life, an object like a milk stool is only rudimentary until you try to make one. The concept of folk art as a catch-all category for certain nonacademic styles dates from the 1920s and is important in understanding twentieth-century aesthetics, but it has little to do with nineteenth- or eighteenth-century life or perceptions of world view.[10]

Another obvious example is the nagging and virtually meaningless dis-

Figure 14 Tall clock case attributed to Major John Dunlap, Bedford, New Hampshire; movement by Jonathan Mulliken II (1746–1782), Newburyport, Massachusetts, 1780–1792. Cherry and whitewood stringing with white pine. H. 88½", W. 22½", D. 11¼". (Courtesy, Mead Art Gallery, Amherst College.) The deaths of Jonathan Mulliken in 1782 and of John Dunlap ten years later help to determine the date of the clock's manufacture. The clock descended in Dunlap's family until the 1930s and is probably the "House Clock 14 £" listed in his probate inventory.

tinction between city and country furniture. This categorization is important to us as late-twentieth-century people, who live in an urbanized society. We face the problems and expense of urban decay as well as the joys that a few hundred dollars can bring to an evening on the town. But what did city *versus* country mean to American society before 1920 when more people lived on the farm than in suburbia? Their possessions tell a different story. For example, we recognize mahogany as an expensive, imported wood widely used in urban furniture after the mid-eighteenth century, and we usually define Connecticut cabinetwork as rural. Yet some eighteenth-century Connecticut furniture is made of mahogany, breaking down two sets of suppositions about early craftsmanship (see figs. 47, 48).[11]

Several other misconceptions cloud our perspective on objects and limit our enjoyment and understanding of old things. As a culture of consumers, we are continually distracted by visual quality and the connotations of status in objects. For example, clocks were one of the leading status symbols in eighteenth-century households. But the clock cases made by the Dunlap family in southern New Hampshire are invariably cited as squat, bizarre attempts at craftsmanship, although expensive ones (fig. 14). Some might ask, "Why did they waste their money?" In this instance, Major John Dunlap (1746–1792) obviously did not draw on the comfortable proportions of a classical column for the clock case, as was usually done, but neither did he reject architectural precedent. His case is designed like a pedimented frontispiece or doorway based on the academic correlations recommended by William Salmon in *Palladio Londinensis* (1734).[12]

Design aside, we have a tendency to value the physical qualities of the object over the complexity of the craftsman's ideas, materials, and the context in which he worked. Benjamin Cheney, Jr. (1725–1815) and Timothy Cheney (1731–1795) began making clocks in East Hartford, Connecticut, about 1750 (fig. 15).[13] Perhaps because their father was a joiner, they developed the concept of offering options in clocks to expand their clientele: thirty-hour wooden movements as well as more expensive, eight-day, brass clocks. From across the parlor, both products look essentially the same. Upon close inspection, the depth of the hood concealing the wooden movement is much deeper to accommodate its cumbersome parts (fig. 16). Some dials even have false painted winding holes to complete the deception of an eight-day clock. The thirty-hour version is wound by pulling up the weights on the rope behind the waist door. The cases of the economy model are often made of native pine (though hardwood examples are also known) stained to imitate mahogany or cherry. Two centuries later, these clocks are usually rejected by collectors on the basis of quality, although the ingenious wooden mechanism and the marketing concept behind it were among the more sophisticated ideas afoot in the marketplace of eighteenth-century New England.

Likewise, we also tend to value the quality of ornament over the quality of construction, the sole province of the craftsman, who might select one method over another for reasons of structural integrity or the availability of materials. The chest illustrated in figure 17 has ornamental paint to simulate

Figure 15 Tall clock made by Benjamin Cheney Jr. and inscribed "B. Cheney/Hartford" (on dial), East Hartford, Connecticut, ca. 1790. White pine with oak, cherry, maple, pine, iron, steel, and brass. H. 88¼", W. 20½", D. 13". (Courtesy, Historic Deerfield, Inc.; photo, Amanda Merullo.)

Figure 16 Clock movement made by Benjamin Cheney Jr., East Hartford, Connecticut, ca. 1790. Oak, cherry, maple, pine, iron, steel, and brass. H. 17¼", W. 13½", D. 9". (Courtesy, Historic Deerfield, Inc.; photo, Amanda Merullo.)

Figure 17 Chest of drawers, New England, ca. 1810. (*a*) Front and (*b*) back views. White pine. H. 39¼", W. 36¾", D. 18¼". (Courtesy, Shelburne Museum; photo, Ken Burris.)

inlay and stringing, but its most costly, labor-intensive feature is against the wall. The backboards are dovetailed to the case sides rather than simply nailed into a rabbet or beveled to fit into a groove.

Similarly, simple but highly functional objects are rarely appreciated unless they are Shaker made. The curious pine shelving illustrated in figure 18 is actually the product of clever design. Made to butt up against the long side of a table, it is lightweight and mobile and is intended to create a desk complete with a central "prospect" and space for storing ledgers and papers. The decisions resulting from the need for a mobile desk led to distinctive workmanship.

Figure 18 Desk, northeastern United States, 1825–1875. White pine. H. 46¼", W. 40", D. 12". (Courtesy, Shelburne Museum; photo, Ken Burris.)

Quality obtained from efficient production is invariably overlooked. Plans of some sort were always used to create design. Specified measurements or the replication of shapes assisted by templates made craftsmen more efficient and faster. These plans could be quite detailed; other times, notes were sketched on the back of a board long since used for kindling. In either case, the replication of form is an under-used clue in identifying shop traditions and methods, except perhaps in the connoisseurship of pewter made in long-lost molds. For example, a secretary made in William Lloyd's (1779–1845) shop at Springfield, Massachusetts, in 1804 has a writing surface and base adapted from existing templates for a card table (fig. 19).[14]

Obviously, multiple objects from a shop tradition like Lloyd's go far in defining the range of workmanship practiced by established craftsmen. Nevertheless, we invariably define skill or quality on the basis of a single surviving object or type of object. Windsor chairmaker Stephen Tracy (1782–1865) of Lisbon, Connecticut, and Cornish, New Hampshire, is a good example. He was the nephew and probable apprentice of Colonel Ebenezer Tracy (1744–1803) of Lisbon, a highly skilled specialist who is the most famous of all Windsor chairmakers. Hundreds of chairs by the Tracys and their apprentices have survived, and the assumption might be that they only made chairs. Although seating furniture dominated, Stephen's ledger shows that he also made agricultural implements and case furniture, including the fashionable bow-front bureau perhaps built for Erastus Adams in 1806 (fig. 20).[15]

Figure 19 Secretary made by William Lloyd and Luther Bliss, Springfield, Massachusetts, 1804. Cherry, mahogany veneer, and whitewood inlay with white pine. H. 70 1/8", W. 36 1/4", D. 18 1/8". (Private collection; photo, David Stansbury.)

Figure 20 Chest of drawers made by Stephen Tracy, branded "S.TRACY" and stamped "EADAMS [reversed S]," Lisbon, Connecticut, or Cornish, New Hampshire, ca. 1806. Cherry with white pine. H. 34 7/8", W. 39 3/8", D. 20 3/4". (Courtesy, Historic Deerfield, Inc., Mr. and Mrs. Hugh B. Vanderbilt Fund for Curatorial Acquisitions; photo, Amanda Merullo.)

There is also a strong tendency to overlook historical reality. The Shakers, for example, are renown for the clean, efficient designs of their furniture. The sect is especially well known for chairs, which they made in quantity for "the world." Today, anything with crisp lines is defined as Shaker. The chair illustrated in figure 21 was factory made in the Renaissance revival taste about 1890 at the Shaker community in Canterbury, New Hampshire.[16] The clue to its origins are the tilters on the rear legs to make leaning backwards less damaging to the floor. At face value, this chair is the last one to fulfill the dreams of a traditional collector of Shaker furniture.

Just as we might focus on a single object to define the range of one man's work over several years and perhaps in several places, we also regularly fix on the moment of creation as the only significant point in the history of an artifact. However, possessions move through time and are affected by the environment and changing perceptions of their beauty or usefulness. Frequently, a significant component of an item is swept away during restoration because it was not part of the original craftsman's or owner's intent. The loss of paint layers is a good illustration, but structural details that say a great deal about modernization are also often lost to "repair." What was once a common upgrading of design can become quite rare because most examples have been restored to their original appearance. The chair illustrated in figure 22 was made originally for Governor Caleb Strong (1745–1819) of Northampton, Massachusetts, about 1780. His children or grandchildren came along in the 1820s or 1830s and thought it should have modern scrolled arms to make it appear less old-fashioned, so a craftsman

Figure 21 Side chair, Canterbury, New Hampshire, 1875–1900. Oak. H. 32½", W. 17¾", D. 16¾". (Collection of Shaker Village, Inc., Canterbury; photo, Bill Finney, courtesy, New Hampshire Historical Society.)

Figure 22 Armchair, Massachusetts, ca. 1780 and ca. 1825. Cherry with pine. H. 38¼", W. 22", D. 23¼". (Courtesy, Historic Deerfield, Inc., gift of H. William Strong Jr.; photo, Amanda Merullo.)

arguably as competent in neoclassical design as the original maker in the style of his period was hired to do the work.

Style is rooted in the desire to associate with people of power, wealth, or intelligence. When emulation accelerates, fashion becomes hybridized and usually reinvented at lower price levels. In the eighteenth century, this process took less time than we think. Although the products of hybridization may appear ungainly, the effect was quite modern. For example, the Windsor, Connecticut high chest of drawers illustrated in figure 23 is dated "1736," only six years after the documented appearance of the cabriole leg in Boston, and it may not have been the first made by this anonymous craftsman. He used the latest techniques to construct the upper case—dovetails rather than mortise-and-tenon joinery—and gave the cabriole legs bold curves that anticipate William Hogarth's line of beauty, published a generation later. The cabinetmaker, or a local painter-stainer, also ornamented the chest with paint that simulates contemporary Boston "japanning."[17]

The diversity within and the interaction between regions make it clear that defining a place through one object (or vice versa) is a false step in determining a distinctive lifestyle. Multiple objects from a single shop paint a clearer picture of regional relationships and aspirations. For example, the previous high chest of drawers and the dressing table illustrated in figure 24 were made in the same anonymous shop but were ornamented differently. We know that urban patrons often specified furniture with fine walnut veneers, and some householders in Connecticut had similar aspirations. In concept, the cabinetmaker offered a dressing table with a veneer of paint to simulate the imported wood.

Demand for stylish furnishings created new designs in rural New England, sometimes regardless of the availability of goods in nearby urban commercial centers. The small city of Portsmouth, New Hampshire, for

Figure 23 High chest of drawers, Windsor or East Windsor, Connecticut, 1736. Maple with yellow pine. H. 59", W. 41 3/8", D. 22". (Courtesy, Winterthur Museum.)

Figure 24 Dressing table, Windsor or East Windsor, Connecticut, ca. 1735. Materials not recorded. H. 29", W. 38 1/4", D. 24 1/4".(Courtesy, Shelburne Museum; photo, Ken Burris.)

example, did not support successful clockmakers until after the Revolution because the elite imported English or Boston tall clocks. In the country towns nearby, wealthy farmers were unable to acquire these status symbols. Not to be outdone, they patronized blacksmiths, especially in the towns of Kensington and Kingston, who demonstrated a genius for making iron posted-frame clocks that ran for a day in cases inspired by late-seventeenth-century English designs (fig. 25).[18]

Sometimes the broad appeal of certain motifs broke down the presumed boundaries of regions and even technologies to become universal. The flared ears on rococo chairs, for example, were standard fare throughout the eastern seaboard. A group of turners in the Piscataqua region of coastal New Hampshire found an imaginative way to build the same motif into their chair design, even though their lathes limited turning to straight rather than curvilinear parts (fig. 26).[19] Although the finials were destined to remain strictly vertical, these turners made crest rails with flaring ears that assume the appearance of paired fish tails.

The diversity found in objects goes beyond personal or eccentric preference, and the borders of culture, however fluctuating, are defined by more than time and place. Ethnic identity provides distinctions within the mixed culture of a place. For example, threads of Old World material culture and technique were carried by the Scots-Irish to southern New Hampshire and certainly by the Germans to Pennsylvania. These craftsmen made furniture alongside English joiners and were similarly linked to their own cultures by design and technique. John and Samuel Dunlap (1752–1830) in New Hampshire, for example, were trained to make distinctive furniture derived from Scots-Irish designs popular a century and a half earlier (fig. 27). Sim-

Figure 25 Tall clock made by Jonathan Blasdel Jr. (1709–1802), East Kingston, New Hampshire, 1768. Maple with white pine. H. 81½", W. 17½", D. 10". (Courtesy, New Hampshire Antiquarian Society; photo, Bill Finney.)

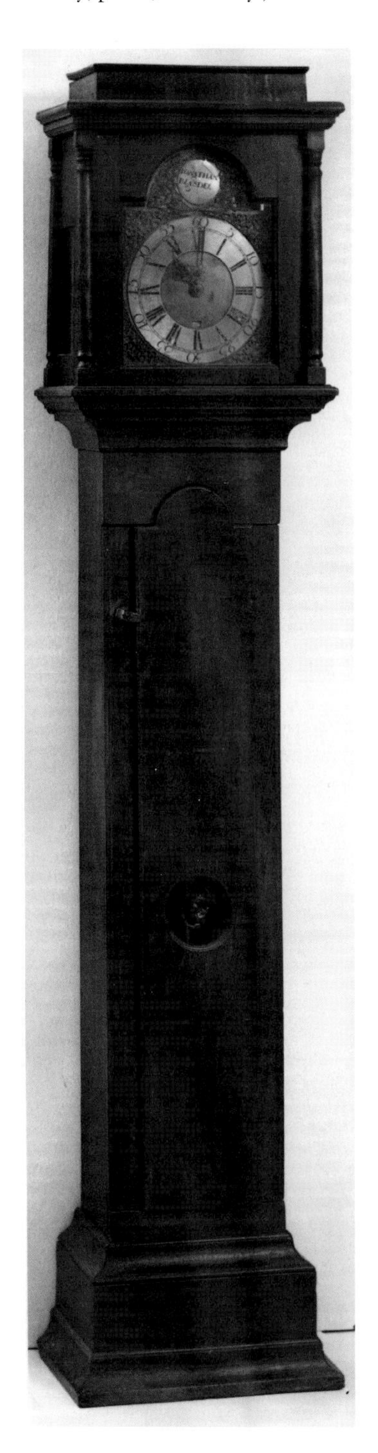

Figure 26 Side chair, Portsmouth, New Hampshire area, 1740–1790. Maple. H. 41½", W. 15¾", D. 13". (Courtesy, Historic Deerfield, Inc.; photo, Helga Photo Studio.)

ilarly, Norwich, Vermont, cabinetmaker George Stedman (b. 1795) offered local clientele (and presumably consumers in his hometown of Chester) the option of cherry furniture inspired, not by English, but by French Louis XVI designs (fig. 28).[20]

The diverse character of rural New England furniture is well rooted in the seventeenth century when society was completely fragmented by the mobility and varying traditions of people from all around Great Britain. At least seven joiners whose divergent origins are known worked in Windsor, Connecticut, during the first generation of settlement. Faced with a vast forest of numerous species of trees, each with special woodworking advantages, they chose to work with oak, the traditional wood of English joinery, and to ornament their furniture in the way that they were trained. One shop made chests built entirely of riven oak in the manner of Gloucestershire work in the west of England (fig. 29).[21]

Figure 27 High chest of drawers made by William Houston and J. Miller in the shop of Major John Dunlap, Bedford, New Hampshire, 1780. Maple with white pine. H. 83¼", W. 41⅞", D. 20 15/16". (Courtesy, Winterthur Museum.) The chest is inscribed "Wllm Houston" and "J Miller 1780."

Figure 28 Chest of drawers "Made by G [eorge] Stedman/ Norwich/ Vt," 1816–1822. Cherry, mahogany veneer, and whitewood inlays with white pine. H. 34⅞", W. 41¾", D. 20⅛". (Courtesy, Winterthur Museum.)

Figure 29 Chest, Windsor, Connecticut, ca. 1650. White oak. H. 23¾", W. 54", D. 23". (Courtesy, Pocumtuck Valley Memorial Association, Memorial Hall Museum, Deerfield, Massachusetts, gift of Mrs. Catherine W. Hoyt; photo, Helga Studio.) The legs and lid are lost.

Ironically, only stagnation encouraged homogeneous design at the regional level. Hadley chests, first made in western Massachusetts at the end of the seventeenth century, constitute the largest group of joined furniture in America; some 250 chests, tables, boxes, and fragments are recorded (fig. 30). The study of these chests by Clair Franklin Luther in *The Hadley Chest* (1935) confirmed the concept of regionalism early in the literature of American antiques. Unfortunately, he had investigated one of the few exceptions to regional diversity in American material culture. Hadley chests were made throughout the Connecticut River towns of west-

Figure 30 Chest with drawer, inscribed "RA," Hadley or Hatfield, Massachusetts, ca. 1700. Red oak with yellow pine. H. 34", W. 47 1/4", D. 20 1/2". (Courtesy, Pocumtuck Valley Memorial Association, Memorial Hall Museum, Deerfield, Massachusetts, gift of Chester Graves Crafts; photo, Amanda Merullo.)

Figure 31 Chest of drawers, Hampshire County, Massachusetts, ca. 1725. Maple and yellow poplar with yellow and white pine. H. 48 3/4", W. 43 1/2", D. 19 1/8". (Courtesy, Historic Deerfield, Inc., Mr. and Mrs. Hugh B. Vanderbilt Fund for Curatorial Acquisitions; photo, Amanda Merullo.)

ern Massachusetts until about 1740 by generations of joiners working in an isolated economy of oligarchy and indebtedness to one family: the Pynchons of Springfield. The members of this founding family patronized specific joiners for both private and public works throughout the towns that they subsidized. The result was the homogenization of design and construction for three or four generations.[22]

Restyling came slowly to Hadley chests. Although the technical preferences for internal construction remained intact, western Massachusetts joiners finally began to emulate fashionable coastal styles in the baroque taste. The joined chest of drawers in figure 31 looks like the upper case of a walnut-veneered high chest made by a cabinetmaker a hundred miles away in Boston. The tradition of consistency was broken after the conclusion of raids by the French and Indians about 1745 and after the emergence of new wealth among related families of patrons, called the "River Gods."[23] They sought fashionable goods and supported native cabinetmakers. It was the eager patron, not the efficient craftsman comfortable with replication, who made the decision to alter the tried and true.

Understanding the willingness to change underscores the importance of the "who" rather than the "what" in objects. Patronage by people of varying economic status or cultural bias, superimposed on one another in their respective towns, created diverse and often contradictory regional expressions. With time, the material culture of the gentry network in each locale came to dominate what is remembered because of the power of status, money, and quality. These things became the expression of an age, but they may not have been totally representative of it.

In this context, the craftsman and the patron were joined by the merchant, who brokered the appearance of fashion and who factored an array of foreign goods into the local economy. With their extensive connections, these people made outlandish objects available through knowledge and the growth of capital. For example, within two years of settlement on the New Hampshire Grants in the mid-1760s, merchant Jonathan Chase (1732–1800) of Cornish was bartering mohair, silk, chocolate, and knee buckles with neighbors eager to put aside the frontier and to enjoy their investments. Down the Connecticut River, a half century after Hadley chests had dominated the parlors of western Massachusetts, Springfield's minister, Reverend Bezaleel Howard (1753–1837), owned a costly and cosmopolitan Boston bombé desk-and-bookcase that undoubtedly became a local standard for acceptable fashion (fig. 32).[24]

The scholarship on regionalism in the eighteenth century is especially muddled. An inordinate amount of rural furniture is attributed to either Connecticut or New Hampshire just because it looks like it. But where are the belongings of the people in Vermont, western Massachusetts, the District of Maine, and upstate New York? In southern New Hampshire and Connecticut, there was a broad middle class quick to emulate the taste of wealthy neighbors. These agricultural societies were prosperous and had choices. But today, only the dominant craft traditions, typically involving multi-generational dynasties, are remembered. These skilled tradesmen

Figure 32 Desk-and-bookcase, Boston, 1770–1788. Mahogany with white pine. H. 97", W. 46¾", D. 23¾". (Courtesy, Springfield Science Museum, gift of Edward A. Andrews.)

pandered to the elite, and the sheer volume of surviving furniture testifies to their marketing strategies.

The most dominant craftsmen responsible for "regional styles" often had pan-regional, coastal ties. In Connecticut, William Manley (ca. 1703–1787) of Wethersfield, who probably introduced the cabriole style of cabinetwork to the Connecticut Valley, moved from Charlestown, near Boston, in 1729 (fig. 33). Benjamin Burnham (1737[?]–after 1773) of Colchester and Eliphalet Chapin of East Windsor Hill both worked in Philadelphia during the 1760s. Chapin's fashionable Delaware Valley–style furniture was the rage in central Connecticut and parts of western Massachusetts for a generation, making it an unlikely illustration of regionalism (fig. 34). The furniture attributed to Eliakim Smith (1735–1775) of Hadley, Massachusetts, was made with Boston proportions and construction details (fig. 35). In southern New Hampshire, the Dunlap family of cabinetmakers were both pan-regional and pan-cultural. They rejected nearby Anglo-Boston styles for the motifs derived from the Scottish Lowlands 150 years earlier (see figs. 14, 27).[25]

Figure 33 Dressing table, Wethersfield, Connecticut, 1745–1760. Sycamore with white pine. H. 27½", W. 33½", D. 23½". (Courtesy, Connecticut Historical Society, gift of George Dudley Seymour.)

Figure 34 High chest of drawers attributed to Eliphalet Chapin and/or Aaron Chapin, East Windsor, Connecticut, ca. 1785. Cherry with white pine. H. 87⅛", W. 40¼", D. 20¼". (Courtesy, Winterthur Museum.)

Hundreds of objects survive by these famous Connecticut and New Hampshire craftsmen. The strength of tradition demonstrates the buying power of patrons more than the independence of craftsmen whose work was a commodity instead of decorative art. An extreme case is the relationship of cabinetmaker John Dunlap with the local sawyer, Job Dow, who apparently had enough capital to act as a furniture broker. He sold thousands of board feet of hardwood and pine to Dunlap in the years before the Revolution. In return, the cabinetmaker built forty-six pieces of furniture for the sawyer between 1769 and 1784 to settle the account, far more than Dow could use at home.[26] The sawyer probably bartered some of the furniture on his own account, in a way competing with the cabinetmaker.

On the other side of the coin, the furniture made by the "little guys" who enjoyed limited patronage now seems either innovative or bizarre, depending upon your perspective. More business might have brought efficiency and fame to their designs. Instead, they fit nicely into our misconception about the work of naive or independent craftsmen. Their products appear awkward next to the furniture of the pan-regional craftsmen, who operated large shops. For example, a chair made in the vicinity of Windsor, not far from Chapin's shop at East Windsor Hill, may seem odd, but it was expensive to produce, with a "crookt back," carved crest rail, and pad feet (fig. 36).[27] The chair incorporates many fashionable details from the vocabulary of pan-regional design, exemplified by its Chinese pagoda-like crest rail and rococo ears. Clearly, its maker was not ignorant of convention.

Such hybrids show the mistake in defining furniture by style alone based on a "chronology" of designs loosely associated with the reigns of kings or with cabinetmakers who published design books, such as Thomas Chippendale and George Hepplewhite. Although these names, no matter how accurate or appropriate, can be useful in learning this material, the assumption that styles are monolithic and sequential is false. Many styles were offered simultaneously, like the work of Thomas Bliss (1767–1839) and John W. Horswill of Charlestown, New Hampshire, who produced both rococo

Figure 35 High chest of drawers attributed to Eliakim Smith, Hadley, Massachusetts, ca. 1770. Cherry with white pine. H. 89¾", W. 39 15/16", D. 20⅜". (Courtesy, Historic Deerfield, Inc.; photo, Amanda Merullo.)

Figure 36 Side chair, East Windsor area, Connecticut, 1770–1790. Cherry and ash. H. 42", W. 19 3/8", D. 13 7/8". (Private collection; photo, John Giamatteo.)

Figure 37 Chest of drawers made by Thomas Bliss and John W. Horswill, Charlestown, New Hampshire, 1798. Cherry with white pine. H. 35", W. 41 1/8", D. 21". (Private collection.)

Figure 38 Easy chair made by Thomas Bliss and John W. Horswill, Charlestown, New Hampshire, 1798. Mahogany and whitewood inlay with oak, maple, and white pine. H. 47 1/8", W. 32 3/4", D. 30 1/4" (Courtesy, New Hampshire Historical Society; photo, Bill Finney.)

and neoclassical furniture during their brief partnership between December 1797 and March 1798 (figs. 37, 38).[28]

Chippendale is an especially poor term for rococo furniture made in rural New England between about 1760 and 1810. This style encompasses the Chinese, Gothic, and "modern" (or French) tastes, yet little furniture made outside of Boston, Salem, and Portsmouth bears the hallmarks of "Chippendale" design: claw-and-ball feet, cabriole legs, and foliate carving that is often asymmetrical. These details are scarce in rural New England, dominated by the "neat and plain," because such ornament was the work of specialists whose products may have seemed foreign, vulgar, or unnecessary in the conservative households of the Yankee upland. In truth, Thomas Chippendale (1718–1779) and his *Gentleman and Cabinetmaker's Director* (1754) were virtually unknown in New England in those days. Although a few urban objects were inspired by plates in the *Director* or by imports based on those plates, the book was not owned anywhere in rural New England.[29]

Most rural design, refined or experimental, was governed by a provincial aesthetic that permeated New England through most of the eighteenth century. This style is organized, rational, and even predictable in its attenua-

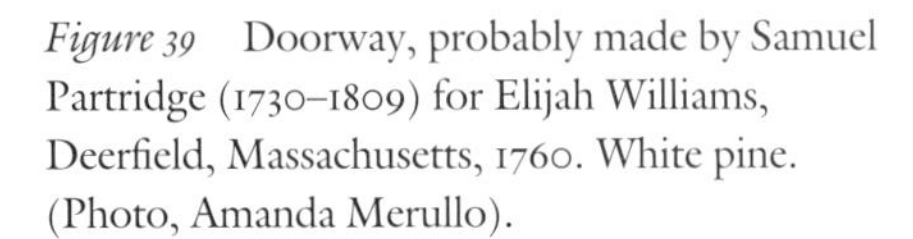
Figure 39 Doorway, probably made by Samuel Partridge (1730–1809) for Elijah Williams, Deerfield, Massachusetts, 1760. White pine. (Photo, Amanda Merullo).

tion, verticality, symmetry, and pretension. It is essentially baroque in its balance, formality, and vertical stance. Like the chair from Windsor, some vocabulary of stylish urban work is usually present, but it is exaggerated.

There is little doubt that a provincial baroque aesthetic governed the constructed surroundings of rural New Englanders throughout most of the eighteenth century. When Major Elijah Williams (1712–1771) built a new house in Deerfield, Massachusetts, with a modern doorway in 1760, he offered passers-by a strong impression of baroque formality.[30] The scrolled doorway emphasizes the axis of the large central-hallway house with ornamental moldings and burgeoning S-curves (fig. 39). A kind of carpenter's baroque easily fashioned from elaborate moldings was perfect for rural patrons drawn to conspicuous consumption. Imaginative and exuberant options were fashioned from standard moldings and fielded panels to achieve a bold, complex, and sculptural overstatement (fig. 40).

To understand baroque design as it was reinterpreted in the New England hinterland between 1720 and 1820, we must turn to the domestic context and conditions that shaped the selection of form and ornament. The designs preferred by this distant but unisolated society were deter-

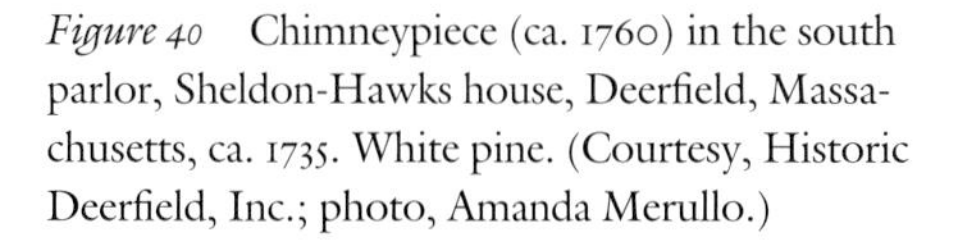

Figure 40 Chimneypiece (ca. 1760) in the south parlor, Sheldon-Hawks house, Deerfield, Massachusetts, ca. 1735. White pine. (Courtesy, Historic Deerfield, Inc.; photo, Amanda Merullo.)

mined by several factors: European precedent, shifting political allegiances and trade connections, agricultural wealth, mobile networks of family members and apprentices, a lack of craft specialization due to labor demands, and the desire for speedy replication of form in order to make a living. Although baroque design for Yankee consumers had its roots in the visual traditions of the courts of William and Mary and Queen Anne—formal, bold, symmetrical, vertical, and vigorous—it was refashioned by the pressures of a prosperous agricultural society made conservative by the rigid annual cycle of farm work and by a lack of specie in a barter economy. Style was also tempered by rote learning and face-to-face relationships. Furniture was local and custom-fit to neighborly expectations and to local architecture. Nevertheless, these Yankees were not out of touch. Only their furni-

Figure 41 Ralph Earl, *Elijah Boardman*, New Milford, Connecticut, 1789. Oil on canvas. 83" × 51". (Courtesy, Metropolitan Museum of Art, bequest of Susan W. Tyler.)

ture, utilitarian ceramics, and most of their iron were manufactured at home. The remaining consumer goods enjoyed in rural New England were foreign imports.[31]

Agriculture provided substantial purchasing power in the fertile valleys of New England. Prosperity sprang from supplying provisions during the Seven Years War in the 1750s and later during the Revolution. Farming was specialized, and cash crops were raised for export. Individual towns became identified with single commodities by the middle of the eighteenth century. In Connecticut, Wethersfield was known for its onions, East Hartford and Glastonbury for tobacco, Windsor for horses and flaxseed. Enfield and Suffield shared their reputation for wheat with Longmeadow and Northampton in western Massachusetts. Farther up the Connecticut Valley, farmer-merchants in Deerfield, Hadley, and Hatfield drove fattened beef to Boston. In western New Hampshire and Vermont, lumber was harvested, especially the tall white pines. In southern New Hampshire, the Scots-Irish had a reputation for their linen.[32]

Much of the population in the rich valley towns lived in big houses on farms. Tax lists show that two-story houses greatly outnumbered one-story houses in Wethersfield in 1773. John Adams (1735–1826) described this prosperous scene on June 8, 1771, when he rode south from Windsor through Hartford to Wethersfield:

> I had spent this Morning in Riding Thro Paradise. My Eyes never behold so fine a Country. From Bissells [tavern] in Windsor to Hartford Ferry, 8 Miles, is one continued Street—Houses all along, and a vast Prospect of level Country on each Hand, the Land's very Rich and the Husbandry pretty good. Here is the finest Ride in America. . . . I wish Connecticut River flowed through Braintree [his home on the south shore of Massachusetts].[33]

The wealth of these New England valleys supported ambitious architecture and furnishings, although the houses were sometimes grander than the people. The interior rooms are often nicely paneled but small and multifunctional. The typical Deerfield parlor in 1775, for example, was sparsely furnished by our standards. It contained on average a bedstead and hangings, six crooked-back (late baroque or "Queen Anne") chairs, a "round" or oval drop-leaf table, andirons, fire tools, a trammel, a few books, two wine glasses, two punch bowls, white tea dishes, and a half-dozen silver teaspoons. Although probate inventories are not complete windows on the past, John Adams's description of the Wethersfield house of his friend, Doctor Eliot Rawson, substantiates the quantitative picture of the Deerfield parlor seventy miles away: "His house is handsome without, but neither clean nor elegant within, in furniture or any Thing else. . . . His dining Room is crowded with a Bed and a Cradle, &c. &c."[34]

Elijah Boardman (1760–1823) of New Milford, Connecticut, in the Housatonic Valley was among the upper tier of merchants who sold raw materials for finished products and who set trends for their neighbors (fig. 41). He represents a phalanx of consumers eager for the trappings of status, which he readily traded at his store and counting house (fig. 42). Such country people moved in a society characterized by a broad middle class, who combined livelihoods as merchants, farmers, and craftsmen, often on a seasonal basis.[35]

The governing convention of rural baroque design—in furniture and portraiture (see fig. 41)—is a vertical emphasis achieved by exaggeration and attenuation. This exaggeration disrupts the whole design but emphasizes its parts to the point where they almost exceed the whole, like the fins on Detroit's automobiles in the 1950s that were meant to emphasize size and movement and to identify cars with airplanes. Boardman becomes an abstracted expression of himself, bigger than life with those long limbs and torso in a picture 83″ tall.

In furniture, the emphasis on the parts highlights the stylishness of the

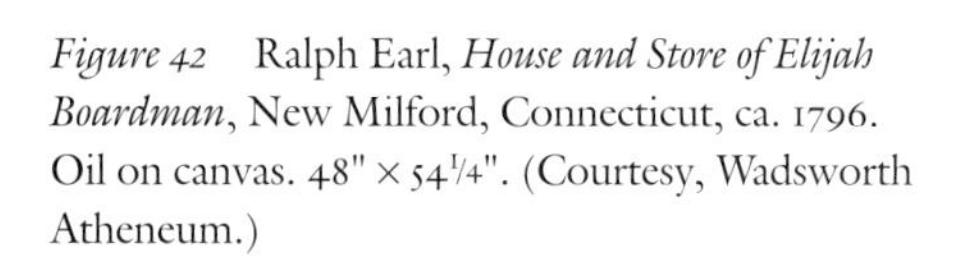

Figure 42 Ralph Earl, *House and Store of Elijah Boardman*, New Milford, Connecticut, ca. 1796. Oil on canvas. 48" × 54¼". (Courtesy, Wadsworth Atheneum.)

Figure 43 Side chair attributed to the Chapin workshops, Hartford County, Connecticut, ca. 1800. Cherry with white pine. H. 38½", W. 19½", D. 15". (Courtesy, Historic Deerfield, Inc.; photo, Helga Studio.)

object, often flagrantly, in the same way that paint color (which these people also used extensively) is used to emphasize detail (fig. 43). The attenuated, usually vertical, eighteenth-century shapes work to good visual advantage in the small, paneled parlors and chambers of rural New England, partly because the furniture for these homes was often made by the same craftsmen during the winter months.[36] In many instances the furniture probably appeared larger owing to the sparse furnishings and low ceilings of most middle-class houses. The western Connecticut desk-and-bookcase shown in figure 44 illustrates the point. The paneled doors and "scroll'd head" give it a strong architectural presence enhanced by familiar baroque ornaments such as the large shell at the base. Unconventional design was an intentional vehicle of stylishness rather than a symptom of ignorance.

Options in exaggerated moldings and S-curves were available to rural furniture buyers throughout this period. Probably made about 1765, the high chest and dressing table illustrated in figure 45 became a rhythmic staccato of S-curves and brass hardware. The complex, scalloped top of the dressing table was the high-style choice for tables and chests, which the cabinetmaker otherwise simply fitted with rectangular tops. The scalloped option in Connecticut Valley furniture, made first in Wethersfield and then northward in Northampton, Hatfield, and Deerfield, is visually exciting, but it constitutes a kind of abstract baroque. The sawn shape is ultimately two-dimensional, reducing the cost of detailed, free-hand carving, although it aspires to more. A generation later, the old baroque formality was still preferred in hill towns like Conway, Massachusetts, where Jonathan Smith Jr. (b. 1770) made a doorway-like chest-on-chest in 1803 (fig. 46).[37]

After the Revolution, improvements in transportation and technology swept through the valleys of rural New England. The creation of capital

Figure 44 Desk-and-bookcase, Woodbury, Connecticut, 1770–1800. Cherry with white pine. H. 96", W. 40", D. 21 5/8". (Courtesy, Winterthur Museum.)

Figure 45 High chest of drawers and dressing table, Hatfield, Massachusetts, area, ca. 1765. Cherry and yellow birch with yellow and white pine. H. 80¾", W. 38¾", D. 20½"; H. 29", W. 36", D. 24½". (Courtesy, Historic Deerfield, Inc.; photo, Amanda Merullo.) The high chest of drawers and dressing table were made for John and Content Little Hastings, who were married in 1764.

through export agriculture centralized community life in the 1780s, and a network of small market towns replaced John Adams's view of a continuous street of valley farms before the Revolution.[38] By the 1790s, some inland market towns had grown into small, pretentious cities, like Middletown and Hartford, Connecticut; Springfield, Massachusetts; and Concord, New

Figure 46 Chest-on-chest-on-frame made by Jonathan Smith Jr. for Simon and Lydia Batchelder DeWolf, Conway, Massachusetts, 1803. Cherry with white pine. H. 83½", W. 37½", D. 23¼". (Courtesy, Historic Deerfield, Inc.; photo, Amanda Merullo.)

Figure 47 High chest of drawers, southern Hartford County, Connecticut, ca. 1785. Mahogany and mahogany veneer with white pine. H. 88½", W. 44½", D. 24¼". (Courtesy, Historic Deerfield, Inc., Mr. and Mrs. Hugh B. Vanderbilt Fund for Curatorial Acquisitions; photo, John Giamatteo.)

Hampshire. Several other large towns and county seats boasted newspapers and academies. Whereas before, any sense of a regional style had been borne on the backs of mobile apprentices and journeymen, the new furniture moved independently with improved travel and communication. In 1794, the cabinetmaking firm of Samuel Kneeland (1755–1828) and Lemuel Adams (d. 1821) advertised in the *Vermont Journal*, 160 miles up the Connecticut River at Windsor, that they "can furnish them [potential customers] with every kind of Cabinet Work, made in the newest and most approved fashions from Europe, . . . cased and delivered at the water side Hartford."[39] Consumerism accelerated with the growth of trade and specie, and repetition in the production of furnishings standardized form and design.

The consumer revolution changed perception of self and the governing logic of order and precedent. In the sphere of design, the reign of baroque by rote repetition entered a confident age of crisp, integrated, academic, classical architecture. The treatment of ornament moved from exaggerated parts to integrated statements. Craftsmen confidently adopted the academic, classical designs made popular by the promoters of Andrea Palladio's principles of architecture perfected in the sixteenth century. Although introduced to western New England in the 1760s, Palladian taste was not popularized until Williams Sprats (1747–1810), a Scot architect from Edinburgh,

Figure 48 Desk-on-frame, southern Hartford County, Connecticut, ca. 1785. Mahogany with white pine and yellow poplar. H. 44", W. 40", D. 21". (Courtesy, Yale University Art Gallery, gift of C. Sanford Bull.)

found himself a prisoner of war at Hartford in 1779 and designed a mansion house for Barnabas Deane. Before moving to Vermont, where he died in 1810, Sprats lived for fifteen years in Litchfield County, Connecticut, where he designed Elijah Boardman's grand house in New Milford (see fig. 42).[40]

The wrenching shift from baroque exaggeration to Palladian order in western New England furniture is illustrated by a mahogany high chest of drawers probably made at Middletown, Connecticut, about 1785 (fig. 47). The pilastered design of the high chest is both classically inspired and proportioned. The chest is rigidly symmetrical and has a squared, less vertical stance than earlier furniture, emphasizing its monumentality. An academic underpinning integrates the parts with the whole. The overall height is twice the overall width. The measurements of the lower case form a 3:4:5 right triangle. Most importantly, the height of the lower case is in the same proportion to the height of the upper case as the upper case is to the overall height of the high chest. The "golden mean" in ancient proportion calls for the shorter line to relate to the longer line as the longer line relates to the whole. The ratio is 5:8 and forms the foundation of this Palladian high chest of drawers. Numbers aside, the vocabulary of Palladian architectural design sometimes joined its sense of proportion. For example, abstract Ionic columns are integrated into the serpentine facade on a mahogany desk (fig. 48) from the same shop as the high chest of drawers.[41]

The urbanization of New England after the Revolution created a new way of life and a new appearance for it. Baroque formality was merged with Palladian structure and later ornamented with neoclassical design. Orderliness and agricultural prosperity were joined with consumerism and manufacture. The result for most of rural New England, especially in the hill towns beyond the river valleys, was the continued marriage of local resources and ornament to imported concepts.

After the Revolution, a new hybrid was born. Neoclassical designs were attractive for their roots in ancient republics and for association with the new nation. The visual legacy of the eighteenth century lingered in rural New England alongside the new designs. One example is the front room of the house built by Major Joseph Griswold (1777–1843) at Buckland, Massachusetts, in 1818 (fig. 49).[42] Confident consumerism drew on the new motifs with the assurance that two mantlepiece designs stacked on a single chimney breast, perhaps as illustrated in an architectural pattern book, were better than one. He acknowledged the past with the abstract leaf carving on the upper stiles. Griswold's eagerness to blend new designs with the old harbored no rejection of urban taste: just the opposite. He fashioned his own urban style, displaying the confidence with which rural people had always manipulated cosmopolitan taste.

New England is fertile ground for defining culture through artifacts and manuscripts because so much survives. The wealth of this material reveals a cultural complexity that permeated all aspects of life. The marriage of skills, materials, and intent hybridized all that had gone before to create something new. Consequently, conflicting "regional characteristics" invariably arise to defy categorization during exercises in connoisseurship and cultural

Figure 49 Chimney breast made by Joseph Griswold, Buckland, Massachusetts, 1818. White pine. (Photo, Amanda Merullo.)

analysis (which should be paired more closely than they are). Every player behind the production and use of New England furniture and architecture left their mark and inadvertently documented the human condition in their time and place. Although we are easily diverted by the beauty or bizarreness of objects, the human component holds valuable information for determining what life was like in "the back of beyond."

ACKNOWLEDGMENTS The author thanks William Hosley for his encouragement and commentary on this paper and Luke Beckerdite and Kim King Zea for careful readings of the text.

1. For a range of discussions regarding regionalism, homogeneity, and isolation, see Milieu B. Vance, "The Regional Concept as a Tool for Social Research," in *Regionalism in America*, edited by Merrill Jensen (Madison, Wis.: University Press of Wisconsin, 1951), pp. 119–40; Michael K. Brown, "Scalloped-Top Furniture of the Connecticut River Valley," *Antiques* 117, no. 5 (May 1980): 1092–99. See also, Robert Blair St. George, "Artifacts of Regional Consciousness in the Connecticut River Valley, 1700–1780," and Richard D. Brown, "Regional Culture in a Revolutionary Era: The Connecticut Valley, 1760–1820," in *The Great River: Art & Society of the Connecticut Valley, 1635–1820*, edited by Gerald W. R. Ward and William N. Hosley Jr. (Hartford: Wadsworth Atheneum, 1985), pp. 29–39, 41–48.

2. Ward and Hosley, eds., *The Great River*, pp. 247–48. John Witherspoon, *The Works of the Reverend John Witherspoon*, 4 vols. (Philadelphia, 1802), 3:583. The author thanks Kenneth Hafertepe for bringing this reference to his attention. According to the *Oxford English Dictionary*, "neat" in the eighteenth century was defined as "elegance of form or arrangement, with freedom from all unnecessary additions or embellishment; of agreeable but simple appearance; nicely made or proportioned." For examples of southern "neat and plain" furniture, see Wallace B. Gusler, *Furniture of Williamsburg and Eastern Virginia, 1710–1790* (Richmond: Virginia Museum of fine Arts, 1979), figs. 56, 76, 78–81, 86–88, 92, 105, 109, 113. Ronald L. Hurst and Jonathan Prown's forthcoming catalogue of southern furniture at Colonial Williamsburg will address the topic at length.

3. Philip D. Zimmerman, "Regionalism in American Furniture Studies," in *Perspectives on American Furniture*, edited by Gerald W. R. Ward (New York: W.W. Norton, 1988), esp. pp. 19–38.

4. Philip Zea, "Craftsmen and Culture: An Introduction to Vermont Furniture Making," in Charles A. Robinson, *A Checklist of Vermont Furniture Makers* (Shelburne, Vt.: Shelburne Museum, 1994), pp. 18–20. Kenneth Joel Zogry, *The Best the Country Affords: Vermont Furniture, 1765–1850*, edited by Philip Zea (Bennington, Vt.: Bennington Museum, 1995), passim.

5. John Gaines II and Thomas Gaines I, Account Book, 1707–1761, Winterthur Museum Library; Philip Zea, "Rural Craftsmen and Design," in Brock Jobe and Myrna Kaye, *New England Furniture: The Colonial Era* (Boston: Houghton Mifflin Company, 1984) pp. 63–64; Robert E. T. Hendrick, "John Gaines II and Thomas Gaines I, 'Turners' of Ipswich, Massachusetts," M.A. thesis, University of Delaware, 1964, pp. 67, 78, 95–96.

6. Donna Keith Baron, "Furniture Makers and Retailers in Worcester County, Massachusetts, Working to 1850," *Antiques* 143, no. 5 (May 1993): 786, 789, 792, 794; William G. Lord, *History of Athol, Massachusetts* (Athol, Mass.: by the author, 1953), pp. 282, 284, 490–91. Donna-Belle Garvin, James L. Garvin, and John F. Page, *Plain & Elegant, Rich & Common: Documented New Hampshire Furniture, 1750–1850* (Concord, N.H.: New Hampshire Historical Society, 1979), pp. 132–33, 142; Brock Jobe, ed., *Portsmouth Furniture: Masterworks from the New Hampshire Seacoast* (Boston: Society for the Preservation of New England Antiquities, 1993), pp. 114–21. A similar Haverhill sideboard by Stephen Adams (1778–1859) is also known. See *American Collector* 6, no. 5 (June 1937): 7.

7. Donna-Belle Garvin, "A 'Neat and Lively Aspect': Newport, New Hampshire as a Cabinetmaking Center," *Historical New Hampshire* 43, no. 3 (Fall 1988): 202–24; *New-Hampshire Spectator* (Newport), May 1828; Garvin, Garvin, and Page, *Plain & Elegant*, pp. 134–35, 144.

8. Cary Carson, "Doing History with Material Culture," in *Material Culture and the Study of American Life*, edited by Ian M.G. Quimby (New York: W.W. Norton, 1978), pp. 41–64.

9. Philip Zea, "Erastus Grant: The Emergence of a Connecticut Valley Cabinetmaker," *1987 Western Reserve Antiques Show Catalogue* (Cleveland, Ohio: Western Reserve Historical Society, 1987), pp. 18–20; Houghton Bulkeley, "George Belden and Erastus Grant, Cabinetmakers," in *Contributions to Connecticut Cabinetmaking* (Hartford: Connecticut Historical Society, 1967), pp. 72–81. The distinction of being the earliest documented piece of western Massachusetts furniture with neoclassical detail is shared with a tall clock case made in 1799 by Daniel Clay (1770–1848) of Greenfield, Massachusetts, now in the collection of Historic Deerfield, Inc. See Dean A. Fales Jr., *The Furniture of Historic Deerfield* (New York: E. P. Dutton, 1976), p. 267.

10. Beatrix T. Rumford, "Uncommon Art of the Common People: A Review of Trends in the Collecting and Exhibiting of American Folk Art," in *Perspectives on American Folk Art*, edited by Ian M. G. Quimby and Scott T. Swank (New York: W.W. Norton, 1980): pp. 13–53; Kenneth L. Ames, *Beyond Necessity: Art in the Folk Tradition* (Winterthur, Del.: Winterthur Museum, 1977), esp. pp. 62–65; Sumpter T. Priddy III., *American Fancy* (forthcoming).

11. For example, see Ward and Hosley, eds., *The Great River*, pp. 219–20, 227.

12. William Salmon, *Palladio Londinensis* (London, 1734), pl. 26.

13. Philip Zea and Robert C. Cheney, *Clock Making in New England, 1725–1825: An Interpretation of the Old Sturbridge Village Collection* (Sturbridge, Mass.: Old Sturbridge Village, 1992), pp. 23–25, 28; Ward and Hosley, eds., *The Great River*, pp. 349–51.

14. For example, see William N. Hosley Jr., "Timothy Loomis and the Economy of Joinery in Windsor, Connecticut, 1740–1786," in Ward, ed., *Perspectives on American Furniture*, p. 132. Gail Nessell Colglazier, *Springfield Furniture, 1700–1850: A Large and Rich Assortment* (Springfield, Mass.: Connecticut Valley Historical Museum, 1990), pp. 28–29, 36–37.

15. Nancy Goyne Evans, "The Tracy Chairmakers Identified," *Connecticut Antiquarian* 33, no. 2 (December 1981): 14–21; William R. Child, *History of Cornish, New Hampshire*, 2 vols. (Concord, N.H.: Rumford Press, 1910), 2:372–74; Stephen Tracy Day Book, Lisbon, Conn. and Cornish, N.H., 1805–1849, p. 10, private collection.

16. Jean M. Burks, "The Evolution of Design in Shaker Furniture," *Antiques* 145, no. 5 (May 1994): 732–41; Mary Lyn Ray, *True Gospel Simplicity: Shaker Furniture in New Hampshire* (Concord: New Hampshire Historical Society, 1974), fig. 32; Mary Lyn Ray, "A Reappraisal of Shaker Furniture," in *Winterthur Portfolio* 8, edited by Ian M.G. Quimby (Charlottesville: University Press of Virginia, 1973), pp. 107–32.

17. Brock Jobe, "The Boston Furniture Industry, 1720–1740," in *Boston Furniture of the Eighteenth Century*, edited by Walter Muir Whitehill (Boston: Colonial Society of Massachusetts, 1974), esp. pp. 39–47. William Hogarth, *The Analysis of Beauty* (London: J. Reeves, 1753), pl. 1; Ward and Hosley, eds., *The Great River*, pp. 210–11; J. L. Cummings, "Painted Chests from the Connecticut Valley," *Antiques* 34, no. 4 (October 1938): 192–93.

18. Jobe, ed., *Portsmouth Furniture*, pp. 193–200. See also Philip Zea, "Piscataqua Clocks: Marking Change Through Time," paper presented at "'That Little World' Portsmouth: The Art and Culture of the Piscataqua Region: A Symposium," Currier Gallery of Art, Manchester, N.H., September 26, 1992, pp. 12–16; Zea and Cheney, *Clock Making in New England*, pp. 15–17.

19. Jobe, ed., *Portsmouth Furniture*, pp. 289–91.

20. Philip Zea and Donald Dunlap, *The Dunlap Cabinetmakers: A Tradition in Craftsmanship* (Mechanicsburg, Pa.: Stackpole Books, 1994), pp. 6–45; Benno M. Forman, "German Influences in Pennsylvania Furniture," in Scott T. Swank, *Arts of the Pennsylvania Germans*, edited by Catherine E. Hutchins (Winterthur, Del.: Winterthur Museum, 1983), pp. 102–70. David Hewett, "G. Stedman—The Elusive Vermont Cabinetmaker," *Maine Antique Digest* 14, no. 3 (March 1986): 1D–4D.

21. Henry R. Stiles, *The History and Genealogies of Ancient Windsor, Connecticut*, 2 vols. (Hartford: Case, Lockwood & Brainard Company, 1891–92), 2:76–77, 126, 393, 700–702; Sylvester Judd, *History of Hadley, Including the Early History of Hatfield, South Hadley, Amherst, and Granby, Massachusetts* (Springfield, Mass.: H. R. Huntting and Company, 1905), Part 2, pp. 111–12; Patricia E. Kane, "The Joiners of Seventeenth Century Hartford County," *Connecticut Historical Society Bulletin* 35, no. 3 (July 1970): 78–80; Jonathan L. Fairbanks and Robert F. Trent, eds., *New England Begins: The Seventeenth Century*, 3 vols. (Boston: Museum of Fine Arts, 1982), 2:121, 3:506–7; Ward and Hosley, eds., *The Great River*, pp. 185–86, 190–93, 201–2. William Buell (d. 1681) was born in County Huntingdon. Thomas Holcombe (d. 1657) was born in Devonshire. Thomas Bissell (d. 1689) may have come from Somersetshire. Richard Lyman Jr. (d. 1662 in Northampton, Mass.) and Samuel Porter Sr. (d. 1689) left different villages in Essex, and Henry (1598–after 1685) and Francis Stiles (b. 1602) were born in Bedfordshire and emigrated from London. Ward and Hosley, eds., *The Great River*, pp. 193–94.

22. Clair Franklin Luther, *The Hadley Chest* (Hartford: Case, Lockwood & Brainard Company, 1935). Philip Zea, "The Fruits of Oligarchy: Patronage and the Hadley Chest Tradition in Western Massachusetts," in *Early New England Furniture: Essays in Memory of Benno M. Forman*, edited by Brock Jobe (Boston: Society for the Preservation of New England Antiquities, 1987), pp. 1–65; Philip Zea and Suzanne L. Flynt, *Hadley Chests* (Deerfield, Mass.: Memorial Hall Museum, 1992).

23. Zea, "The Fruits of Oligarchy," pp. 14, 18–19. Kevin M. Sweeney, "Mansion People: Kinship, Class, and Architecture in Western Massachusetts in the Mid Eighteenth Century," *Winterthur Portfolio* 19, no. 4 (Winter 1984): 231–55; Kevin M. Sweeney, "River Gods in the Making: The Williamses of Western Massachusetts," in *The Bay and the River, 1600–1900*, edited by Peter Benes (Boston: Boston University, 1982), pp. 101–16.

24. Jonathan Chase Papers, Ledger 1, pp. 1–50, New Hampshire Historical Society, Concord; Zea, "Rural Craftsmen and Design," p. 47; Child, *History of Cornish, New Hampshire,* 2:62–63. Ward and Hosley, eds., *The Great River*, pp. 243–44.

25. Kevin M. Sweeney, "Furniture and Furniture Making in Mid-Eighteenth-Century Wethersfield, Connecticut," *Antiques* 125, no. 5 (May 1984): 1156; Ward and Hosley, eds., *The Great River*, pp. 212–13; Henry R. Stiles, ed., *The History of Ancient Wethersfield, Connecticut*, 2 vols. (New York: Grafton Press, 1904), 2:495; Robert F. Trent, "The Colchester School of Cabinetmaking, 1750–1800," in *The American Craftsman and the European Tradition, 1620–1820*, edited by Francis J. Puig and Michael Conforti (Minneapolis, Minn.: Minneapolis Institute of Arts, 1989), pp. 112–35; Joseph Lionetti and Robert F. Trent, "New Information about Chapin Chairs," *Antiques* 129, no. 5 (May 1986): 1082–95; Thomas P. Kugelman, and Alice K. Kugelman, "The Hartford Case Furniture Survey," *Maine Antique Digest* 21, no. 3 (March 1993): 36A–38A; Alice Kugelman, Thomas Kugelman, and Robert Lionetti, "The Chapin School of East Windsor, Connecticut: The Hartford Case Furniture Survey, Part II," *Maine Antique Digest* 22, no. 1 (January 1994): 12D–14D. Ward and Hosley, eds., *The Great River*, pp. 226–27. Two generations of craftsmen, working before and after the Revolution, made case furniture ornamented with carved vines in western Massachusetts. Eliakim Smith is a viable candidate for the earlier craftsman. A partial 1850s transcription of his account book in the Judd Manuscript at the Forbes Library, Northampton, Massachusetts, demonstrates that he made elaborate furniture forms. A cherry breakfast table of comparable work was owned by descendants of Smith when examined by the author in 1979. The work of the second generation (identity unknown), as illustrated in *The Great River*, appears to have been produced with somewhat less skill in southern Hampshire County in the Springfield area during the last quarter of the eighteenth century. Another craftsman, William Mather (1766–1835) of Whately, Massachusetts, also worked in a similar style. See Bernard and S. Dean Levy, catalogue 6 (1988): 85. Zea and Dunlap, *Clock Making in New England*, pp. 36–40.

26. John Dunlap, Account Book, Goffstown and Bedford, N.H., 1768–1789, as transcribed in Charles S. Parsons, *The Dunlaps & Their Furniture* (Manchester, N.H.: Currier Gallery of Art, 1970), pp. 230–31.

27. Ward and Hosley, eds., *The Great River*, pp. 238–39.

28. Garvin, Garvin, and Page, *Plain & Elegant*, pp. 124–27, 141, 146–47.

29. Morrison H. Heckscher and Leslie Greene Bowman, *American Rococo, 1750–1775: Elegance in Ornament* (New York: Metropolitan Museum of Art, 1992), pp. 137, and 167, 169, 182–83; Jobe and Kaye, *New England Furniture,* pp. 19–20. See also Morrison H. Heckscher, "Philadelphia Chippendale: The Influence of the *Director* in America," *Furniture History* 21 (1985): 283–95.

30. Amelia F. Miller, *Connecticut River Valley Doorways: An Eighteenth-Century Flowering* (Boston: Boston University for the Dublin Seminar for New England Folklife, 1983), pp. 48–49; Ward and Hosley, eds., *The Great River*, pp. 66, 81–97.

31. For examples of foreign imports with histories of ownership in the Connecticut Valley, see Ward and Hosley, eds., *The Great River*, pp. 194–95, 270–71, 306–8, 311–14, 318–21, 325, 338, 374–75, 380–82, 384–85, 421–29, 432–39, 441–43.

32. Thomas R. Lewis, "The Landscape and Environment of the Connecticut River Valley," in Ward and Hosley, eds., *The Great River*, pp. 12–13; Kevin M. Sweeney, "Gentlemen Farmers and Inland Merchants: The Williams Family and Commercial Agriculture in Pre-Revolutionary Western Massachusetts," 1986 *Dublin Seminar for New England Folklife*, edited by Peter Benes (Boston: Boston University, 1988), pp. 60–73; Kevin M. Sweeney, "From Wilderness to Arcadian Vale: Material Life in the Connecticut River Valley, 1635–1760," in Ward and Hosley, eds., *The Great River*, pp. 21–24; Winifred Barr Rothenberg, *From Market-Places to a Market Economy: The Transformation of Rural Massachusetts, 1750–1850* (Chicago and London: University of Chicago Press, 1992), pp. 79–111; J. Ritchie Garrison, *Landscape and Material Life in Franklin County, Massachusetts, 1770–1860* (Knoxville: University of Tennessee Press, 1991), pp. 18–35; *All Sorts of Good Sufficient Cloth: Linen-Making in New England, 1640–1860* (North Andover, Mass.: Merrimack Valley Textile Museum, 1980), pp. 5–32.

33. Sweeney, "Mansion People," p. 242. *Diary and Autobiography of John Adams*, 4 vols., edited by L. H. Butterfield (Cambridge, Mass.: Belknap Press of Harvard University Press, 1961), 2:28.

34. Barbara C. Batson, "Wells-Thorn Refurnishing Plan" (unpublished National Museum Act Internship Paper, 1985, on file at the Henry N. Flynt Memorial Library, Historic Deerfield, Inc., Deerfield, Mass..), pp. 15–24. *Diary and Autobiography of John Adams*, 2:31.

35. Elizabeth Mankin Kornhauser, *Ralph Earl, The Face of the Young Republic* (Hartford, Conn.: Wadsworth Atheneum, 1991), pp. 47, 73–76, 154–55, 217–18. Zea, "Rural Craftsmen and Design," pp. 47–72.

36. Zea, "Rural Craftsmen and Design," pp. 56–67.

37. Brown, "Scalloped-Top Furniture," pp. 1092–99; Sweeney, "Wethersfield," pp. 1156–63; Ward and Hosley, eds., *The Great River*, pp. 222–25. Philip Zea, "The Emergence of Neoclassical Furniture Making in Rural Western Massachusetts," *Antiques* 142, no. 6 (December 1992): 844–45.

38. Margaret E. Martin, "Merchants and Trade of the Connecticut River Valley, 1750–1820," *Smith College Studies in History* 24, nos. 1–4 (October 1938–July 1939): 7–17, 52–54, 61–65, 198–210.

39. *Vermont Journal* (Windsor), March 17, 1794.

40. Andrea Palladio, *Quattro Libri dell'Architettura* (1570); William B. O'Neal, "Pattern Books in American Architecture, 1730–1930," in *Palladian Studies in America*, edited by Mario di Valmarana (Charlottesville: University Press of Virginia, 1984), 1:47; Ward and Hosley, eds., *The Great River*, pp. 66–67 and nos. 17, 18, 22, 24, 25, 107; Zea, "Neoclassical Furniture Making," pp. 844–49. William Lamson Warren, "William Sprats and His Civil and Ecclesiastical Architecture in New England," *Old-Time New England* 44 (Winter 1954): 65–78, and (Spring 1954): 103–14; William Lamson Warren, "William Sprats, Master Joiner: Connecticut's Federalist Architect," *Connecticut Antiquarian* 9 (December 1957): 11–20; Ward and Hosley, eds., *The Great River*, pp. 67–68 and no. 22; Trent, "Colchester," pp. 132–33.

41. In the lower case of the high chest, the overall height is 34", the overall width is 44", and the diagonal is 54." The diagonal measurement also matches the height of the upper case. The author thanks Cheryl Chappell for sharing her research into the design of this object. For a similar analysis, see Zea, "Neoclassical Furniture Making," pp. 845, 851; Ward and Hosley, eds., *The Great River*, p. 227.

42. Thomas S. Michie, "Joseph Griswold, Views of a Cabinetmaker Through his Account Book" (unpublished manuscript Historic Deerfield Summer Fellowship Paper, 1977, Henry N. Flynt Memorial Library, Deerfield, Mass.).

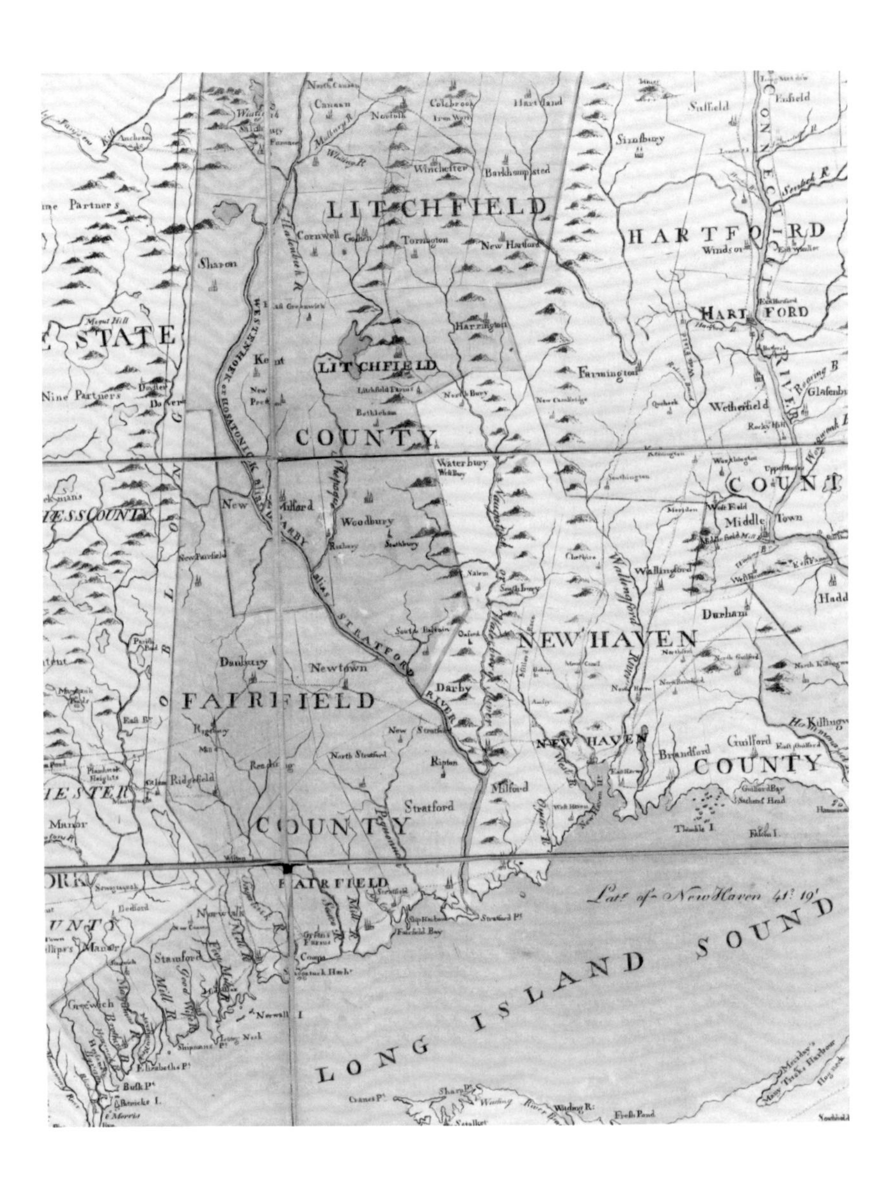

Figure 1 Bernard Romans, map of Connecticut, 1777. (Courtesy, Beinecke Library, Yale University.)

Edward S. Cooke Jr.

The Social Economy of the Preindustrial Joiner in Western Connecticut, 1750–1800

▼ SAMUEL GOODRICH, the author of the many Peter Parley stories published in the second quarter of the nineteenth century, grew up in the southwestern Connecticut hill town of Ridgefield during the late-eighteenth and early-nineteenth centuries. Reflecting on his childhood home several decades later, Goodrich commented upon the local agrarian economy, the role of the yeoman-craftsman, and the "simple character" of the domestic furnishings:

> Nearly all the inhabitants of Ridgefield were farmers, with the few mechanics that were necessary to carry on society in a somewhat primeval state. Even the person not professionally devoted to agriculture had each his own farm, or at least his garden and home lot, with his pigs, poultry, and cattle. . . . The household, as well as political, economy of those days lay in this,—that every family lived as much as possible within itself.[1]

Among those not professionally devoted to farming were blacksmith David Olmstead and joiner, or cabinetmaker, Elisha Hawley. These craftsmen served both economic and cultural roles. Their "articles of use" were important items of exchange in the specie-poor economy. On a deeper level, the artifacts they produced "expressly" for their fellow townspeople became cherished possessions. Goodrich fondly recalled the identity of the local craftsmen who helped create his family's domestic environment.[2]

Although Goodrich lamented the primitive material state of his youth, particularly in contrast to the abundant domestic refinement of his later years, his remarks on the local economy point out the importance of artisans within an interdependent network of independent households. In western Connecticut (fig. 1) between 1750 and 1800, a truly mixed agricultural economy incorporated grains, animals, and crafts. It is therefore important to examine craftsmen and the context of their work within this multi-faceted economy. I use the term social economy to describe this context because it refers to a particularized web of relations and activities that preceded a capitalist political economy. The products of local craftsmen emanated from and responded to a specific set of social relationships. The term social economy recognizes the importance of craftwork to the decisions of a household on the allocation of resources for production and exchange. It was a time, as Michael Foucoult suggests, in which the value of work and objects was gauged more by social standards than by monetary ones. In such an integrated community, skill took on meanings far different from today's notions of quality.[3]

The creation and use of objects are integral parts of a dynamic social process, not just static events or ends unto themselves. Artifacts evolve and gain meaning out of cultural values and social relationships and, in turn, shape and maintain cultural values and social relationships. During a period of limited advertising and uneven, fluctuating exposure to several fashion systems, the local arena was where the meanings of goods were selected, adapted, invested, or divested. Furniture, in particular, serves as a signifier: it can provide functional enjoyment or comfort for a person or household; it can indicate surplus exchange power; it can manifest memories of past experiences and social relationships; it can unify or differentiate peoples; it can embody abstract ideals such as accomplishment or achievement, social power, or stability; and it can serve as an owner's legacy to be passed on into the future.[4]

Joiners, who lived in every town and whose products combined enduring utility and changing fashion, worked at the interface of traditional household or community values and external market forces. During the last half of the eighteenth century, joiners in western Connecticut were linked by a common technical tradition. The largest shops consisted of two benches in a 300 to 400 square-foot area and a work force of six. Most shops tended to be slightly smaller, with one bench and two or three joiners. Probate inventories from the region also reveal the similarities of joiners' tools: the major distinction of the larger shops is a greater number of certain tools, like molding planes, rather than the type of tool. A basic and effective chest of tools for preparing, assembling, and finishing furniture seems to have been accessible to most joiners with their own shops. Artifactual evidence from the region's furniture reveals that joiners could draw upon a number of techniques to construct furniture—mortise-and-tenons, post-and-rungs, dovetails, or nails—or to decorate furniture—sawn profiles, molding, turned ornament, carving, or inlay. Often the craftsman combined a variety of techniques on the same piece of furniture. The size of the shop and workforce, the relative low cost of tools and basic materials, and the variety of techniques gave the preindustrial joiner of the region a great deal of flexibility during this period of "low technology" craft production. Drawing upon a broad technical repertoire and a shop tradition that stressed economical use of human skill, the joiner worked skillfully and efficiently to create a wide range of furniture. He could respond quickly to a client's demands or to new fashion without drastic retooling.[5]

Despite the joiners' use of similar tools, technologies, and work spaces, considerable variety prevailed among the furniture made and owned in western Connecticut from 1750 to 1800. Not only are there differences in furniture forms and decoration between towns, but also within towns. We thus need to identify what restricted or encouraged the artisan's choice of form, technique, or decoration. The specific context in which a joiner worked is crucial to any understanding of these selections and adaptations. His web of social and economic relations determined his composition, tool selection, techniques, work rhythms, levels of production, and the look of the final product. The craftsman's choices were grounded within a very specific set of learning experiences, economic systems, and social norms and obligations. By focusing attention on how the joiner learned his trade and then refined or expanded his skills and attitudes, we can begin to analyze the workings of the social economy of the region.

Acquisition of Skills

Apprenticeship, a system that clarifies especially well the social basis for the joiner's trade during the preindustrial period, was the primary method for learning the craft. In the eighteenth century, apprenticeship differed significantly from its modern or contemporary form. Today, a person voluntarily enters into an apprenticeship with a company to learn a specific aspect of the trade. The company pays the apprentice a minimal wage during the learning process and defines all relationships between company and apprentice by wage rates and working hours. The company essentially cares only about the apprentice's performance on the job and how quickly he will pay back the investment. Room, board, and life outside of work are the apprentice's own responsibilities.[6]

Preindustrial apprenticeship was fundamentally a social contract in which mutual obligations and expectations bound the two parties. The young lad followed certain prescribed rules of living in return for instruction in a trade. Like the son of a farmer, the apprentice was willing to give up certain personal freedoms and to perform certain tasks for a paternal figure with little direct recompense, because he expected to become a master himself. The master willingly taught the youth and took him into his household, because the apprentice's commitment permitted the master to increase the variety and scale of operations and to maximize opportunities during his peak years of physical activity. Apprenticeship ensured the availability of extra labor for preparatory tasks such as sawing and dressing stock as well as the ability to undertake larger, more logistically complicated tasks such as fabricating large case furniture, paneling interiors, or hauling boards. In addition, young apprentices even served as a form of human credit. During slack periods in his own shop, the master "rented out" his apprentices to others in the community for simple woodworking tasks or even for agricultural labor. In such a case, the youth was not working on his own time but rather as a member of the master's household. The apprentice's labor thus built up indebtedness within the community that the master could draw on as need arose.

Even apprenticeship selection was based upon the social network; a young craftsman in his twenties took on the sons of neighbors or relatives. A joiner in his thirties turned to his own adolescent sons for apprentices. Those with daughters but no sons often arranged for a daughter to marry an apprentice or a member of another shop, thereby consolidating or controlling the trade for the next generation. Once the elder craftsman had set his own children up as independent adults, he had less interest in his production and earning power. At this later point in his career, the joiner became an individual craftsman, helping out in local shops when needed or undertaking light work or repair work.[7]

The apprenticeship agreement between Lazarus Prindle and Joseph Peck

Jr., both of Newtown, sheds light upon this training process in a time when life and work were interwoven and work arranged along household lines. On June 5, 1793, Peck, then fifteen years old and with his father as witness, bound himself to Prindle for a two-year training period. In return for instruction, Peck promised to serve faithfully, keep his master's secrets, waste none of his master's goods, avoid unexcused absences, and obey his master's lawful commands. In addition, Peck pledged not to commit fornication, to contract matrimony, to play at dice or other illegal games, to haunt taverns or playhouses, nor to buy or sell anything on his own during the term of his apprenticeship. In short, Peck completely resigned himself to Prindle's authority.

For his part, Prindle, then thirty years old and without a son ready to apprentice, swore to teach and instruct the apprentice in the trade and mystery of a joiner. Furthermore, Prindle provided Peck with lodging, food, and washing by treating him as a surrogate son within the household. Upon the completion of his training, Peck would receive a good suit of clothes and take his place as a productive, good-standing member of the community.[8]

The "art, trade & mystery" of the joiner's craft encompassed a wide range of attitudes, responsibilities, and activities. In an era before differentiation and specialization drew lines of distinction between design, workmanship, decoration, and marketing, the rural joiner oversaw and participated in the entire furniture-making process from conception through sale. The apprentice acquired these values and skills through a process that combined observation and imitation. Due to the casual interaction that took place in the small shop, the boy could see the decisions, actions, and results of the master or any other craftsmen who worked in that shop. In this manner, the apprentice internalized his master's approaches and techniques. Less consciously, the apprentice also adopted certain attitudes about working wood. From a broad range of possibilities, the apprentice therefore learned and practiced the solutions favored and used by his master. In a time of human power and relatively low technology, a reliance on internalized solutions to structural problems, systematic and habitual motions, and familiar sequences helped to ensure efficient, satisfactory work. This workmanship of habit made craftwork economically viable. As a result, reflexive actions acquired and developed during training became an integral part of the joiner's chest of tools. These conventions serve as diagnostic features that help group surviving furniture and identify it as the work of a particular shop tradition.[9]

A joiner's later experiences supplemented, but never totally subsumed, the basic technical foundation acquired during his time as an apprentice. His performance, however, was not totally confined to mere replication of his master's work; rather, he worked within a dynamic tradition of furniture making. He selectively gathered ideas about new techniques or approaches from the products of other shops in the same town or nearby, or from observations made during travel, the challenge of replicating imported furniture, meeting the new demands of a client, or repairing a piece of furniture made in another shop.[10] These new ideas, inevitable within a New England society far more mobile than has been perceived, were grafted onto existing structural habits or filtered through local working conventions.

In Stratford, for example, two shops dominated the local furniture market: that of Brewster Dayton and that of the Hubbell family. Dayton (working in Stratford ca. 1762–1796) was born across Long Island Sound in Brookhaven, New York, and apprenticed with an English-trained immigrant joiner in Stratford. His early experiences exposed him to the Anglo-Dutch work of Long Island and the vernacular Georgian work of his master. Ebenezer Hubbell (1726–1812), the master of the Hubbell shop during the last half of the eighteenth century, probably trained with his father Josiah, a joiner who helped build the side galleries for the town's meetinghouse in 1715. His training thus took place entirely within Stratford.[11]

Case furniture documented or attributed to the Dayton and Hubbell shops reveals a specific set of Stratford features: carved feet with square pads, central toes flanked by two smaller toes on each side, and a tightly curved crooked leg; deeply carved shells in the lower drawers of desks and chests; blocks of wood nailed to the inside surface of these drawer fronts to provide extra depth for the shell carving; and extensive use of wooden trunnels (pegs) rather than iron nails to secure drawer bottoms, moldings, and drawer supports. However, the work of each shop is distinctive for its individual workmanship and forms. Slight differences in decorative work also distinguish the two shops: Dayton's carved feet feature a central spade-shaped toe and are blockier than Hubbell's more modeled feet, Dayton's

Figure 2 Bottom half of a chest-on-chest attributed to Brewster Dayton, Stratford, Connecticut, 1770-1790. Cherry with yellow poplar and oak. H. 44¼", W. 40", D. 20". (Courtesy, Middlesex County Historical Society; photo, Edward S. Cooke Jr.)

Figure 3 Desk-and-bookcase, probably by Ebenezer Hubbell, Stratford, Connecticut, 1760-1780. Cherry with yellow poplar, white pine, yellow pine, and butternut. H. 93 1/4", W. 40", D. 23 1/4". (Courtesy, Connecticut Historical Society, Hartford.)

legs are slightly taller and therefore less sinuous, his shells are rather flat with simple ribs whereas Hubbell's are deeper with more undulating ribs, and Dayton's base moldings tend to be thicker than the thinner, more complex cymas by Hubbell (figs. 2, 3). Dayton also developed certain conventions for his construction: he often smoothed the inside surfaces of a carcass side with a toothing plane, added a butterfly key to strengthen the glued butt joint of a carcass side consisting of two boards, and chamfered the top edges of his drawer sides and backs. None of these features are found on furniture from the Hubbell shop. The similarities and differences suggest the way in

Figure 4 Chest of drawers, Litchfield, Connecticut, 1780–1800. Cherry with white pine. H. 34", W. 35 5/8", D. 19 1/2". (Courtesy, Mattatuck Museum.)

Figure 5 Detail of the bottom of the chest illustrated in fig. 4.

Figure 6 Chest of drawers, Litchfield, Connecticut, 1780–1800. Cherry with white pine and yellow poplar. H. 32 3/8", W. 36 3/8", D. 18 3/4". (Courtesy, Mattatuck Museum.)

Figure 7 Detail of the bottom of the chest illustrated in fig. 6.

which contemporaries in the same town could draw from different training to develop a similar language with distinct dialects.[12]

A similar relationship is evident in the work of two as yet unidentified shops in the Litchfield area (figs. 4–7). Case furniture from these shops is linked by very idiosyncratic base construction whereby diagonal braces are tenoned into the inner surface of the legs and nailed along the bottom of the carcass. Both shops also feature unusually graduated drawers and fashionable decoration such as ball-and-claw feet, fluting or quarter columns on

Figure 8 Chest of drawers signed by Bates How, northwestern Connecticut, 1795. Cherry with white pine. H. 38 1/2", W. 39 3/4", D. 17 1/4". (Courtesy, Yale University Art Gallery, Mabel Brady Garvan Collection.)

the front corners, or extensive carving. Yet there are distinct differences in the work of the two shops: one features longer braces, drawer sides dovetailed to the drawer fronts and drawer backs dovetailed to the drawer sides, and more crisply executed carving (figs. 4, 5); the other features shorter braces, drawer sides dovetailed to the drawer fronts and backs, softer carving, and drawer bottoms with a rabbeted edge rather than a chamfered edge (figs. 6, 7). More finished joinery and the use of wooden pegs to secure the drawer bottoms to the drawer backs also distinguishes the latter shop. The differences cannot be explained by the role of a shared specialist but, rather, suggest the development of a shop tradition in the hands of an apprentice or the work of contemporaries who had similar training but employed different types of joiners in their respective shops.[13]

A similar relationship can be seen in the work of Bates How of Canaan (fig. 8) and Reuben Beeman of Kent (fig. 9). Signed work by these joiners reveals many similarities: squat, carved ball-and-claw feet, extensive reliance on rope carving along base moldings and quarter columns, similar dovetailing of drawers, and backboards dovetailed to the back edges of the carcass sides. In spite of these shared idiosyncracies, there are noticeable differences between the shops. How's signed chest features extensive use of screws to attach the moldings and quarter columns and an abundance of knotty, second-grade white pine boards. Beeman's work lacks the reliance on screws and scrap pine and has a distinctive drawer detail: the sides taper

Figure 9 Chest-on-chest signed by Reuben Beeman, Kent, Connecticut, 1795–1805. Cherry with white pine. H. 88½", W. 43". (Courtesy, Christie's.)

toward the upper edge, thereby providing more material where the groove for the drawer bottoms is run. The differences between the How and Beeman shops suggest that craftsmen with different training responded in similar ways to the market in the hill towns of northwestern Connecticut.[14]

Rhythms of Work

Under apprenticeship, young joiners also learned how to organize their tasks and rhythms in accordance with local custom. A master introduced the boy to and subtly schooled him in local economic cycles, labor conventions, and sources of materials and credit. It is therefore essential to understand the particular context in which the tools and skills were used. Although most rural New England communities followed some sort of mixed agriculture, each economy varied based on the location of the town, time of its founding, size, social structure, and local materials. From the time of the earliest settlements, making chests, chairs, and tables was one facet of the agricultural cycle, and such work fit in neatly with the responsibilities of animal and grain husbandry and fishing.

In the older coastal communities of western Connecticut, stretching from Milford to Norwalk, limited coastal trade made imported products and materials available. Several Stratford storekeepers imported chairs made by Edward Larkin of Charlestown, Massachusetts, in the 1740s and 1750s, and the 1763 probate inventory of Captain Joseph Squier of Fairfield lists "6 Chairs boston make." Inventory references also point out the increased availability of black walnut from the Middle Atlantic and southern regions and mahogany from the West Indies during the second half of the eighteenth century. Although Captain John Brooks of Stratford, who conducted trade with the Caribbean in the 1770s and 1780s, shipped six chairs made by Henry Beardslee to St. Croix in 1785, joiners' work along the Long Island Sound was not as dependent upon maritime and shipbuilding rhythms as in maritime centers such as Marblehead, Massachusetts. Coastal trade was only a small part of an economy based on agriculture, animals, fishing, and small shop craftwork. Lewis Burritt (1772–1839), an accomplished joiner who made inlaid mahogany case furniture, participated in the varied Stratford economy of the 1790s and early 1800s. Besides making furniture, he hayed and pulled flax, made and mended oyster rakes, and made hat blocks and farming tools.[15]

Shop joiners in the more recently settled lands of western Connecticut organized their work in accordance with local agricultural rhythms. Widespread ownership of and experience with such tools as axes, saws, broad axes, and the like enabled the professional joiner to draw on a number of neighbors during the slack farming months of December, January, and February to fell, score, sled, split, and saw the plentiful supplies of cherry, maple, yellow poplar, oak, and white pine. Winter was the ideal time for such activity: farmers had more free time and eagerly accepted such occasional work, the wood cut best at that time, and logs were easily sledded on the snowy ground. Most preparation and assembly of furniture took place between harvest and spring planting. The joiners could count on uninterrupted time so that workmanship habits and the set-up of lathes or bench clamps in the small shops could be used to efficient advantage. One such discrete task was the production of great quantities of turned chair parts when the lathe was set up and slightly green wood was available. Case furniture could be produced throughout the year, but the work seems to have

Figure 10 Fiddleback chair, Stratford, Connecticut, 1760–1800. Maple, yellow poplar, and ash. H. 38⅝", W. 19", D. 14". (Courtesy, Discovery Museum; photo, Gavin Ashworth.)

Figure 11 Fiddleback chair, Newtown, Connecticut, 1760–1800. Maple, yellow poplar, and ash. H. 40⅛", W. 19½", D. 14". (Private collection; photo, Gavin Ashworth.)

been concentrated between February and April and August and November. The first period followed the cutting of new wood and allowed the joiner to work the wood while slightly green, an advantage in turning and in some types of carving. The second period was when the clientele of farmers could calculate their harvest yield and therefore could gauge what they could afford to spend on furniture.[16]

The seasonal rhythms and local economies affected the types of furniture produced. Turned chairs were often produced and exported by urban craftsmen such as Edward Larkin but were also the ideal chair type to be produced in a rural-based, mixed agricultural community. There was always a market for chairs: they tended to suffer from abuse, were more affordable than more complicated furniture forms, possessed a fair amount of visual flair, and enjoyed greater demand due to changing social customs. In addition, they were easier to compose and make than case furniture. Due to practical considerations such as seat height and dimensions, the maker worked in a more circumscribed habitual manner when making chairs and tables than when making storage furniture. Standard dimensions provided the general parameters of design. Variations tended to be more in degree than kind, often concentrated in the appearance of the legs and back.

Rural joiners, who had the winter months free, could produce considerable quantities of turned chairs (figs. 10–12). They set up their lathes and turned parts efficiently and quickly by using a strike pole or marking stick to lay out the sections of turned elements and by maximizing the rhythm of their turning tools and lathe. They could also rive out quantities of wood for the slats or use a template to cut out the banisters and crest rails. It was thus possible and advantageous to stockpile certain parts such as stretchers, posts, and slats. Several jobs, such as bottoming and painting, could be subcontracted to others within the community. Joiners in western Connecticut often delegated such irregular work to young joiners just establishing themselves, older joiners in the twilight of their careers, or other members of the community. This subcontracting was not simply a means of reducing price but also of distributing work during the slack months, providing work for aging craftsmen, tightening the web of local exchange, and allowing the craftsman to organize his work and focus on furniture making during the winter months and other opportune times.[17]

Turned chair production was not a specialized task but rather standard output for a largely local market. Its production speed and the use of local labor and materials also enabled craftsmen to make case furniture in the

Figure 12 Fiddleback chair, Woodbury, Connecticut, 1760–1800. Maple, yellow poplar, and ash. H. 42 1/8", W. 20 1/2", D. 14". (Courtesy, New Haven Colony Historical Society.)

winter months. Unlike chairs, case furniture was a more complex, open-ended product. Per capita ownership of such forms in comparison with the sets of chairs listed in accounts and inventories indicates there was relatively limited demand for large storage forms. Most households had several pieces of storage furniture, but there were consistently many more chairs and tables. There were also a number of options regarding form, size, and configuration of drawers and compartments. Finally, large drawered or doored furniture required more material and labor. Limited demand and the high cost of labor contributed to certain patterns of production in rural shops. A plentiful supply of butted and nailed chests—easily assembled from boards sawed at the local sawmill—has survived but so has a variety of joined case furniture such as high chests, dressing tables, and chests of drawers.[18]

The number of complex storage forms listed in the written documents and the evidence of the many surviving examples suggest that western Connecticut joiners employed a number of strategies to produce case furniture efficiently. Foremost was their reliance on local sawmills to provide boards in desired dimensions, thereby precluding the need to resaw or plane the lumber to usable thicknesses. In Newtown and Woodbury, surviving artifacts reveal the joiners' use of blanks that required only slight planing before use. Some boards used for drawer linings or backboards still retain their water-powered saw marks. In Newtown, most cherry boards were sawn 3/4" thick, and yellow poplar and oak, 1/2" thick; in Woodbury, cherry tended to be 7/8" thick, yellow poplar, 1/2 or 7/8" thick, oak, 1/2" thick, and white pine, 3/8" thick. With boards delivered in proper thickness, the joiner could more easily lay out and cut his joints. Jigs such as a marking gauge to mark mortise-and-tenon joints and a bevel gauge to lay out consistent pins and tails for dovetails made preparations easy. Workmanship habits made the cutting of tenons or dovetails proceed quickly. We tend to romanticize about the construction process, but the joiners of this period could perform like human machines.[19]

The probate inventories also indicate widespread ownership of templates and patterns. Although many scholars have believed that template use was an urban phenomenon typical of large-scale production, patterns also proved worthwhile in a rural shop with infrequent or seasonal production. Using templates to lay out crooked legs, bracket feet, and skirt profiles saved considerable time within a small shop, and, combined with the mental templates of rote structural work, enabled the small-shop joiner to make a desk in about a week and a half and a case of drawers in about three weeks.[20]

The organizational structure of the joiner's shop was also critical to its successful operation. The written records identify two basic coexisting approaches to furniture production in western Connecticut: the family-based shop and the individual shop. In the family shop, a master craftsman took on neighbors or kin and then sons, as they matured, to staff their shops. Such shops were part of a household economy that also included improved land for crops and pasturage for animals. Acreage varied but usually included one to five acres of improved land and five to thirty acres of unimproved land.

The historical evidence of such family dynasties as the Durands of Milford, the Hubbells and Beardslees of Stratford, and the Prindles and Fabriques of Newtown attests to the success of such an approach.

For other joiners, continuing in the community was not desirable or possible. Drawn by the promise of a newly developing area or pushed out of a stagnant or overcrowded center, some joiners lacked the means or connections to purchase sufficient land to establish their own mixed agricultural/craft household. Many bought or even rented small lots of one acre or less. To compensate for their lack of productive land, such craftsmen were under more pressure to make a living from their services. They thus concentrated more on craftwork and irregular handyman work. The instability of their lifestyles meant that the family often lasted less than a generation in a town and continued to move along.

Social Aspects of Composition

With the exception of shops in the commercial centers such as Boston and Newport, the production of furniture in eighteenth-century New England was essentially a face-to-face negotiation between the joiner and his customers. The customer would purchase a piece already assembled or specify a certain combination of features. In the latter case, the patron would have a more active role in the craftsman-client relationship, but the joiner still determined the form, decoration, and trim from his repertoire or through his own understanding of the desired style. The artisan controlled the "nature of work"—the physical knowledge of materials and techniques and its application—whereas the community controlled the "context of work." The joiner allocated his time and skills among the members of the community as he saw fit, while the community constantly judged his performance and bestowed him with a reputation. It was therefore important for the craftsman to understand and respond to his community. After all, the local clientele ultimately determined the need for and success of a single joiner or the viability of several joiners.[21]

Apprenticeship introduced boys to the role of the joiner within that particular community and exposed them directly to the opinions and expectations of the town. Schooled in socialization as well as technical skills and conventions, the young artisan developed a personal expression that blended empirical craft techniques and local aesthetics. It is essential to gain an understanding of the local context—the existing views of material life, local notions of appropriateness, and limits of variability. A joiner's cultural acumen and judgment of the market allowed him to practice a dynamic craft, but this dynamism was dependent on his patrons. Just as a kit of tools and learned techniques shaped the craftsman's range of possibilities, so did the needs, aspirations, and expectations of his clientele.[22]

Due to the social context of the craft, most joiners found it easiest to remain in the town in which they were trained. Knowledge of local preferences, established accounts with neighbors or relatives, and familiarity with local labor and materials certainly gave local joiners an edge. A less tangible advantage was his internalization of local aesthetics. Within a familiar environment, he continued to learn attitudes and techniques for design and fabrication. His training conditioned him to recognize that particular community's needs and provided him with the skills currently in demand. If new techniques were observed or introduced by a newly arrived craftsman, the locally trained joiner perceived these changes from a viewpoint similar to the majority of his customers. Work performed in such a context tended to be traditionally based, but not unchanging.

On the other hand, a joiner trained in one community but active in another often had different experiences. His learned techniques and the customers' demands may not have aligned so neatly. To continue his trade, such a joiner had to be more willing to alter his internalized approaches, especially those concerned with decoration and forms. To survive he incorporated different techniques seen in work by other craftsmen, paid more attention to new forms produced elsewhere, or gave greater weight to his customers' requests. If he worked in a community with joiners trained in a number of different traditions, he had many techniques from which to draw.[23]

To understand the social context of furniture making, it is essential to reconstruct the social and economic structure of the community over time and to identify the backgrounds of the joiners. Particular attention should be paid to periods of dynamic growth or internal stasis and to turning points in these trends. For example, the prosperous coastal town of Stratford experienced considerable cultural flux during the 1710s and 1720s: the Anglican church established its first Connecticut parish there, several teachers at Yale College who converted to Anglicanism in 1722 had close ties with the community, there was trade with Boston merchants and with Anglo-Dutch traders on Long Island, and two immigrant English joiners, Thomas Salmon and Samuel French, settled in the town. French and Salmon introduced a British vernacular tradition that blended with Boston and New York work to become a distinctive Stratford Georgian style. This style became the standard for much of the century as an Anglican–Old Light coalition established a cultural hegemony in the 1740s.[24]

Stratford's selective conservatism affected clients and makers alike. Inventory references after 1750 were sprinkled with evidence of new fashionable and expensive furniture forms such as sideboards, breakfast tables, and easy chairs, signifying the availability of these products and an awareness of them. These forms appeared infrequently, however. People of all income levels owned substantial quantities of furniture, but they favored traditional forms. They purchased expensive case furniture, particularly cases of drawers, dressing tables, and desks, and large quantities of chairs, especially turned and crooked-back chairs. For much of the last half of the century, the conservatism even influenced younger households, who acquired traditional furniture. During the first decade of the nineteenth century, joiner Lewis Burritt made several inlaid mahogany tables, but he still satisfied the traditional demands. He made chests, cherry chests of drawers or desks, and even fiddleback and york chairs. The latter had been fashionable chair forms in the 1740s.[25]

Brewster Dayton, who trained with an English joiner and had access to

Figure 14 Chest of drawers signed by Brewster Dayton, Stratford, Connecticut, 1784. Cherry with yellow poplar. H. 87", W. 39 3/4", D. 20 1/8". (Private collection; photo, Edward S. Cooke Jr.)

Figure 13 Chest of drawers signed by Brewster Dayton, Stratford, Connecticut, 1784. Cherry with sycamore, yellow poplar, and white pine. H. 86 1/2", W. 39 3/4", D. 20 3/8". (Courtesy, Winterthur Museum.)

many sophisticated forms and techniques, restricted his performance in Stratford. Much of his work was rooted in a vocabulary established before 1750. The proportions, tympanums, and crowns of his two signed cases of drawers from 1784 (figs. 13, 14) closely resemble those features on Long Island furniture of the 1740s. To this Anglo-Dutch work he blended the carved feet and scrolled knees introduced by his master. Dayton's probate inventory and various account book references also indicate that he made slat-back, fiddleback, and crooked-back chairs, all of which are based on traditional turned chair forms. Even the primary woods of his furniture—particularly sycamore and subgrade cherry—reflect his reliance on local networks. The artifactual evidence points out the limitation of the local clientele.[26]

The Hubbell shop of Stratford evidently enjoyed slightly greater latitude. Whereas the surviving Dayton work features only pad or carved feet, the Hubbells offered a variety of feet for their case furniture: pad feet, bracket feet, carved feet, and ball-and-claw (figs. 3, 15–17). Furniture attributed to that shop is also distinguished by a greater variety of primary woods. Of all the identifiable Stratford shops, it is the only one to use walnut and mahogany during the last half of the century. Ebenezer's brother-in-law, Captain John Brooks, a merchant who was the "principal inhabitant of Stratford," provided the Hubbell shop with these imported woods. The handling of the ball-and-claw feet also suggests an external influence. The Hubbell feet closely resemble Philadelphia work, as does a set of joiners' chairs that might have been made in the Hubbell shop (fig. 18). Chairs of

Figure 15 Married chest of drawers (top probably by Brewster Dayton; bottom probably by Ebenezer Hubbell), Stratford, Connecticut, 1770–1790. Top: cherry with yellow poplar and white pine; bottom: walnut with cherry and white pine. H. 72 1/4", W. 40 1/2", D. 20 1/8". (Private collection; photo, Edward S. Cooke Jr.) All of the drawers in the lower section are replacements.

this type are listed in John Brooks's probate inventory of 1777, which included "New furniture at Hubbells"—"1 Case Black Walnut Draws £8:10:0, 6 Cringle Back do Chairs @ 20/ £6, 1 great Chair £1:5:0." Although the Hubbell shop could make high-style case furniture and joiners' chairs, the bulk of their work was executed in a simpler fashion. Most surviving chairs that relate to the single set of joiners' chairs are fiddleback and crooked-back versions.[27]

In contrast to the stylistic cohesion of Stratford was the stylistic frenzy of the Woodbury area between 1750 and 1800. In the middle of the century, Woodbury experienced considerable growth because it served as a gateway

Figure 16 Desk, probably by Ebenezer Hubbell, Stratford, Connecticut, 1760–1780. Cherry with white pine and yellow poplar. H. 42 5/8", W. 36 3/16", D. 21 3/4". (Courtesy, Discovery Museum; photo, Gavin Ashworth.)

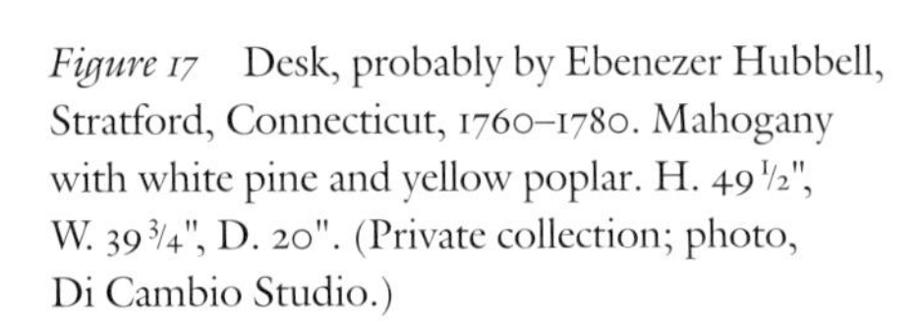

Figure 17 Desk, probably by Ebenezer Hubbell, Stratford, Connecticut, 1760–1780. Mahogany with white pine and yellow poplar. H. 49 1/2", W. 39 3/4", D. 20". (Private collection; photo, Di Cambio Studio.)

Figure 18 Joiner's chair, possibly by Ebenezer Hubbell, Stratford, Connecticut, 1770–1790. Cherry, yellow poplar, and ash. H. 39 3/4", W. 22", D. 17 1/8". (Courtesy, Barry G. Freeman.)

Figure 19 Chest of drawers signed by Silas Butler, Woodbury, Connecticut, 1755. Cherry with white pine. H. 86", W. 40", D. 20". (Courtesy, Wadsworth Atheneum.)

and center for the newly settled and developing Litchfield County. Established proprietors controlled land distribution, but new inhabitants, including craftsmen, arrived from all parts of Connecticut. Much of the surviving furniture from the middle of the century reveals the varied origins of the population. A case of drawers made in March 1755 by Silas Butler (fig. 19) blends Connecticut Valley (the legs and skirt in particular) and

Figure 20 Chest of drawers, Woodbury, Connecticut, 1760–1780. Cherry with red oak, white pine, and yellow poplar. H. 80", W. 39 5/8", D. 19 5/8". (Courtesy, The New Haven Colony Historical Society.)

Figure 21 Great round-top chair, Woodbury, Connecticut, 1750–1770. Maple, yellow poplar, and ash. H. 42 1/4", W. 22 1/2", D. 15". (Courtesy, First Congregational Church, Woodbury; photo, Edward S. Cooke Jr.)

coastal Connecticut (the architectonic crown molding and carved shells) traditions. The work of another shop (fig. 20) and chairs (fig. 21) belonging to some of the leading citizens manifest a similar synthesis of traditions. The coherent look of the case furniture and the traditional character of the chairs mirror the evidence in the probate inventories of the 1750s and 1760s. Furniture listed in these estates resemble those of the surrounding communities and include painted turned chairs, chests, chests with drawers, simple tables, and cases of drawers.[28]

Figure 22 Crooked-back chair, Woodbury, Connecticut, 1780–1800. Cherry, yellow poplar, and ash. H. 41 1/2", W. 20 1/8", D. 13 3/4". (Private collection; photo, Gavin Ashworth.)

Figure 23 Joiner's chair, Woodbury, Connecticut, 1780–1800. Cherry, yellow poplar, and ash. H. 38", W. 19 7/8", D. 15 5/8". (Private collection; photo, Cortes and Company.)

In the 1760s an entrepreneurial class of proprietors in Woodbury began to organize the export of beef and pork for the New York market during the Seven Years War. After hostilities ceased, the merchants continued to ship meat to New York for local consumption and for export to the West Indies. During and after the Revolution, these Woodbury merchants expanded their business, providing food and blankets for the war effort and shipping dairy products such as cheese and butter, as well as meat, to New Haven and New York from the 1780s through the first quarter of the nineteenth century. Woodbury's stratified social structure, a development of the mid-eighteenth century, was ideally suited for the export trade. Proprietary families such as the Hinmans, Stiles, Osborns, Tomlinsons, and Bacons controlled the disposition and rental of lands to the new immigrants and orchestrated the gathering of surplus agricultural products. These merchants did, however, suffer from local and extralocal pressures. Due to weather fluctuations and family allocations, the merchants could not count on consistent quantities of surpluses. Elaborate credit relationships with New York and New Haven merchants and the changing needs of a distant market also provided an element of vulnerability.[29]

The tenuous socioeconomic status of the proprietary merchants gave rise to a certain status anxiety that affected furniture taste in Woodbury. As the proprietary class became competitive, they exerted an influence upon the context of craftwork. They sought expensive furniture, distinguished by elaborate decoration, time-consuming workmanship, and an expansive variety of forms. Many of the local elite began to purchase crooked-back

Figure 24 Tea table, Woodbury, Connecticut, 1780–1800. Cherry. H. 27", top diam.: 33". (Private collection, photo, Gavin Ashworth.)

(fig. 22) and joiners' chairs (fig. 23), tea tables (fig. 24), and a variety of large case furniture including desk-and-bookcases. Jabez Bacon, who reportedly controlled the New York pork market, may have even sought to control fashion in town by sponsoring Windsor chairmaker Nicholas Jebine, who emigrated from New Haven in 1794. Jebine rented a house and shop on land that had been leased to Bacon. Documentation that Jebine provided Bacon with Windsor chairs and the inclusion of sixty Windsors in Bacon's store inventory of 1807 provides additional evidence that Bacon had close ties with Jebine. Several surviving Windsors owned in Woodbury resemble New Haven work (fig. 25).[30]

The stratified social structure not only stimulated the demand for a wide variety of work and styles but also helped to ensure the presence of joiners who were willing partners in the competitive furniture trade. The proprietary system did not allow many yeomen craftsmen to prosper in Woodbury. The biographies of joiners active in Woodbury reveal considerable turnover in the trade; few were trained locally or remained in town. Craftsmen immigrated from various parts of Connecticut, worked for several years, and then moved on. Joiners such as William H. Peabody of Norwich, John Whitehead Gould of Branford, or Billious Hill of Goshen purchased or rented only an acre of land or less and therefore could not establish themselves within the mixed agricultural economy. As a result, they depended almost entirely upon their craftwork and allocated their time and energies accordingly. It was a period of intensified industry and specialization in cabinetmaking. With varied backgrounds and constant mobil-

Figure 25 High-back Windsor armchair, probably by Nicholas Jebine, Woodbury, Connecticut, 1790–1810. Maple, white pine, and red oak. H. 36 1/4", W. 16 1/4", D. 16 9/16". (Courtesy, Yale University Art Gallery, Mabel Brady Garvan Collection.)

Figure 26 Desk-and-bookcase, Woodbury, Connecticut, 1780–1800. Cherry with white pine and yellow poplar. H. 84", W. 38", D. 20 3/4". (Private collection; photo, Edward S. Cooke Jr.)

Figure 27 Chest of drawers, Woodbury, Connecticut, 1780–1800. Cherry with red oak. H. 33 1/4", W. 34 3/8", D. 20 1/2". (Courtesy, Hartford Steam Boiler Inspection and Insurance Company; photo, Gavin Ashworth.)

Figure 28 Chest of drawers, Woodbury, Connecticut, 1790–1810. Cherry with yellow poplar. H. 37", W. 44", D. 18 3/4". (Private collection; photo, Edward S. Cooke Jr.)

Figure 29 Desk-and-bookcase, Woodbury, Connecticut, 1780–1800. Cherry with yellow poplar and red oak. Dimensions not recorded. (Courtesy, Kenneth Hammit.)

Figure 30 Desk-and-bookcase, Woodbury, Connecticut, 1780–1800. Cherry with yellow poplar, white pine, and ash. H. 85 5/8", W. 39 3/4", D. 22". (Private collection; photo, Cortes and Company.)

Figure 31 Chest of drawers, Woodbury, Connecticut, 1780–1800. Cherry with red oak, yellow poplar, and white pine. H. 90", W. 44", D. 22 3/4". (Courtesy, Colonial Williamsburg Foundation.)

ity among joiners working in an increasingly competitive trade, Woodbury's furniture trade was unusually complex and dynamic, a good match for its entrepreneurial, image-conscious, outward-oriented proprietors. One shop worked in a Philadelphia-inspired manner (fig. 26), while another shop distinguished itself by offering a wide variety of goods that reflected familiarity with many different regional traditions (figs. 27–32).[31]

Figure 32 Chest-on-chest, Woodbury, Connecticut, 1780–1800. Cherry with yellow poplar and red oak. H. 82 1/2", W. 40 3/4", D. 19 3/4". (Private collection; photo, Edward S. Cooke Jr.)

Even though permanence and learned techniques often resulted in traditional but evolving styles, and mobility and chosen techniques often resulted in rapid stylistic change, we should avoid drawing simple polarities. All furniture blends the familiar and the new; what is different is the proportion of each and where change is permitted. Similarly, in studying Connecticut furniture, we should not automatically draw a distinction between the traditional, Old Light western part of the colony and the cosmopolitan, New Light eastern section. The analysis of specific craftsmen-community relationships is essential.

The Cultural Significance of Joiners

In eighteenth-century rural New England, a world characterized by increasing population density, flourishing coastal trade, and chronic agricultural underemployment, a craft skill such as furniture making served an increasingly important function. Craft skills had always been an integral part of families' strategies for estate settlement, but certain trends in the eighteenth century endowed it with new importance. The expanding population, shrinking supply of unsettled land, and increased accumulation and consumption of household goods shifted the balance of craft and farm work. Whereas craft employment had been subordinate to agriculture, by the end of the eighteenth century craft activity advanced to the lead. As many household farms became smaller and the increased population demanded more goods, craft skills gained stature. Whether in a stagnant or a dynamic rural area, furniture makers personified the adaptive resiliency that became a celebrated trait of the New England character in the eighteenth century. Furniture making reflected and embodied the prevalent values of the period: the familial priority of permanence and stability and the pragmatic need to conduct some entrepreneurial activity with the external market.[32]

Many New Englanders placed particular emphasis on permanence and stability. By the mid-eighteenth century, the subdivision of family lands throughout several generations had taxed the limited land resources and was creating impractically sized farms. To preserve stability, agrarian families adopted various strategies to keep their children on the family land or within a community of kin. Fathers provided sons with craft training and thereby enabled them to earn a living with a smaller plot of arable land. Part-time artisan work thus provided the means to subdivide family lands further while maintaining economic viability and preserving the family identity in town. Combining craftwork and farming allowed a particular family to balance numbers and resources and to strengthen ties within the community. Craft shops produced needed goods for the expanding population and drew on the services of other community members.[33]

In families with several generations of woodworkers, joiner's skills provided both a livelihood and a legacy. Craft skills and tools—like land for sons of farmers and furnishings for daughters—became another form of "property" that could be transmitted through the family network. Like real and personal estate, skills and tools allowed the succeeding generation to establish its own productive household unit while maintaining cross-generational rights and responsibilities. The success of this artisan strategy can be seen in the several families who produced several generations of joiners within each town: the Durands in Milford, Hubbells in Stratford, and Prindles in Newtown.[34]

Other New Englanders placed slightly less emphasis on geographic permanence. If pressure for land continued unabated, the father could acquire land in a nearby town or on the frontier. Then the father assisted his son's migration by deeding him the land. Sons with joiner's skills probably found such relocation easier. Demand for joiner's work permitted some sons to establish themselves in a nearby community, close to kin support. For instance, John Fabrique, a Newtown cordwainer, provided two sons with woodworking skills. David and Bartimeus Fabrique were then able to practice the house joiner's trade in Newtown and the adjacent communities of Derby, Southbury, Woodbury, Roxbury, and New Milford. Other families developed multi-generational dynasties of house and shop joiners who formed regional networks. Among the many examples of such families in western Connecticut were the Beardslees, Prindles, and Booths.[35]

Those who moved further away often moved with other kin or people from the same town. Joiners in such a group preserved the group's cultural identity by providing familiar products. Like the English joiner who emigrated to New England in the 1630s, the rural Connecticut joiner who moved north or west in the early-nineteenth century created physical and psychological comfort for others in a new environment. Lemuel Porter, a Waterbury joiner, moved west to Tallmedge in the Western Reserve in 1818 and built a church and several houses that recreated the feel of Litchfield, Connecticut.[36]

Craft skills could also be used in more innovative ways. Instead of being pushed into the joiner's trade by familial pressures, some sons were pulled into it. The growing population fostered a growing need for furniture, and such structural shifts gradually and unevenly affected cultural values. Some sons of farmers took advantage of the available opportunities. Lacking the strength of family tradition, farmers' sons like Arcillus Hamlin may have been less tied to tradition and therefore more innovative in their work. Hamlin, the son of a Sharon farmer, worked as a joiner in Newtown. His 1827 inventory listed many items that were unique or rare for Newtown joiners such as trunks, sheets of veneer, and bureaus. Such free agent joiners were also more willing to migrate as individuals. William H. Peabody, born in Norwich, worked for a few years in Stratford, sold his shop in Stratford and moved to Woodbury, worked in Woodbury for twelve years, and then returned to Stratford. Joiners like Hamlin and Peabody may have perceived their skills as a marketable commodity for an individual rather than as an adaptive strategy for family continuity and identity.[37]

Woodworkers' sons who inherited skills and tools sometimes made different uses of these inherited traditions as economic patterns changed and altered their attitudes. Justin Hobart Jr., the son of a Fairfield shop joiner, received his father's home and shop in 1797 but preferred to seek his fortune as a journeyman cabinetmaker in New York City. His entrepreneurial attitude was expressed in several letters to his sister Mary. In some of the early letters from 1797, Hobart reported of constant work and good earnings, however, within three years he lamented:

> I dont think that I shall work Journey work any longer their is no profit in it I dont Earn but Just Enough to pay my Expenses and I believe I can doe that in the Country . . . I have work on hand that will take me about 6 weeks to finish and then I intend to quit working Journey work for a Spell . . . if their is going to Bee so many traders in Fairfield it will Doe for me to Carry on the Cabinet Business their they Cant get that away from me.

Nevertheless, Hobart remained in New York a while longer, for in 1804 he took on John Jackson as an apprentice.[38]

Silas Cheney, a member of another woodworking family from Manchester, Connecticut, moved to Litchfield in 1799, probably with the intent to exploit the growing economy in northwestern Connecticut. Such awareness was fully revealed by his establishment of a rural manufactory for the production of furniture. He employed several journeymen and apprentices at one time and for outwork drew on woodworkers in nearby Connecticut and Massachusetts towns. A Lenox, Massachusetts, woodworking shop, West & Hatch, provided Cheney with parts for kitchen and Windsor chairs. One of Cheney's journeymen, Lambert Hitchcock, went on to refine some of these practices in the large-scale production of turned, flag-seated fancy chairs.[39]

In the eighteenth century, similarities in technical repertoires, tool ownership, and shop layout linked the joiners of western Connecticut. However, these artisans made different uses of the same processes and equipment according to traditions in which they were trained and the context of their mature work. By identifying the diagnostic details of craft traditions, it is possible to follow the flow and confluence of ideas and people over the New England landscape. Changes in consumption patterns or production rhythms often coincided with shifting commercial relations and increased involvement with external markets. Documentary evidence of craftsmen and communities, used in conjunction with artifactual evidence, offers explanations about why different towns supported different types of joiners and contrasting tastes in furniture during the eighteenth century.

1. Samuel Goodrich, *Peter Parley's Own Story* (New York: Sheldon & Company, 1866), pp. 31, 33.

2. Ibid., pp. 18, 320–45. Goodrich's phrase "articles of use" is noteworthy, for it resembles the Marxist concept of use value. For a historiographical review that characterizes the intense non-market exchanges of rural New England households, see Alan Kulikoff, "The Transition to Capitalism in Rural America," *William and Mary Quarterly* 46, no. 1 (January 1989): 122–26.

3. John Schlotterbeck first used the term "social economy" to analyze the diverse local economy in Virginia during the second quarter of the nineteenth century: "The 'Social Economy' of an Upper South Community: Orange and Greene Counties, Virginia, 1815–1860," in *Class Conflict and Consensus: Antebellum Southern Community Studies*, edited by Orville Burton and Robert McMath Jr. (Westport, Conn.: Greenwood Press, 1982), pp. 3–28. My forthcoming book *Making Furniture in Preindustrial America: The Social Economy of Newtown and Woodbury, Connecticut* (Baltimore: Johns Hopkins University Press, 1996), elaborates upon and refines the term, drawing important insights from sociologists and folklorists who study craftsmen. On the social value of work, see Michael Foucoult, *The Order of Things: An Archeology of the*

Human Sciences (New York: Random House, 1973). For an example of a contemporary skilled craftsman who works within a similar network, which cannot be defined by economic transactions alone, see Douglas Harper, *Working Knowledge: Skill and Community in a Small Shop* (Chicago: University of Chicago Press, 1988).

4. Grant McCracken, *Culture and Consumption: New Approaches to the Symbolic Character of Consumer Goods and Activities* (Bloomington: Indiana University Press, 1988), pp. 58–59, 118–29; Mary Douglas, *The World of Goods: Towards an Anthropology of Consumption* (New York: W. W. Norton, 1979), pp. 4, 5, 59–65; and Mihaly Csikszentmihalyi and Eugene Rochberg-Halton, *The Meaning of Things: Domestic Symbols and the Self* (New York: Cambridge University Press, 1981), pp. 58–64.

5. For greater detail, see Cooke, *Making Furniture in Preindustrial America*, chapter 1.

6. Robert Seybolt, *Apprenticeship & Apprenticeship Education in Colonial New England & New York* (New York: Columbia University Teachers College, 1917); Paul Douglas, *American Apprenticeship and Industrial Education* (New York: Columbia University Press, 1921); and Ian Quimby, *Apprenticeship in Colonial Philadelphia* (New York: Garland Publishing, 1985).

7. Mutual obligations affected not only craft training but the whole realm of social and economic activities: Philip Greven, *Four Generations: Population, Land, and Family in Colonial Andover, Massachusetts* (Ithaca, N.Y.: Cornell University Press, 1970); James Henretta, "Families and Farms: *Mentalite* in Pre-Industrial America," *William and Mary Quarterly* 35, no. 1 (January 1978): 3–32; and John Waters, "Patrimony, Succession, and Social Stability: Guilford, Connecticut in the Eighteenth Century," *Perspectives in American History* 10 (1976): 131–60. On the role of apprentice woodworkers within the life cycles of their masters, see Edward Fix, "A Long Island Carpenter at Work: A Quantitative Inquiry into the Account Book of Jedediah Williamson," *Chronicle of the Early American Industries Association* 32, no. 4 (December 1979): 61–63, and *Chronicle of the Early American Industries Association* 33, no. 1 (March 1980): 4–8; and Ann Dibble, "Major John Dunlap: The Craftsman and His Community," *Old-Time New England* 68, nos. 3–4 (Winter-Spring 1978): 50–58.

8. Apprenticeship agreement between Lazarus Prindle and Joseph Peck Jr., June 5, 1793 (privately owned).

9. The importance of observation, learning fundamental formulas, and internalizing a master's values is stressed by upholsterer Andrew Passeri in "My Life as an Upholsterer, 1927–1986," in *Perspectives in American Furniture,* edited by Gerald W. R. Ward (New York: W. W. Norton, 1988), pp. 169–203. Philip Zimmerman points out the role of workmanship of habit in "Workmanship as Evidence: A Model for Object Study," *Winterthur Portfolio* 16, no. 4 (Winter 1981): 283–307.

10. Works that indicate how a craftsman broadened his performance include George Sturt, *The Wheelwright's Shop* (1923; reprinted, New York: Cambridge University Press, 1963); and R. Gerald Alvey, *Dulcimer Maker: The Craft of Homer Ledford* (Lexington: University Press of Kentucky, 1984). Pertinent works on American furniture makers include John Bivins Jr., *The Furniture of Coastal North Carolina, 1700–1820* (Winston-Salem, N.C.: Museum of Early Southern Decorative Arts, 1988); William Hosley Jr., "Timothy Loomis and the Economy of Joinery in Windsor, Connecticut, 1740–1786," in Ward, ed., *Perspectives in American Furniture*, pp. 127–51; Brock Jobe, "Urban Craftsmen and Design," in Brock Jobe and Myrna Kaye, *New England Furniture: The Colonial Era* (Boston: Houghton Mifflin, 1984), pp. 3–46; Robert F. Trent, *Hearts & Crowns* (New Haven, Conn.: New Haven Colony Historical Society, 1979); and Philip Zea, "Furniture," in *The Great River: Art & Society of the Connecticut Valley*, edited by Gerald W. R. Ward and William Hosley Jr. (Hartford, Conn.: Wadsworth Atheneum, 1985), pp. 185–91.

11. Edward Cooke Jr., "Craftsman-Client Relationships in the Housatonic Valley, 1720–1800," *Antiques* 125, no. 1 (January 1984): 272–80; Edward S. Cooke Jr., "The Work of Brewster Dayton and Ebenezer Hubbell of Stratford, Connecticut," *Connecticut Historical Society Bulletin* 51, no. 4 (Fall 1986): 196–224; and Edward S. Cooke Jr., "New Netherlands' Influence on the Furniture of the Housatonic Valley," in *The Impact of the New Netherlands Upon the Colonial Long Island Basin*, edited by Joshua Lane (Washington, D.C., and New Haven, Conn.: Yale-Smithsonian Seminar on Material Culture, 1993).

12. Ibid.

13. For published examples, see *Litchfield County Furniture* (Litchfield, Conn.: Litchfield County Historical Society, 1969), pp. 36–37, 64–65.

14. For the most recent published treatment of these shops, see Gerald W. R. Ward,

American Case Furniture in the Mabel Brady Garvan and Other Collections at Yale University (New Haven, Conn.: Yale University Art Gallery, 1988), pp. 142–44.

15. Account Book of Joseph Shelton of Stratford, 1728–1789, pp. 22, 30 (Yale University Library, New Haven, Conn.); Account Book of Ephraim Curtis of Stratford, 1743–1775, p. 264 (Connecticut Historical Society, Hartford, Conn.); and Fairfield District Probate Records, vol. 14, p. 520 (Fairfield Town Hall, Fairfield, Conn.). Information on woods drawn from a survey of Fairfield District Probate Records, vols. 4–20. On local economic activities, see Connecticut Archives: Industry and Connecticut Archives: Trade Maritime Affairs (Connecticut State Library, Hartford, Conn.). On the Stratford examples, see Account Book of John Brooks Jr. of Stratford, 1784–1824 (Discovery Museum, Bridgeport, Conn.) and Account Book of Lewis Burritt of Stratford, 1794–1838 (Stratford Historical Society, Stratford, Conn.). For comparative insights on Marblehead joiners who worked according to maritime rhythms, see Account Book of Joseph Lindsey of Marblehead, 1739–1764 (Winterthur Museum Library, Winterthur, Del.); Jobe, "Urban Craftsmen and Design," pp. 12–13; Account Book of Nathan Bowen of Marblehead, 1775–1779 (Winterthur Museum Library, Winterthur, Del.); Philip Chadwick Smith, ed., *The Journals of Ashley Brown (1728–1813) of Marblehead* (Boston: Colonial Society of Massachusetts, 1973), 2: 646; and Richard Randall Jr., "An Eighteenth Century Partnership," *Art Quarterly* 23, no. 2 (Summer 1960): 152–161.

16. These observations are based on readings of account books from western Connecticut in the collections of the Bethlehem Historical Society, Connecticut Historical Society, Connecticut State Library, Fairfield Historical Society, Litchfield Historical Society, Milford Historical Society, New Haven Colony Historical Society, Newtown Historical Society, Old Sturbridge Village Library, Winterthur Museum Library, and Yale University Library. The best sources are the Account Book of John Durand of Milford, 1760–1783 (Milford Historical Society, Milford, Conn.) and the Account Book of Elisha Hawley of Ridgefield, 1786–1800 (Connecticut Historical Society). Even as late as 1844, it was customary for cabinetmakers in Greenfield, Massachusetts, a community no longer dominated by farming, to work evenings from September to March. These extended winter hours allowed a shop to produce sufficient pieces and parts for much of the following year. See Christopher Clark, "The Diary of an Apprentice Cabinetmaker: Edward Jenner Carpenter's 'Journal' 1844–45," *Proceedings of the American Antiquarian Society* 98, part 2 (1989): 325, 359.

17. In addition to the account books cited in note 16 above, see Account Book of David and Abner Haven of Framingham, Massachusetts, 1786–1841 (Winterthur Museum Library); Benno Forman, "Delaware Valley 'Crookt Foot' and Slat-Back Chairs: The Fussell-Savery Connection," *Winterthur Portfolio* 15, no. 1 (Spring 1980): 41–64; and Bernard Cotton, *The English Regional Chair* (Woodbridge, Suffolk: Antique Collectors' Club, 1990), pp. 13–31.

18. The best summary of the distinctive aspects of case furniture is Gerald W. R. Ward, *American Case Furniture,* pp. 3–17. Few scholars have specifically addressed the production rhythms involved in case furniture, but see Jeanne Vibert Sloane, "John Cahoone and the Newport Furniture Industry," *Old-Time New England* 72 (1987): 88–122; and Margaretta Lovell, "'Such Furniture as Will Be Most Profitable': The Business of Cabinetmaking in Eighteenth-Century Newport," *Winterthur Portfolio* 26, no. 1 (Spring 1991): 27–62

19. For a contemporary perspective on the efficiency and exactness possible from empirical knowledge and repetitive action, see Sam Maloof, *Sam Maloof: Woodworker* (New York: Kodansha International, 1983). Maloof maintains that he can cut dovetails for a piece of case furniture in less time than it would take him to set up and use a jig for a router or table saw.

20. On the view that templates were an urban characteristic, see Forman, "Delaware Valley 'Crookt Foot' and Slat-Back Chairs," p. 51; and Zimmerman, "Workmanship as Evidence," pp. 283–308. Estimates on production time are drawn from Hosley, "Timothy Loomis and the Economy of Joinery," pp. 137–39 and 150–51; and Account Book of Oliver Avery of Norwich, 1788–1839 (Winterthur Museum Library).

21. Douglas Harper uses the terms "nature of work" and "context of work" in *Working Knowledge: Skill and Community in a Small Shop.*

22. My understanding of the social basis of design and workmanship is derived from Clifford Geertz, *Local Knowledge: Further Essays in Interpretive Anthropology* (New York: Basic Books, 1983); Michael Jones, *The Hand Made Object and Its Maker* (Berkeley and Los Angeles: University of California Press, 1975); Henry Glassie, *Folk Housing in Middle Virginia* (Knoxville: University of Tennessee Press, 1975); Christian Norberg-Schulz, *Intentions in Architecture* (Cambridge, Mass.: M. I. T. Press, 1968); and Louis Chiaramonte, *Craftsman-*

Client Contracts: Interpersonal Relations in a Newfoundland Fishing Community (St. John's: Memorial University of Newfoundland, 1970).

23. Barbara Ward explains the terms learned techniques and chosen techniques in "The Craftsman in a Changing Society: Boston Goldsmiths, 1690–1730" (Ph.D. dis., Boston University, 1983), pp. 40–44,100–104.

24. Cooke, "Craftsman-Client Relationships"; Cooke, "The Work of Brewster Dayton and Ebenezer Hubbell"; Cooke, "New Netherlands' Influence on Furniture of the Housatonic Valley."

25. Edward S. Cooke Jr., "The Selective Conservative Taste: Furniture in Stratford, Connecticut, 1740–1800" (M.A. thesis, University of Delaware, 1979); and Account Book of Lewis Burritt of Stratford, 1794–1838 (Stratford Historical Society, Stratford, Conn.).

26. Cooke, "Craftsman-Client Relationships"; Dean Failey, *Long Island is My Nation* (Setauket, N.Y.: Society for the Preservation of Long Island Antiquities, 1976); and Michael Podmaniczky, "Examination Report of Brewster Dayton High Chest 68.772" (Winterthur Museum, 1989; copy in possession of author).

27. Cooke, "Brewster Dayton and Ebenezer Hubbell"; and Fairfield County Court Records, 1768–1773 (Connecticut State Library), p. 307.

28. Cooke, *Making Furniture in Preindustrial America.*

29. Ibid. For a similar response in eastern Connecticut, see Robert F. Trent, "The Colchester School of Cabinetmaking, 1750–1800," in *The American Craftsman and the European Tradition 1620–1820*, edited by Francis Puig and Michael Conforti (Minneapolis; Minneapolis Institute of Arts, 1989), pp. 112–35; and Robert F. Trent, "New London County Joined Chairs: Legacy of a Provincial Elite," *The Connecticut Historical Society Bulletin* 50, no. 4 (Fall 1985): 15–186.

30. Cooke, *Making Furniture in Preindustrial America.*

31. Ibid.

32. On the legacy of woodworking skills in the seventeenth century, see Robert B. St. George, "Fathers, Sons, and Identity: Woodworking Artisans in Southeastern New England, 1620–1700," in *The Craftsman in Early America,* edited by Ian Quimby (New York: W. W. Norton, 1984), pp. 89–125. The emphasis on the adaptive nature of New Englanders in the eighteenth century is best demonstrated by Christopher Jedrey, *The World of John Cleaveland* (New York: W. W. Norton, 1979); Douglas Jones, *Village and Seaport* (Hanover, N.H.: University Press of New England, 1981); and Fred Anderson, "A People's Army: Provincial Military Service in Massachusetts During the Seven Years War," *William and Mary Quarterly* 40, no. 4 (October 1983): 499–527.

33. The traditional emphasis on the lineal family and its influence upon adaptive strategies is discussed in Jedrey, *The World of John Cleaveland;* Jones, *Village and Seaport*; Robert Gross, *The Minutemen and Their World* (New York: Hill and Wang, 1976); and Henretta, "Families and Farms," pp. 3–32.

34. Benno Forman, "The Crown and York Chairs of Coastal Connecticut and the Work of the Durands of Milford," *Antiques* 105, no. 5 (May 1974): 1147–54; Cooke, "Selective Conservative Taste," p. 44; Account Book of John Brooks, Jr. of Stratford, 1784–1824, pp. 20, 81; and Bridgeport Probate District, Docket 2232 (Connecticut State Library). For information on the Prindle family, see Edward S. Cooke Jr., *Fiddlebacks & Crooked-backs: Elijah Booth and Other Joiners in Newtown and Woodbury, 1750–1820* (Waterbury, Conn.: Mattatuck Museum, 1982), p. 90. A similar pattern of craft families and traditionalism existed on eighteenth-century Long Island (Failey, *Long Island is My Nation*, pp. 191–200).

35. Cooke, *Fiddlebacks & Crooked-backs*, appendixes A and B for information on the Booths, Fabriques, and Prindles. The Beardslees included Henry and Andrew of Stratford, John of Trumbull, John of Newtown, and John of Woodbury who apprenticed with Bartimeus Fabrique. Account Book of John Brooks, Jr. of Stratford, 1784–1824, p. 31; Account Book of Henry Curtiss of Stratford, 1749–83 (Stratford Historical Society, Stratford, Conn.), p. 82; Account Book of Philo Curtiss of Stratford, 1795–1824 (Boothe Homestead, Stratford, Conn.), p. 6; Stratford Probate District, Docket 151 (Connecticut State Library); Newtown Probate District, Docket 69 (Connecticut State Library); and Account Book of Bartimeus Fabrique of Southbury, 1785–1820 (Yale University Library), pp. 31–35, 47.

36. Robert F. Trent, "New England Joinery and Turning Before 1700," in *New England Begins: The Seventeenth Century*, edited by Robert F. Trent and Jonathan Fairbanks (Boston: Museum of Fine Arts, Boston, 1982), 3: 501–50; Robert B. St. George, "Style and Structure in the Joinery of Dedham and Medfield, Massachusetts, 1635–1685," *Winterthur Portfolio* 13 (1979):

1–46; and I. T. Frary, *Early Homes of Ohio* (1936; reprint, New York: Dover Publications, Inc., 1970), pp. 90–95. *Plain & Elegant Rich & Common* (Concord, N.H.: New Hampshire Historical Society, 1979), a catalogue of documented New Hampshire furniture, implies that many joiners who migrated to that state retained the traditions of their training. This study, as well as William Hosley Jr., "Vermont Furniture, 1790–1830," *Old-Time New England* 72 (1987): 245–86, points out that more work needs to be done on the concept of cultural transfer in New Hampshire and Vermont.

37. Newtown Probate District, Docket 970 (Connecticut State Library); H. Franklin Andrews, *The Hamlin Family* (Exira, Iowa: H. Franklin Andrews, 1902); Samuel Orcutt, *A History of the Old Town of Stratford and the City of Bridgeport Connecticut* (New Haven, Conn.: Tuttle, Morehouse & Taylor, 1886), p. 494; Stratford Land Records (Stratford Town Hall, Stratford, Conn.), 28:402–3 and 411; and Woodbury Land Records (Woodbury Town Hall, Woodbury, Conn.), 32:138; 35:58.

38. Hobart Family Papers (Fairfield Historical Society, Fairfield, Conn.).

39. Account Books of Silas Cheney of Litchfield, 1799–1821 (Litchfield Historical Society, Litchfield, Conn.); and John Kenney, *The Hitchcock Chair* (New York: Clarkson N. Potter, Inc., 1971).

Kevin M. Sweeney

Regions and the Study of Material Culture: Explorations Along the Connecticut River

▼ THIS ESSAY CONSISTS OF three reflections on the material culture of a particular region: the Connecticut River Valley of Connecticut and neighboring western Massachusetts. It examines seventeenth-century Wethersfield, Connecticut, case furniture; explores the origins of some classic expressions of eighteenth-century furniture; and concludes with a once commonplace type of artifact, the worm fence. An analysis of these selected items as texts illuminates the problematic relationship between the study of material culture and the study of a region. In particular these objects challenge the uncritical use of such terms as "traditional" and "folk," which are usually embedded in studies of regional material culture.

Despite the pitfalls, an approach to a region's culture that is sensitive to problems inherent in the concept of regionalism and in the historical study of material culture can be used to raise questions about cultural innovation as well as the persistence of cultural patterns. In New England, a regional approach, particularly one using material culture, provides a way out of the parochial embrace of studies focusing on a single town and its community. Translocal communities become much more obvious when defined by craft and class and when the field of vision is expanded to include more geography and more evidence, especially of the material sort.

To realize the potential of this approach one has to disentangle the regional study of material culture from the study of regionalism. Ideologically, the study of regionalism in America owes much to the concerns of the 1930s. In almost all of its various manifestations, be they literary, artistic, or scholarly, the concept of regionalism expressed a search for the essence of America and a yearning for community stability amidst the disruptions and discouragements of the Depression. In the words of one scholar, America's regions appeared to embody "a communal form of living that existed apart from the formal institutions and the pressures of industrial capitalism."[1]

For some scholars, the study of regionalism became a self-conscious search for a simpler, more spiritual culture that could be contrasted to the complex and materialistic world of twentieth-century industrial capitalism. The prominent sociologist and theorist of regionalism, Howard W. Odum, treated regions as "an extension and an attribute to the 'folk,'" and, therefore, regions served as "living, physical area tabernacles for the folk cultures of the world to maintain a quality culture in a quantity world." Because regional cultures were basically folk cultures, Odum saw them as "natural," "isolated," and "relatively homogeneous." Other sociologists similarly defined regions as "comprised of a constellation of communities" characterized by "a homogeneity of economic and social structure," "whose people are bound together by mutual dependencies arising from common interests."[2]

The original emphasis on presumed isolation, homogeneity, shared values, and community has continued to influence the study of regions by students of folklife, anthropologists, historians, and others who often do not share the ideological agendas of the first students of regionalism. Even recent studies of traditional or folk material culture and regionalism often embrace a vision of homogeneous communities that are relatively or completely isolated from outside influences and in which change occurs very slowly, if at all. In New England, this vision is reinforced by the persistent belief in the initial establishment by the Puritan settlers of prelapsarian communities—whether John Winthrop's "city upon a hill" or the modern social historian's "Christian Utopian closed corporate community."[3]

Such a view of culture and region makes explanations of cultural change particularly problematic. Explanations of changes in material culture can end up contributing to the long-established tradition of viewing New England's colonial history as a story of declension. Alternatively, cultural change is explained by cataclysms or semantic sleights of hand that a growing number of historians find unconvincing. As historian Joyce Appleby observed, "The normative quality given continuity and persistence then leads to an interpretation of change as the promoter of tensions, fear, anxiety, and guilt."[4]

For a number of students of early American material culture, the third quarter of the eighteenth century is a period of dramatic cultural change. These scholars see a profound change in the character of artifacts as well as a change in the quantity of artifacts. The changes are seen as reflecting and encouraging the acceptance of a "Georgian world view." Archaeologist James Deetz finds this new world view to be "mechanical where the older was organic, balanced where the older had been asymmetrical, individualized where the older had been corporate."[5] The acceptance of this Georgian world view marked the replacement of a traditional, homogeneous, folk culture by an individualistic, popular culture. This Anglicized or "re-Anglicized" popular culture also supplanted the regional variations that distinguished folk material culture in seventeenth- and early-eighteenth-century New England.

Although evidence drawn from the Connecticut Valley could be used to interpret changes during this period as such a reordering of the region's material and intellectual universe, to do so misinterprets the material culture of the seventeenth and early eighteenth centuries. The region's material culture in 1750 or 1680 cannot be characterized as "traditional" or "folk" if these terms are meant to suggest a slowly changing material culture shaped in isolation by a relatively homogeneous society and undiversified economy.[6] Marked from the outset by hierarchical distinctions in form, gravestone motifs and furniture styles went through three or four changes between 1635 and 1760. Housing also varied by class and went through more subtle changes during the same period of time. From the earliest period, artifacts produced and used in the region were shaped by three distinguishable but interrelated social groups: the craft dynasties, the gentry elite, and the yeomen farmers. Throughout the seventeenth and eighteenth centuries, commercial agriculture, mercantile activity, and specialized preindustrial production shaped and constantly modified the region's material culture. Most artifacts produced and consumed in this context were products of an Anglicized popular culture, though in important ways distinctive variants of it.[7]

The period from 1635 to 1670 witnessed the transplanting of English culture in its various localized embodiments to the Connecticut River Valley. The character of this process, which occurred throughout New England, is described in a number of studies by David Grayson Allen, James Deetz, Robert Blair St. George, Robert Trent, and others.[8] The usual emphasis in these studies is on the direct transference of English artifactual prototypes to relatively homogeneous and, for some, rather "traditional" communities.

The picture that emerges from a study of the social landscape and material culture of the Connecticut Valley during the seventeenth century is a bit different. The physical survivals and documentary evidence create a picture of diverse communities that often quarreled over matters of religion and supported several distinct shop traditions of woodworkers. These patterns of behavior are not necessarily related, but the diversity suggested by both types of evidence fits poorly with pictures of homogeneous, corporate communities so popular in the historical studies of New England towns produced during the 1970s. Because of the focus on relatively homogeneous and atypical communities such as Hartford and Windsor, diversity, turbulence, and the special character of the early history of the Connecticut Valley often get overlooked.[9]

The 1634 settlement at Wethersfield, which makes claim to be the first English town settled in the Connecticut Valley, can perhaps make a better case for typicality. Wethersfield was not settled by a united church of Puritans shepherded out of Massachusetts by a charismatic pastor. John Oldham, a trader, and John Chester, a minor English gentleman, led the original ten adventurers who came to Wethersfield from Watertown, Massachusetts. The members of the initial group and subsequent settlers came from a variety of English backgrounds, and the origins of the town's first woodworkers reflected this diversity. Surviving objects and the backgrounds of carpenters, joiners, turners and shipwrights document the presence of joinery traditions originating in East Anglia, the north of England, and the West Country, and of building practices from East Anglia, the Hampshire-Wiltshire region, and possibly London.[10]

The shops were typically family organized and perpetuated by master-apprentice relationships that passed from a father to a son or a son-in-law or a nephew. The family rather than the town determined the cultural horizons influencing individual craftsmen. The development of family networks, which even in the mid-1600s transcended town boundaries, determined the diffusion and persistence of particular craft practices that influenced the construction and appearance of furniture and houses. The marriage of joiner Samuel Steele to joiner James Boosey's daughter linked Wethersfield and Farmington woodworkers before 1650; members of the Gilbert family of carpenters, joiners, and glazers lived and worked in Windsor, Wethersfield, Hartford, Springfield, Northampton, and possibly New Haven; and joiners from the Dickinson family moved up the Connecticut River into western Massachusetts and back to Wethersfield by the late 1670s.[11]

Disparate English shop traditions persisted in seventeenth-century Wethersfield. There was no such thing as a Wethersfield style or a Connecticut Valley style at the time. Surviving furniture and documentary sources provide evidence for the existence in Wethersfield of five or six different joinery shops. By the late seventeenth century, locally produced furniture often revealed the influence of more than one English tradition as woodworkers responded to new influences. Local transformations as well as lit-

Figure 1 Box, possibly by John Nott, Wethersfield, Connecticut, 1640–1680. Oak. H. 7½", W. 23¾", D. 16". (Luke Vincent Lockwood, *Colonial Furniture in America* [New York: Charles Scribner's Sons, 1901], p. 251, fig., 221.)

Figure 2 Chest with drawers, Wethersfield, Connecticut, 1675–1700. Oak with pine. H. 40", W. 48", D. 20". (Courtesy, Historic Deerfield, Inc.; photo, Amanda Merullo.) In *The Furniture of Historic Deerfield* (New York: E. P. Dutton & Co., 1976), p. 167, Dean A. Fales Jr. speculated that the chest may have descended from Hannah Talcott (1665–1741), who married Major John Chester at Wethersfield in 1686, to their daughter Sarah.

Figure 3 Chest with drawers, Wethersfield, Connecticut, 1704. Oak with pine. H. 37 1/4", W. 48", D. 21". (Courtesy, Art Institute of Chicago, Wirt D. Walker Fund.)

eral transplanting of English shop traditions shaped the character of Wethersfield furniture.

An oak box decorated with carved flowers and the letter "N" probably represents the work of first-generation joiner John Nott (d. 1682). The box, which descended in the Nott family, is known from an illustration in Luke Vincent Lockwood's *Colonial Furniture in America* (fig. 1).[12] The profiles of the tulips bear an obvious relationship to those in secondary locations on "sunflower" chests from the Wethersfield area. Especially striking is the similarity between the box's two smaller tulips and the tulip found on the muntin of the lower drawer of a joined chest that reportedly descended in the John Chester family of Wethersfield (fig. 2), as well as the similarity between the box's four larger tulips and the smaller tulips on the flanking panels of the facade of a carved and painted chest dated 1704 (fig. 3). The carving on the Nott box is also set off by a background stippled in a manner similar to that on many "sunflower" chests.

The box's decoration and John Nott's origins in the north of England suggest that he may have been the source for the tulips, roses, and vines that became prominent features of the "sunflower" and Hadley chests made during the late seventeenth and early eighteenth centuries. Several scholars have suggested that the origins of both Connecticut Valley carving traditions lay in the north of England, and Nott was well situated to influence woodworkers who produced both types of chests. From his arrival in the late 1630s to his "retirement" about 1675, he appears to have been the town's most prominent woodworker and his joinery shop next to the meetinghouse was a Wethersfield landmark.[13]

Totally unrelated to this box is a joined chest, with low relief carving, owned in Glastonbury, which was a part of Wethersfield until 1693 (fig. 4). It may represent a tradition from the west of England, where joiners fre-

Figure 4 Chest, Wethersfield, Connecticut, 1670–1690. Red oak with yellow pine. H. 26", W. 48½", D. 20¼". (Courtesy, Webb-Deane-Stevens Museum; photo, Gavin Ashworth.)

Figure 5 Door, Wethersfield, Connecticut, 1640–1680. Yellow pine. H. 70⅜", W. 38¼", D. 1¼". (Courtesy, Connecticut Historical Society.)

quently used similar combinations of motifs. The finished, four-panel back of the chest, which is closer to English joinery practices than the single framed panel commonly found on "sunflower" chests, suggests that the chest is the work of a first-generation joiner. It is, however, a late example of first-generation work, for it has millsawn bottom boards, dating the chest no earlier than the late 1660s when the first sawmills began operation in Wethersfield.[14]

Another early shop having possible West Country origins may have produced a nine-panel joined door from a house in Rocky Hill, which was Wethersfield's Stepney parish until 1843 (fig. 5). The door documents the richness and the diversity of joinery work found in early Wethersfield and suggests that some early woodworking traditions had a regional, as opposed to a purely local, pattern of diffusion. The muntins of this door are ornamented with rope moldings that strongly resemble the decoration on the lower rail of a joined chest with a recovery history in Windsor, Connecticut (fig. 6). Despite its location, this chest (and a related chest with a Windsor history at Memorial Hall in Deerfield, Massachusetts) have been linked to a group of New Haven chests. The group, which exhibits elements associated with furniture from the West Country of England, is believed to be the work of first-generation joiners active between 1640 and 1680.[15]

A press that descended in the Goodrich family of Wethersfield provides even more dramatic evidence of the presence of outside influences and the arrival of new designs there during the late seventeenth century (fig. 7). Although the Nott box, the Glastonbury chest, and the Rocky Hill door are late expressions of a carved mode of Mannerism (introduced into England in the 1520s), the Goodrich press has applied ornament, which is characteristic of a later phase of that style (introduced into England in the later 1500s and early 1600s). On seventeenth-century New England furniture, the use of geometrically patterned moldings, prisms, and glyphs usually suggests

Figure 6 Chest, probably Windsor, Connecticut, 1640–1680. White oak and white pine (top) with tulip poplar. H. 27", W. 48", D. 19¾". (Courtesy, Yale University Art Gallery, The Mabel Brady Garvan Collection.)

Figure 7 Press, Wethersfield, Connecticut, 1670–1690. Oak with yellow pine. H. 67", W. 68", D. 19". (Courtesy, Hartford Steam Boiler Inspection and Insurance Company; photo, Gavin Ashworth.)

the presence of London-trained artisans or New England artisans trained or influenced by London woodworkers.[16] A member of the Goodrich family may have inherited the press or purchased it from a joiner working in another town or city. If locally made, the press probably represents the work of an outsider, since its ornament and construction differ from the three shop traditions described above.

The most likely source of the applied-ornamental style in Wethersfield is Peter Blin (ca. 1640–1725), a joiner credited with the production of many Wethersfield "sunflower" chests. The circumstantial evidence for this association is strong. Blin arrived in Wethersfield around 1675, just before the Reverend Joseph Rowlandson (d. 1678) acquired a "sunflower" cupboard with turned and applied ornament and about the time John Nott "retired." In addition, most of Blin's contemporaries were locally trained, or they arrived in Wethersfield after 1678. Traditionally, scholars credited Blin with the introduction of motifs drawn from either the north of England or Huguenot sources, but they barely considered the geometric moldings and applied turnings on "sunflower" chests, both of which suggest London sources. Even though Blin was probably Francophone, it is more likely that his family had its roots in the French-speaking communities of the Low Countries or the Channel Islands. Blin family tradition also maintains that he came to New England from London instead of from the north of England; therefore, John Nott is a more plausible bearer and disseminator of a North Country carving tradition.[17]

The late Mannerist applied style, exemplified by the ornament on the Goodrich press, did not totally supplant the earlier carved style. The largest group of late-seventeenth-century Wethersfield furniture—the forty to eighty chests and seven cupboards with "sunflower" motifs—has carved Tudor roses, tulips, and thistles *and* (with two exceptions) applied spindles and bosses (fig. 8). Production of these case pieces required joinery and turning skills, and although Peter Blin apparently was proficient in both trades, other evidence suggests that more than one tradesman produced

Figure 8 Chest with drawers, Wethersfield, Connecticut, 1675–1690. Oak with pine. H. 37¾", W. 45⅞", D. 19⅜". (Courtesy, Connecticut Historical Society.)

these chests and cupboards. Variations in the motifs and execution of the carved panels and minor variations in the drawer construction of some chests indicate the work of different hands. During the late seventeenth century, Wethersfield also supported at least two other turners, Joseph Andrus (or Andrews) (1651–1706) and Nathaniel Foote (1647–1703), the latter of whom had business dealings with Blin.[18] Part of this group of case pieces may represent the work of Foote and Obediah Dickinson (1641–1698), a joiner who probably trained in Wethersfield, left town, then returned about 1680.[19] The size of the "sunflower" group and the existence of chests with strong histories of ownership outside Wethersfield suggests production from different shops as well as individual shops employing several workmen.

Regardless of their makers' identity, the "sunflower" chests and cupboards reveal the complex character of late-seventeenth-century furniture, which makes the use of the term traditional or "folk" problematic. The chests and cupboards in this group combine high-style motifs based on the manipulation of classical forms with older vernacular motifs such as flowers and hearts. Carved motifs such as Tudor roses and Scottish thistles reflect the influence of the larger political community of which Wethersfield was a distant part. The presence of tulips and vines, based in part on North Country motifs probably dating to the previous century, with more up-to-date spindles and moldings painted to suggest exotics—ebony and possibly snake wood—indicates that both innovation and the preservation of tradition were conscious choices made in the presence of alternatives (see fig. 8). Even though its material composition seems to suggest an insular community, the furniture's ornamentation documents on-going contact with the outside, and, therefore, instead of embodying a long-established and geographically restricted "tradition," this kind of chest gave expression to a "horizon," a "pattern characterized by widespread distribution of a complex of cultural traits that lasts a relatively short time."[20]

Innovation generally occurs first in decoration, whereas form is usually the place where tradition is manifested and retained. With the "sunflower" chests, both form and decoration are modified and adapted from various sources. The basic chest form, with its undivided storage space and lift-top, dates to the Middle Ages, possibly to Antiquity. The addition of one or two drawers to the vast majority of the Wethersfield "sunflower" chests resulted from the appearance locally in the 1670s of the chest of drawers, a form first produced in the 1630s for members of the English urban middle class. The addition of drawers to the traditional chest form thus bespoke urban influences, a practical need to store and differentiate a growing quantity of smaller items, and a willingness to spend more to obtain a more expensive form. The relative cost of a "sunflower" chest compared to a six-board chest that provided an equivalent amount of storage space indicates a growing level of prosperity and a rising standard of living. The numbers in which the chests survive from a community that had only sixty to eighty households during the late seventeenth century suggests that they were widely distributed in Wethersfield.[21]

Despite the evidence of some innovation within the dominant shop tradition, most furniture made and owned in Wethersfield during the late 1600s and early 1700s adhered closely to late-seventeenth-century forms and styles. Joined chests with and without drawers and board chests were the most common types of case furniture, and older types of seating, such as stools and forms, remained in use. The number of chairs in local households increased, and during the early 1700s, a few residents owned cane chairs and leather chairs, possibly imported from Boston. All of the locally made case furniture from this period is joined rather than being dovetailed. Joiners, carpenters, and turners who were born and trained in Wethersfield made the bulk of the furniture used in the town. Though susceptible to outside influences, the Wethersfield woodworkers active between 1680 and 1730 were essentially an in-grown, if not inward-looking, group.[22]

The situation began to change as the population and prosperity of Wethersfield increased during the next fifty years. The town's population grew from less than 2000 in 1730 to almost 3500 by 1774. Shipping tonnage owned by residents increased dramatically between 1730 and 1780. In the 1770s, six merchants traded directly with the West Indies, and five to six ships sailed from the town. By the eve of the American Revolution, Wethersfield had become an urban village, the second most densely populated town in the colony. The principal beneficiaries of this increased commercial activity and population growth appear to have been those who worked in the town's expanding service sector. One-fourth to one-third of the male taxpayers in Wethersfield proper (the town's First Society) derived a part of their income from nonagricultural sources such as commercial, professional, and craft activity, and by the 1770s, the town ranked among the top quarter of Connecticut towns as measured by artisan activity.[23] The presence of a relatively large number of craftsmen provided opportunities for cooperation and inspired the competition that produced more innovative and often more cosmopolitan cultural expressions.

During the mid-1700s, woodworkers moved to Wethersfield to set up shop as chairmakers, joiners, and shipwrights. The arrival of woodworkers, especially those from eastern Massachusetts, influenced the character of furniture, of buildings, and possibly, though the evidence does not survive, of ships. The traits commonly associated with high-style, eighteenth-century Connecticut Valley furniture and house joinery were not indigenous products that spontaneously generated in the rich alluvial soil of the river's bottomlands. They resulted from a combination of an economically attractive environment for migrating craftsmen bearing new designs and the patronage of merchants, professionals, and yeomen with pretensions and some means, but not unlimited means. The resulting combination of influences created cosmopolitan yet restrained provincial expressions.

The first group of newcomers migrated from eastern Massachusetts. Early in the 1720s, Hezekiah May (1696–1783) of Roxbury, Massachusetts, arrived in town, apparently to do the joinery work on the Newington Parish meetinghouse. He stayed and eventually became one of the town's leading house joiners and builders. His reputation ran from Saybrook at the mouth of the Connecticut River to Hatfield in western Massachusetts. Hezekiah's

Figure 9 Dressing table attributed to Return Belden, Wethersfield, Connecticut, 1740–1760. Sycamore with white and yellow pine. H. 27⅜", W. 35", D. 24½". (Courtesy, Porter Phelps Huntington Historic House Museum; photo, Gavin Ashworth.)

Figure 10 Side chair, Wethersfield, Connecticut, 1740–1770. Maple; remnants of original black paint. H. 40", W. 19¾", D. 14". (Courtesy, Brooklyn Museum, Dick S. Ramsay Fund.) This chair is from a set of at least five originally owned by Dr. Ezekiel Porter (1706–1775) of Wethersfield. A very similar set descended in the Buck family of Wethersfield.

son Samuel (1724–1792) and his grandson William (1749–1809) followed the same trade. Charlestown, Massachusetts, cabinetmaker William Manley arrived around 1730, maintained a shop for fifteen years, and trained apprentices such as Return Belden (1721–1764). Thomas Brigden (1703–1781), a contemporary of Manley's from Charlestown, established a chairmaker's shop in the early 1740s that continued into the early 1800s.[24]

Eastern Massachusetts design and construction techniques had a profound influence on Wethersfield and, more broadly, on Connecticut Valley furniture and homes. The deeply scalloped skirts of high chests made in Wethersfield between 1740 and 1760 and the use of central drawer runners and double-beaded drawer sides document the indebtedness of Wethersfield furniture makers to Boston designs and construction practices (fig. 9). Surviving examples of locally owned and made crooked-back chairs also reveal the influence of designs from eastern Massachusetts (fig. 10). Architectural historian Abbott Cummings characterized Wethersfield's Buttolph-Williams house (ca. 1721) as displaying "one of the most extensive arrays of features associated with Massachusetts Bay".[25] The scalloped cupboard and the twist-turn newel post in the Joseph Webb house (ca. 1752) relate directly to interior joinery work in Boston's Thomas Hancock house (ca. 1737) and its contemporary neighbors.

Influences came to Wethersfield from areas other than eastern Massachusetts. Chairs and case furniture made between 1730 and 1780 suggest the presence of chairmakers and cabinetmakers with ties to coastal and southeastern Connecticut. For example, the Atwood family and Thomas Brigden made crown chairs—a distinctive seating form more commonly associated with coastal Connecticut—and references to this chair type appear in pro-

Figure 12 Side chair, probably Norwalk, Connecticut, 1750–1760. Maple and ash. H. 43¾", W. 19", D. 15." (Courtesy, Webb-Deane-Stevens Museum; photo, Gavin Ashworth.)

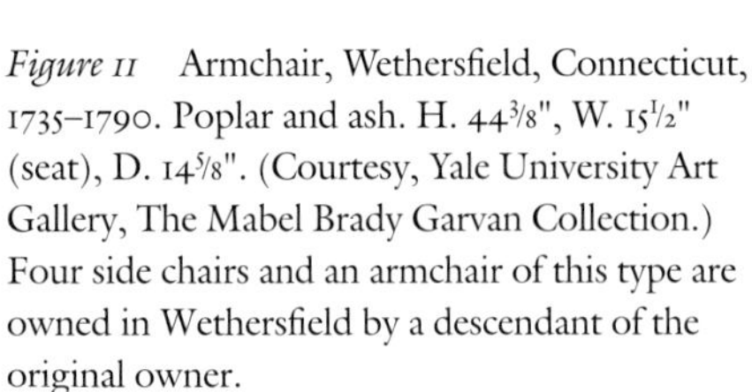

Figure 11 Armchair, Wethersfield, Connecticut, 1735–1790. Poplar and ash. H. 44⅜", W. 15½" (seat), D. 14⅝". (Courtesy, Yale University Art Gallery, The Mabel Brady Garvan Collection.) Four side chairs and an armchair of this type are owned in Wethersfield by a descendant of the original owner.

bate inventories as early as 1732. The turnings of crown chairs with Wethersfield histories bear some relationship to the turnings of crown chairs made along the Connecticut coast from the 1730s to the 1760s (fig. 11). The actual ties to the coast are not yet documented, though a maple "heart-and-crown" chair owned in a Wethersfield branch of the Wolcott family is identical to one attributed to a member of the Durand family of Norwalk (fig. 12).[26] Like the crooked-back chairs, these turned chairs were not distinctive Connecticut Valley expressions in form or ornamentation.

The diffusion of this more vernacular chair type suggests the still poorly understood processes by which the design of certain commonplace objects became increasingly standardized during the 1700s. One suspects that slat-back or ladder-back chairs would reveal even more similarities in design and construction, though the low rates of survival of these types of chairs make comparisons between locales difficult. Still, John Kirk's research uncovered affinities between slat-back chairs from the Wethersfield area and those of southwestern Connecticut, and "fiddleback chairs" and "york chairs" are also found in both regions (fig. 13).[27]

It is easier to analyze the origins of design elements and construction techniques in high-style chairs, which usually exhibit more distinctive features. Three sets of compass seat "Queen Anne" chairs hint at a still elusive connection between Philadelphia or provincial British craft practices and those of the Hartford-Wethersfield area. Two sets of Wethersfield-owned chairs with seat rails made of boards laid flatwise, secured by horizontal joints, and tenoned through the rear stiles are known. The first set, owned

Figure 14 Side chair, Wethersfield, Connecticut, 1750–1770. Cherry and maple. H. 41", W. 15¼", D. 17½". (Courtesy, Brooklyn Museum, Henry L. Batterman Fund.) This is one of a set of chairs possibly owned by Dr. Ezekiel Porter of Wethersfield (see also fig. 10) and probably owned by his son-in-law, Colonel Thomas Belden (1732–1782).

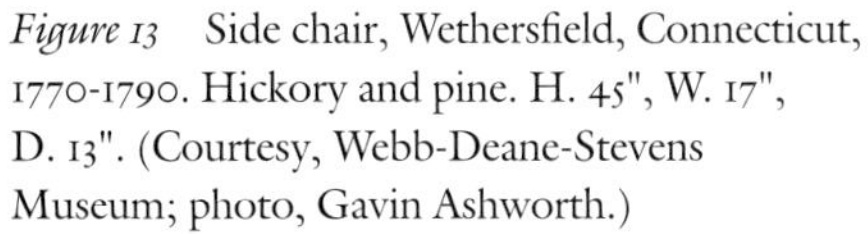

Figure 13 Side chair, Wethersfield, Connecticut, 1770-1790. Hickory and pine. H. 45", W. 17", D. 13". (Courtesy, Webb-Deane-Stevens Museum; photo, Gavin Ashworth.)

by Sarah Noyes Chester, was probably not made in Wethersfield; the second set, owned in the Porter and Belden families, may have been (fig. 14). A third set of slip-seat chairs with through-tenoned seat rails survives with a history of ownership in a branch of the Wells family of Wethersfield. These chairs, which have very deep seat rails, employ the more usual New England practice of constructing seat frames with boards set on edge instead of laid flatwise (fig. 15). The design and construction of the chairs in this third set suggest the work of another local craftsman who selectively adopted visual features of "Philadelphia-style" seat construction—flat seat rails and through tenoning—but modified them to suit his work habits. The existence of the three sets with visual similarities but marked differences in proportions and construction is the product of a competitive environment in which copying by parallel shops and not the expansion of a single shop tradition by the training of apprentices accounted for the diffusion of the style.[28]

This competitive environment and the demands of consumers encouraged the movement of Wethersfield woodworkers throughout the towns along the Connecticut River. Their movements helped diffuse the construction practices and stylistic elements commonly associated with high-style, eighteenth-century Connecticut Valley furniture and house joinery. William Manley and Return Belden sold furniture in western Massachusetts (see fig. 9). When he left Wethersfield around 1745, Manley resettled in the Wintonbury (today Bloomfield) section of Windsor. Wethersfield joiner and shipwright Timothy Boardman (1727–1792) established himself in Mid-

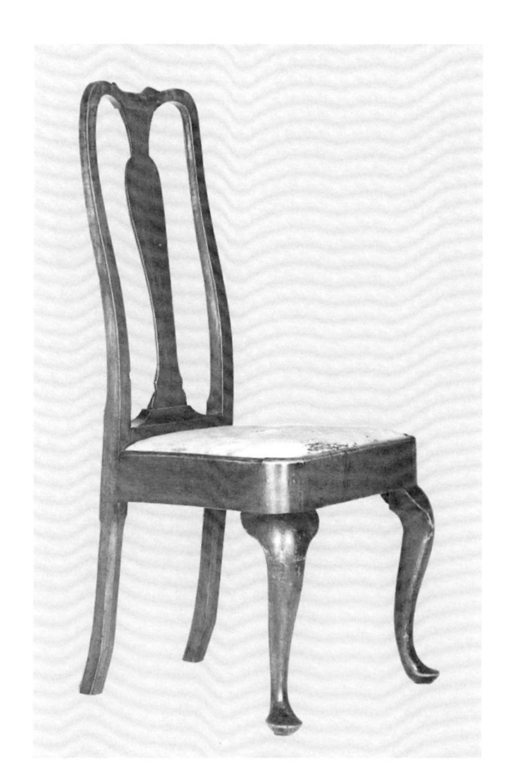

Figure 15 Side chair, Wethersfield, Connecticut, 1735–1760. Cherry. H. 40½", W. 18½", D. 15¼". (Private collection; photo courtesy, Connecticut Historical Society.) This chair is from a set of at least five. The slip seats of two chairs have most of their original foundation upholstery and remnants of their needlework covers.

dletown around 1752, and at least one high chest with a Middletown history bears a strong resemblance to certain Wethersfield high chests of the same period (fig. 16). Thomas Brigden, a son of the Wethersfield chairmaker of the same name, set up shop in Middletown during the 1760s and produced crooked-back chairs.[29]

The movement of Wethersfield furniture and craftsmen along the Connecticut River was not just an instance of following the course of least resistance, and thus an example of geographic determinism. The existence of gentry networks that followed the river influenced the movement of ideas, furniture, and craftsmen. Purchase of Wethersfield furniture by the Porters and Williamses in western Massachusetts can be traced to the presence in Wethersfield of Porter and Williams cousins. When Israel Williams of Hatfield needed advice on the design of a meetinghouse or a home for himself, he turned to his brother Elijah Williams of Wethersfield, who consulted the Wethersfield joiner Hezekiah May and a Scots-born contractor, James Mitchell (1701–1776). Because of these ties, Samuel Partridge of Hatfield apparently came to Wethersfield for his training as a joiner. After his return home, Partridge trained other woodworkers in western Massachusetts.[30] Because of the number and apparent prominence of woodworkers in Wethersfield and craft and family ties that linked Wethersfield to towns from the mouth of the Connecticut River to those in western Massachusetts, local woodworking shops had an impact on the other towns along the river that was equaled only by Hartford and possibly Middletown in the period before the American Revolution.

The complex material world of mid-eighteenth-century Wethersfield and the other towns of the Connecticut Valley was also captured in a more mundane artifact. It is hard to imagine a more seemingly "traditional" or "folk"

Figure 16 High chest of drawers, possibly Middletown, Connecticut, 1760–1780. Cherry with pine and tulip poplar. H. 86", W. 29½", D. 21". (Courtesy, Middlesex County Historical Society; photo, Gavin Ashworth.)

artifact than the worm fence, which is also known as a snake fence or Virginia fence (fig. 17). The form appears to be timeless, or at the very least an obvious seventeenth-century solution to the early colonists' need for eas-

Figure 17 Southwest View of Bernardston, Massachusetts, ca. 1838. (From John W. Barber, *Massachusetts Historical Collections* [Worcester, Mass.: Dorr, Howland, 1839].)

ily constructed fencing.[31] The worm fence has a history, however, and it is a suggestive one. It has been overlooked because this type of fencing is no longer common within the region; it is not a particularly Connecticut Valley product; and it is, from a traditional art historical or decorative arts perspective, a "styleless" or plain artifact that is not related in form or design to English prototypes.

The worm fence is, nevertheless, a revealing artifact. Evidence from account books indicates that these fences appeared in the region around 1750. Sylvester Judd, who wrote his history of Hadley, Massachusetts, during the second quarter of the nineteenth century, came to a similar conclusion. The fence's introduction and its period name, "Virginia fence," document once again that the Connecticut Valley was open to outside influences—in this instance an idea that can be traced from the Chesapeake region through the middle colonies and into the valley.[32] Not all simple or plain artifacts were traditional and not all outside ideas or material forms arrived as "high-style" objects. Unfortunately, the methods of transmission that are so clear in some cases remain very obscure in this instance.

The date of this artifact's introduction into the region can be determined, and its appearance then is particularly suggestive. The mid-1700s was a period of agricultural innovation that saw the introduction of new fodder crops, such as turnips, and new tools, such as grain cradles. It also saw a lot of people ending up in court for encroaching on highway rights-of-way and for illegally enclosing common lands. Fences at that time were matters of dispute and conflict, and it was into this environment that the easily constructed "Virginia fence" was introduced. The fence embodied a quick and affordable solution to problems resulting from complex causes. The fence's apparent simplicity belies the complexity of the social and economic environment of which it became an integral part. It is thus hard to call such fences "folk" or even "traditional" or to see them as expressions of "strong traditional cultures," "changing slowly and interacting with their neighbors to a very limited degree."[33]

The material evidence in the Connecticut Valley and in other areas in the American colonies provides confirmation for English historian Peter Burke's "simple model of a complex process," which argues "that the commercial revolution led to a golden age of traditional popular culture (material culture, at least), before the combined commercial and industrial revolutions destroyed it." When describing the artifacts produced by eighteenth-century German immigrants in Pennsylvania, historian Scott Swank goes even further and categorizes "so-called peasant or folk art" as being "primarily rural bourgeois art." He sees conditions very similar to those existing in the Connecticut Valley as necessary for the production of such art, for he concludes that "preindustrial bourgeois attitudes, certain types of economic activity, geographic concentration, and a particular level of prosperity appear to be characteristic of each of the societies that produced significant quantities of art." To this list can be added the importance of communications and the constant interaction with individuals and ideas from outside the region.[34]

Failure to recognize or accept the complex, commercial aspects of preindustrial popular culture and its physical expression, vernacular material culture, requires one to posit a dramatic transformation some time during the eighteenth century. Archaeologist James Deetz and others are forced into explanations that invoke the arrival of market economy, the "new importance of the individual," or "re-Anglicization" to explain the change. Such approaches slight the formative and continuing role popular culture and vernacular material culture played in shaping elements of family and collective identities. Such explanations also look upon the apparent mid-eighteenth-century Anglicization of early American material culture as a new and all-pervasive process. Gentry families and craft dynasties who played central roles in this process acted as filters, not sponges. As Burke observes, such changes in popular culture were not so much "substitutive" as "additive."[35]

Ignoring the commercial contexts in which much of vernacular material culture was produced, consumed, and distributed also artificially separates the study of certain categories of artifacts. The production of gravestones in New England expanded dramatically during the mid-1700s, but this development is not considered in contemporary historians' studies of the eighteenth-century's "consumer revolution," because such objects are too often categorized as "folk" and thus removed from the view of historians interested in consumer goods. At the same time, the importation into the American colonies of commercially produced, blue, resist-dyed textiles followed a distinctive regional pattern, but students of regional material culture often overlook these goods because they were manufactured in England.[36] The distribution and consumption of both categories of goods, however, were influenced by the same economic and cultural systems.

Study of the vernacular material culture of a particular region needs to move beyond a focus on artifacts that are peculiar to a given region to a more inclusive approach that focuses on those objects that are representative but not necessarily distinctive. A variety of locally produced objects and those produced outside of but used within a given region must be studied together. Examples from different media need to be juxtaposed—even placed in opposition—to capture the diversity and conflict within a particular region, not just record similarities and presumably shared values. The artificial distinctions that often prompt scholars to ask different questions of gravestones and imported English textiles have to be broken down.[37]

This essay deliberately emphasizes the dynamic character and historical contingencies of cultural processes in an effort to challenge the often ahistorical and uncritical acceptance of artifacts or cultural patterns as "traditional" or "folk." Nothing should be uncritically accepted as traditional or folk. Even common fences have histories that can be recovered. Furthermore, a region suggests a part of a whole, and one should not lose sight of the larger framework, whether looking at the Connecticut Valley, the entire New England region, or some other region of preindustrial America.[38]

1. Michael C. Steiner, "Regionalism in the Great Depression," *Geographical Review* 73, no. 4 (October 1983): 430–46; Vernon Carstensen, "The Development and Application of Regional-Sectional Concepts, 1900–1950," in *Regionalism in America,* edited by Merrill Jensen (Madison: University of Wisconsin Press, 1951), pp. 99–118; Richard H. Pells, *Radical Visions and American Dreams: Culture and Social Thought in the Depression Years* (New York: Harper and Row, 1973), pp. 101–5, Robert L. Dorman, *Revolt of the Provinces: The Regionalist Movement in America, 1920–1945* (Chapel Hill: University of North Carolina Press, 1993). See also Joan Shelley Rubin, "A Convergence of Vision: Constance Rourke, Charles Sheeler, and American Art," *American Quarterly* 42, no. 2 (June 1990): 203. Quotation in Pells, *Radical Visions and American Dreams*, p. 103.

2. Howard W. Odum, "Folk and Regional Conflict as a Field of Sociological Study [1930]" and "The American Blend: Regional Diversity and National Unity [1949]," in *Folk, Region, and Society: Selected Papers of Howard W. Odum,* edited by Katharine Jocher et al. (Chapel Hill: University of North Carolina Press, 1964), pp. 247, 193. Howard W. Odum and Harry Estill Moore, *American Regionalism: A Cultural-Historical Approach to National Integration* (New York: Henry Holt and Company, 1938), pp. 416–19. Howard W. Odum, "Folk Culture and Folk Society [1947]," in Jocher, ed., *Folk, Region, and Society*, p. 225. See also Odum and Moore, *American Regionalism*, pp. 15, 16, 29–31. Rupert B. Vance, "The Regional Concept as a Tool for Social Research," in Jensen, ed., *Regionalism in America*, p. 123.

3. Kenneth Lockridge, *A New England Town: The First Hundred Years, Dedham, Massachusetts. 1636–1736* (New York: W. W. Norton, 1970), p. 16.

4. Joyce Appleby, "Value and Society," in *Colonial British America: Essays in the New History of the Early Modern Era,* edited by Jack P. Greene and J. R. Pole (Baltimore: Johns Hopkins University Press, 1984), p. 308.

5. James Deetz, *In Small Things Forgotten: The Archeology of Early American Life* (New York: Anchor/Doubleday, 1977), p. 40.

6. For such characterizations of folk or vernacular art, see Henry Glassie, "Folk Art," in *Folklore and Folklife: An Introduction,* edited by Richard M. Dorson (Chicago: University of Chicago Press, 1972), p. 258; Henri Focillon, "Introduction" to *Art Populaire*, in Robert F. Trent, *Hearts and Crowns: Folk Chairs of the Connecticut Coast 1720–1840* (New Haven, Conn.: New Haven Colony Historical Society, 1977), pp. 15–20. See also Johannes Fabian and Ilona Szombati-Fabian, "Folk Art from an Anthropological Perspective," in *Perspectives on American Folk Art*, edited by Ian M. G. Quimby and Scott T. Swank (New York: W. W. Norton for the Winterthur Museum , 1980), p. 252.

7. Kevin M. Sweeney, "Gravestones," in *The Great River: Art and Society of the Connecticut Valley, 1635–1820*, edited by Gerald W. R. Ward and William N. Hosley, Jr. (Hartford, Conn.: Wadsworth Atheneum, 1985), pp. 485–523; Kevin M. Sweeney, "Where the Bay Meets the River: Gravestones and Stonecutters in the River Towns of Western Massachusetts, 1690–1810," in *Markers III: The Journal of the Association for Gravestone Studies*, edited by David Watters (Lanham, Md.: University Press of America, 1985), pp. 1–46; William N. Hosley Jr., "Architecture," in Ward and Hosley, eds., *The Great River*, pp. 63–133.

8. David Grayson Allen, *In English Ways: The Movement of Societies and the Transferral of English Local Law and Custom to Massachusetts Bay in the Seventeenth Century* (Chapel Hill: University of North Carolina Press, 1981); Robert B. St. George, "Style and Structure in the

Joinery of Dedham and Medfield, Massachusetts, 1635–1685," in *American Furniture and Its Makers Winterthur Portfolio* 13, edited by Ian M. G. Quimby (Chicago: University of Chicago Press, 1979), pp. 1–46; Jonathan L. Fairbanks and Robert F. Trent, eds., *New England Begins: The Seventeenth Century*, 3 vols. (Boston: Museum of Fine Arts, Boston, 1982).

9. See, for example, Philip J. Greven Jr., *Four Generations: Population, Land, and Family in Colonial Andover, Massachusetts* (Ithaca, N.Y.: Cornell University Press, 1970); and Lockridge, *A New England Town*. Even in his study of religious contention entitled *Valley of Discord: Church and Society along the Connecticut River, 1636–1725* (Hanover, N.H.: University Press of New England, 1976), Paul Lucas subscribes to the belief that "most of the early towns [in the Connecticut Valley] were founded by wandering congregations" (p. 40), a generalization contradicted by the settlements begun at Farmington, Lyme, Middletown, Saybrook, Springfield, and Wethersfield.

10. Sherman W. Adams and Henry R. Stiles, *The History of Ancient Wethersfield, Connecticut* (New York: Grafton Press, 1904), 1:17–79, 135–65, 246–333; and for an insightful treatment, see John P. Demos, *Entertaining Satan: Witchcraft and the Culture of Early New England* (New York: Oxford University Press, 1982), pp. 340–67. Kevin M. Sweeney, "From Wilderness to Arcadian Vale: Material Life in the Connecticut River Valley, 1635–1760," in Ward and Hosley, eds., *The Great River*, p. 18.

11. On Steele and Boosey, see Adams and Stiles, *History of Ancient Wethersfield*, 2:123–24, 665–66. On the Gilberts, see ibid., 2:353–55; Henry R. Stiles, *The History and Genealogies of Ancient Windsor, Connecticut*, 2 vols. (Hartford, Conn.: Press of Case, Lockwood & Brainard Company, 1892), 2:288; Patricia E. Kane, "The Joiners of Seventeenth Century Hartford County," *Connecticut Historical Society Bulletin* 35, no. 3 (July 1970): 70. On the Dickinsons, see Adams and Stiles, *History of Ancient Wethersfield*, 2:284–91. See also Philip Zea, "The Fruits of Oligarchy: Patronage and the Hadley Chest Tradition in Western Massachusetts," in *New England Furniture: Essays in Memory of Benno M. Forman, Old Time New England* 72 (Society for the Preservation of New England Antiquities, 1987); 1–65.

12. Luke Vincent Lockwood, *Colonial Furniture in America*, 3d ed., 2 vols. (New York: Charles Scribner's Sons, 1901), 1:251, fig. 221.

13. Nott or Knott was born in Nottingham, England. See George S. Roberts, *Historic Towns of the Connecticut River Valley* (Schenectady, N.Y.: Robeson & Adee, 1906), p. 157. John Kirk suggested southern Lancashire, Derbyshire, and, to a lesser extent, Lincolnshire as the origin for the motifs. Nottingham is between Derbyshire and Lincolnshire. See John T. Kirk, "Sources of Some American Regional Furniture," *Antiques* 88, no. 6 (December 1965): 795; and John T. Kirk, *Connecticut Furniture, Seventeenth and Eighteenth Centuries* (Hartford, Conn.: Wadsworth Atheneum, 1967), p. xiii. Most recently Kirk pointed to the Yorkshire, Lancashire, and Westmoreland region. See his *American Furniture and the British Tradition to 1830* (New York: Alfred A. Knopf, 1982), pp. 98–118, esp. figs. 295, 296. Robert F. Trent has also pointed to the Lancashire-Cheshire region. Robert F. Trent, "New England Joinery and Turning before 1700," in Fairbanks and Trent, eds., *New England Begins*, 3:501. Nott retired from public life in the mid-1670s when he stopped serving as a selectman. He drew his will two years before his death in 1681, suggesting that he may not have been in good health. See Estate of John Nott, 1681, Hartford Probate District, file no. 3983, Connecticut State Library, hereafter cited as CSL; Adams and Stiles, *History of Ancient Wethersfield*, 1:289, 2:521.

14. Anthony Wells-Cole to Kevin M. Sweeney, April 26, 1984. The first sawmill within the boundaries of Wethersfield was operating by 1669. This mill was on the east side of the Connecticut River in what is today Glastonbury. The second, established on the west side of the river in Wethersfield proper, was authorized in 1677 and operating by 1680 at the latest. See Adams and Stiles, *History of Ancient Wethersfield*, 1:640–41.

15. Robert F. Trent, "Acquisitions," *Notes & News, The Connecticut Historical Society* 8, no. 4 (July-August 1983): 2–3. Patricia E. Kane, *Furniture of the New Haven Colony: The Seventeenth Century Style* (New Haven, Conn.: New Haven Colony Historical Society, 1973), fig. 5, pp. 18–19; Gerald W. R. Ward, *American Case Furniture in the Mabel Brady Garvan and Other Collections at Yale University* (New Haven, Conn.: Yale University Art Gallery, 1988), fig. 20, pp. 83, 84. For joined furniture that is probably related, see Kane, "The Joiners of Seventeenth Century Hartford County," p. 79, fig. 10; Wallace Nutting, *Furniture Treasury,* 3 vols. (1928–33; reprinted, New York: MacMillan, 1948–49), 1:fig. 7; Kirk, *Connecticut Furniture*, p. 7, figs. 9, 26. For the chest at Memorial Hall in Deerfield, see Dean A. Fales Jr., *The Furniture of Historic Deerfield* (New York: E. P. Dutton, 1976), p. 165, fig. 351. This chest was owned in

the Hoyt family of Deerfield, a family with Windsor, Connecticut, antecedents and no obvious New Haven connections. See George Sheldon, *A History of Deerfield, Massachusetts* (Deerfield: privately printed, 1895–96), 2:213–18. When discussing carving on the chest owned by Yale, Kane wrote, "The enrichment of the convex molding on the stiles and the lower rail of this chest with gouge carving, diagonal lines, and dots also suggest that it may have been made as early as 1640 when the Elizabethan tradition of carving was still strong" (Kane, *Furniture of the New Haven Colony*, p. 19). These same features are found on the Rocky Hill door.

16. Trent, "New England Joinery and Turning before 1700," pp. 501–4; and Robert F. Trent, "The Emery Attributions," *Essex Institute Historical Collections* 121, no. 3 (July 1985): 213–15.

17. The attribution of the "sunflower" chests to Blin is based on the linking of a chest that descended in the Bulkeley family to a 1681 entry in the Reverend Gershom Bulkeley's account book. Houghton Bulkeley, "A Discovery on the Connecticut Chest," *Connecticut Historical Society Bulletin* 23, no. 1 (January 1958): 17–19. Susan Schoelwer raises serious questions about several of the assumptions in Bulkeley's attribution of his family's chest to Blin. See Susan Prendergast Schoelwer, "Connecticut Sunflower Furniture: A Familiar Form Reconsidered," [Yale University Art Gallery] *Bulletin* (spring 1989): 27. Her essay contains the best informed and most thoughtful discussion of the group of "sunflower" chests and cupboards. For the association of Blin with carving from Huguenot or North Country sources, see Fairbanks and Trent, eds., *New England Begins*, 2:267; Ward and Hosley, eds., *The Great River*, pp. 187, 198–201; Ward, *American Case Furniture*, p. 93. Benno M. Forman first suggested that the flowers were marigolds and a Huguenot emblem based on evidence in Mrs. James M. Lawson, "The Emblematic Flower and Distinguishing Color of the Huguenots," *The Proceedings of the Huguenot Society of America* 2 (1891–1894): 237–45. Initially, I too believed that Blin was the bearer of a Huguenot or North Country carving tradition, but Schoelwer's article, Jane Blin's research, conversations with Neil Kamil, and my own research on John Nott have prompted me to reassess Blin's probable role in shaping the "sunflower" chests. Stiles claims that he was "of French (prob. Huguenot) origin" (Adams and Stiles, *History of Ancient Wethersfield*, 2:104). James Hill claims that Peter Blin was born in London around 1640, even though he could not find confirmation of this fact (James W. Hill, *Blin: A Short Genealogy of One Line of the Blin Family, Descended from Peter Blin, the Settler, of Wethersfield, Connecticut* [Peoria, Ill.: by the author, 1914], p. 3). Jane Blin's research suggests that Peter Blin may have been born in Leyden in 1639 to Huguenot parents who soon moved to London (Jane Blin, "Notes on Blin, Blynn, Blen, Blinn," [unpublished ms., Connecticut Historical Society, 1979], pp. 1, 3).

18. It has been variously estimated that from thirty to one-hundred chests and six to eight cupboards survive. See Kane, "The Joiners of Seventeenth Century Hartford County," p. 75; Ward, *American Case Furniture*, pp. 93, 382; Schoelwer, "Connecticut Sunflower Furniture," p. 34. On the motifs, see Kirk, "Sources of Some American Regional Furniture," pp. 790–95. For a discussion of the variation in carving, see Schoelwer "Connecticut Sunflower Furniture," p. 132. My examination of "sunflower" chests has led to similar conclusions. Foote Account Book, pp. 141, 145, 149, Wethersfield Historical Society.

19. Schoelwer, "Connecticut Sunflower Furniture," pp. 28–29. It is, however, unlikely that either man returned to Wethersfield before the November 1678 death of the Reverend Joseph Rowlandson, who died possessed of a cupboard in the "sunflower" style. It is the timing of the return of these woodworkers to Wethersfield, not just their dates of death, as Schoelwer suggests, that precludes the possibility that either man was the originator or sole producer of the chests and cupboards in this style. Dickinson returned to Wethersfield in 1679. Adams and Stiles, *History of Ancient Wethersfield,* 2:286. Lucius M. Boltwood in "Genealogies of Hadley Families" gives "about 1681" as the date of Foote's return to Wethersfield (Sylvester Judd, *History of Hadley* [Springfield, Mass.: H. R. Huntting & Company, 1905], p. 52). Schoelwer also makes this point in "Connecticut Sunflower Furniture," p. 29.

20. Kirk, "Sources of Some American Regional Furniture," pp. 790–95. See discussions in Fairbanks and Trent, eds., *New England Begins*, 2: 267; Ward, *American Case Furniture*, pp. 94–95. I am following James Deetz in his use of "archeological tradition" and "horizon in archaeology," though this essay's discussion of seventeenth-century Wethersfield material culture challenges his characterization of seventeenth-century New England material culture as "traditional" or "folk." See Deetz, *In Small Things Forgotten*, pp. 40–41.

21. On tradition and innovation, see Kenneth L. Ames, *Beyond Necessity, Art in the Folk Tradition* (New York: W. W. Norton for the Winterthur Museum, 1977), pp. 66–71, 76–78; Benno M. Forman, "The Chest of Drawers in America, 1635–1730: The Origins of the Joined

Chest of Drawers," *Winterthur Portfolio* 20, no. 1 (spring 1985): 1–2, 14–15; Kevin M. Sweeney, "Furniture and the Domestic Environment in Wethersfield, Connecticut, 1639–1800," in *Material Life in America. 1600–1860*, edited by Robert B. St. George (Boston: Northeastern University Press, 1988), pp. 268, 270. Ward indicates that forty-one of the chests have two drawers in *American Case Furniture*, p. 93. The estimate of the number of households in late-seventeenth-century Wethersfield is based on the 1670 Grain Census for Hartford, Wethersfield, and Windsor in the *Wyllis Papers Collections of the Connecticut Historical Society* 21 (Hartford, Conn.: Connecticut Historical Society, 1924): 197–99.

22. Sweeney, "Furniture and the Domestic Environment," pp. 266–76. For the development during this period of a similar pattern, see Robert B. St. George, "Fathers, Sons, and Identity: Woodworking Artisans in Southeastern New England, 1620–1700," in *The Craftsman in Early America*, edited by Ian M. G. Quimby (New York: W. W. Norton for the Winterthur Museum, 1984), pp. 112–13.

23. Evarts B. Greene and Virginia D. Harrington, *American Population Before the Federal Census of 1790* (New York: Columbia University Press, 1932), p. 58. Adams and Stiles, *History of Ancient Wethersfield*, 1:541, 545–46, 555–95; Bruce Daniels, *The Connecticut Town: Growth and Development, 1635–1790* (Middletown, Conn.: Wesleyan University Press, 1979), pp. 55–56, 140–41, 152–53, 194–95. Kevin M. Sweeney, "Using Tax Lists to Detect Biases in Probate Inventories," in *Early American Probate Inventories The Dublin Seminar for New England Folklife Annual Proceedings 1987*, edited by Peter Benes (Boston: Boston University, 1989), p. 38.

24. Adams and Stiles, *History of Ancient Wethersfield*, 2:134–35, 495, 500–501; "Connecticut Cabinetmakers Part II," *Connecticut Historical Society Bulletin* 33, no. 1 (January 1968): 2; J. Frederick Kelly, *Early Connecticut Meetinghouses,* 2 vols. (New York: Columbia University Press, 1948), 2:46. Ledger No. 5 Belonging to Elisha Williams & Co. [1738–1756], p. 69, Wethersfield Historical Society.

25. Kevin M. Sweeney, "Furniture and Furniture Making in Mid-Eighteenth-Century Wethersfield, Connecticut," *Antiques* 125, no. 5 (May 1984), pp. 1157–59. Kevin M. Sweeney, "Chairs and Chair Making in Early Wethersfield," in *"Please Be Seated,"* edited by Beth Ann Spyrison (Wethersfield, Conn.: Webb-Deane-Stevens Museum, 1993), p. 21. Quotation in Abbott L. Cummings, "Connecticut and Its Building Traditions," paper presented at the Association for the Study of Connecticut History Annual Meeting, "Reshaping Traditions: Native Americans and Europeans in Southern New England," November 7, 1992, p. 2.

26. Sweeney, "Chairs and Chair Making in Early Wethersfield," pp. 20–21; Sweeney, "Furniture and Furniture Making in Mid-Eighteenth-Century Wethersfield, Connecticut," pp. 1162–63. See crest rail on fig. 27 and stretchers on fig. 30 in Trent, *Hearts & Crowns,* pp. 56, 58; for a similar observation see Robert F. Trent and Nancy Lee Nelson, "New London County Joined Chairs 1720–1790" *The Connecticut Historical Society Bulletin* 50, no. 4 (fall 1985): 133. For a similar chair, see Trent, *Hearts and Crowns*, p. 51, fig. 21.

27. Kirk, *Connecticut Furniture*, pp. 110–11, nos. 192–95; fig. 13 resembles the york chairs pictured in Trent, *Hearts & Crowns*, pp. 67–68, figs. 41–42; for references to fiddleback chairs in Wethersfield, see Estate of Janna Deming, 1796, Hartford Probate District, file no. 1600, and Capt. Ashbel Riley, 1798, Hartford Probate District, file no. 4489, CSL.

28. Sweeney, "Furniture and Furniture Making in Mid-Eighteenth-Century Wethersfield, Connecticut," pp. 1161–62; Sweeney, "Chairs and Chair Making in Early Wethersfield," pp. 21–22; Patricia E. Kane, *300 Years of American Furniture* (Boston: New York Graphic Society, 1976), pp. 78–80; Trent and Nelson, "New London County Joined Chairs 1720–1790," pp. 39–51, 55–62, 87, 90–91, 106–8, nos. 1–10, 20–21, 29, 30.

29. Ledger No. 5 Belonging to Elisha Williams & Co. [1738–1756], pp. 42, 119. Adams and Stiles, *History of Ancient Wethersfield*, 2:114; Estate of Timothy Boardman, 1792, Middletown Probate District, file no. 447, CSL; the high chest resembles the Wethersfield high chest pictured in Sweeney, "Furniture and Furniture Making in Mid-Eighteenth-Century Wethersfield, Connecticut," pp. 1160–61, fig. 9. Sweeney, "Chairs and Chair Making in Early Wethersfield," p. 21.

30. Ledger No. 5 Belonging to Elisha Williams & Co. [1738–1756], pp. 42, 119. Kevin M. Sweeney, "Mansion People: Kinship, Class, and Architecture in Western Massachusetts in the Mid Eighteenth Century," *Winterthur Portfolio* 19, no. 4 (winter 1984): 239–43. Amelia F. Miller, "Connecticut River Valley Doorways: An Eighteenth-Century Flowering," in *The Bay and the River: 1600–1900. The Dublin Seminar for New England Folklife: Annual Proceedings 1981*, edited by Peter Benes (Boston: Boston University, 1982), pp. 70–72.

31. John R. Stilgoe, *Common Landscape of America 1580–1845* (New Haven, Conn.: Yale University Press, 1982), pp. 64–65, 188–90; Susan Allport, *Sermons in Stone: The Stone Walls of New England and New York* (New York: W. W. Norton, 1990), p. 37; Bernard L. Herman, *The Stolen House* (Charlottesville: University Press of Virginia, 1992), pp. 140–41. This is assumed in William Cronon, *Changes in the Land: Indians, Colonists, and the Ecology of New England* (New York: Hill and Wang, 1983), pp. 119–20. In the middle colonies and in the Shenandoah Valley of Virginia, worm fences replaced earlier post and rail fences. See Esther Louise Larsen, "Pehr Kalm's Observations on the Fences of North America," *Agricultural History* 21, no. 2 (April 1947): 76–77; Robert D. Mitchell, *Commercialism and Frontier: Perspectives on the Early Shenandoah Valley* (Charlottesville: University Press of Virginia, 1977), pp. 136–37.

32. Judd, *History of Hadley*, p. 432. Larsen, "Pehr Kalm's Observations on the Fences of North America," pp. 76–77; Henry Glassie, *Pattern in the Material Folk Culture of the Eastern United States* (Philadelphia: University of Pennsylvania Press, 1968), pp. 225–28.

33. Sweeney, "From Wilderness to Arcadian Vale," pp. 23–25; Kevin M. Sweeney, "Gentlemen Farmers and Inland Merchants: The Williams Family and Commercial Agriculture in Pre-Revolutionary Western Massachusetts," in *The Farm: The Dublin Seminar for New England Folklife Annual Proceedings 1986*, edited by Peter Benes (Boston: Boston University, 1988), pp. 62–64. In the Shenandoah Valley, the adoption of the worm fence in the last quarter of the eighteenth century was associated with improvements to farmsteads. See Mitchell, *Commercialism and Frontier*, pp. 136–37. Quotation in Deetz, *In Small Things Forgotten*, p. 38.

34. Peter Burke, *Popular Culture in Early Modern Europe* (New York: Harper & Row, Publishers, 1978), pp. 245–46. Scott Swank et al., *Arts of the Pennsylvania Germans* (New York: W. W. Norton for the Winterthur Museum, 1983), p. viii. At times even Howard Odum attacked the "fallacy which identifies regionalism with localism or with areal homogeneities due primarily to isolation, either in space through lack of communication and extra-regional relationships, or in time as in the case of primitive peoples." See Odum, "The American Blend: Regional Diversity and National Unity [1949]," in Jocher, et al., eds., *Folk, Region, and Society*, p. 197.

35. Deetz, *In Small Things Forgotten*, pp. 38, 40, 43, 59–60, 89–90. Burke, *Popular Culture in Early Modern Europe*, p. 257.

36. Florence H. Pettit, *America's Indigo Blues: Resist-printed and Dyed Textiles of the Eighteenth Century* (New York: Hastings House, 1974), pp. 170, 176, 178, 180.

37. For more along these points, see Swank et al., *Arts of the Pennsylvania Germans*, pp. vii–x, 3–34, 61–101.

38. Vance, "The Regional Concept as a Tool for Social Research," pp. 119–40. See also Odum, "The American Blend: Regional Diversity and National Unity [1949]," pp. 192–201.

Donna K. Baron

Definition and Diaspora of Regional Style: The Worcester County Model

▼ IF A REGION had a strong sense of cultural and economic identity and a large, well-established furniture-making tradition, does it necessarily follow that a distinctive regional furniture style evolved? Studies of Plymouth County, Massachusetts, the Connecticut River Valley, and eastern Connecticut, among others, tend to support this conclusion; however, a wide ranging analysis of evolving socioeconomic patterns in Worcester County, Massachusetts, suggests that this pattern did not always hold true. In certain cases, timing, demographics, and macro-economic forces may have impeded the development of an identifiable regional style.

Worcester County in Massachusetts lies between the eastern counties around Boston and the great Connecticut River Valley. Stretching from New Hampshire on the north to Connecticut and Rhode Island on the south, the region was first settled during the third quarter of the seventeenth century. Repeated Indian attacks prevented substantial settlement until nearly 1720, however.

Settlers came from both the east and west, claiming first the cleared Native American fields in the valleys and last the wooded highlands. Throughout the eighteenth century, the county's economy was based on agriculture and the local exchange of craft goods. In 1839, John Warner Barber wrote, "Till within a few years almost all the people were farmers, and the great body still cultivate the soil. For the last few years many of the inhabitants have been employed in manufactures."[1]

The change observed by Barber had been more profound than he realized. In 1790, Worcester County had forty-nine towns and 56,807 inhabitants, but the county was still largely wilderness. Most of the terrain was woodland; in 1781, tax assessors estimated that over three-quarters of it was "unimproved." Travelers passed through substantial forested stretches to find patches of land opened for tillage and pasture. Clear views and lines of sight between farmsteads were rare.[2]

Given the comparatively small population of the region and the resultant limited demand for many kinds of goods, most craftsmen farmed. Although some families existed on a subsistence level, others were more economically secure. Just prior to the American Revolution, a British traveler wrote that some families in the county "enjoy many of the necessaries of life upon their own farms. [They] yield food, much of cloathing, most of the articles of building, with a surplus sufficient to buy such foreign luxuries as are necessary to make life pass comfortably."[3]

Despite twentieth-century myths, New England farmers were never totally self-sufficient. Instead, they produced surplus commodities and exchanged them for goods and foodstuffs that could not be fabricated, grown, or produced at home. During the late-eighteenth century, farmers increasingly responded to enhanced market opportunities, producing larger surpluses and transporting them longer distances for exchange.[4]

Worcester County changed in profound ways in the sixty years following the American Revolution. Between 1790 and 1840, the population nearly doubled from 56,807 to 95,313. This increase meant that there were both more consumers and more producers. The period also witnessed "the increasingly thorough penetration of the marketplace, if not always the machine, into production and consumption."[5] The significance of this change is most apparent in the industrialization of textile manufacturing. Driven by the impetus for capital investment, English textile technology (already present in Rhode Island and eastern Massachusetts) found a home on the streams and rivers of towns in the southern part of the county. In other trades, as in farming, the impact of industrialization was less dramatic but of equal or greater economic and social importance.

The shoe-making, straw-braiding, printing, and furniture-making trades were broadly effected by newly organized systems of production, the use of a range of processes from factory to outwork, an extension of markets, improvements in transportation, an expanded use of cash, and a general increase in market orientation. In his study of broom making in Hadley, Massachusetts, Gregory Nobles referred to this phenomenon as "rural production for urban markets." Briefly stated, the process involved using locally available resources, like hides, straw, or wood, and comparatively inexpensive but often skilled rural labor to produce goods marketable in the cities.[6]

As the manufacture and distribution of shoes, braid, books, and chairs increased, Worcester County became more prosperous. New jobs in shops, mills, and homes provided an alternative to farming. With more jobs, families often had more income and, perhaps, more inclination to invest in household goods—a demand filled in part by locally manufactured products.

Probate inventories reveal a substantial increase in the number and variety of household goods owned by central Massachusetts residents. One study determined that in the 1790s there were an average of 10.9 chairs per probated household. By the 1830s this average increased to 20.6 chairs, and the numbers of tables and case pieces nearly doubled. In addition, washstands and other inexpensive furniture forms began appearing on inventories taken during the 1820s.[7]

The road system in Worcester County improved as a result of capital investment by manufacturers following the American Revolution. Roads were, however, only the first step in the creation of a new transportation system. The improved highways encouraged the establishment of regular stage service between communities and between the county and major urban areas. As increased production led to increased shipment, businessmen sought less expensive and more efficient alternatives to wagons. As a direct result of this need, the Blackstone Canal between Worcester and Providence opened in 1828 and the first railroad reached Worcester in 1837. Although relatively few county residents traveled on these new systems prior to 1850, the canal and railroad did transport goods into and from the region.[8]

Furniture was among those goods with a long history of production in the county. The earliest furniture makers were farmers and woodworkers who made tables and chairs, built houses and barns, made and repaired farm tools, and provided a variety of related services for their neighbors. Probate inventories and deeds document furniture makers in Worcester County by 1760. Since no pre-1790 business accounts or signed furniture are known and the first newspaper was not published in the county until 1775, deeds provide the best means of identifying furniture makers. In deeds recorded in 1760, the only term that clearly referred to a craftsman with the tools and expertise to make furniture was "shop joiner"; however, a "cooper," "wheelwright," "house joiner," or "husbandman" might also have been a furniture maker. To date, more than seventy furniture makers working in the eighteenth century have been identified. The itemized probate inventories of fifteen of these men strongly suggest that many early furniture makers were farmers and that some practiced two or more trades.[9]

Identifying the work of Worcester County furniture makers before 1790 has proven impossible, yet, sophisticated architectural woodwork from southern Worcester County confirms that some of these artisans were extremely proficient. In Sturbridge several houses contain extraordinary paneling, including built-in sets of drawers. The Shumway house (ca.

Figure 1 Chimney wall paneling and fireplace surround from the Shumway house, Sturbridge, Massachusetts, ca. 1780. (Courtesy, Museum of Fine Arts, Boston.)

Figure 2 Fireplace surround and corner cupboard in the Nathaniel Walker house, Sturbridge, Massachusetts, ca. 1765. (Courtesy, Old Sturbridge Village; photo, John O. Curtis.)

1780–1786) parlor has a set with flanking pilasters above the fireplace (fig. 1). This room was part of a two-story, center-chimney farmhouse in Fiskdale, part of Sturbridge. Although architectural sets of drawers were rare, elaborate, well-made paneling was relatively common even in unpretentious houses. The one-and-a-half story, gambrel-roof, Nathaniel Walker house

Figure 3 Side chair, possibly Worcester County, ca. 1770. Walnut with pine (slip seat). H. 37 3/4", W. 20 2/4", D. 17 3/8". (Courtesy, Old Sturbridge Village; photo, Henry E. Peach.) The side chair is from a set of six, all having original needlework seat covers.

(ca. 1760–1770) in Sturbridge had raised fielded panels, bolection molding, and a corner cupboard (fig. 2).[10] Any craftsman with the tools and skill to design, fabricate, and install the Shumway or Walker interiors also had the ability to make furniture.

Architectural details of this type can be firmly associated with their place of origin, but this identification is not necessarily true for the few known pieces of eighteenth-century furniture reportedly used in the county. The most important group consists of three case pieces and a set of chairs that descended in the John Chandler family of Woodstock,

Figure 4 Chest of drawers, possibly Worcester County, ca. 1760. Mahogany with unidentified secondary woods. H. 31", W. 36 1/4", D. 21 3/4". (Courtesy, Old Sturbridge Village; photo, Henry E. Peach.

Figure 5 Ladder-back armchair, possibly Worcester County, 1730–1780. Woods unidentified. H. 38 3/4", W. 23". (Courtesy, Old Sturbridge Village; photo, Henry E. Peach.) The rockers are nineteenth-century additions.

Connecticut, and Worcester and Lancaster, Massachusetts (figs. 3, 4). All are stylish and relate visually to forms made in eastern Massachusetts. Without documentation, it is impossible to determine whether they were purchased in the Boston area or made in Worcester County, perhaps by a Boston-trained cabinetmaker.[11]

Other than the Chandler group, only a few pieces of eighteenth-century furniture have Worcester County histories, and their date of arrival there is unknown. Perhaps the earliest is the turned slat-back armchair illustrated in figure 5. This example and a closely related side chair have recovery histories in the Charlton/Sturbridge area.[12] The massive posts and sausage-turned arm supports may indicate an early date and manufacture in eastern Massachusetts or may suggest, instead, retardetaire production by a woodworker or shop joiner in Worcester County. Also associated with the county are a pair of turned leg, "crooked-back" side chairs owned by the Chase fam-

Figure 6 Photograph showing the Chase family of Southbridge, Massachusetts, on their front lawn with a pair of crooked-back side chairs dating 1740–1760. (Courtesy, Old Sturbridge Village.)

ily of Sturbridge and Southbridge. A photograph taken about 1900 shows these chairs on the front lawn of the Chase homestead (fig. 6).

With so few and such disparate pieces to study, it is difficult to draw any conclusions about an evolving Worcester County style before 1800. The lack of evidence leads to the inevitable question—Why is there so little furniture? Survival is certainly one factor, both of furniture and of information. During the nineteenth and early-twentieth centuries, many local families left the county, and in the process some possessions were sold and family associations were lost. Other pieces were carried west or to cities where, over the generations, traditions about where or for whom they were made were forgotten.

More importantly, the level of patronage in Worcester County during the eighteenth century may have been insufficient for the development of a distinctive regional style. Most residents were middle-class farmers whose houses were modestly furnished. In Sturbridge inventories, the first clock, dressing table, desk-and-bookcase, and high case of drawers do not appear until after 1800.[13] Only the most affluent householders, who were members of the local social and political elite, had large sets of chairs, several cases of drawers, or expensive desks. These were the same people who traveled to Boston regularly on business or to serve in the legislature and who had strong family ties to eastern Massachusetts. Consequently, they were more likely than other Worcester County residents to purchase furniture in Boston or to commission Boston-style furniture from local craftsmen.

The possibility that there was little demand for stylish furniture that looked "local" cannot be discounted. New England regional styles tended to evolve in areas where a sizable group of affluent customers encouraged cabinetmakers to explore distinctive design concepts. During the eighteenth century, Worcester County had only a small affluent class that was culturally and socially linked to Boston. Although there were furniture makers of considerable skill in the county, without patronage a distinctive and recognizable regional style could not evolve.

Following the Revolution, the nature of patronage in Worcester County began to change. As the population grew and became more prosperous during the 1790s and early 1800s, the demand for furniture increased. Gradually, cabinetmakers and chairmakers who limited themselves to furniture production replaced furniture-making woodworkers and shop joiners.[14] By 1790 both cabinetmakers and chairmakers worked in some communities, although some furniture-making woodworkers remained in the trade for almost another thirty years.

The first full-time cabinetmakers in Worcester County were either general woodworkers who narrowed their business efforts to concentrate on furniture making or were apprenticed cabinetmakers who never practiced a secondary trade. Some of the latter, particularly those who lived in other counties until they were of marriageable age, undoubtedly served apprenticeships outside Worcester County. During the 1790s, most Worcester County cabinetmakers were not born in the town where they set up their businesses, but were married in that town within a few years of acquiring

Figure 7 Swelled-front bureau signed and dated "Alden Spooner Athol 1807." Cherry and ash with unidentified conifer. H. 35½", W. 39½", D. 21¼". (Courtesy, Old Sturbridge Village; photo, Henry E. Peach.)

Figure 8 Swelled-front bureau signed "Spooner & Fitts Athol," 1808–1813. Cherry and maple veneer with unidentified conifer. H. 42¾", W. 44¾", D. 23⅛". (Courtesy, Old Sturbridge Village; photo, Henry E. Peach.)

property. Evidence also suggests that cabinetmakers were moving into the region from eastern Massachusetts from the end of the American Revolution until around 1800. Prior to 1790, only a few cabinetmakers can be firmly identified as Worcester County natives.[15]

The impact of these demographic and economic forces is manifest in documented Worcester County furniture from the first half of the nineteenth century. Even for this period, there are only about fifty pieces of cabinet shop furniture (as opposed to joiner's work) and one-hundred examples of chair shop seating known. The earliest dated piece of Worcester County furniture is a tall clock case made in 1795 by Elisha Harrington (1760–1817) of Spencer, Massachusetts. It has an eight-day brass movement and is surprisingly sophisticated, with elegant bracket feet and complex inlay. The case design is related to many Roxbury, Massachusetts, examples, particularly those housing Willard-type clocks; however, Harrington was a county-born craftsman about whose training nothing is known.[16]

Artisans in other communities produced comparable work at about the same time. Alden Spooner (1784–1877) was born in Petersham and worked for more than forty years in Athol. His earliest known piece is a fashionable "swelled-front bureau," signed and dated 1807 (fig. 7). Only Spooner's use of native primary woods and several distinctive construction techniques differentiate this bureau from those made in eastern Massachusetts. A second case of drawers made during his partnership with George Fitts is even more like Boston and North Shore examples (fig. 8).[17]

Other Worcester County furniture made in emulation of Boston styles includes a desk labeled by Ezekiel Brigham of Grafton in 1812 (fig. 9), a card

Figure 9 Desk by Ezekiel Brigham, Grafton, Massachusetts, ca. 1812. Mahogany and mahogany veneer with unidentified conifer. H. 44¼", W. 41", D. 17⅝". (Courtesy, Old Sturbridge Village; photo, Thomas Neill.)

Figure 10 Swelled-front bureau by George W. Holmes, Sturbridge, Massachusetts, 1820-1830. Cherry with unidentified conifer. H. 42⅜", W. 42¾", D. 21⅜". (Courtesy, Old Sturbridge Village; photo, Thomas Neill.)

table made in the same town by Jonathan Fairbanks, and a group of three swelled-front bureaus from the Sturbridge area, one of which is signed "George W. Holmes/Sturbridge, MA" (fig. 10). Each is well designed and competently made—in the words of Ezekiel Brigham's label, "cabinet work of a middling good workman."[18] As with the earlier period, however, this furniture is too scarce and too widely scattered to draw conclusions about more than a single shop. Even Alden Spooner's hand is hard to trace, although in recent years furniture attributed to "Spooner and Fitch" has been advertised in auctions from Maine to Maryland.

There is little to differentiate this body of furniture from that made in parts of Middlesex and Essex Counties. After mahogany became widely available in rural areas, the best Worcester County furniture resembled middling Boston furniture; however, much locally made furniture was not nearly as stylish. Common furniture was rarely signed or labeled, but it appears in quantity in makers' account books. Light stands for $1, common bedsteads for $3, "kitching" tables for $3—this was the furniture with which most county residents filled their homes.

Furniture found in the Emerson Bixby house in Barre Four Corners is undistinguished but typical (figs. 11–13). A blue-painted, common bedstead may be the one Bixby purchased from Barre cabinetmaker Luke Houghton, who recorded the transaction in his account book (fig. 11). The other Bixby pieces, although undoubtedly of local origin, are unattributable.[19] Furniture similar to this is still found in farmhouses and local auctions in southern Vermont and New Hampshire, parts of New York State, central and western Massachusetts, and rural Connecticut and Rhode Island. It was utilitarian and made without reference to changing styles.

Distinctive regional characteristics become more obscure in furniture made after 1820. From 1820 to 1845, newspaper advertisements and cabinetmakers' accounts increasingly refer to Grecian card tables, Grecian work stands, Grecian chairs, and Grecian sofas, as well as to French bureaus and French bedsteads (fig. 14). The widespread and frequent use of "Grecian" and "French" as advertising catch-phrases suggests that there was a market for sophisticated cosmopolitan goods.[20] Customers wanted what was fashionable, and cabinetmakers accommodated them by adopting these styles, or at least their names, while continuing to make common bedsteads, three- and four-foot tables, chests with two drawers, and other traditional utilitarian forms.

The burgeoning demand for "exotic" styles was especially apparent in the newly emerging trade of chairmaking. Between 1790 and 1850, more than 1,200 men and unknown numbers of women and boys worked in the furniture trade, including about 400 cabinetmakers, 36 furniture retailers, and nearly 800 workers involved in some aspect of the chairmaking business. Although there are no production figures available for cabinet furniture, the numbers for chairs are staggering. In 1820, 70,000 chairs were manufactured annually in the town of Sterling alone. By 1850, six towns in the northern part of the county had an annual chair production of more than 800,000.[21]

Figure 11 Bedstead, probably Barre, Massachusetts, ca. 1830. Maple and pine; original blue-green paint. H. 31½", L. 74¾", W. 51¾". (Courtesy, Old Sturbridge Village; photo, Henry E. Peach.)

Figure 12 Ladder-back chair, probably Barre, Massachusetts, 1800–1840. Woods unidentified. H. 41¾", W. 17¾", D. 13⅝". (Courtesy, Old Sturbridge Village; photo, Henry E. Peach.) The chair is from a set of six.

Figure 13 Chest, probably Barre, Massachusetts, 1810–1840. Pine; original painted decoration. H. 18", W. 43⅞", D. 18". (Courtesy, Old Sturbridge Village; photo, Henry E. Peach.)

Figure 14 Advertisement published in the 1844 *Worcester Almanac, Directory & Business Advertiser* by Lansford Wood, a cabinetmaker and furniture wareroom operator. (Courtesy, Old Sturbridge Village; photo, Thomas Neill.)

Specialized chairmaking was, of course, neither invented in nor unique to Worcester County. During the seventeenth century, Boston chairmakers produced multiple parts and assembled them in a systematic manner, maintained a stock-in-trade, and engaged in speculative ventures with merchants, upholsterers, ship captains, and others involved in the export trade.[22] In Worcester County, specialization first emerged during the late

Figure 15 Common chair by Joel Pratt Jr., Sterling, Massachusetts, 1820–1840. Pine (seat) and unidentified hardwoods. H. 32½", W. 16", D. 15⅞". (Courtesy, Old Sturbridge Village; photo, Thomas Neill.) The chair is from a set of six.

1790s when at least six men identified themselves as chairmakers, two specifically as Windsor chairmakers. By 1815, Worcester County chairmakers had advanced specialization further than any of their predecessors and earlier than their best-known Connecticut competitor.

Two models of production emerged. The first developed in Sterling and comprised geographically dispersed turning shops, which were often water powered and associated with sawmills. The turned "stuff" was sold to "chairmakers," who organized the assembly, painting, and distribution. Shops rarely had more than a half dozen hands. A second system, which more closely resembled the familiar Hitchcock model, emerged during the mid-1830s in Gardner and surrounding towns. Work was increasingly centralized; large shops employed turners, assemblers, and painters.[23]

Two basic types of chairs were produced in both kinds of shops. "Common" chairs had sawn plank seats with turned pillars (back posts), legs, stretchers, and rods (back spindles) and sawn backs (fig. 15).

Figure 16 Fancy chair, Worcester County, Massachusetts, 1830–1850. Flag (seat) and unidentified hardwoods. H. 33 1/4", W. 17 3/8", D. 14 7/8". (Courtesy, Old Sturbridge Village; photo, Jan Stittleburg.) Worcester County chairmakers probably referred to such chairs as "screwed back." This example descended in an Auburn (Ward), Massachusetts, family.

Depending on the specific style, such chairs retailed for $1 to $1.25. "Fancy" chairs had woven flag or cane, seats with turned legs, posts, stretchers, and, sometimes, backs (fig. 16). Ranging in price from $2 to $2.50 each, they cost twice as much as common chairs. In addition, many shops also made related rocking chairs (fig. 17), night chairs, and settees (fig. 18).[24]

Population figures indicate that the 70,000 chairs produced in Sterling in 1820 were not intended for local consumption. The market was farther afield. Although the developing commercial and mill communities of the county probably provided the first market, Boston, Salem, and Providence soon became more important. By 1830, few local cabinetmakers still turned chairs because it was cheaper and more efficient to buy them wholesale.

Chair racks (wagons) carrying about 200 chairs each were traveling overland to Boston, while manufacturers shipped thousands of chairs down the Blackstone Canal from Worcester to Providence. Others were shipped to Hartford for sale. During the mid-1830s, wareroom operator Isaac Wright

Figure 17 Common rocking chair by Levi Pratt of Fitchburg, Massachusetts, 1830–1840. Pine (seat) and unidentified hardwoods. H. 31", W. 17¼", D. 24¼". (Courtesy, Old Sturbridge Village; photo, Thomas Neill.)

Figure 18 Settee by Charles Webster Bush, Gardner, Massachusetts, 1835–1845. Pine (seat) and unidentified hardwoods. H. 34", W. 83", D. 15". (Courtesy, Old Sturbridge Village; photo, Thomas Neill.) This settee is the earliest known example of labeled Gardner seating furniture.

Figure 19 "Common" chair by John David Pratt, Lunenburg, Massachusetts, 1825–1840. White pine (seat) and unidentified hardwoods; original yellow paint and stenciled decoration. H. 34 13/16", W. 17 1/4", D. 15 7/8". (Courtesy, Old Sturbridge Village; photo, Thomas Neill.) The chair is from a set of four.

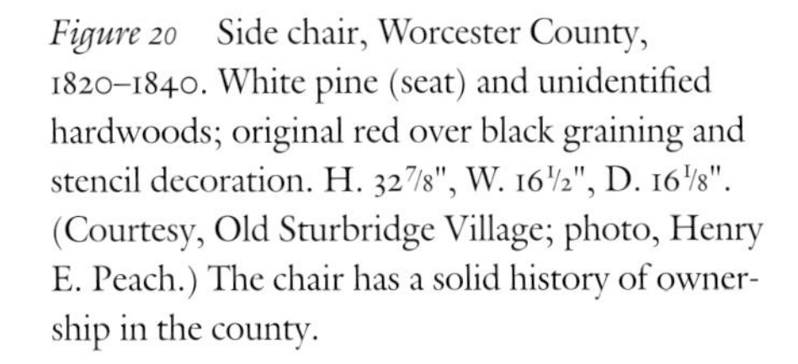

Figure 20 Side chair, Worcester County, 1820–1840. White pine (seat) and unidentified hardwoods; original red over black graining and stencil decoration. H. 32 7/8", W. 16 1/2", D. 16 1/8". (Courtesy, Old Sturbridge Village; photo, Henry E. Peach.) The chair has a solid history of ownership in the county.

purchased common chairs from Sullivan Hill of Spencer, Massachusetts, among others. In 1840, Joel Pratt Jr. of Sterling opened his own chair store in Hartford.[25]

From New England ports, merchants distributed these chairs around the world. An 1827 report cites the southern states and the West Indies as destinations, and shipping records suggest that some went to Africa and the East Indies; furthermore, a newspaper editorial accused chairmakers of denuding the county's forests to send chairs to England and Europe.[26]

Even in the nineteenth century, it may have been difficult to identify these chairs as having been made in Worcester County. Few chairmakers labeled their products, and those who did rarely included a place name. Also, many chairs were sold unpainted or even as unassembled "chair stuff." Chairs decorated in Worcester County show a limited palette and stencil repertoire

Figure 21 Fancy chair, possibly Worcester County, 1830–1840. Woods unidentified. H. 33½", W. 17½", D. 16". (Courtesy, Western Reserve Historical Society.)

(figs. 19, 20); however, these same characteristics probably do not hold true for those chairs decorated elsewhere.

One example may be a fancy chair signed "S. Kendall" on the rear seat cover strip (fig. 21). Since the signature is hand painted in script, not stenciled, it appears to be that of the painter, possibly Samuel Kendall. Kendall and his brother, Ezekiel, moved from Sterling to Boston when they were twenty-nine and thirty-one years old. They left behind two brothers, a brother-in-law, and a least three cousins who were chairmakers. These family ties and Samuel and Ezekiel's frequent periods of residency in Sterling between years in Boston raise the possibility that they imported chairs from Worcester County then painted and sold them in Boston.[27]

Two chairs at the Rhode Island Historical Society may also represent this practice. They are signed by their decorator, Christian M. Nestell, who trained in New York City. Although the chair frames resemble some with Worcester County makers' labels, the decoration is very different. It is possible that Nestell, who worked in Providence from 1824 to 1836, bought chairs shipped down the Blackstone Canal to Rhode Island.[28]

The chairmaking network was often rather complex and far flung. Jacob Felton (b. 1787) was a Fitzwilliam, New Hampshire, chairmaker who bought parts from at least four Sterling chairmakers—Edward Burpee, Thomas Baker, Thomas Lewis, and John Lynds—and a Mr. White in Gardner. Edward Burpee had apprenticed with Joel Pratt Jr. in Sterling who, in turn, purchased chair seats from Rial Haywood of Fitzwilliam. Felton's trade network for selling his chairs extended even further. Two of his primary customers were George S. Miller of Boston and Anthony VanDoorn of Brattleboro, Vermont.[29]

Worcester County chairmakers were dependent on distant markets, and they tailored their products accordingly. Elbridge Gerry Reed, a Sterling turner and assembler, frequently recorded making "Balti" or Baltimore chairs. In 1828, Henry Miller, owner of the Worcester Chair Factory, had an agent in New York City send him chairs specifically so patterns could be taken.[30]

In addition to exports, migrating artisans contributed to the dissemination of Worcester County chair styles. Beginning in the late eighteenth century, craftsmen left the county for Boston, New Hampshire, Maine, Pennsylvania, and Ohio. Signed pieces made in these areas by transplanted chairmakers are similar to those made in Worcester County. In some cases, the emigrant chairmakers clearly maintained craft links with their hometowns.

The precise number of craftsmen who relocated remains unclear, but the examples discovered thus far suggest that Worcester County had a substantial indirect impact on chairmaking and related trades in several areas. Given the well-established economic links between Worcester County and Boston, that city was a logical choice for both urban distribution facilities and chairmakers looking for greater commercial opportunities. Even nineteenth-century observers noted that it was less expensive to make chair parts in the country where wood and labor were cheap and water power abundant.[31] Comparison of lists of Boston and Worcester County chairmakers and Boston city directories reveal a number of overlapping family names.

Published histories of Gardner, Massachusetts maintained that the Heywood brothers built chairs in Gardner and sold them in Boston. Recent research has confirmed that brothers Levi and Benjamin Heywood were in Boston during the late 1830s and early 1840s, probably retailing the chairs made by their brothers Seth and Walter in Gardner, although the brothers seem to have moved back and forth between the cities quite regularly.[32] Other, as yet unconfirmed, connections include the May, Bush, Gates, Holden, Willard, Pierce, and Whitney families. In each case there are many Worcester County chairmakers of that name and a few Boston chairmakers or chair dealers.

For other regions, the Worcester County connections are much less speculative than for Boston. Peter Wilder (1761–1843) was twenty years old when

Figure 22 Scrolled-arm rocking chair by Abijah Wetherbee, New Ipswich, New Hampshire, 1815–1840. Pine (seat) and unidentified hardwoods. H. 43½", W. 23⅛", D. 22¼". (Courtesy, New Hampshire Historical Society.)

he left Lancaster, Massachusetts, for Keene, New Hampshire. Following brief sojourns in Brattleborough, Vermont, and Boston, he moved to New Ipswich, New Hampshire. He established a chair "factory" there around 1808 with his son-in-law, Abijah Wetherbee. Abijah was a native of Lunenburg, Massachusetts, and a rocking chair bearing his label looks remarkably like one labeled "John D. Pratt/Lunenburg" (fig. 22).[33] The late Charles Parsons located many labeled Wilder chairs, several of which resemble documented Sterling chairs. This is, perhaps, no coincidence. Sterling separated from Lancaster in 1781, and the Wilder property included land in the new town. Having arrived in southern New Hampshire, Peter Wilder and his sons and son-in-law were central figures in the development of the chairmaking industry in that region.

Figure 23 Scrolled-arm rocking chair by John Bradley Hudson and John Loring Brooks, Portland, Maine, 1815–1823. Pine, maple, and mahogany. H. 45", W. 20¾", D. 27". (Courtesy, Metropolitan Museum of Art, gift of Mr. and Mrs. Arnold Skromme.)

Another regional chair industry developed in Maine. Of the 673 individuals working in the Maine furniture-making industry in 1850 (including sixty-six chairmakers), eighty-one—sixty-six cabinetmakers, seven chairmakers, and five turners—were born in Massachusetts.[34] Only a few have been fully traced, but a connection to the Worcester County chairmaking business is clear.

John Loring Brooks (b. 1793), the son of Sterling chairmaker Ammi Brooks (1765–1815), worked as a chairmaker in Portland, Maine, by 1815. Before 1823 he worked in partnership with another Massachusetts born chairmaker, John Bradley Hudson (fig. 23). Sterling, Massachusetts, native Samuel Kilburn White (1798–1849) worked in Maine by 1820 (fig. 24). Both he and Brooks moved when in their early twenties, presumably after com-

Figure 24 Common chair by Samuel Kilburn White, Fairfield or Dexter, Maine, ca. 1836–1840. Probably basswood (seat) and birch. H. 33", W. 17", D. 18½". (Courtesy, Maine State Museum.)

pleting their apprenticeships. Maine probably afforded greater opportunities and less competition for chairmakers than Worcester County.[35]

Ashburnham natives Jonathan O. Bancroft (1806–1866) and Walter Corey were two of the most successful Maine chairmakers. When Bancroft's Ashburnham chair factory burned in 1832, he sold chairs in Boston for a short time. In 1836 he joined his brother-in-law, Walter Corey (1809–1891), who had recently moved to Portland, Maine. Within a few years they were operating a wareroom, a horse-powered chair factory, and a water-powered saw, planing, and turning mill. Few of the 20,000 chairs they produced annually survive, but some fit the description "common turned back" and "common screwed back" found in the account of chairmaker Elbridge Gerry Reed (fig. 25).[36]

Figure 25 Common chair attributed to Walter Corey, Portland, Maine, 1830–1840. White pine (seat) and unidentified hardwoods. H. 32 7/8", W. 15 3/4", D. 15 1/4". (Courtesy, Old Sturbridge Village; photo, Henry E. Peach.)

Worcester County chairmakers sought economic opportunity even further away than New Hampshire and Maine. In the early 1820s, Abel Rice of Hubbardston, Massachusetts, moved to Susquehanna County, Pennsylvania, with the families of his adult sons—chairmakers Amos Jones, Abel, and Daniel. His daughter, Betsy, her husband, chairmaker James Greenwood, and Daniel Rice's brother-in-law, Harry Roper, also moved. The Rice brothers opened a chairmaking business in Harford, Pennsylvania. Their nephew, Aaron Willard Greenwood, worked in their shop for several years before establishing his own chair factory. Meanwhile, Harry Roper moved on to Brooklyn, Pennsylvania, where he ran a chair shop. Apparently, the family maintained contact with chairmaking relatives in Worcester County. According to the 1850 census, a Joseph Greenwood from Massachusetts—probably cousin Joseph Willard Greenwood of Hubbardston—worked for A. W. Greenwood. The only known labeled chair from the group of chairmakers resembles those made in a South Gardner, Massachusetts, factory owned by another branch of the Greenwood family.[37]

Recently published studies show that Pennsylvania chairmakers were central to the development of the Ohio chair industry in the 1830s and 1840s. Since Worcester County chairmakers moved to both states, both direct and indirect influences seem probable. Stephen Kilburn (1786–1867) was born in Sterling, Massachusetts. By 1820 he moved to nearby Templeton where he was a "fancy chairmaker," producing 12,000 chairs annually using "peculiar water privileges" (fig. 26). Between 1823 and 1825, Kilburn moved to Adams, New York and by 1840 he had relocated to New London, Ohio. Tradition suggests that he made chairs in New York State, but his Ohio chairmaking business is well documented. Jane and Edward Hageman's description of surviving Stephen Kilburn chairs in *Ohio Furniture Makers, 1790–1860*, could easily apply to labeled Sterling chairs: "They have four spindles between the uprights in the back with pronounced bamboo style turnings. The large saddle seat has an incised line around the edge. The cross piece at the top is attached with wood pegs. The legs taper at the bottom."[38]

Further research may reveal other examples of where and how Worcester County chairmakers and their designs spread throughout the northern

Figure 26 Side chair by Stephen Kilburn, probably Sterling or Templeton, Massachusetts, 1820–1825. Materials and dimensions not recorded. (Courtesy, Historic Deerfield; photo, Jennifer Mange.)

United States; nevertheless, the pattern is clear. Chairs once possibly unique to central Massachusetts were being made in many places by the mid-nineteenth century. If there were Worcester County–style chairs, they became American-style chairs.

As a result of the economic boom following the Revolutionary War, Worcester County had a sizable and growing affluent class and an increasing demand for stylish furniture by 1800. Forty years earlier, these factors might have led to the development of a distinctive regional style; however, the intervention of external market forces prevented that from happening. Between 1785 and 1800 there was a substantial influx of cabinetmakers from eastern Massachusetts—men who were familiar with Boston-area styles and construction technologies. At the same time, the county's economy was gradually shifting from production for local consumption to manufacture for urban markets. Finally, by 1820 furniture making changed as a result of the almost simultaneous popularization of late neoclassical style and the advent of new technologies and tools such as water-powered lathes and veneer saws. As furniture makers responded to this succession of changes, Worcester County lost its opportunity to develop a regional style.

Although some traditional cabinetmakers continued to work after 1850, the craft was dying. Organizational and marketing skills became increasingly more important than craft skills, yet, as the craft faded, the industry flourished. By 1840 furniture warerooms replaced cabinetshops as the place where most county residents, like their urban and East Coast counterparts, bought furniture. Unseen anonymous craftsmen who had little or no contact with the customers produced most of the ready-made furniture sold in warerooms. Traditional cabinetmakers who survived this change did so in part by accommodating their customers' desire for instant gratification. They offered ready-made furniture as well as bespoke furniture and repair services.

Within the specialized trade of chairmaking, increased standardization and ever-growing markets fueled the demand for chairs. The result was greatly increased investment and productivity. By 1850 Worcester County chairmakers produced more than 800,000 chairs annually and shipped them all over the world.

Why did all this happen in Worcester County? Other areas had skilled craftsmen, adequate sources of lumber, water power, good transportation systems, and economies based on the production of goods for urban markets. There is no simple answer to this question. In Worcester County all these factors were present in abundance. The overall economy expanded at just the right time to encourage extensive exploitation of labor, material, power, transportation, and markets. With capital and infrastructure in place, the industry was so solidly established that, despite temporary setbacks, the subsequent need to import wood, the costs of converting from water power to steam and then to electricity, and increased labor costs did not really hurt the business until after the Second World War. Worcester County furniture making, then, is a case study in the making of a new American economic and material world. Local distinctiveness, connectiveness, and traditional skills were lost, but the benefits were material abundance, choice, and variety for most county residents and substantial wealth for some.

1. Unless otherwise noted all newspapers, deeds, probate inventories, and federal censuses cited are on microfilm in the Research Library of Old Sturbridge Village (hereafter cited OSV). John Warner Barber, *Massachusetts Historical Collections* (Worcester, Mass.: Dorr, Howland & Co., 1839), p. 550.

2. Jack Larkin, "From 'Country Mediocrity' to 'Rural Improvement': Transforming the Slovenly Countryside in Central Massachusetts, 1775–1840," in *Everyday Life in the Early Republic*, edited by Catherine E. Hutchins (Charlottesville, Va.: University of Virginia Press for the Winterthur Museum, 1992).

3. *American Husbandry*, 2 vols. (London: printed for J. Bew, 1775), 1:50, as quoted in Andrew H. Baker and Holly V. Izard, "New England Farmers and the Marketplace, 1780–1865: A Case Study," *Agricultural History* 65, no. 3 (summer 1991): 91–92.

4. See Baker and Izard, "New England Farmers and the Marketplace"; Robert A. Gross, "Culture and Cultivation: Agriculture and Society in Thoreau's Concord," *Journal of American History* 69, no. 1 (June 1982): 42–61; and Jack Larkin, "Massachusetts Enters the Marketplace 1790–1860," in *A Guide to the History of Massachusetts,* edited by Martin Kaufman, John W. Kaufman, and Joseph Carvalho III (New York: Greenwood Press, 1988), pp. 69–82.

5. "Population Tables—Worcester County," in *The Gazetteer of Massachusetts* (Boston: John Hayward, 1846), pp. 322–30. Larkin, "Massachusetts Enters the Marketplace," p. 70.

6. See Blanche Evan Hazard, *The Organization of the Boot and Shoe Industry in Massachusetts Before 1875* (New York: A. M. Kelly, 1969); Jack Larkin, "The Merriams of Brookfield: Printing in the Economy and Culture of Rural Massachusetts in the Early Nineteenth Century," *Proceedings of the American Antiquarian Society* 96 (April 1986): part 1, pp. 39–74; Mark Sipson, "An Introduction to Leather Processing and Shoemaking," unpublished paper, ca. 1979, OSV; and Caroline Sloat, "A Great Help to Many Families: Straw Braiding in Massachusetts Before 1825," in *House and Home*, edited by Peter Benes (Dublin, N.H.: Dublin Seminar for New England Folklife, 1988), pp. 89–100. Gregory Nobles, "Rural Manufacture and Urban Markets: A Case Study of Broom-making in Nineteenth Century Massachusetts" (paper presented at the annual meeting of the Organization of American Historians, Cincinnati, 1983), as cited in Larkin, "The Merriams of Brookfield."

7. These figures, provided by Jack Larkin, are based on an analysis of probate inventories undertaken by OSV (see Probate Inventories for the towns of Brimfield, Palmer, Chester, Sturbridge, Shrewsbury, and Barre, Massachusetts, 1790–1850, and Probate Inventory Sample of Worcester County Farmers, Mechanics, and Merchants 1790–1850, transcripts and analyses at the Department of Research, Collections, and Library [hereafter cited DRCL], OSV). For a more detailed discussion of this data, see Larkin, "Transforming the Slovenly Countryside."

8. For assistance and advice, regarding this introductory text, the author thanks Jack Larkin, Myron Stachiw, Frank White, and Karen Blanchfield.

9. Shop joiner Nathaniel Wyman married in Lancaster in 1742, and shop joiner Stephen Jewit married in Oxford in 1757 (*Oxford Vital Records* [Worcester, Mass.: Franklin P. Rice, 1907], p. 187). Information on occupations is taken from Worcester County deeds 1790–1799 and 1825–1830 (compiled by David Proulx), data base in DRCL, OSV. The estates of Asa Stearns (Hardwick, 1795, 26:247) and David Hosley (Lancaster, 1802, 32:475) included agricultural equipment, livestock, and woodworking tools. The inventories of other woodworkers, including Joseph Carpenter (Uxbridge, 1813, 257:297), John Hills (Leominster, 1784, 20:376), and Joshua Wetherel (Dudley, 1802, 31:43), listed farming tools but not woodworking tools; however, all these men identified themselves as furniture makers in deeds. Jeremiah Reed (New Braintree, 1803, 31:520) and Nathaniel Wyman (Lancaster, 1801, 30:503) had woodworking tools but no farm-related implements listed in their probate inventories. The aforementioned David Hosley was a wheelwright and housewright as well as a furniture maker (32:475), whereas Ezra Kendall (Sterling, 1828, 67:272) owned cooper's, wheelwright's, blacksmith's, and shop joiner's tools. The author thanks Holly Izard and Frank White for assisting with sample studies of earlier deeds.

10. Although the Walker house was destroyed and the Shumway woodwork has been moved, a related interior is in situ in nearby Woodstock, Connecticut, which was once part of Worcester County. A chamber of the Chandler house (ca. 1770–1780) in South Woodstock has the facade of a high case of drawers complete with cabriole legs on a plastered wall.

11. A high case of drawers and dressing table were acquired by Nina Fletcher Little from a Chandler descendant in the mid-1950s (Nina Fletcher Little, *Little by Little* [New York: E. P. Dutton, 1984], pp. 200–1). At the same time, Mrs. Little arranged for OSV to acquire a four-drawer chest and set of chairs with original Irish stitch embroidered seats. The furniture belonged to the Hon. John Chandler (1720–1800), judge of probate and Loyalist, whose estate was confiscated in 1779 when he fled to England. His heirs retained or recovered various pieces, which remained in Petersham and South Lancaster until 1956. The Chandler family pieces from the Little Collection were sold at The Bertram K. Little and Nina Fletcher Little Collection, Part 1 (Sale 6526), Sotheby's, New York, January 1994, lots 428–31.

12. The armchair (OSV 5.2.113) was purchased from the estate of a local family. The side chair (private collection) was purchased from a picker who reportedly got it at an old farm in Charlton.

13. The author thanks Holly Izard who is transcribing and analyzing all itemized probate inventories of Sturbridge residents from 1740 to 1850.

14. Between 1790 and 1799, craftsmen used the terms "shop joiner," "winsor chair maker," and "cabinetmaker" to identify themselves.

15. Of the thirty-nine men who listed themselves as cabinetmakers in deeds during the 1790s, thirty-five were not born in the town where they bought land. Most were recently married or married within a few years of their arrival in town, suggesting an influx of mature, young craftsmen. Only seven of the thirty-five can be definitively traced to other locations prior to their 1790s deeds. Nathan Bangs moved from Leverett to Barre; David Wight Sr. moved from Medway to Sturbridge; brothers Isaac and Jacob Fisher moved from the Wrentham area to the Lancaster area; Elijah Stone Jr. moved from Framingham to Rutland and Barre; and brothers Jonathan and John Tower moved from Sudbury to Rutland. The earlier Worcester County–born cabinetmakers include: Isaac Johnson (1742–1779); Elisha Harrington (1760–1817) of Brookfield; Sewall Hall (b. 1767) and Justus Warner (b. 1768) of New Braintree; and Amasa Holden (b. 1773) of Shrewsbury. In addition, Oliver Wight (b. 1765) of Sturbridge (born in Medway but moved to Sturbridge at age nine) and Nathaniel Wyman (b. 1746) of Lancaster identified themselves as shop joiners and presumably trained with their fathers who were also shop joiners.

16. This clock is illustrated in Skinner's Americana Catalogue, Bolton, Massachusetts, January 16, 1993, lot 132. Elisha Harrington was born in Brookfield in 1760 and married in that town in 1785. By 1792 (the birthdate of his second child), he was a resident of Spencer. He described himself as a cabinetmaker in both Brookfield and Spencer deeds, but by 1807 he referred to himself as a "gentleman." His probate inventory includes a work bench, seven planes, one draw shave, an old saw, and fifty feet of maple boards. The significance of the "No 64" that appears on the handwritten label is not clear.

17. Both cases are cherry and cherry veneer rather than mahogany, and the cross-banding on the 1807 chest appears to be ash—an unlikely inlay wood for eastern Massachusetts. The later chest has mahogany banding and what is probably purchased stringing. Atypical construction details include glue blocks on the drawer bottoms, exaggerated bracing of the French feet, and crudely inlet inlay. A neoclassical sofa by Spooner has an elegantly curved back but lacks the stay-rail needed to hold the upholstery.

18. The Brigham desk is at OSV. The author is aware of two card tables with Fairbanks signatures. One, dated 1816, is in a private collection; the other is at OSV along with the three bureaus mentioned. Brimfield, Massachusetts, dealers Susan and Richard Raymond report having seen related chests in area houses.

19. In 1971, the contents of the Emerson Bixby house were given to OSV by descendants. The house was subsequently donated and has been moved to the museum. Since the 1870s (following the death of Emerson and Laura Bixby), the house had been used only during summer holidays. The furnishings were all either original to the structure or had been purchased at local estate sales. Houghton recorded, "to a rocking chair $2.23, to 1 work table $2.00, to a common bedstead $1.75, to 1 3 feet table $2.00" (Luke Houghton Account Book, September 1828–March 1837, Barre Historical Society, Barre, Massachusetts).

20. Newspapers studied include those published in Worcester, Barre, Southbridge, Fitchburg, and Athol, Massachusetts, between 1775 and 1850. These papers are primarily in the collections of the American Antiquarian Society with random issues at OSV. Editions of the Worcester city directories in the collections of OSV and the Worcester Historical Museum were also consulted.

21. See data base of Worcester County furniture makers, DRCL, OSV. According to the *United States Census of Manufactures, 1820* (Washington, D.C.: United States Census Office, 1820), twenty-three men in Sterling produced approximately 70,000 chairs. In 1832 the towns of Ashburnham, Sterling, Templeton, Gardner, Hubbardston, Princeton, Rutland, and Spencer produced at least 363,500 chairs (Louis McLane, *Documents Relative to the Manufactures in the United States* [1832; reprinted, New York: Augustus Kelly, 1969], pp. 474–577. The *Branches of Industry for Worcester County* (Boston: Dutton and Wentworth), pp. 42–73, asserted that the same towns manufactured 525,200 in 1837. The figure for 1850 excludes Rutland and Spencer and is drawn from the Census of Manufactures.

22. For more on the speculative manufacture and distribution of chairs, see Benno M. Forman, *American Seating Furniture, 1630–1730* (New York: W.W. Norton, 1988); Edward S. Cooke Jr., *Fiddlebacks and Crooked-backs: Elijah Booth and Other Joiners in Newtown and Woodbury 1750–1820* (Waterbury, Conn.: Mattatuck Historical Society, 1982); Philip Zea, "Furniture," in *The Great River, Art & Society of the Connecticut Valley 1635–1820,* edited by

Gerald W. R. Ward and William N. Hosley Jr. (Hartford, Conn.: Wadsworth Atheneum, 1985); Benno M. Foreman, "The Crown & York Chairs of Coastal Connecticut and the Work of the Durands of Milford," *Antiques* 105, no. 5 (May 1974): 1147–54; Patricia Kane, *Three Hundred Years of American Seating Furniture* (New York: Graphic Society, 1976); Robert Trent, *Hearts and Crowns: Folk Chairs of the Connecticut: Elijah Booth and Other Joiners in Newton and Woodbury, 1720–1840* (New Haven, Conn.: New Haven Colony Historical Society, 1977).

23. OSV has done extensive research on chair production in Sterling during the 1820s and 1830s, utilizing various sources including the account books of chairmakers Joel Pratt Jr. and Elbridge Gerry Reed (both in private collections), Sterling tax records (Sterling Historical Society), and the deeds and inventories of approximately a hundred chairmakers.

The author thanks the staff of the South Gardner Historical Society, notably Warren Sinclair and Windsor Robinson, for their assistance in locating and using primary documents in private collections.

24. The definitions and prices are extrapolated from references in the Elbridge Gerry Reed accounts and the Daybook of Lansford Wood of Worcester 1832–1844 (both in the American Antiquarian Society) and Isaac Wright of Hartford 1834–1837 (Connecticut Historical Society).

25. Isaac Wright accounts cited in William N. Hosley Jr., "Wright Robbins & Winship and the Industrialization of the Furniture Industry in Hartford, Connecticut," *Connecticut Antiquarian* 35, no. 2 (December 1983): 12–19. Broadside for J. Pratt Jr. & Son, Hartford, location unknown.

26. *Worcester Magazine and Historical Journal* (1827); Index of Early Southern Artists and Artisans, Museum of Early Southern Decorative Arts, Winston-Salem, N.C.; Thomas Holmes Papers 1813–1818, Essex Institute, Salem, Massachusetts; Karen Blanchfield, *Transporting for Trade: Tracking Worcester County Furniture from Shop to Sale, 1790 to 1850*, unpublished paper, 1991, done for Boston University, copy on file at OSV. Norman R. Bennett and George E. Brooks Jr, eds., *New England Merchants in Africa: A History Through Documents 1802–1865* (Boston: Boston University Press, 1965). *Patriot* (Barre, Mass.), September 20, 1844.

27. E. Page Talbott, "Check List of Boston Cabinetmakers, 1810–1835," *Antiques* 141, no. 5 (May 1992): 845–50. Boston City Directories, 1820, 1825, 1831, 1832.

28. Collections files of the Rhode Island Historical Society, Providence, R.I. See Brian Cullity, *Plain and Fancy, New England Painted Furniture* (Sandwich, Mass.: Heritage Plantation of Sandwich, 1987), fig. 30.

29. The Jacob Felton Daybook, 1836–1838 is in the OSV collections. Initial analysis was undertaken by Sandra Christoforidis. Kenneth Joel Zogry provided additional information about Anthony VanDorn.

30. Reed Day Book. Henry Rice to Henry W. Miller, February 4, 1828, manuscript collection, Worcester Historical Museum.

31. Edward Hazen, *Panorama of Professions and Trades* (Philadelphia: Uriah Hunt, 1836), p. 227.

32. William D. Herrick, *History of Gardner* (Gardner, Mass.: The Committee, 1878), pp. 168–69; Esther G. Moore, *History of Gardner, Massachusetts, 1785–1867* (Gardner, Mass.: Hatton Publishing, Inc., 1967), pp. 222–28; *Vital Records of Gardner, Massachusetts* (Worcester: Franklin P. Rice, 1970); Talbott, "Check List of Boston Cabinetmakers," p. 850.

33. Charles S. Parsons, "Wilder Chairs," unpublished paper, February 1973, photocopy in DRCL, OSV. Jane C. Giffen, "New Hampshire Cabinetmakers and Allied Craftsmen, 1790–1850," *Antiques* 94, no. 1 (July 1968): 78–87; *Plain and Elegant, Rich and Common: Documented New Hampshire Furniture, 1750–1850* (Concord, N.H.: New Hampshire Historical Society, 1979), pp. 116–17.

The Wetherbee chair is in the New Hampshire Historical Society. The current location of the Pratt chair is unknown.

34. Data from the 1850 United States Population Census, quoted in Edwin Churchill to Donna K. Baron, January 8, 1993.

35. Edwin A. Churchill, *Simple Forms and Vivid Colors: Maine Painted Furniture 1800–1850* (Portland, Maine: Maine State Museum, 1983), pp. 86, 94, 96. An effort is underway to compare lists of furniture makers in both areas.

36. *Ashburnham, Massachusetts Vital Records* (Worcester: Franklin P. Rice, 1904); *Gazette* (Fitchburg, Mass.), November 6, 1832, and January 29, 1833; Earle G. Shettleworth Jr. and

William D. Barry, "Walter Corey's Furniture Manufactory in Portland, Maine," *Antiques* 121, no. 5 (May 1982): 1199–1207; Churchill, *Simple Forms & Vivid Colors*, p. 88.

37. The Rice/Roper/Greenwood story was pieced together with the assistance of Karen Blanchfield, Ruth Hoffman of the Sterling, Massachusetts, Historical Society, and Betty Smith of the Susquehanna Historical Society who provided pages of genealogical information and local history. Correspondence and notes on file at OSV.

38. Jane Sikes Hageman and Edward M. Hageman, *Ohio Furniture Makers 1790 to 1860*, vol. 2 (Cincinnati, Ohio: by the authors, 1989), p. 15. *United States Census of Manufactures, 1820*; *Sterling Massachusetts Vital Records*. Hageman and Hageman, *Ohio Furniture Makers*, 2:149–50.

Neil D. Kamil

Hidden in Plain Sight: Disappearance and Material Life in Colonial New York

▼ OCTOBER 29, 1716 MONDAY. *New York . . . I walked round this town. There is here three churches, the English church, the French and the Dutch church. . . . The French have all the privileges that can be in this place and are the most in number here. They are of the council, of the parliament, and in all other employments here.*

John Fontaine, Huguenot traveler

"Ingate" and "Outgate": Dialogues about Words and Things

The current state of New England regional studies indicates that traditional notions of dominance and cultural homogeneity are finally undergoing revision. Recent scholarship suggests that the once "monolithic" Puritan region was settled intermittently by diverse groups of migrants, not only from a variety of East Anglian settlements, but from all over England and America. Given our awareness of the limitations of this traditional assumption, it is ironic that historians of colonial America who venture into the middle Atlantic region must again confront similarly reductive and one-dimensional ethnic models.[1]

The most enduring scheme of ethnic reductiveness in middle Atlantic regional studies is the one that posits successive Dutch and then English cultural hegemony in colonial New York, with 1664—the date of the English imperial conquest of the colony—representing the chronological break between the two periods. Transatlantic historians might well ask, how does one even begin to define the pluralistic, shifting Netherlands in such monolithic "Dutch" terms? One must also consider persuasive quantitative evidence that, although New Netherland came into being as a Dutch West India Company, the colony never had an effective ethnic Dutch majority. Indeed, many of the earliest colonists were French-speaking Huguenots and Walloons who came in search of refuge and economic opportunity. Immigrants from all over Protestant Europe, African slaves, and local native groups combined to make New York City and its dauntingly large hinterland among the most pluralistic societies in colonial America. This social and geographic context has enormous implications for understanding the fluid history and culture of New York Colony.[2]

The stereotype of "pure Dutchness" owes much to the nostalgic ethnic myths and fairytales popularized by New York's nineteenth-century essayist and historian Washington Irving (1783–1859), particularly his *Dietrich Knickerbocker's A History of New York* (1809). This perception powerfully shaped the historiography of New York and limited the analysis of the colony's many other important and linguistically distinct subgroups, which were engaged in constant cultural conflict and accommodation on many levels of interaction. The real story of New York's material culture was not about Dutchness or Englishness per se but rather about ethnic and cultural diversity, within which both the Dutch and the English played their proper roles.[3]

Figure 1 Side chair, Boston, ca. 1700. Maple and oak; original leather upholstery. H. 34¼", W. 17¾", D. 14¾". (Courtesy, Wadsworth Atheneum.) In New York, Boston leather chairs of this type outnumbered carved examples approximately six to one.

The French words for "furniture" ("mobilier" or "meubles") are defined literally as "moveables," and one way to begin understanding such ambiguous issues as regional identity in diverse colonial settings, ethnic stereotypes, and cross-cultural conflict and accommodation is by considering the journey (or diffusion) of an instantly recognizable colonial artifact—the Boston "plain" leather chair (fig. 1). Thanks largely to the work of furniture historian Benno M. Forman, we now know that because of intercoastal trade the Boston leather chair—a shoddily made, provincial adaptation of the fashionable, London cane chair—probably was the single most influential moveable produced in colonial America between the Restoration and the end of the French and Indian War. Forman's main concern was what he and most other art historians of his generation called connoisseurship, an intensely "presentist" word directed towards highly subjective questions of universal quality and difficult to define or contextualize historically; nevertheless, because of his research, we can readily separate leather chairs made in Boston, New York, Philadelphia, and other coastal style centers and focus on new sets of questions and concerns.[4]

What, after all, was the leather chair's significance as it was carried as merchant cargo from place to place in the colonies, inspiring local copies nearly everywhere it was sold? Why were "style" and "fashion" such key words for the artisans, merchants, and consumers of leather chairs in the port towns of early-eighteenth-century America?

Historically, the Boston leather chair's significance centers on its role as an important English symbol for colonial elites. Made primarily for export to the middle Atlantic region and the South by a network of Boston chairmakers and upholsterers, the chair remained at the nucleus of New England's coastal furniture trade for more than a century. New York City and western Long Island were among the most important markets; however, only the elite owned leather chairs. A survey of 560 inventories probated between 1700, when the new, high-backed leather chair first made its appearance, and 1760, when appraisers consistently described a later version of that form as *old*, *very old*, or *old-fashioned,* indicates that only thirty-one households (5.5 percent) possessed leather chairs.

These were important households, however; the average valuation of estates that list leather chairs was £982.8.[5] The chairs were clearly luxury items, and they ranged in value from 10*s* to £3 or more apiece depending on model and condition. Most significantly, households valued near the average were seldom without at least one leather chair, indicating that they were a necessary symbol of status for New York's elite. Owners were generally "merchants" or "gentlemen" who lived in the city, where 77.4 percent of all leather chairs were inventoried. The remainder were evenly distributed in Flushing, Jamaica, and Hempstead, the largest towns on western Long Island. These towns were also the traditional strongholds of New York's prosperous Quaker community.

So widespread was the trade in leather chairs that some colonial officials protested to the British Board of Trade that New England artisans and merchants were undermining the spirit of the Navigation Acts by infringing on England's natural prerogative to provide her colonies with manufactured goods. In a contentious report presented to Parliament on January 22, 1733, Lieutenant Governor William Gooch of Virginia complained that "scrutoires, chairs and other wooden manufactures . . . are now being exported from thence to the other plantations, which, if not prevented, may be of ill consequence to the trade and manufactures of this kingdom."[6] Gooch's report clearly reflects the fact that his constituents in the Chesapeake produced tobacco, grain, and cattle for export, not chairs.

To compensate for the lack of an overarching staple, New England merchants and artisans produced and exported chairs and other manufactured goods so aggressively that transatlantic economic historians now conclude New England's mercantile strategy was to assume consciously the role of English metropolis in the New World. According to historians John J. McCusker and Russell R. Menard, "New England resembled nothing so much as old England itself. And that, of course, was the problem. . . . It was in the expansion of domestic processing and manufacturing, of a far-reaching export business . . . that New Englanders . . . mounted a growing challenge to the hegemony of the metropolis."[7]

By 1700, the middle Atlantic, southern, and Caribbean plantation economies, which exploited slave labor to extract and refine staple commodities, had far outdistanced New England in terms of direct credits with metropolitan England and the empire's Atlantic market. The Massachusetts General Court had become conscious of this imbalance as early as the empirewide depression of the 1630s and 1640s. In New England, the depression intensified as immigration (the colony's main source of liquid capital) dropped off following the great Puritan migration of the 1630s. Having observed that "our ingate [imports]" were "to exceed our outgate [exports]" such that "the ballance needs be made up," the court passed the Edict of 1646. This decree allowed for the active development of local manufactures in explicit competition with the metropolis, thus addressing the crippling structural problem in the colony's balance of trade.[8] The export of such new manufactures as clothing, shoes, boots, ironware, and chairs was one of the only means available for New England merchants and artisans to boost exports back into balance.

Shortly after the edict, upholstered chairs were among the most common items of New England manufacture carried south on sloops from Boston. Indeed, by the 1670s, references to the earliest form of low-backed, leather upholstered *New England* chair or "stool" (fig. 2) appear in Maryland inventories. By 1700, appraisers in every colony were specifically referring to leather chairs as either *Boston, New England*, or *Boston Made*. The artifactual

Figure 2 Side chair, Boston, 1650–1700. Birch and maple with ash. H. 35", W. 18", D. 15". (Courtesy, Winterthur Museum.)

language of the Boston leather chair thus proved distinctive enough to warrant the acceptance of new terminology into colonial discourse. In the small world of North American commerce, the chair became a medium for intercolonial communication.[9]

But what could chairs communicate? What were the cultural associations that the word "Boston" carried with the chair on its journeys south into the regions of staple production? What, beyond its point of origin, were the signifiers of its Bostonness? Such implicit cultural associations attending the chair trade were imperative to Boston's mercantile strategy. From 1646 until at least the 1730s, Boston acted as the mother country's cultural broker, albeit without her approval. As far as furniture was concerned, Boston was a veritable Anglo-colonial metaregion for elites in other colonies seeking fashionable goods.

Acting as surrogates for the core culture on its colonial periphery, Boston merchants and artisans proclaimed their unique power to produce and disseminate authentic novelties of English metropolitan style. Such novelties were a necessity for aspiring colonial elites consumed with anxiety about falling behind their counterparts in London. As historian William Smith Jr. observed in his *History of the Province of New-York From the First Discovery to the Year 1732* (1757), "In the city of New-York, through our intercourse with the Europeans, we follow the London fashions; though by the time we adopt them, they become disused in England. Our affluence . . . introduced a degree of luxury in tables, dress, and furniture, with which we were before unacquainted. But we are still not so gay a people, as our neighbors in Boston."[10]

Nowhere was Boston's stake in controlling the discourse of novelty and style more evident than in the frequent correspondence between Boston merchant and upholsterer Thomas Fitch (1668/9–1736) and Benjamin Faneuil (b. La Rochelle 1658, d. New York 1719). Faneuil was Fitch's principal agent in New York and a French Huguenot merchant exiled from the great Protestant fortress town of La Rochelle—a place that looms large in the transatlantic history of the Reformation and Counter Reformation. Benjamin, his immensely wealthy son Pierre (b. New York 1700, d. Boston 1742), and brother André (b. La Rochelle 1657, d. Boston 1737) established one of the most important refugee trading firms in early-eighteenth-century America. The Faneuil family's importance resulted not only from the emergence of a strong Boston–New York coastal axis but also from the family's longstanding transatlantic financial connections to other relatives and members of its patronage network still living in La Rochelle, as well as in Rotterdam and New France.[11]

Fitch's letters concern multiple shipments of leather chairs from Boston to New York, and they demonstrate how important the coastal furniture trade was to Boston's merchant elites and their clientage networks in the early eighteenth century. They also inform and complicate historian Robert J. Gough's reconsideration of the arbitrary geographical boundaries usually assigned to the "middle colonies." Gough suggests that the middle colonies were actually comprised of two distinct "human regions":

> New York, parts of western Connecticut, eastern New Jersey, and the northeast corner of Pennsylvania comprised one region. Most of Pennsylvania, part of Maryland, and all of western New Jersey and Delaware formed another. Each region had peculiar characteristics, and the inhabitants of each interacted mostly with themselves. What inter-regional contacts they did have tended to be with the South, for the Philadelphia-centered region, and with New England, for the New York-centered region. Each region was different from the South and from New England in important respects, to be sure, but for different reasons and in different ways.[12]

Although this essay underscores a strong interregional socioeconomic and cultural connection between New England and New York during the late seventeenth and early eighteenth centuries, it also considers transatlantic extensions of New York's human region.

Transatlantic concerns clearly influenced Fitch's performance as cultural broker and the acceptance of that performance in New York. Fitch maintained social distance and cultural dominance over Faneuil precisely because of his self-proclaimed knowledge about what was stylish in London and Boston. Fitch's letter of April 22, 1707, in which he chastized Faneuil for ordering something out of fashion in both London and Boston, is the best example of the asymmetry of the patronage relationship between this fully Anglicized Boston merchant and his French refugee client: "Sir . . . leather couches are as much out of wear here as steeple crowned hats. Cane couches or others we make like them . . . are cheaper, more fashionable, easy and useful."[13]

Faneuil and some of his fellow New Yorkers, however, did not sit idle while Fitch and others flooded the affluent New York market with Boston leather chairs. Fitch was so overwhelmed with orders from New York by 1706 that he wrote Faneuil, "I would have sent yo some chairs but could scarcely comply with those I had promised to go by these sloops"; yet, three years later there was a glut of leather chairs on the market for the first time. On September 9, 1709, Fitch began a series of anxious letters that despaired of Faneuil's inability to sell his consignment: "I wonder the chairs did not sell; I have sold pretty many of that sort to Yorkers, . . . and tho some are carved yet I make it six plain to one carved; and can't make the plain so fast as they are bespoke. So you can assure them that are customers that they are not out of fashion here. . . . I desire that you would force the sale of the chairs. . . . I also submit the price of them to your patience. It's better to sell them than to let them lie." Fitch added, "It might be better to have them rubbed over that they may look fresher," even though the expense of polishing would come out of his rapidly diminishing profit margin.[14]

Figure 3 Side chair, New York City, 1705–1710. Maple and oak. H. 46¾", W. 18", D. 18¾". (Courtesy, Winterthur Museum.)

Boston plain leather chairs had enjoyed uninterrupted popularity in New York for more than a decade (or for more than forty years, if one includes earlier related seating forms), so Fitch's exasperation was understandable. Even his old trumpcard to sway the presumably unanglicized elites in New York—his protestation about the chairs' stylishness in Boston—failed to bolster sales. What had changed? To begin, New York chairmakers began producing a modified version of the Boston leather chair by the end of the seventeenth century (fig. 3). Subsequently, several New York shops produced a number of variants, all incorporating recognizable features of the Boston chair. By 1709, they supplied enough competition to cut into Fitch's formerly secure market. We thus begin to see, on a very local level and in just one sort of export manufacture, early evidence of the unraveling of Massachusetts's mercantile strategy outlined in the Edict of 1646.

As historians Jack P. Greene, John McCusker, and Russell Menard have demonstrated, even those regions engaged primarily in the exploitation of staple agriculture diversified by developing an artisanal component to compete with New England's export market in manufactured goods. Relative population growth is a good general indicator of the potential for regional development of the artisan sector. In 1660, New England's total population (including slaves) exceeded 33,000, while the middle colonies' was less than 6,000 (a ratio of over 5:1). But by 1710, while New England's population had grown to 115,000, the middle colonies' increased to nearly 70,000 (a ratio of less than 2:1). Beginning in 1705, a flurry of correspondence criss-

Figure 4 Map of Aunis-Saintonge, France. (Artwork, Wynne Patterson.)

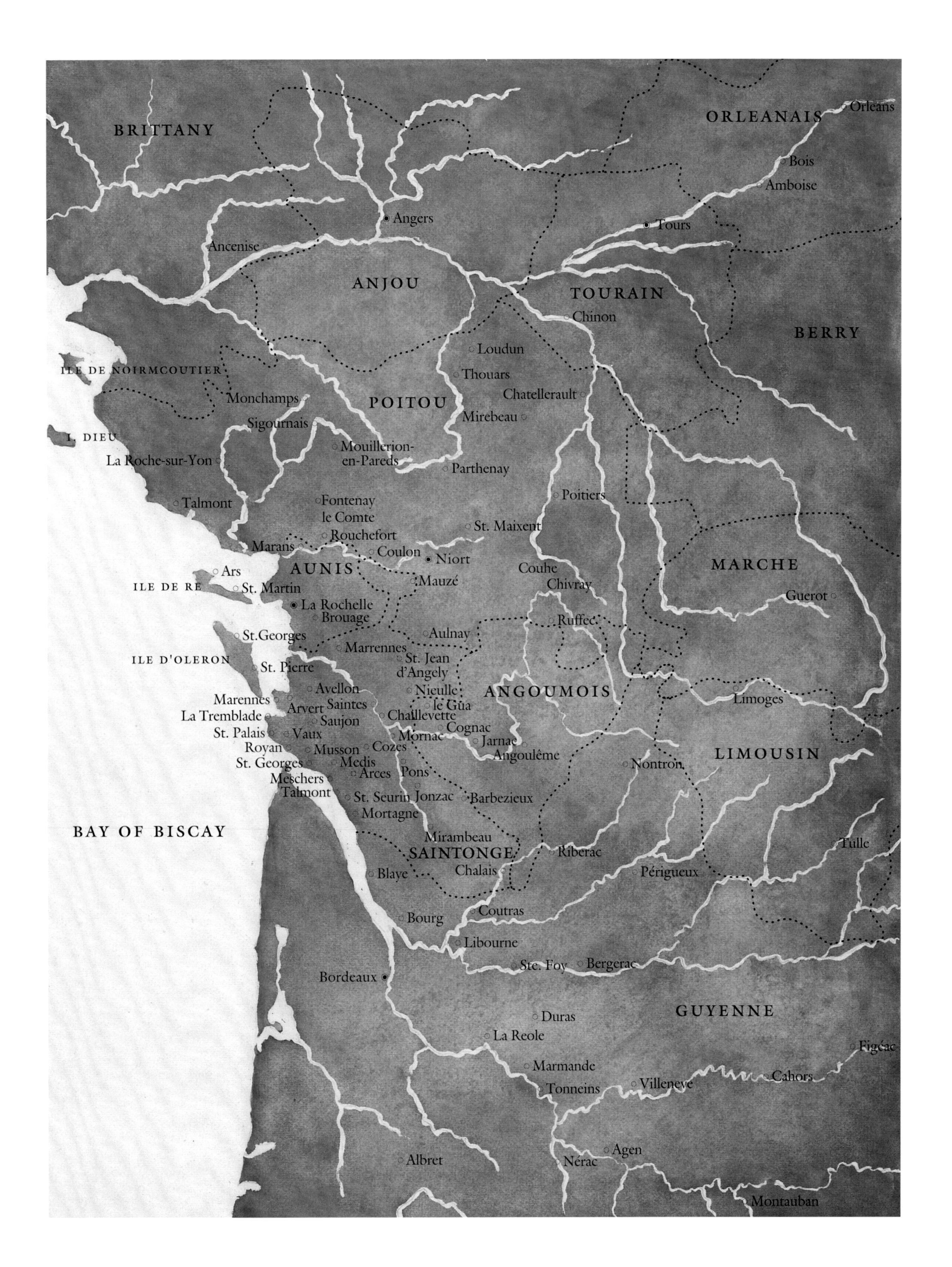
BRITTANY
ORLEANAIS
Orleans
Bois
Amboise
Angers
Tours
Ancenise
ANJOU
TOURAIN
Chinon
BERRY
Loudun
Thouars
ILE DE NOIRMCOUTIER
Monchamps
POITOU
Chatelleroult
Sigournais
Mirebeau
I. DIEU
Mouillerion-
en-Pareds
La Roche-sur-Yon
Parthenay
Talmont
Poitiers
Fontenay
le Comte
Rouchefort
St. Maixent
Marans
Coulon
Niort
AUNIS
Ars
Couhe
MARCHE
Mauzé
Chivray
ILE DE RE
St. Martin
Guerot
La Rochelle
Brouage
Ruffec
St.Georges
Aulnay
Marrennes
ILE D'OLERON
St. Pierre
St. Jean
d'Angely
Avellon
Nieulle
ANGOUMOIS
Marennes
Limoges
Arvert
Saintes
le Gûa
La Tremblade
Chaillevette
Saujon
Cognac
St. Palais
Vaux
Mornac
Jarnac
LIMOUSIN
Royan
Musson
Cozes
Angoulême
Nontron
St. Georges
Medis
Arces
Pons
Meschers
Talmont
St. Seurin
Jonzac
Barbezieux
Mortagne
BAY OF BISCAY
Mirambeau
Tulle
SAINTONGE
Riberac
Blaye
Chalais
Périgueux
Coutras
Bourg
Libourne
Ste. Foy
Bergerac
Bordeaux
GUYENNE
Duras
La Reole
Figéac
Marmande
Villeneve
Cahors
Tonneins
Agen
Albret
Nérac
Montauban

crossed the Atlantic, indicating for the first time that London's Board of Trade saw New York's growing manufacturing sector as a potential threat to British mercantilism.[15] New York had begun to replicate elements of Boston's mercantile strategy successfully enough to gain notice both in Boston and the metropolis.

Still, why would New York be among the first colonies to support an artisan sector powerful enough to respond so rapidly to a formidable mercantile engine largely in place in New England since the 1640s? Given Fitch's condescending attitude toward Faneuil, it seems ironic that many of the artisans and merchants who ultimately usurped Fitch's enterprise were from southwestern France, particularly coastal Aunis and Saintonge, La Rochelle's hinterland (fig. 4). La Rochelle was the birthplace of Benjamin Faneuil, and the Aunisian and Saintongeais refugee immigrants—many of whom shared Old World trade or family associations—comprised the majority of his craft network.[16] La Rochelle was also the last great Protestant fortress town to resist the Catholic state, until it fell to Richelieu and Louis XIII in a year-long siege in 1628—a genocidal Counter Reformation event that claimed the lives of nearly 20,000 heretics with brutal efficiency. The fall of La Rochelle effectively broke the back of Huguenot military resistance in the western provinces, thus setting the stage for Louis XIV's Revocation of the Edict of Nantes in 1685, which outlawed reformed religion in France and signaled the beginning of the final, massive Huguenot dispersion to Protestant northern Europe and the New World.

Figure 5 Side chair, Boston, 1690–1705. Maple and oak. H. 41¾", W. 20", D. 18". (Courtesy, New York State Education Department, Albany.)

The Year 1685 and New York's "Old" Culture

Although 1685 was the starting point for the largest migration of Huguenot artisans from Aunis-Saintonge to New York, the foundation for the city's leather chairmaking industry was laid earlier, since its pluralistic artisan sector developed along with its population. Until the late 1680s, the vanguard of the "Protestant international" in New Amsterdam–New York had consisted of family networks of merchants and artisans from Dutch, Germanic, and Scandanavian regional cultures, Walloon refugees from the Spanish Netherlands (who spoke a French dialect), and "old" diaspora Huguenots who founded churches in exile among sympathetic hosts throughout the North Atlantic reformed community by the 1550s.[17] The Huguenots of the dispersion were the final and primary catalyst that enabled New York's artisans to compete successfully with Boston imports and challenge that city's role as disseminator of metropolitan style and fashion.

On April 16, 1705, Fitch wrote Faneuil, "Please to inform me in yor next whether Turkey worke chairs would see with yo, If yo think they will shall send yo some from 15 to 20*s* a ps here."[18] Presumably, these chairs were

Figure 6 Side chair, New York City, 1660–1700. Maple and oak; original seal skin upholstery. H. 36¾", W. 18¾", D. 15½". (Courtesy, Old Saybrook Historical Society; photo, Gavin Ashworth.) The ball-and-cove and vase turnings on this chair differ from those on seventeenth-century Boston examples such as figs. 2 and 5. Seal skin was used when leather was unavailable.

Figure 7 Side chair, New York City, 1660–1700. Oak and black ash; original leather upholstery. H. 34", W. 18¼", D. 15½". (Courtesy, John Hall Wheelock Collection, East Hampton Historical Society; photo, Joseph Adams.) This chair descended in the Wheelock family of East Hampton, Long Island.

Boston-made, high-backed stools similar to the one illustrated in figure 5. Although no response to Fitch's letter survives, Faneuil probably replied negatively, since this type of chair was outdated in London and Boston.[19] Fitch often remarked that New York was behind fashion, and he probably assumed that turkeywork chairs might still be stylish there.

Fitch evidently underestimated and misunderstood the development and sophistication of New York tradesmen and consumers. Inventories indicate that high-backed stools were out of fashion by 1701. Huguenot "Captain" Nicholas Dumaresq[ue]'s inventory, taken on June 12, 1701, listed "four old high Leather Chairs" and "one old Low chair." Given the proximity and similar language of these listings, the "old Low chair" probably resembled the ones illustrated in figures 2 and 6–9. Appraisers often used the term "old" interchangeably with "old-fashioned," and in this case, "old" probably referred to style rather than condition.[20]

By 1701, two predecessors of the new plain leather chairs were anachronistic in both Boston and New York. What is most significant, however, is that a great variety of low-backed leather, turkeywork, and other woolen

Figure 8 Side chair, New York City, 1660–1685. Red oak. H. 37", W. 18", D. 15 1/8". (Courtesy, Pocumtuck Valley Memorial Association, Memorial Hall Museum, Deerfield, Massachusetts; photo, Helga Studio.) The inverted vase-and-barrel turnings on this and another related example at the Wadsworth Atheneum followed Amsterdam prototypes in an era when Netherlandish design was on the wane in New York City.

upholstered chairs were apparently manufactured in New York during the late seventeenth century (figs. 6–9), but not enough to challenge effectively the Boston trade. Nevertheless, several shops from various cultural traditions were clearly established to lay the socio-material foundation for New York's powerful cultural response—spearheaded by the Huguenot immigration from Aunis-Saintonge after 1685—to the introduction of Boston leather chairs like those exported by Fitch (fig. 1).

If the "old high Leather chairs" in Dumaresque's inventory were made in one of New York's earliest shops, rather than in Boston, they may have resembled the armchair frame illustrated in figure 10. Evidence suggests that this late-seventeenth-century "high [upholstered] chair" is a rare colonial

Figure 9 Side chair, New York City, 1685–1700. Maple and oak. Dimensions not recorded. (Private collection; photo, Gavin Ashworth.) The turnings on this chair are closely related to those on late-seventeenth-century London cane chairs and early-eighteenth-century New York leather chairs, such as the one illustrated in fig. 3.

interpretation of the Parisian "grand" chair, a form that appeared mainly in France and on the Continent around 1670 (the grand chair seemed, anomalously, not to have proven fashionable in London). More importantly, this example is a New York–made predecessor for the high-backed leather chair form introduced during the early eighteenth century (fig. 1).[21]

In formal terms, the design of the grand chair's turned front stretcher relates directly to the side stretchers of a New York escritoire (fig. 11) with a Dutch inscription detailing a business transaction and the date 1695 under its lid. The escritoire and the grand chair, however, could date as early as the mid-1680s, when the word "escritoire" first begins to appear in New York inventories. This escritoire has long been considered a keystone for understanding late-seventeenth-century urban New York cabinetmaking. Collected from a house on Cortelyou Road in the Flatbush section of Kings County early in this century, it may have been made in Brooklyn or brought there from New York City.[22]

Figure 10 Grand Chair, New York City, 1680–1695. Maple stained red. H. 44¼", W. 22½", D. 17¼". (Private collection; photo, Christopher Zaleski.)

Certainly the escritoire, like the grand chair, may have originated in either place, because competent artisans capable of working in "urban" idioms existed on both sides of the East River—a waterway that connected rather than separated these areas. The accessibility of lower Manhattan to the northern tip of Brooklyn—a brief ride on the Long Island ferry across the lower East River, and so easily accessible to the docks or the business end of New York City—is confirmed by the diary of John Fontaine, an Anglo-Irish Huguenot of southwestern French parentage who wrote on October 29, 1716: "About eleven we came to the ferry which goes over to New York. There is a fine village [Brooklyn] upon this island opposite to New York. The ferry is about a quarter of a mile over, and water runs very rapidly here, and there is good convenient landings on both sides. About 12 we landed at New York." Fontaine's appraisal of Manhattan's roads was far less encouraging: "[They] are very bad and stony, and no possibility for coaches to go only in the winter when the snow fills all up and makes all smooth,

Figure 11 Escritoire, New York City or northern Kings County, 1685–1695. Red gum and mahogany with yellow poplar. H. 35¼", W. 33¾", D. 24". (Courtesy, Metropolitan Museum of Art, Rogers Fund, 1944.) The turnings on the side stretchers are closely related to those on the front stretcher of the grand chair illustrated in fig. 10.

Figure 12 Detail of the finial of the grand chair illustrated in fig. 10. (Photo, Christopher Zaleski.)

Figure 13 Detail of a drawer pull on a kas, New York City or northern Kings County, ca. 1730–1750. (Courtesy, Milwaukee Art Museum, Layton Art Collection.)

Figure 14 Side chair, New York City, 1705–1710. Maple and oak; original leather upholstery. H. 47¾", W. 18½", D. 18¾". (Chipstone Foundation; photo, Gavin Ashworth.)

Figure 15 Detail of the finial of the side chair illustrated in fig. 14. (Photo, Gavin Ashworth.)

then they can make use of their wheel carriages. There is but two coaches belonging to this province though many rich people, because of the badness of the roads."[23]

By the late seventeenth century, Kings County surveyors had established a passable network of roads, which connected all the major western towns to the Long Island ferry. The stylistic relation of New York City to Kings County furniture is thus a difficult problem to unravel with utter assurance. Consider the problems that accompany the neat separation of kasten with New York City and Kings County histories. These artifacts share many of the same details. Intraregional interaction is also suggested by the distinctive finial of the New York grand chair (fig. 12), which has much in common with drawer pulls found on a number of early New York City or Kings

County kasten (fig. 13) and with the standard finial on its successor, the New York plain leather chair (figs. 14, 15). Moreover, between the English takeover and the Revocation, cross-generational, transatlantic, cultural continuities, solidified by strategic marriages that connected families, shops, regions, and neighborhoods, clearly played a significant role in the linkage and maintenance of New York's most enduring continental craft networks. Some seventeenth-century Kings County artisans from New York's "old," pre-1685 Huguenot culture, including members of the Lott family of southwestern France, Amsterdam, and Kings County—plausible makers of both the escritoire and the grand chair—worked for elite patrons in New York City while simultaneously developing cheap land and maintaining numerous slaves in the more homogeneous continental towns across the river in Brooklyn. Quaker merchants and artisans followed a similar bifurcated yet symbiotic pattern on western Long Island since the time of Peter Stuyvesant's restrictions on Quaker "conventicles," which led to the publication of the Flushing Remonstrance on December 27, 1657.[24]

Figure 16 Detail of the understructure of the trapezoidal seat of the grand chair illustrated in fig. 10. (Photo, Christopher Zaleski.)

Material evidence strongly suggests that the maker of the grand chair (fig. 10) was of continental descent. The unusual carved arms with concave elbow rests relate less to turned and upholstered metropolitan prototypes than to joined great chairs made in the British midlands and west country. However, a more closely analogous arm occurs on an early-eighteenth-century turned armchair of vernacular French or Germanic origin.[25] There is also the distinct possibility that the New York armchair represents the collaborative work of a turner and a joiner—perhaps individuals from different cultural backgrounds. If so, this would further complicate the quest for ethnic origins in what is most likely a creolized chair.

Two of the most intriguing components of the chair are its trapezoidal seat and recessed back, which frames three squared, partially unfinished spindles (the surfaces have deep horizontal saw marks). The chairmaker constructed the trapezoidal seat by chamfering the front and rear ends of the seat lists and thick side stretchers at opposite though parallel angles, to accommodate the wider front (fig. 16). An alternative method commonly used on British and Boston examples was to leave the ends of the side elements cut flush, an economical technique that allowed for thinner stock, while chamfering the inside back of the two front posts beneath the seat, thus angling the posts instead of the stretchers (figs. 17, 18). It would be simplistic, however, to conclude that one solution was "continental" and the other "British," since these conceptually opposite construction techniques commonly appear on chairs attributable to both Boston and New York.

Peter Thornton has demonstrated how seventeenth-century French and Low Country chairs had "bucket" seats or backs designed to contain removable, mattress-like *carreaux* (or "squabs"). The three rough-hewn spindles on the New York grand chair were not meant to be visible but rather to serve as tying posts for the *carreau's* fasteners, probably made of woven ribbon or "tape." Both transatlantic and cross-generational structural continuities are suggested by the height available for the *carreau* on the grand chair's back, which measures 15½ inches, as does the height of its seat. Reciprocal, one-

Figure 17 Side chair, Boston or New York City, ca. 1700. Maple and oak. H. 47", W. 20", D. 21". (Private collection; photo, Christopher Zaleski.) This chair, branded "PVP" for Philip Verplank of Fishkill, New York, is related to three carved leather chairs at Washington's Headquarters, Newburgh, New York. The latter are also branded "PVP."

Figure 18 Detail of the understructure of the side chair illustrated in fig. 17. (Photo, Christopher Zaleski.)

to-one vertical symmetry remains constant on New York's high-back leather chairs as well (see figs. 3, 45d), although not on Boston plain chairs. Boston chairs accentuate verticality, such that the height of the back typically exceeds that of the seat. The back structure of an unusual southern armchair at Colonial Williamsburg suggests that it also had a *carreau*; however, the framing members of the back are larger, and they are smooth planed and molded. The latter example possibly represents the work of a Huguenot tradesman from one of the large French settlements in the South Carolina Low Country.[26]

Although the upholstery materials used on the seat of the New York grand chair are unknown, nail holes indicate it had a sacking bottom (rather than girtwebbing) that was probably covered tightly by leather or a woolen. Print sources suggest that a high cushion may have surmounted the seat, ris-

Figure 19 Side chair, New York City, 1705–1710. Maple with oak. H. 45⅝", W. 18⅛", D. 15¼". (Courtesy, Milwaukee Art Museum, Layton Art Collection; photo, Richard Eells.) This chair reportedly descended in the Pieter Vanderlyn family of Kingston, New York. Pieter immigrated to New York City from the Netherlands in 1718. His arrival date suggests he may have acquired the chair from an earlier owner.

Figure 20 Detail of the "French hollow" back of the side chair illustrated in fig. 20. The curvature is similar to that of the early carved leather chair illustrated in fig. 39.

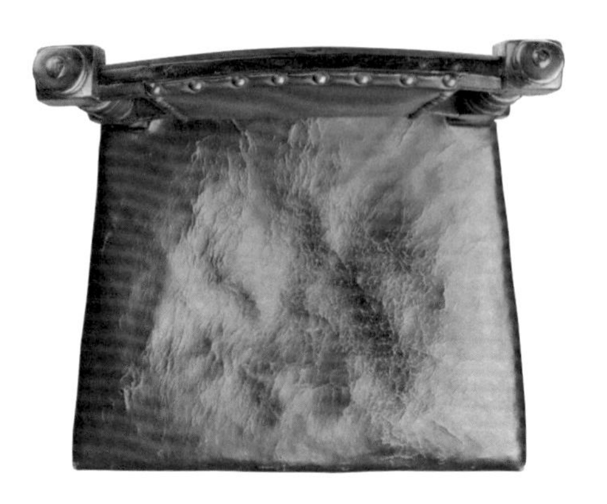

ing to fill the gaping hole between the top of the frame's seat lists and the bottom of its lofty stay rail. Presumably, the *carreau* and seat cushion had matching textile covers. In his discussion of continental seating styles, Thornton cites "a French chaire hollow in ye back." To accommodate the shape of the sitter's shoulders and ribs, such chairs had concave backs formed by subtly curving the crest and stay rails backward.[27] This feature principally occurs only on early-eighteenth-century New York leather chairs (see figs. 19, 20) and may represent a Huguenot innovation.

The New York grand chair suggests by its very singularity that only a few were made. The advent of "new fashioned," high-backed London cane (fig. 21) and Boston leather chairs, combined with the Parisian grand chair's apparent rejection in London, assured that the latter form quickly passed

Figure 21 Cane chair, London, ca. 1700. Beech. Dimensions not recorded. (Private collection; photo, Neil D. Kamil.)

Figure 22 Side chair, New York City, ca. 1700. Maple. Dimensions not recorded. (Private collection; photo, Gavin Ashworth.) The front stretcher is related to that of fig. 10. The feet and a portion of the right leg are missing.

Figure 23 Side chair, New York City, ca. 1700. Maple. Dimensions not recorded. (Private collection; photo, Gavin Ashworth.) This chair is closely related to the one illustrated in fig. 22.

out of fashion in New York. Fitch's 1701 letter to Faneuil stressing the availability of presumably cheap, high-backed turkeywork chairs currently out-of-fashion in the metropolis indicates that he was intent on capturing what remained of the dwindling New York market for these luxury items. Evidently, the new, high-backed "Boston" plain leather chair was just coming into fashion in New York around the turn of the century.

Two high-back leather chairs made in New York about 1700 (figs. 22, 23) have the same seventeenth-century turning sequences as the grand chair

Figure 24 Joined great chair, New York, 1650–1700. Oak. H. 43", W. 23¾", D. 21". (Courtesy, Wallace Nutting Collection, Wadsworth Atheneum, gift of J. P. Morgan; photo, Joseph Szaszfai.) The left arm and seat are replaced, and the feet are missing.

(fig. 10). These are the only known high-back chairs of the later variety with these early turnings. Anomalous survivals such as these were undoubtedly considered anachronistic by the early eighteenth century, particularly when compared with new turning patterns drawn from fashionable London cane chairs. Fashion did not erase all memory of the grand chair however. For example, arm supports with bilaterally symmetrical balusters—a classical form that was updated and called a "double poire" (double pear) by French architect Charles Augustin d'Aviler in his *Cours d'Architecture* (1710)—appear on several early-eighteenth-century, high-back New York leather armchairs (see fig. 30).[28] The earliest New York example with this turned element is a joined great chair (fig. 24). Made a decade or two earlier than the grand chair, it attests to the longevity of this turning pattern; however,

Figure 25 Armchair with carving attributed to Jean Le Chevalier, New York City, 1705–1710. Maple with oak and hickory. H. 47½", W. 25½", D. 27". (Courtesy, Historic Hudson Valley; photo, Gavin Ashworth.) The finials are incorrect nineteenth century restorations; the feet are more recent.

the "double poire" and urn finial with its proud boss turned in the round (figs. 10, 12) were the only parts of the short-lived New York grand chair consistently repeated on later upholstered furniture.

Human Geography and Material Life

By 1701 Fitch had enlisted Faneuil to act as a middleman and to persuade New Yorkers of every ethnic stripe that the leather chair was no less popular in English Boston than in heterogeneous New York. In that capacity Faneuil was able to maximize his personal power, as had generations of other multilingual Rochelais merchants in northern Europe and the British archipelago. Evidence suggests that Faneuil may have endured Fitch's arrogant scorn to his eventual profit while serving as the upholsterer's submissive apprentice in the subtleties of Anglo-Boston material culture. The profit, of course, came when Faneuil and his network of Huguenot artisans understood the social and cultural connotations of the Boston leather chair and quietly made it their own through adaptation and innovation.

The most compelling artifact asserting the role artisans from Aunis-Saintonge played in the New York leather chair industry after 1701 is a carved armchair made for Stephanus Van Cortlandt (1643–1700) or his son, Philip (1683–1748) (fig. 25).[29] Found among the family collections of the Van Cortlandt Manor in Croton, southern Westchester County, the armchair appears in a late-nineteenth-century photograph of the second-story hall.

Among the most distinctive features of the armchair are its carved crest rail and stretcher, both of which have angular scrolls with stylized flowers at the interstices and acanthus leaves shaded with a parting tool (a V-shaped carving tool). The crest rail and stretcher are virtually identical to those of a contemporary armchair that descended in the Chester-Backus families of

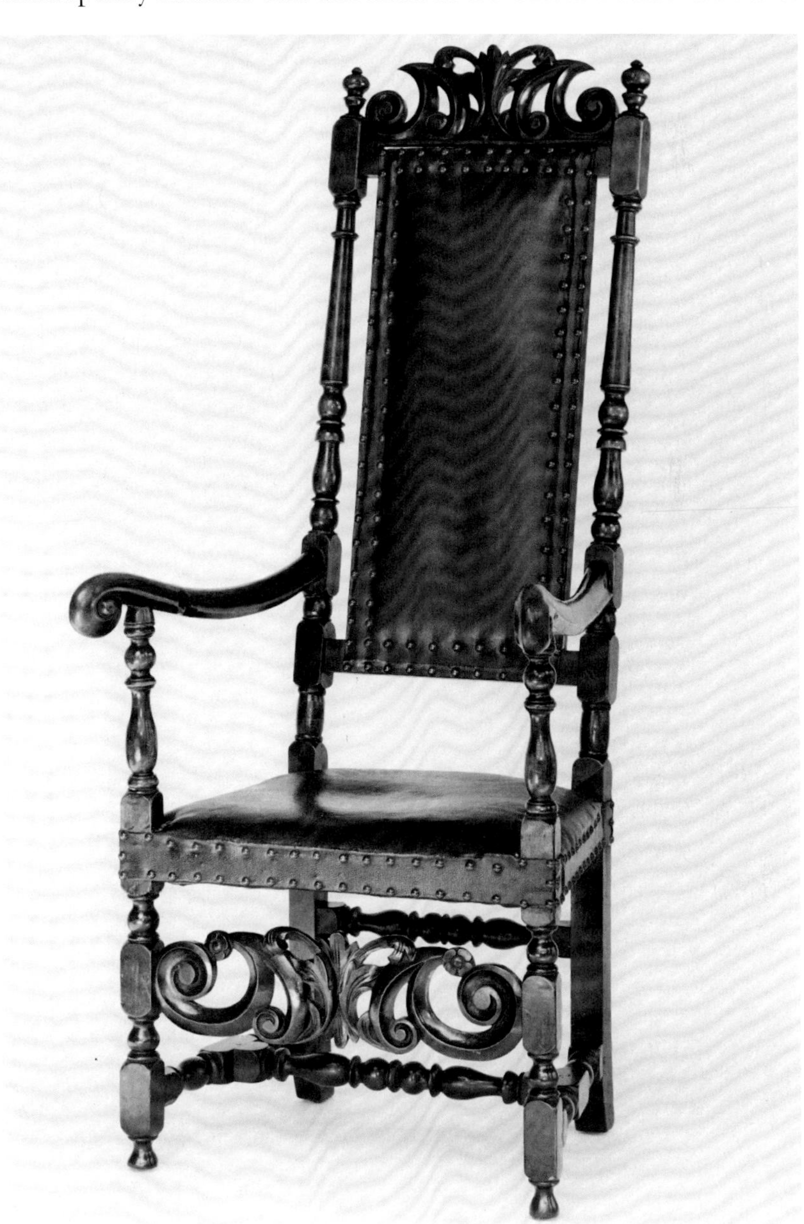

Figure 26 Armchair with carving attributed to Jean Le Chevalier, New York City, 1705–1710. Maple with oak. H. 53¾", W. 27/8", D. 163/8". (Courtesy, Museum of Fine Arts, Boston, gift of Mrs. Charles L. Bybee; photo, Edward A. Bourdon, Houston, Texas.) This chair was damaged by fire while in the Bybee collection.

Figure 27 Armchair with carving attributed to Jean Le Chevalier, New York City, 1705–1710. Maple with oak. H. 52", W. 24¾", D. 17½". (Chipstone Foundation; photo, Gavin Ashworth.) The low placement of the carved front stretcher is reminiscent of late seventeenth-century French fauteuils as well as some varieties of contemporary London cane chairs, which took French court furniture as a stylistic paradigm under the influence of refugee Huguenot artisans, especially after 1685. The left scroll volute of the crest is a replacement.

Figure 28 Side chair with carving attributed to Jean Le Chevalier, New York City, 1705–1710. Maple with oak. Dimensions not recorded. (Private collection; photo, Gavin Ashworth.)

Figure 29 Composite detail showing (from top to bottom) the crest rails of the chairs illustrated in figs. 26, 27, and 28 and the stretcher of the chair illustrated in fig. 25.

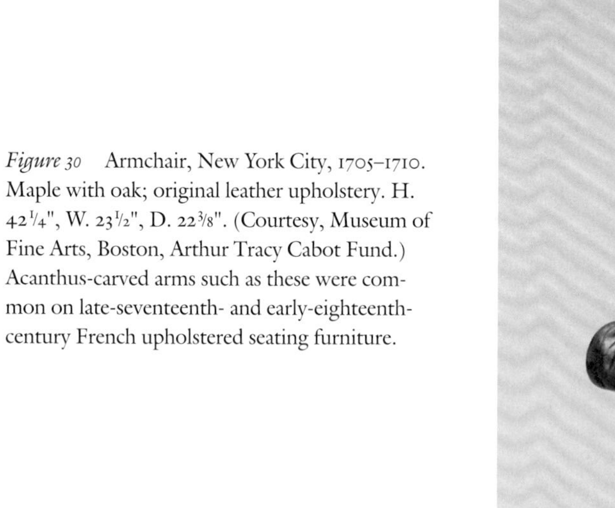

Figure 30 Armchair, New York City, 1705–1710. Maple with oak; original leather upholstery. H. 42¼", W. 23½", D. 22⅜". (Courtesy, Museum of Fine Arts, Boston, Arthur Tracy Cabot Fund.) Acanthus-carved arms such as these were common on late-seventeenth- and early-eighteenth-century French upholstered seating furniture.

Albany (fig. 26), the armchair illustrated in figure 27, and the side chair fragment illustrated in figure 28 (see also fig. 29).[30] The acanthus leaves on all of these examples are also similar to those on the arms of a more conventional New York leather armchair (fig. 30), but the technical relationships are insufficient to attribute them conclusively to the same hand. Nevertheless, the turnings on the latter example and the Chester-Backus armchair are directly related to those on the standard New York version of the Boston leather chair (fig. 3).

Several different turners and chairmakers were involved in the production of these leather chairs, although at least four are linked to a single carver. All have trapezoidal seats that are constructed differently. The Chester-Backus chairmaker joined the side stretchers and front posts in a manner once thought exclusive to Boston leather chairmakers (fig. 26; see also fig. 18); the chairmaker of figure 27 utilized the same techniques as the maker of the New York grand chair (see fig. 16); and the Van Cortlandt chairmaker awkwardly combined both methods—perhaps indicating an idiosyncratic, "creolized" solution or mere confusion over the application of a difficult new constuction technique (fig. 25).[31]

There is strong circumstantial evidence that these chairs were carved in the shop of Jean Le Chevalier, a Saintongeais Huguenot who provided carving for the royal custom house barge in 1700. Le Chevalier was born around 1670, probably in the region of Mortagne, in Saintonge. The Chevalier family was deeply involved in the Reform movement in the small coastal seafaring villages of Mauzé, Soubise, St. Seurin, and Mortagne from the sixteenth century until the family's emigration to London and New York in the late seventeenth century. Although he did not arrive in the colonies until around 1688, the stage for his entrance into New York's artisan community may have been set twenty years earlier by another Jean Chevalier, probably his grandfather.[32]

The elder Jean Chevalier and a relative named Thomas (possibly his brother) were apparently in Martinique in January 1661. The following month, "John Cavlier" married "Eleanor La Chare [sic]" in New York City. She was probably the daughter of Salomon La Chaire, who served as notary of New Amsterdam from 1661 until 1662 and was a powerful member of the city's bureaucracy. Like so many of New Netherlands' earliest colonists, Salomon was a Walloon, born on the Lindengracht in Amsterdam. His father was Pierre La Chaire, a weaver from La Haye, Normandy, who became connected with the Normandy branch of the Le Chevalier family when he married Marguerite "Cavulier" in Amsterdam. The elder Jean Le Chevalier's social and political connections undoubtedly helped him secure important public contracts, like framing and repairing the royal coat of arms on the front of city hall in 1675. Such commissions also increased his exposure to the city's Anglican elites.[33]

This complex, transatlantic web of patronage, ramified by marriage and familial interconnections, provides fragmentary evidence of a migrating colonial craft network. Salomon La Chaire's brother, Jan, was a carpenter who emigrated from Valenciennes, a town in northeastern France bordering Flanders, and who arrived in New Amsterdam on September 2, 1662. Jean Chevalier (Cavlier) thus married a cousin of another family of refugee woodworking artisans, setting the stage for his grandson's entrée into a preexisting New York craft network. This network probably originated generations earlier in heretical outposts of northern and southwestern France before extending its web to Amsterdam, London, and finally to colonial America.[34]

On June 27, 1692, Jean Le Chevalier Jr. married Marie de la Plaine in the Dutch Reformed Church in New York. When their two daughters were born in 1693 and 1695, however, they were baptised in the new French Church. Le Chevalier's name appears often in the records of the French Church after 1688 (the date of his arrival), a strong indication of the multiple public and private allegiances that many New York City Huguenots maintained with dominant local cultures. Marie de la Plaine was the daughter of Nicholas de la Plaine, a Huguenot from the Seigneurie de la Grand Plaine, near Bressuire, just north of La Rochelle in the Poitou. Nicholas was living in New Amsterdam by April 1657 when he took the oath of allegiance to the Dutch government. By marrying into a French Protestant family established during the period of Dutch ascendancy, Le Chevalier forged additional ties with New York's "old" French culture. Marie's brother, Joshua (Delaplaine), was one of New York's most successful joiners, thus Jean may have also benefited from the commercial associations established by his brother-in-law.[35]

An alien under British colonial law, Le Chevalier received letters of denization in New York on September 28, 1695, and was made a freeman the following October. On June 11, 1700, "John Chevalier joiner" sued "gentleman" Duie [*sic*] Hungerford for "non-payment for making [a] Screwtore, table and other joiners work." Evidently, Le Chevalier was an extremely versatile tradesman capable of producing a variety of joined forms, carving, and turning. Something may be learned about his training as a turner from a note attached to the inventory of Magdalena Bouhier (also "Bouyer," from Marennes in Saintonge) taken on July 15, 1698, and designated "To John Le Chavallir by tornors tools of s[ai]d heredity 12s." Although Magdalena's husband Jean was a clothmaker, a close male relative or a previous husband may have taught Le Chevalier the "art and mystery" of turning. The turners tools "of s[ai]d heredity" could refer to the set of tools often given an apprentice at the end of his term. It is uncertain whether Le Chevalier served his apprenticeship in France, London, or New York.[36]

Le Chevalier's personal history suggests that he learned his trade both within the nuclear family and without, in shops belonging to closely related southwestern Huguenot craft networks. We know, for example, that he was apprenticed to a member of Magdalena Bouhier's family and so was trained as a turner in the Saintongeais tradition, that he probably learned to carve from either his grandfather or father (assuming his grandfather "Jan" trained his father), and that he was connected to at least two Huguenot craft and patronage networks through marriage. He was also well known to the entire New York Huguenot community through his active participation in the French Church. In addition to close social and occupational ties with his native community, Le Chevalier was connected with older New York continental cultures through his long association with the Dutch Calvinist Church. Nevertheless, evidence suggests that many of his patrons were New York elites of British descent and other craftsmen.

From the fall of 1700 until the summer of 1701, the British Custom House and the fort in New York underwent extensive renovation. On October 15, 1700, "Jno Chivaleer Carpenter" received £6 "for work done in the Custom house," and he earned £86.11 "for Joiner's work done ye Fort" the following June. At least five other carpenters and joiners worked on the custom house and its interior, but Le Chevalier received the highest payment.[37]

Le Chevalier gained access to New York's Anglicized elites through public projects and by supplying piecework for English joiners such as John

Ellison Sr., one of the most successful and well respected Anglican woodworkers in the city. Among the debtors and creditors listed in Ellison's ledger and inventory are several prominent local artisans including Le Chevalier, who may have sold him turned or carved components or entire chair frames.[38] Le Chevalier's public commissions and his close association with Ellison also suggest that he was one of the most important early New York carvers. Indeed, no other carver is documented in New York at the turn of the century. Given the relatively low demand for carving in early-eighteenth-century New York (Fitch's correspondence suggests that he sold six plain leather chairs for every carved one), it is plausible that Le Chevalier and his shop were capable of providing most of the carving needed by New York chairmakers and joiners. New York merchants and chairmakers did not develop an extensive export trade, so it is unlikely that the city could support more than a few professional carvers.

Although it can only be inferred that Le Chevalier made leather chair frames, there is direct evidence that at least two other Huguenots with connections to southwestern France made leather chairs—Richard Lott and Jean Suire (John Swear). The earliest references to Lott are in Thomas Fitch's letterbooks. On September 9, 1706, Fitch sent "Richard Lott NYC" a "bill Lading and Invo[ice] of one bale of upholstery being what yo bought amounting to forty two pound 7/9d shipd as yo odder'd . . . hpe will get safe to [New] York." Apparently, Lott, who was refered to as an "upholsterer" and "chairmaker" by 1707, imported most of his upholstery materials from Boston. The following month, Fitch wrote Lott, "I had not one brass nail nor tack by all these ships Tho a supply of other goods. That I shall be forced to buy Some here if can get them and if I can meet with any shall send yo some."[39]

On April 22, 1707, Fitch wrote Faneuil, to whom Fitch had transferred Lott's debt, "I hope Lott has paid all: as to his chairs being somewhat lower priced, ye reason is they were not Russia, but New Eng. leather, he had done here." Fitch apparently understood that Lott and his fellow New York chairmakers were a source of competition, but he continued to sell him the upholstery materials. Fitch's patronage of both Faneuil and Lott may have exemplified an "unintended performance," since the combination of chairs imported from Boston and those produced locally saturated the New York market with leather chairs by 1709.[40]

Fitch may have been partially mistaken, or perhaps intentionally misleading, in his analysis of why Lott's chairs were "somewhat lower priced." Although Lott imported upholstery materials from Boston, several factors gave him a competitive advantage over Fitch: Lott did not have custom duties and other carrying costs to factor into his price; he did not make chairs for venture cargo, therefore he assumed far less risk than Fitch who, by 1709, had a number of unsold chairs on consignment in New York; and Lott was intimately connected with and answerable to the local market. The latter may have required him to produce chairs that were better made and more ornate than conventional Boston examples—ones closer to the Huguenot-inspired, prototypical London cane chair (fig. 21).[41]

Little is known about Lott other than what is found in the Fitch letter-books and court records. The progenitor of his family in New York was probably Peter Lott, who emigrated from the Lott River Valley in south central France, not far from Saintonge, in 1652 and settled in Flatbush, Kings County. Since Richard Lott became a freeman in 1707, he must have been born around 1686, probably in Flatbush. Assuming that Peter Lott was his grandfather, Richard would have been a second-generation New Yorker from the "old" French culture, a relative rarity among early-eighteenth-century Huguenot artisans, most of whom emigrated in the 1680s. Peter may have left France in response to one of Richelieu's periodic military forays against Protestant strongholds south of the Loire Valley. The southwestern experience certainly supports the hypothesis that the persistent wars of religion caused thousands of Huguenots to leave in distinct waves long before the Revocation of the Edict of Nantes. Peter may also have been a woodworker. Several of the Kings County Lotts were woodworkers, some until well into the eighteenth century.[42]

New York chairmaker and joiner Jean Suire emigrated from St. Seurin de Mortagne, a tiny coastal village just north of the Gironde River in Saintonge. A Jean Suire appears often in Mortagne's consistorial records as an active participant in local church activities from St. Seurin. The Suire name remains common in coastal Saintonge and Aunis and is distinctly regional. It may be counted repeatedly in the archives of merchant and artisan heresy in southwestern France, where the Suires were usually recorded as woodworking or textile-producing tradesmen and occasionally as small shopkeepers. Members of the family were prone to conflict with both religious and secular authorities, to whom they were very well known. As early as 1661, La Rochelle's police undertook the "Expulsion of the Reformed: Suire, of Marans [a fishing village just north of La Rochelle]." In 1748, police in La Rochelle fined "Suire and his wife, publicans['cabaretiers']"—suspected as secret, "newly converted" Huguenots who remained in France after the Revocation—"for having served drinks to apprentice shoemakers and operated [for this purpose] during prohibited times and by night." Were the Suires serving heresy along with their wine? Did their public house provide a meeting place for Huguenot artisans denied access to the city's guilds since the events of 1628? It is not difficult to imagine that Jean Suire may have been forced to leave Saintonge because of similar activities.[43]

Nothing is known about Jean's route from St. Seurin, how long he may have resided in England or Holland, or the specific circumstances that caused him to immigrate to America. He was naturalized in New York in 1701, where he lived and worked in the West Ward until his premature death in March 1715. Suire's name seldom appears in the public records, although on December 6, 1715, he signed the Oath of Abjuration to George I. Virtually everything known about Jean's working life in the New World is contained in his inventory, a rich record that documents the shop of an industrious New York joiner, chairmaker, upholsterer, shoemaker, and sleighmaker. Evidently he died in his prime, for he left many things "done in part" or "not finish'd."[44] Suire was certainly not alone in practicing multiple trades. The theory that specialization was an urban phenomenon and that real diversity only existed in rural areas is refuted by the inventories of several New York woodworkers. Personal, familial, economic, and cultural factors, as well as geography, all influenced artisans' decisions about diversification.

Suire's estate was inventoried on March 12, 1715, by two English appraisers who knew him as "John Swear late of this City Joyner." The correct spelling of Suire's name and his ethnicity might have been lost had not his wife, "Marjan Suirre," signed the document and made several notations in French. The latter consist of computations from her husband's account books taken shortly before she and her son Cezar left the city and moved north to the Huguenot settlement at New Rochelle.

Suire's possessions suggest that he was relatively successful. The Anglo-French word "Due" mixed with Marjan's creolized French denotes outstanding debts totaling over £75.

1 ps Oxenbrix 93 Ells Brown . . . 5.8.6.
1 crokas & wooden Screen 8 Leaves . . . 1.18.0
a parcel fo Iron worke 16 box Locks 30 small
Locks & 8 pair of Chest hinges 9 dozen of .0.0
Brass Drops & 3 dos. Scutchins a parcel of Nails & brads
11 short thread Laces . . . 0.4.0
a parcel of Joyners Tools viz sws chizels gouges plaines &c . . . 10.0.0
2 pair scales and weights . . . 1.0-.0
8 Indian drest Deerskins . . . 1.3.0
2 skins of Neat Leather & 1 pair Shoes . . . 1.0.0
a parcel of Lumber . . . 1.0.0
1/2 barrel Lamp black 1 bird cage and one small box of paint . . . 0.18.0
part of a New Bedstead . . . 0.6.0
3 Small Cupboards not finish'd . . . 1.7.0
1 Jug with about 1 gallon Varnish . . . 0.9.6
1 old grindstone . . . 0.4.6
28 square ps Timber
50 boards whitewood & Gum & some black wallnutt . . . 3.10.0
1 Sleigh without Irons . . . 1.4.0
1 Negro about 8 yeares . . . 12.0.0
1 chest Drawers not finish'd . . . 0.18.0
2 old cross cutsaws 2 old guns & a parcell of rushes for chairs . . . 0.8.0
80 yds bristole stuff . . . 3.0.0

Pour argen recu 15//14//3
Pour Due Sur Le Livre 16//4//9
Pour Due Sur le Livre 59 – 0.8
Marjan Suirre

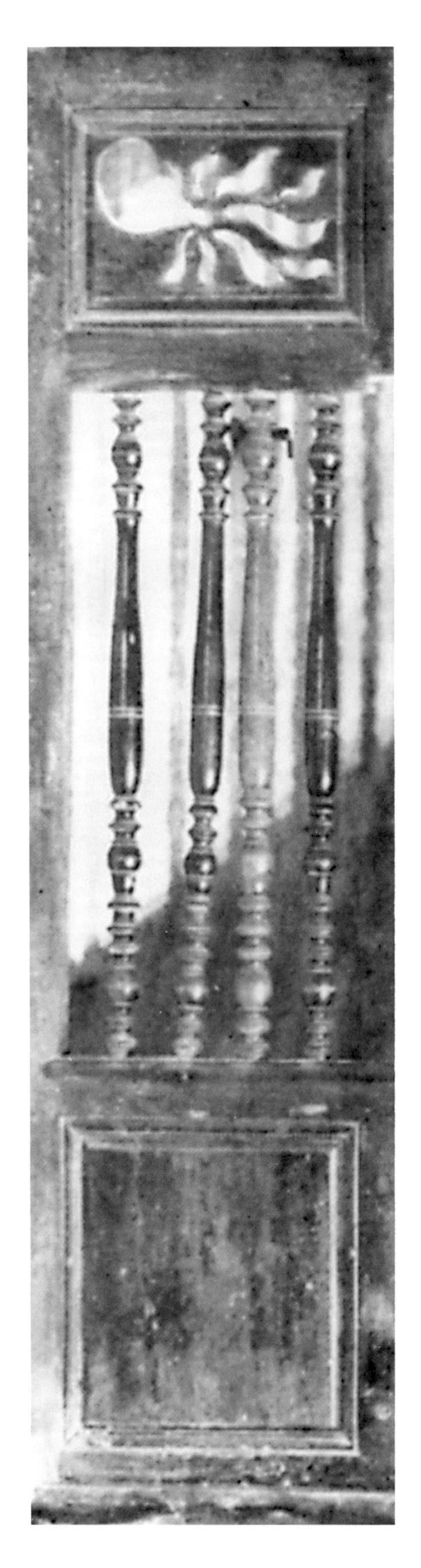

Figure 31 Details of the baptismal screen in the church of St. Étienne, Ars-en-Ré, Île de Ré, France, 1625–1627. Oak. (From *Inventaire Général des monuments et des Richesses Artistiques de la France, Commission Régionale de Poitou-Charentes, Charente-Maritime, Cantons Île de Ré*; photo, Christopher Zaleski.)

Suire's inventory, including household goods, totaled £126.9.1, and his joiner's tools were among the most expensive inventoried in New York City during the late seventeenth and early eighteenth centuries, indicating that he probably had the means to produce elaborate furniture forms. Lumber on hand included whitewood (yellow poplar), gumwood (or "bilsted"), and black walnut, along with "28 square ps Timber," probably intended for turning. The "parcell of rushes for chairs" and other upholstery materials, such as leather, "oxenbrix," "crokas," and "bristole stuff," indicate that Suire was both a joiner and a chairmaker. Most intriguing are the "8 Indian drest Deerskins" and "2 Skins of Neat Leather." The Indian deerskins may have been used for upholstery, but it is also possible that Suire stocked them for making shoes.[45] The "neat leather" was probably for chair upholstery, since Fitch and other upholsterers commonly used that term to denote furniture-grade material. The locks, hinges, brass drops, and "Scutchins" were expensive articles of hardware, largely imported from England, and the "Lamb black, small box of paint [and] 1 gallon Varnish" were finish components.

An artisan with a cultural background similar to Suire's may have constructed the Van Cortlandt armchair (fig. 25). Of all the New York examples known, it is the least indebted to Anglo-Boston prototypes and the closest to Saintongeais antecedents. With its undulating arms that sweep downward from a block high on the sharply raked rear posts and its low massing of details (an unusual combination of features for an Anglo-American leather armchair), the basic form of the Van Cortlandt armchair is generically related to seventeenth- and eighteenth-century French provincial fauteuils and to fauteuils made by French tradesmen in the upper St. Lawrence and lower Mississippi River valleys. The turned elements on the back posts are strikingly similar to those on the balusters of the baptismal screen or *clôture des fonts baptismaux* (fig. 31) in the medieval parish church of St. Étienne, in the canton of Ars-en-Ré on Île de Ré. The woodwork in the church dates between 1625 and 1627, just before the siege of La Rochelle. After the siege, the most openly practicing Huguenots were systematically purged from the regional guilds.[46]

The interior woodwork of the church of St. Étienne is essential for understanding the turning patterns favored by southwestern French Huguenots during the seventeenth century. Very little seventeenth-century interior woodwork from the war-torn region of Aunis-Saintonge (where churches were favored targets for iconoclasts) remains in situ. Moreover, Île de Ré lies just off the coast of La Rochelle, in Aunis, and is perfectly situated along the traditional trade routes used by Protestant merchants and mariners as they traveled north through the Bay of Biscay to Britain, the Netherlands, and ultimately the New World. This interior reflects the interaction of metropolitan woodworking traditions from La Rochelle and other Reformed metropolises in northern Europe and vernacular traditions from Saintonge, carried up the coast by journeymen woodworkers who regularly made the short journey to the island by sea in search of seasonal work. Despite the fact that St. Étienne was Roman Catholic, Huguenots were in the majority

Figure 32 Black chair, Long Island Sound region, perhaps southeastern Westchester County, 1705–1730. Maple and ash. Dimensions not recorded. (Dey Mansion, Wayne Township, New Jersey; photo, Neil D. Kamil.)

Figure 33 Black great chair, probably Tarrytown, Westchester County, 1705–1730. Woods unidentified. H. 44½", W. 25", D. 26¼". (Courtesy, Historic Hudson Valley.)

in the port towns where they dominated most of Île de Ré's artisan guilds by 1625. During the renovation of the Church of St. Étienne, Huguenot material culture was probably more pervasive on Île de Ré and in La Rochelle, its powerful patron and protector, than ever before.

The unusual turning sequences shared by the chair posts and screen balusters are distinguished by an attenuated ovoid element bracketed by delicate filets and spools that rise into sharply ridged and molded bands. The maker of the Van Cortlandt chair rejected the attenuated balusters common on Saintongeais prototypes in favor of the radically cut-down, tapered, and stacked column common to leather chairs and London cane chairs, which were influenced by Huguenot designers and turners in England. His turnings therefore blend Saintongeais forms with Huguenot-inspired London ones.[47]

The positive and negative spaces created by the balusters of the baptismal screen are similar to those formed by the back posts of a side chair that descended in the Schuyler and Dey families of New York and New Jersey (fig. 32) and the spindles of an armchair with a history of ownership in Tarrytown in Westchester County, New York (fig. 33). Both probably represent the work of chairmakers trained in southwestern coastal traditions. Commonly referred to as "black" or "colored" chairs, such forms were almost invariably painted and fitted with simple rush seats. Suire, for exam-

Figure 34 Couch, New York City or coastal Rhode Island, 1700–1715. Maple. H. 42⅛", W. 74⅜", D. 25⅛". (Courtesy, Winterthur Museum.)

ple, had all the materials necessary for the production of black chairs, including lumber prepared for turning, "1/2 barrel Lamp black . . . and one small box of paint," and "a parcell of rushes for chairs." New York inventories indicate that black chairs were commonly used in combination with cane chairs (though rarely with leather chairs), so they represented a relatively inexpensive, turner's alternative to upholstered furniture.[48] Evidently, Suire and his Huguenot contemporaries made chairs for consumers of all income levels.

Turnings similar to those of the "black chairs" (figs. 32, 33) are typically associated with coastal Connecticut chairmaking, but evidence suggests that similar work was produced along the entire coastline of the culturally permeable Long Island Sound as well as in the Connecticut River Valley towns that traded with communities commercially linked to the sound. The couch illustrated in figure 34 reflects the shifting, transatlantic human geography of the Long Island Sound. Probably made in either Rhode Island or New York, it belonged to Ezekiel Carré, a Huguenot minister who was a native of Île de Ré until 1686 when he emigrated with twenty-five other French refugee families to the short-lived settlement of Frenchtown in East Greenwich, Rhode Island.[49]

Perhaps the best material evidence documenting the extensive migration of refugee turners and chairmakers from southwestern France to the Long Island Sound region is from the cross-generational shops of the Durand family of St. Froul (a town of four hundred in seventeenth-century coastal Saintonge) and Milford, Connecticut, and of the Coutant family of Île de Ré and New Rochelle in southern Westchester County, New York. Benno Forman, Robert Trent, and Kathleen Eagen Johnson have documented the production of these shops, including their turned alternatives to metropolitan leather chairs. More importantly, they have also demonstrated an overlap between the end of the so-called "heart-and-crown" phase of coastal Connecticut chairmaking at midcentury and the beginning of the "York" (New York) phase of chairmaking in the Hudson, Connecticut, and Delaware River valleys and the Long Island Sound region.[50]

Given what we know about the refugee origins of these shops, it is plausible that many of the relationships between these diverse artifacts reflect common familial, craft, and patronage ties that originated in southwestern France. However, this is *not* to say that only Huguenot artisans produced turner's chairs—or, for that matter, New York leather chairs. Instead the evidence suggests that, at the very least, a process of Anglo-French creolization was active in the cultural and material life of New York City and the Long Island Sound region. Peter Thornton has documented a similar process among French refugee artisans living in London after 1685.[51] In both instances, creolization occurred as a result of face-to-face interaction in French-speaking artisan networks of refugees from the same regional diaspora and through common artisanal discourse. In New York, the latter included the ubiquitous use (in several different combinations) of architectonic, superimposed balusters.

Huguenot turners such as the Coutants, for example, were undoubtedly

Figure 35 Detail of the confessional in the church of St. Catherine, Loix, canton of Ars-en-Ré, Île de Ré, early eighteenth century. Oak. (From *Inventaire Général des monuments et des Richesses Artistiques de la France, Commission Régionale de Poitou-Charentes, Charente-Maritime, Cantons Île de Ré*; photo, Christopher Zaleski.)

Figure 36 Side chair attributed to Pierre or Andrew Durand, Milford, Connecticut, 1710–1740. Maple and ash. H. 45¼", W. 19½", D. 14¾". (Anonymous collection; photo, New Haven Colony Historical Society.)

familiar with early-eighteenth-century baluster and molding shapes such as those decorating a confessional (fig. 35) in the parish church of St. Catherine, also in the canton of Ars-en-Ré on Île de Ré. This French regional turning style, introduced to England and the New World by refugee woodworkers from the Continent, is manifest in the prototypical "first-generation heart-and-crown chair," made in Milford by Andrew Durand (1702–1791) or his master, possibly Pierre Durand (fig. 36). The latter may have emigrated to America as early as 1702.[52] The Durands and Coutants were thus connected over the course of more than a century by two bodies of water—the Bay of Biscay and Long Island Sound—as well as by common languages and artisanal traditions carried west in the Huguenot diaspora from Aunis-Saintonge.

Just as New York City Huguenot chairmakers began to wrest a share of the local market for metropolitan upholstered furniture from Anglo-Boston merchants and artisans, rural Huguenot shops began to dominate the regional market for inexpensive stylish alternatives to urban leather-upholstered seating. Both drew patterns from similar Old World sources but adapted them to different economic and social milieu. Although southwestern French patterns were often cloaked under the guise of the dominant Anglo-Boston fashion for leather chairs, many details endured and were adapted to inexpensive vernacular forms. In some rural settings, French turning styles persisted long after the "mannerist" superimposed baluster style became anachronistic in the metropolis.

The baptismal screen in the church of St. Étienne (fig. 31) also yields important information about the human geography of southwestern French Huguenots in New York and the Long Island Sound region. Architectural carving installed during the same period as the screen (see figs. 41, 42) foreshadows, at the very least, the emergence of New York plain leather chairs, heart-and-crown chairs, and, perhaps most of all, their Anglicized antecedents. Indeed, the heart-and-crown chair may have been the most enduring adaptation of a southwestern Huguenot artifactual language that began on the coast of the Bay of Biscay around the middle of the sixteenth century and ended on the coast of Long Island Sound in the middle of the eighteenth. The New York leather chair was just as profoundly indebted to that artifactual language as was its rural counterparts, only its debt was much more dissonant and ambiguous.

Benno Forman was the first to recognize ambiguities in how the historical and formal structures of New York leather chairs interacted. Forman understood that any inquiry into the nature of New York's material life must focus on the complex, contingent relation between history and form—the "life of form." Yet, he was unable fully to apply this methodology to the pluralistic New World societies of the middle Atlantic region and the South. His struggle with the conceptual problems pluralism posed focused ultimately on his thwarted formal analysis of the one "European" leather chair (fig. 37) that he considered absolutely central to the "origins of the New York style."[53]

This "European" chair had many of the standard features of the New York leather chair that differed fundamentally from standard Boston models: superimposed baluster posts wherein the turner's scansion is sharply punctuated by compressed caps, filets, reels, and ellipsoids (see fig. 3); compressed, urnlike finials surmounted by distinctively rotund bosses (see figs. 12, 15); leather upholstery pulled through a slit in the crest rail and nailed in the back—a device that appears on virtually all standard New York leather chairs with carved crests and rectangular back panels (see figs. 26–29); thick, double side stretchers that connect with a rear stretcher tenoned at the same level as the bottom side stretcher—a feature that appears on most, but not all New York plain leather chairs (see fig. 3); symmetrical balusters on the posts below the seat and often, in lieu of a cylinder, on the turned juncture of the rear posts between the bottom of the back and the top of the seat (see figs. 14, 19); and a concave or "French hollow" back (see fig. 20). "If this European chair is English," Forman wrote, "then the style of the New York chairs is English, and the New York high-back leather chairs took their inspiration from a part of the English tradition unknown or less influential

Figure 37 Side chair, probably London, 1685–1700. Woods and dimensions not recorded. (Photo, Symonds Collection, Decorative Arts Photographic Collection, Winterthur Museum.)

in Boston. If, on the other hand, this European chair is continental, then the New York chairs are northern European in inspiration." But, when Forman looked to Holland, a logical northern European source for immigrant New York craftsmen, the stylistic origins of the chair became more ambiguous. Chairs with verifiable Netherlandish provenances shared remarkably similar features with the European leather prototype, its London cane derivatives, and New York leather chairs.[54]

Forman also reached an intellectual cul de sac when he attempted to ascertain the origins of a finial turning shared by a Dutch highchair, the New York–made Chester-Backus armchair, *and* some Boston chairs: "The Dutch highchair also has a finial almost identical to that on the . . . [Chester-Backus chair]. Were these attributes brought to New York by an emigrant craftsman from Holland? The picture is further complicated by a version of the finial of the Dutch highchair and the [Chester-Backus] chair that is also common on Boston-made chairs in this period. How did that come about? Did this particular form of the finial make its way from Holland to England and thence to Boston and New York?"[55] Regrettably, the human context disappeared over three hundred years before these chairs caught Forman's eye.

Part of the problem lies in the quest to locate static territorial origins for the New York leather chair, indeed for New York history per se. Both were products of converging *human* geographies; of unstable, shifting, and above all infinitely mutable Atlantic communities, atomized and dispersed across Britain and Protestant northern Europe by vicious religious wars that beset Europe and colonial America from the sixteenth to the eighteenth centuries. Historical context, contingency, and above all human interaction dictated that *all* and *none* of the place names cited in Forman's analysis were the genesis of the New York leather chair. Thus the New York leather chair, like the "European" leather chair and the London cane chairs that preceded it, was not purely French, English, Dutch, Bostonian, or American. Instead the New York leather chair is a material manifestation of the interactive discourse of cultural convergence, quotation, and creolization, whereby different regional cultures communicated their perception of difference to themselves and others.

Figure 38 Side chair, London, 1685–1700. Beech. H. 48¾", W. 21⅞", D. 17⅝". (Courtesy, Museum of Fine Arts, Boston; gift of Mrs. Winthrop Sargent, in memory of her husband.)

Forman's intuitions about the "European" chair and the physical evidence embodied in it ultimately help portray Huguenot artisans as cultural creoles who used available artifactual languages in an innovative process of negotiation and conservative adaptation to accommodate changing contexts and power relations throughout the early modern Atlantic world. Forman speculated, on the basis of its russia leather upholstery, that the "European" chair was "probably" made in urban England. This attribution is validated by its close relation to London high-back cane and turkeywork chairs (compare figs. 21, 38). The carved and turned elements on the cane chair in particular share much with New York leather chairs, as do details on many other types of London cane chairs. The post turnings—vases surmounted by a sharply articulated reel and baluster—on the European chair are related to all but one New York leather chair illustrated here (fig. 25), as well as to the Durand side chair (fig. 36) and an important group of New York City tables. The turkeywork chair (fig. 38) also has a slit crest rail and carved elements associated with the "European" leather chair (fig. 37) and its London cane and New York leather contemporaries, and its frame is strikingly similar to that of a carved New York side chair with "barley twist" posts and stretchers (fig. 39). The fleur-de-lis and the sunflower motif on these chairs (see figs. 39, 40) spread from France in courtly and religious iconography that preceded the Huguenot dispersion and became part of the decorative vocabulary in England and Scotland during the sixteenth century. On these early chairs, however, the fleur-de-lis and sunflower may relate specifically to Huguenot artisanal culture and patronage.[56]

Assuming that the "European" leather chair (fig. 37) was made in London, the *earliest* date assignable to its "boyes and crown" crest rail and

Figure 39 Side chair, New York City, 1685–1700. Maple. H. 48", W. 20¼", D. 22". (Chipstone Foundation; photo, Gavin Ashworth.)

stretcher is extremely significant. The term "boyes and crown," which probably derives from the same craft and etymological tradition as "heart and crown," first appears in the accounts of the English royal household after 1685, in references to carving on new cane chairs made for James II and William and Mary. This date coincided with the Revocation of the Edict of Nantes, after which Huguenot refugee artisans flooded into London. Publisher, architect, and interior designer Daniel Marot (1661–1752) was one of many highly skilled Huguenot artisans who received royal patronage during the mid-1680s. Although he and his father Jean certainly helped introduce the court style to England and Holland, many French baroque

Figure 40 Detail of crest rail, posts, and finial of the side chair illustrated in fig. 39. (Photo, Gavin Ashworth.)

designs, such as the "boyes and crown," are too generic to attribute specifically to them. Even the Marots did not invent many of the designs they published; rather, their work represents an ingenious and marketable compilation of Huguenot design dialects carried north from the courts of Paris and Versailles as well as from small towns and regional centers such as Aunis-Saintonge.[57]

The appearance of the "boyes and crown" in London in 1685 and its stylistic relationship to earlier architectural carving in the church of St. Étienne (figs. 41, 42) strongly suggest that this motif, like most of the decorative vocabulary on the wooden frames of the "European" leather chair and its New World counterparts, was developed in both metropolitan and colonial contexts through direct interaction with southwestern Huguenot craftsmen and their merchant patrons such as Jean Suire, Jean Le Chevalier, Richard Lott, the Durands, and Benjamin Faneuil. After 1685, most refugee craftsmen resided in Huguenot artisan communities in metropolitan England (as did the family of Jean Le Chevalier) or, before 1664, in Holland (as was the case with the family of Richard Lott). The duration of their stay generally depended on economic prospects, political conditions, and the existence of familial or craft networks in other areas of Europe or America.

The carved elements of the choir screen in the church of St. Étienne (fig. 41) are therefore also important for understanding the movement of artisans and ideas.[58] The facade contains sixteen square, rectangular, and demilune panels depicting scenes of Christ the evangelist and his apostles (fig. 41a). The biblical representations are punctuated by acanthus foliage (fig. 41b) or Italianate grotesques (figs. 41c, 42). The latter are carved naturalistically in deep, three-dimensional relief and are framed by sharp, complex, applied moldings.

Half of the carved panels are friezes representing opposing winged cherubs with flowing curly hair, goatlike hooved legs, and aquatic serpents'

Figure 41 Details of three carved panels on the choir screen in the church of St. Étienne, Ars-en-Ré, Île de Ré, components ca. 1629: (a) Christ gathering his flock; (b) acanthus-leaf foliage; (c) winged cherubs holding an urn. Oak and walnut. (From *Inventaire Général des monuments et des Richesses Artistiques de la France, Commission Régionale de Poiton-Charentes, Charente-Maritime, Cantons Île de Ré*; photo, Christopher Zaleski.)

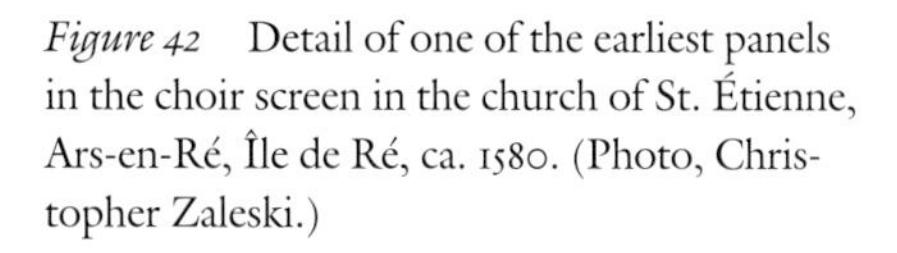

Figure 42 Detail of one of the earliest panels in the choir screen in the church of St. Étienne, Ars-en-Ré, Île de Ré, ca. 1580. (Photo, Christopher Zaleski.)

tails. Most (see fig. 41c) hold between them an urn containing tiny flowers that are remarkably similar to those unique to some New York carved leather chairs. The latter typically conjoin the opposing halves of S scrolls (fig. 29). The lower half of the urn has a mature flower flanked by opposing foliate volutes joined by a clearly delineated band, perhaps forming a rosy cross. The articulation of this motif, often represented in both Rosicrucian and Huguenot iconography of the seventeenth century, recalls the carved fleur-de-lis on the London high-back turkeywork chair (fig. 38), as well as the carved crest rail of a seventeenth-century joined great chair (figs. 43, 44) found in Southampton, Long Island, in 1875.[59]

Figure 43 Joined great chair, probably New York City, ca. 1675. Oak. H. 42½", W. 25", D. 22½". (Courtesy, Winterthur Museum.) Jean Le Chevalier's grandfather, "Jan Cavelier," was one of the most important carvers in New York during the era when this chair was made.

Fourteen of the carved screen panels date from the late 1620s, about two generations before the "boyes and crown" appeared in London. The two remaining panels, which date from the late sixteenth century, also depict winged cherubs with goat feet and serpents' tails (fig. 42). Since they probably served as the prototype for the later panels, this Italianate imagery may have appeared in the Aunis-Saintonge area as early as the 1580s. Although the "boyes and crown" on the "European" leather chair is not by the same hand as the later church carving, it is clearly the work of a Huguenot refugee—or a Huguenot trained "native"—who emerged from the same southwestern French regional craft traditions.

Forced out into the Atlantic world, Huguenot craftsmen sought to form new identities through artisanal interaction. Long experience at crafting heresy at the French court, the core of French absolutism, had demonstrated that skill in manipulating the material languages of concealment and display was absolutely necessary to maintain a semblance of cultural equilibrium in the new world of asymmetries. For the Huguenots, asymmetry

Figure 44 Detail of the carved crest rail of the great chair illustrated in fig. 43. (Courtesy, Winterthur Museum.) The compressed, diamond-shaped aperture surmounted by a lunette at the nexus of the opposing scrolls is repeated in the carving of the sunflower on the crest rail of the New York leather chair illustrated in figs. 39, 40.

and the quest for equilibrium had become a permanent condition of life in "the desert." The desert was, after all, a place to await the millenium at the end of time—the Huguenots' only real "home" in history. The apocalyptic moment of perfect social and spiritual harmony would accompany Christ's return and, with it, the annihilation of all difference. Concealment, the armature of a displaced, shifting identity, would then simply dissolve into transparency.

Hidden in Plain Sight

New York's successful response to the importation of Boston leather chairs began with the massive influx of French Huguenot merchants and craftsmen into New York City from the Aunis-Saintonge region of southwestern France following the Revocation of the Edict of Nantes in 1685. Within a decade, New York had a mature community of Huguenot artisans, many of whom arrived in kinship networks that migrated virtually intact in the same craft diaspora that transformed notions of courtly style in England and Holland. In this context, the Huguenot diaspora of the 1680s compares favorably with the migration of Puritan craft networks to Boston and other parts of southeastern New England during the 1630s. By the end of the seventeenth century, New York also had a well-developed community of "native" artisans including "old," pre-1685 French or Walloon refugees who migrated west during earlier periods of confessional violence. These craftsmen linked the newcomers with French-speaking groups that were already established in New Amsterdam prior to the English takeover in 1664. Comprised of individuals from both artisan sectors, New York's leather chairmakers and their merchant patrons were perfectly positioned to compete effectively in the heterogeneous market for luxury goods that Boston's merchants and artisans had dominated since the mid-seventeenth century.

As Fitch and Faneuil's correspondence about the rigorous demands of metropolitan style and fashion indicates, commercial success in New York was contingent upon interaction and convergence with the dominant Anglicized culture. Fragmented and asymmetrical, the process of convergence manifested itself in discrete yet perceptible cultural boundaries arranged specifically within the internal spatial dynamics of the chairs themselves. The chairs, therefore, encoded a sort of narrative; a "fictional consensus" between competing merchant-elites and artisan communities that represented competing cultures on the colonial core and periphery—a material discourse interacting with multiple histories whereby both specific and generic perceptions of metropolitan style encompassed fundamental questions of identity, social distance, and boundaries in a pluralistic new world society.

This problem was, however, a transatlantic one wherein marginalized cultures acted to subvert and redefine core cultures in relation to themselves, particularly in arenas of social and economic action that remained viable after political and military battles were lost. By the early eighteenth century, the negotiation of shifting identities between "natives" and "foreigners" had a long history in absolutist France owing to the enduring presence of Huguenots and Jews. Both "foreigners" and "natives" pinned their hopes on shifting, circular dialogues: "foreigners" hoped for manipulation toward change from below, "natives," for maintenance (or extension) of the status quo from above. "A 'native resident,'" wrote French Chancellor Henri d'Aguesseau in 1742, "is the opposite of a 'foreigner'; and as opposites ought to define one another, in defining the term 'foreigner' we will know the full limits of the 'native resident.'"[60] Although they could not remain pure "opposites" in a Protestant America that granted them refuge, New World Huguenots found meaning in the negotiation of an identity in which their historical status as perpetual "foreigners" was a defining element.

In Aunisian and Saintongeais Huguenot society, artisans had a powerful formative influence on virtually every facet of economic life in the countryside and in lay spiritual life as well. Tradesmen pursued strategies that linked local religious discourse and materialism at the most basic levels of experience. Yet, the one-dimensional, linear framework employed by many historians of the American Huguenot experience virtually "predetermines" the rapid decline, assimilation, and "disappearance" of Huguenot culture in New York. Although this monolithic approach documents simple superficial evidence of their absorption into the dominant English culture, it is too shallow to confront change as process. Because it overlooks or misinterprets the Huguenot experience in southwestern France, it provides no foundation for understanding the complex, dynamic processes of transatlantic convergence and creolization in the middle colonies. The most fundamental stumbling block for the assimilationists, however, is their perception of Huguenot culture as transparent; they take traditional Huguenot masking behavior—or "disappearance"—at face value. As early as 1611, a bemused Catholic observer at the great Huguenot assembly at Saumur cautioned

Figure 45 Composite diagram of the New York side chair illustrated in fig. 3. (Drawing, Neil D. Kamil; art work, Wynne Patterson.)

(a) Trapezoid representing the ground plan of the central axes of the four posts considered from an axiometric perspective.

(b) Dimensions of the trapezoid providing basic units of measurement.

(c) Trapezoid extended vertically to form framework in three dimensions.

(d) Chair's overall dimensions indicating a one-to-one symmetrical relationship between the seat height and the height of the leather back panel (compare to figure 10).

(e) Backward rake of the rear posts viewed from the side.

(f) Proportional system of horizontal elements viewed from the side: overall symmetry and balance, as opposed to the verticality of the Boston prototype, is achieved by equidistant, tripartite repetition traversing areas both above and below the seat (bc / gh / lmn); balancing and then reducing the three spaces beneath the seat using the largest measurements available in the system to accentuate a "bottom heavy" effect (jk / kl / lmn); and the static repetition of the turner's pattern above the seat (ji / gf / ed /; hg / cb /; fe / dc / ba).

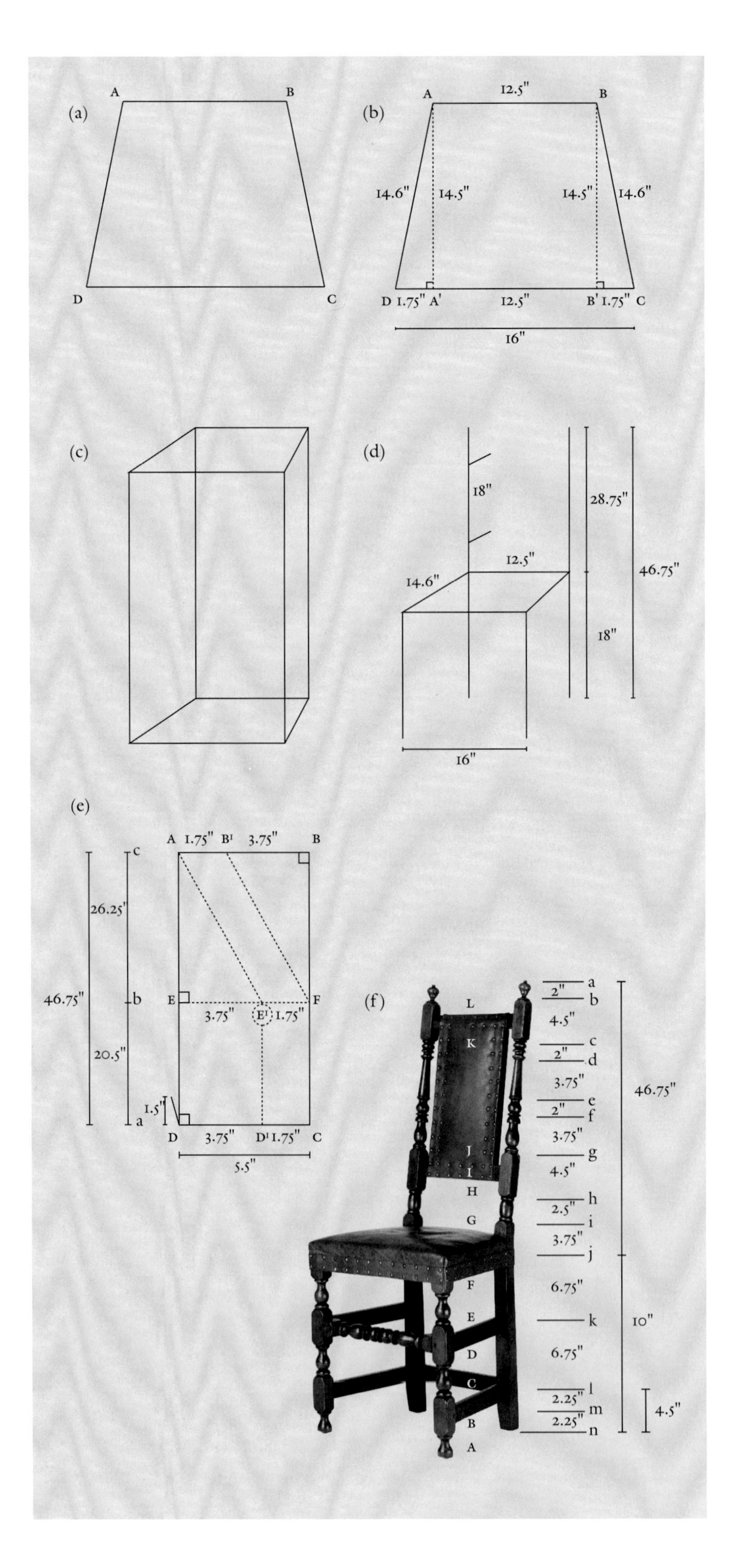

against the danger of such generalizations: "When the Protestant beseeches the king *très humblement* [he does so with] hand held high, sword drawn from its scabbard."[61]

Nearly three centuries of continuous religious war and violent reversals of power in the region caused southwestern Huguenots to become anything but transparent. To survive they had to develop strategies of interaction with others that were devious, obfuscating, and subterranean; they had to remain invisible while close to the heart of power. This strategy is reflected in the Bourbons' use of disease metaphors, such as "virus" or "cancer," to describe "poisonous" insidious "attacks" by heretics hidden within the "body" of the state and to justify brutal, cleansing excisions. By the mid-sixteenth century, southwestern Huguenots had developed a mobile, mutable, largely artisanal culture that expressed its values, attitudes, and beliefs obliquely, usually in material form, by converging invisibly, yet within plain sight, with the most powerful symbols of the dominant host culture. A marginalized people, they chose to display their personal symbols on the margins of their work.

When New York Huguenots such as Jean Le Chevalier, Richard Lott, Jean Suire, and Benjamin Faneuil, appropriated the Boston leather chair, they radically transformed only the surface treatment of the frame (the cheapest and most inconspicuous or *marginal* component), leaving the generic structure and leather panels of the Boston prototype undisturbed (fig. 45); however, the compositional logic of the New York leather chair conveys a dissembling, almost subversive quality. By subdividing the smooth, classical scansion of the Boston chair frame and substituting symmetry where there was asymmetry, the producers of the standard New York plain leather chair inverted the primary aesthetic intended by the producers of the Boston prototype—the abrupt, centrifugal verticality that represented the very essence of New England's mercantile reinterpretation of the most novel features of imported Anglo-French metropolitan cane chairs. Because the language of the chair was defined by its upholstery, and because he was not restrained by the economics of production for export, the New York chairmaker could make significant changes in the disposition of ornament on the frame without making a different chair. New York chairmakers creolized the Boston chair's artifactual language. They borrowed all of its basic lexicon, yet worked to change the generative grammar—fluid substructures that interact with the surface of the lexicon to generate meaning—to suit contingencies associated with their (or their patron's) own sociocultural requirements for the same price (or less) as the Boston leather chair.[62]

The exact percentage of the Boston prototype transformed by New York artisans and upholsterers can be calculated by taking the surface area of the New York chair viewed frontally and subtracting significant "grammatical" change from the Boston prototype. The composite is nearly four parts prototype to one part alteration. Although the New York Huguenot artisan altered only one-fifth of the space of the Boston form, he did so by reactivating "old" cultural turning patterns derived from Anglo-French London cane and leather chairs, earlier New Amsterdam/New York Franco-Walloon chairs, or specific southwestern French regional woodworking paradigms, patterns that would have meaning for artisans and patrons from Aunis-Saintonge. In doing so, he constructed a new socio-material identity that converged multiple, symbiotic, yet partially discrete "human regions" in a single dominant artifact.

Jack P. Greene has argued that colonial British America was an "uncertain, unequal, exploitative, restless, and, in many respects, chaotic world" in which "the psychology of exploitation" was so "normative" that there existed a "symbiotic relationship between independence and dependence." Pluralistic cultures in British America were constantly engaged in a struggle to "establish their mastery over their . . . several distinctive cultural spaces." As an artifact of cultural convergence with perceptible internal boundaries, the New York leather chair was a medium through which the struggle over mastery could be negotiated in an acceptable if not wholly benign manner—as commerce—and ultimately redefined as economic "improvement" useful in elaborate, mutually acceptable (if not mutually inclusive) rituals of "politeness" and "civility." These contexts provided the appropriate discursive conditions for acceptance by upwardly mobile colonial elites.[63]

The elements of the New York chair that evidence the most radical centripetal motion are the very ones that move centrifugally on the Boston prototype: the columns on the back posts and the balusters on the front stretcher. Indeed, the attenuated "classical" columns and smooth surfaces were precisely the spaces chosen for inversion by patrons, artisans, and designers using southwestern Huguenot forms (fig. 46). On the back posts of the Boston chair, the animate motion of the turned line follows its narrow path upward with no opposition, and on the front stretcher the impulse is away from center. By contrast, the molding sequences on the back posts of the New York chair interrupt the upward momentum; impulse ascends, rebounds, and returns to its starting point. The front stretcher, the only component common to almost all New York plain leather chairs, turns movement inward towards center to such a degree that it is virtually the opposite of its Boston counterpart. The same is true of Boston and New York leather chairs with carved crests. Although the scrollwork of the Boston model flows away from center, the New York crest begins its outward movement, but stops, pivots on an acute angle, and returns just as abruptly. These differences represent a dialogue between Anglo-Boston artisans constructing a centrifugal artifactual language and New York artisans from Aunis and Saintonage responding centripetally.[64]

The analysis of leather chairs and other artifacts can be likened to the analysis of text. As such, the historian must strive to reconstitute an artifact's entire scope, including "what they were intended to mean and how this meaning was intended to be taken."[65] As with the New York chair's physical attributes (or symbolic language), intentionality can be turned in upon itself. If read one dimensionally, as Fitch intended his leather chair be read by New York's merchants and consumers, that perception could be manipulated from "below," as part of an oblique dialogue about the contingency

Boston Back Posts

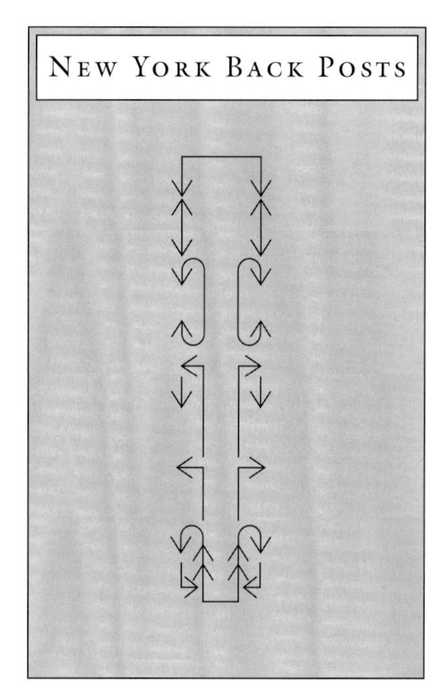

Boston Front Stretcher

Figure 46 Flow diagram representing the formal opposition of turning patterns on Boston and New York plain leather chairs, exemplified by figs. 1 and 3, respectively. (Drawing, Neil D. Kamil; art work, Wynne Patterson.)

of culture, commerce, and ultimately power. The New York plain leather chair was consequently constructed to contain alternative "intentions" responsive to many levels of experience.

One school of perceptual theory maintains that man's fundamental impulse to generalize and order his experience causes him to "abstract single properties and regard them as if they were the whole object." In a pluralistic setting, however, monolithic perceptions are not necessarily generated by the artifacts themselves but are conditioned and potentially refracted and multiplied through social interaction with multiple personal and cultural histories. This "floating chain" of signifiers accommodates areas of instability where contradictory intentions converge and are internalized. Multiple social realities can then be ordered hierarchically as "finite provinces of meaning." New Yorkers were thus socialized to understand that certain phenomena mediated certain artifacts and institutions (or, like the Boston leather chair and the craft community that produced and marketed it, artifactual institutions), and this attitude tended to govern their perceptions.

Clearly, a seductive set of social expectations, associations, and perceptions accompanied the "news" about style, fashion and status that the Boston leather chair and its local variants carried into virtually every elite New York consumer's household under the thrall of Anglicization. The control of knowledge was, therefore, also at stake.[66] The Boston leather chair can thus be interpreted as a strictly coded symbol system with its signifiers, *Boston* and *leather*, plainly defined in the early-eighteenth-century colonial lexicon, making it an artifact accompanied by a verbal and written text to facilitate understanding. The primary signifier of the chair—its rectangular leather back panel—was intended to be perceived first as the center of focus. It possessed the chair's general social, cultural and economic attribute, its sign of Bostonness, and was the one aspect of the chair that was necessary for all viewers to experience. The back panel conveyed the sign in a clearly defined geometric form: a rectangle, preferably made of patterned russia leather, always framed with one or two rows of shiny brass nails. Refractory textiles with crystalline optical qualities, such as russia leather, were highly prized components of the court style. For example, Jean-Francois Niceron's *La Perspective Curieuse ou Magie Artificielle des Effets Merveilleux* (Paris, 1638) diagrammed "the optics" of domestic objects, such as upholstered chairs, "by direct sight." Niceron was particularly interested in the "refraction of crystals" and the "reflection of flat, cylindrical and conical mirrors" as optical paradigms that would be "very useful to painters, architects, engravers, [and] sculptors." On leather chairs, the rake of the back panel, upward in "sight" of the beholder, determined the interplay of pattern and light that reinforced the textile's communicative power.[67]

New York Huguenot artisans capitalized on the production of "polite" objects—things that had both private and public functions—and so had the potential to generate multiple layers of meaning, perceptible to some and obscure to others. By retaining the generic leather back panel, a powerful symbol of British metropolitan style and culture, French chairmakers were able to subvert the secondary codes embodied in the frame of the Boston chair with patterns borrowed from their "old" culture, creating a creolized form that would "pass" in the dominant Anglicized culture while it remained in opposition on a more subliminal level. For most New Yorkers of British descent, the New York leather chair *was* a locally made Boston chair and a requisite status symbol linking them with other Anglicized elites. Huguenots from Aunis-Saintonge, however, undoubtedly perceived vestiges of their own refugee culture attached discreetly to the cognitive edges. Although historians can never fully know the variety of cultural associations that colonial New Yorkers may have carried with them when they took their seats during the early eighteenth century, there is reason to believe that, beyond their obvious practical use, some chairs were made to function interactively, to help mold and direct those associations and so, in a sense, the sitters themselves. Perhaps, for similar reasons, after having "walked round" "English," "French," and "Dutch" New York in 1716, the

Huguenot voyager John Fontaine finally beheld, to his amazement, a "French" town.[68] Everyone could construct their own convergence narrative.

Huguenot artisans and their merchant patrons quietly revealed in New York what they had learned under absolutism. Even the most powerful, seemingly inflexible symbols of dominance afforded valuable opportunities for access, manipulation, and, in the end, appropriation, through the "hidden" mediation of craft. For Faneuil, Lott, Le Chevalier, and Suire, the Boston leather chair, made ubiquitous by the volume, duration, and scope of that city's mercantile activity—indeed, made a "natural" part of colonial America's aesthetic reality—provided an open door to the homes of their hosts. Early New York was a place where, in practice, notions of mastery and totality were notoriously unstable. There, the powerful impulse of Anglicization was transformed into an armature of resistance upon which French refugee merchants and chairmakers harnessed their own concerns about mastery and its limitations.[69]

Ultimately, the Huguenot artisans who migrated from southwestern France to colonial America were part of a dispersed Atlantic culture of almost pure contingency, of infinite adaptation to niches made available by their craft. Never in their history had they lived outside the shadow of a more powerful "other." When considered from the refugee artisan's subterranean perspective of a violent and troubled past, the presumed "disappearance" of southwestern Huguenot culture in early New York becomes the best historical evidence of its continued vitality. What is regionalism, after all, but another word for human geography?

ACKNOWLEDGMENTS Earlier versions of this essay were presented to The Seminar at Johns Hopkins University and the Washington Area Seminar on Early American History and Culture at the University of Maryland at College Park. The author is grateful to members of both seminars for close reading and criticism. The author is especially grateful to Jack P. Greene, Orest Ranum, Sam Cohn, Michael Fried, Nancy Struever, John McCusker, Jean Russo, Roger Gonzales, Kathleen Eagen Johnson, Luke Beckerdite, and the late Benno M. Forman. Fieldwork in the southwest of France was undertaken while on a fellowship from the Fulbright-Hays Commission.

1. Edward Porter Alexander, ed., *The Journal of John Fontaine: An Irish Huguenot Son in Spain and Virginia, 1710–1719* (Charlottesville: University Press of Virginia, 1972), p. 115. These issues are explored in Richard Archer, "New England Mosaic: A Demographic Analysis for the Seventeenth Century," *William and Mary Quarterly* 47, no. 4 (October 1990): 477–502; and David Grayson Allen, *In English Ways: The Movement of Societies and the Transferral of English Local Law and Custom to Massachusetts Bay in the Seventeenth Century* (Chapel Hill: University of North Carolina Press, 1981). For the specific localism of seventeenth-century transferral, see Sumner Chilton Powell, *Puritan Village: The Formation of a New England Town* (Middletown, Conn.: Wesleyan University Press, 1963). For the problem of pluralism and diffusion in seventeenth-century New England material culture, see Robert Blair St. George, *The Wrought Covenant: Source Material for the Study of Craftsmen and Community in Southeastern New England, 1620–1700* (Brockton, Mass.: Brockton Art Center/Fuller Memorial, 1979); and Jonathan L. Fairbanks and Robert F. Trent, eds., *New England Begins: The Seventeenth Century*, 3 vols. (Boston: Museum of Fine Arts, Boston, 1982), esp. vol. 1, Migration and Settlement. The single dissenting voice in recent historiography comes from David Hackett Fischer, who maintains the primacy of East Anglian "hearth culture" in colonial New England in *Albion's*

Seed: Four British Folkways in America (New York: Oxford University Press, 1989), pp. 13–205. Fischer's position has been aggressively challenged by historians on both sides of the Atlantic. The issues in this debate are clearly delineated in Jack P. Greene, Virginia De John Anderson, James Horn, Barry Levy, Ned C. Landsman, and David Hackett Fischer, "Albion's Seed: Four British Folkways in America—A Symposium," *William and Mary Quarterly* 48, no. 2 (April 1991): 224–308.

2. On pluralism in early New York, see Thomas L. Purvis, "The National Origins of New Yorkers in 1790," *New York History* 67, no. 2 (April 1986): 133–50; Nan A. Rothschild, *New York City Neighborhoods: The Eighteenth Century* (New York: Academic Press, 1990); Joyce D. Goodfriend, *Before the Melting Pot: Society and Culture in Colonial New York City, 1664–1730* (Princeton, N.J.: Princeton University Press, 1992); and David S. Cohen, "How Dutch Were the Dutch of New Netherland?" *New York History* 62, no. 1 (January 1981): 43–50. On woodworking artisans, pluralism, and creolization, see Neil Duff Kamil, "Of American Kasten and the Mythology of 'Pure Dutchness': A Review Article," in *American Furniture,* edited by Luke Beckerdite (Hanover, N.H.: University Press of New England for the Chipstone Foundation, 1993), pp. 275–82; Lonn Taylor and Dessa Bokides, *New Mexican Furniture, 1660–1940: The Origins, Survival, and Revival of Furniture Making in the Hispanic Southwest* (Santa Fe, N.Mex.: Museum of New Mexico Press, 1987); and Lonn Taylor, "Hispanic Cabinetmakers and the Anglo-American Aesthetic," *Antiques* 136, no. 3 (September 1989): 554–67.

3. Elizabeth Paling Funk, "Netherlands' Popular Culture in the Knickerbocker Works of Washington Irving," in *New World Dutch Studies: Dutch Arts and Culture in Colonial America, 1609–1776*, edited by Roderic H. Blackburn and Nancy A. Kelley (Albany, N.Y.: Albany Institute of History and Art, 1987), pp. 83–94. Kamil, "Of American Kasten," pp. 275–82.

4. Benno M. Forman, *American Seating Furniture, 1630–1730: An Interpretive Catalogue* (New York: W. W. Norton, 1988), pp. 229–356.

5. These inventories represent nearly the total of those known to survive in English from early New York City and Queens and Kings Counties on western Long Island and in northern Brooklyn. Inventories taken in English begin in 1664. The majority of original documents are currently on deposit in the New York State Archives in Albany; Klapper Library, Queens College, Flushing, N.Y.; the New York Historical Society Library, New York, N.Y.; and the Winterthur Museum Library, Winterthur, Delaware.

6. R. W. Symonds, "The English Export Trade in Furniture to Colonial America, Part I," *Antiques* 27, no. 6 (June 1935): 216. The majority of such reports to Parliament (most of which were authored by English merchants and the London guilds) appeared in the 1760s on the heels of the huge debt British taxpayers accumulated after the end of the Imperial Wars in 1763, finally prompting the ill-fated Parliamentary Reform Acts (see John J. McCusker and Russell R. Menard, *The Economy of British America, 1607-1789: Needs and Opportunities for Study* [Chapel Hill: University of North Carolina Press, 1985], p. 190).

7. McCusker and Menard, *The Economy of British America*, pp. 92–93.

8. Ibid., pp. 96–110.

9. Richard H. Randall Jr., "Boston Chairs," *Old-Time New England* 54, no. 1 (Summer 1963): 12–16; Brock Jobe, "The Boston Furniture Industry, 1720–1740," in *Boston Furniture of the Eighteenth Century*, edited by Walter Muir Whitehill, Jonathan Fairbanks, and Brock Jobe (Boston: Colonial Society of Massachusetts, 1974), p. 40; Robert F. Trent, *Hearts and Crowns: Folk Chairs of the Connecticut Coast, 1720–1840* (New Haven, Conn.: New Haven Colony Historical Society, 1977), pp. 32–35. Six "Boston made leather chaires" are listed in the inventory of James Nappier of New York City, March 26, 1754, Joseph Downs Manuscript Collection, Winterthur Museum Library, acc. 53.190. As early as March 28, 1701, Her Majesy's Custom's Clerks recorded that Benjamin Faneuil of New York City was to pay duty on "12 leather chairs [lately arrived on the sloop Rachell from] Boston where the above goods were made" (*An Account of Her Majesty's Revenue in the Province of New York, 1701–1709: The Customs Records of Early Colonial New York*, edited by Julius M. Block, Leo Hershkowitz, Kenneth Scott, and Constance D. Sherman [Ridgewood, N.J.: Gregg Press, 1966], p. 35). Timothy H. Breene, "An Empire of Goods: The Anglicization of Colonial America, 1690–1776," *Journal of British Studies* 25, no. 4 (October 1986): 470–99.

10. William Smith Jr., *The History of the Province of New-York, Volume One: From the First Discovery to the Year 1732,* edited by Michael Kammen (Cambridge, Mass.: Belknap Press of Harvard University Press, 1972), p. 226.

11. Thomas Fitch Letterbook, microfilm M-1422, Joseph Downs Library, Winterthur

Museum. The original letterbooks are in the American Antiquarian Society, Worcester, Mass., and the Massachusetts Historical Society, Boston. On the siege of La Rochelle and its importance to the history of American Huguenot artisans, see Neil D. Kamil, "War, Natural Philosophy, and the Metaphysical Foundations of Artisanal Thought in an American Mid-Atlantic Colony: La Rochelle, New York City, and the Southwestern Huguenot Paradigm, 1517–1730" (Ph.D. diss., Johns Hopkins University, 1989), chapter 1; on the Fitch-Faneuil relationship, the European background of both, and the trade in leather chairs between Boston and New York, see ibid., chapters 6–7. For the most reliable Faneuil genealogy and the family's transatlantic trading and patronage network, see J. F. Bosher, "Huguenot Merchants and the Protestant International in the Seventeenth Century," *William and Mary Quarterly* 52, no. 1 (January 1995): 84–92. For the best recent work on the Atlantic trading society of La Rochelle's mercantile community in Canada, see J. F. Bosher, *The Canada Merchants, 1713–1763* (Oxford: Clarendon Press, 1987), pp. 3–46 and 109–90; and J. F. Bosher, "The Imperial Environment of French Trade with Canada, 1660–1685," *English Historical Review* 108 (Jan. 1993): 50–81.

12. Robert J. Gough, "The Myth of the 'Middle Colonies': An Analysis of Regionalization in Early America," *Pennsylvania Magazine of History and Biography* 103 (July 1983): 394–95. Gough borrows the term "human region" from Lewis Mumford.

13. Fitch Letterbook.

14. Fitch Letterbook.

15. Population figures from Jack P. Greene, *Pursuits of Happiness: The Social Development of Early Modern British Colonies and the Formation of American Culture* (Chapel Hill: University of North Carolina Press, 1988), pp. 178–80. The middle colonies were among the fastest growing regions between 1660 and 1710 owing largely to the "push factor" caused by the continental Wars of Religion. The concerns of the Board of Trade were focused initially on woolens manufactured on Long Island. See letters from Lord Cornbury to Secretary Hodges in 1705, Caleb Heathcote to the Board of Trade on August 3, 1708, and Governor Hunter to the Board of Trade on November 12, 1715, in E. B. O'Callaghan, *The Documentary History of the State of New York*, 4 vols. (Albany, N.Y.: Weed, Parsons, and Comp., 1850–51), 1:711–14.

16. For a detailed reconstruction of Faneuil's Aunisian and Saintongeais craft network in New York City, see Neil D. Kamil, *Discursive Things: Language, Form and Convergence in New York Colony, 1646–1709* (Baltimore, Md.: Johns Hopkins University Press, forthcoming).

17. David Ormrod, "The Atlantic Economy and the 'Protestant Capitalist International,' 1651–1775," *Historical Research* 66, no. 160 (June 1993): 197–207. See also J. F. Bosher, "Huguenot Merchants, pp. 77–100.

18. Fitch Letterbook.

19. Robert F. Trent, "The Endicott Chairs," *Essex Institute Historical Collections,* 114, no. 2 (April 1978): 117–18.

20. Queens College, Klapper Library, Historical Documents Collection (hereinafter cited QC, KL, HDC), Albany, II, fol. 2–84. When appraisers referred to condition, "old" was often accompanied by specific qualifiers such as "broken" or "much abused."

21. The armchair was sold at the Litchfield Auction Gallery in Litchfield, Connecticut on January 6, 1991. The consignors reportedly purchased it from an unremembered "dealer in Greenwich, Connecticut about forty years ago." The author thanks Frank Cowan and the Litchfield Auction Gallery for this information. On the Parisian "grand" chair, see Peter Thornton, "Upholstered Seat Furniture in Europe, 17th and 18th Centuries," in *Upholstery in America and Europe from the Seventeenth Century to World War I*, edited by Edward S. Cooke Jr. (New York: W. W. Norton, 1987), p. 33, fig. 8.

22. According to the *Oxford English Dictionary*, "escritoire" first appears in English in 1611. The migration pattern of the Cortelyou family is typical of the "old" (pre-Revocation) Huguenot diaspora, which usually made its way to New Amsterdam-New York by way of the Netherlands in the seventeenth century. Jacques Cortelyou was the first of the family to settle in New Amsterdam, where he was surveyor-general for the Dutch West India Company by 1660. It was in this capacity that Jacques executed his axiometric view of New Amsterdam in 1660, which served as the model for the well-known Castello Plan of 1670 (Biblioteca Medicea Laurenziana, Florence). For more on the Cortelyou and Castello plans, see Roderick H. Blackburn and Ruth Piwonka, *Remembrance of Patria: Dutch Arts and Culture in Colonial America 1609–1776* (Albany, N.Y.: Albany Institute of History and Art, 1988), p. 93. Cortelyou was born in Utrecht around 1625; nevertheless, in September 1679 Jasper Dankers wrote:

"Jacques [Cortelyou] is a man advanced in years. He was born in Utrecht, but of French parents as we could readily discover from all his actions, looks, and language. He studied philosophy in his youth [at the University of Utrecht] and spoke Latin and good French. He was a mathematician and sworn land-surveyor. He had also formerly learned several sciences, and had some knowledge of medicine" (Jasper Dankers, *Journal of a Voyage to New York*, as quoted in Maud Esther Dilliard, *Old Dutch Houses of Brooklyn* [New York: Richard R. Smith, 1945], n. p.). On February 16, 1660, Cortelyou laid out twenty-two lots to establish the town of Bushwick (Bos Wyck, or "Town in the Woods"). This Huguenot settlement began when fourteen refugees removed to Brooklyn from New Amsterdam (ibid.).

23. *The Journal of John Fontaine*, pp. 114–15. Fontaine's father was born in the town of Jenouille in Saintonge in 1658. The diary references are for October 26 and October 29, 1716.

24. For an analysis of Kings County and New York City kasten, see Peter M. Kenny, Frances Gruber Stafford, and Gilbert T. Vincent, *American Kasten: The Dutch-Style Cupboards of New York and New Jersey, 1650–1800* (New York: Metropolitan Museum of Art, 1991), pp. 16–21 and entry 8. For the story of the Flushing Remonstrance, see Henry D. Waller, *History of the Town of Flushing* (Flushing, N.Y., 1899), p. 44; Haynes Trebor, *The Flushing Remonstrance* (Flushing, N.Y., 1957), pp. 3–4; and Neil D. Kamil, "New Approaches to Religion, Popular Culture, and Material Life in Early America: The Middle Colonies and the Upper South as a Case Study," in *Religion, Popular Culture and Material Life in the Middle Colonies and the Upper South, 1650–1800*, edited by John J. McCusker and Neil D. Kamil (College Park, Md.: Maryland Colloquium on Early American History, 1990), pp. 34–36.

25. John T. Kirk, *American Furniture and the British Tradition to 1830* (New York: Alfred A. Knopf, 1982), p. 235, fig. 752.

26. Peter Thornton, *Seventeenth-Century Interior Decoration in England, France & Holland* (New Haven and London: Yale University Press, 1978), pp. 180–82. The Huguenot settlement at Manakin, Virginia, located twenty miles above the fall line on the James River (or perhaps other Huguenot settlements in southeastern Virginia), is a second, less likely point of origin for this armchair. I am grateful to Luke Beckerdite for bringing this chair to my attention and for sharing his insights on the role of the large population of French refugee artisans in the furniture production of both Virginia and South Carolina. Beckerdite's research will be the subject of a forthcoming article. For an introduction to the history of the Manakin settlement, see James L. Bugg, "Manakin Town in Virginia: Its Story and Its People" (M.A. thesis, University of Virginia, 1950).

27. Thornton, *Seventeenth-Century Interior Decoration,* pp. 198–202.

28. On the "double poire," see Forman, *American Seating Furniture*, p. 226.

29. The Van Cortlandt leather armchair may have been made for Stephanus Van Cortlandt (1643–1700) shortly before or after the construction of his manor house, built ca. 1697. If so, it probably passed to Philip Van Cortlandt (1683–1748) after his father's death in 1700. Alternatively, the chair may have been made for Philip, since it could date as late as 1720. Upon Philip's death, it was willed to Pierre Van Cortlandt (1721–1814). With the death of Pierre, the armchair passed to Pierre Van Cortlandt II (1762–1843) and subsequently to Pierre III. On the death of Pierre's wife Catherine Beck in 1895, the chair descended to her daughter, Catherine T. R. Van Cortlandt (May 2, 1838–February 19, 1921), who married John Rutherford Mathews (November 29, 1835–December 27, 1898). Finally, the chair passed to their daughter, Isabel Rutherford Mathews (May 1, 1878–July 24, 1909). The chair was one of the few items withheld when the Van Cortlandt Manor furnishings were auctioned by Parke Bernet Galleries in New York on February 6–8, 1941, and March 7, 1942. Instead, it was was sold to John D. Rockefeller Jr., who displayed it in the Beekman Wing of Philipsburg Manor, Tarrytown, New York, the first of the properties that he purchased and conserved for Historic Hudson Valley. Catherine Van Cortlandt Mason Browne sold the manor house in 1945. In 1953, Rockefeller purchased the house for Historic Hudson Valley, and in 1959, he returned the Van Cortlandt leather armchair to the second-story hall, where it remains today. See Joseph T. Butler, *The Family Collections at Van Cortlandt Manor* (Tarrytown, N.Y.: Sleepy Hollow Restorations, 1967), pp. 20, 42–3; "The Ancestral Record of the Family of Van Cortlandt," handwritten ms., Library, Historic Hudson Valley; and Auction Catalogues, Parke Bernet Galleries, New York, February 6–8, 1941, and March 7, 1942. The author thanks Joseph T. Butler, Director and Curator Emeritus of Collections at Historic Hudson Valley, for much of the information used to compile this genealogy.

30. The chair was in the Bybee Collection, Dallas, Texas, when it was nearly destroyed by

fire in the 1970s. The remains of the scorched frame are now in storage at the Museum of Fine Arts, Boston.

31. This construction evidence should further discredit the argument that the New York leather chair was produced either in Boston or in the Piscataqua region of New Hampshire. The Piscataqua origin, advanced by some dealers and antiquarians during the 1960s, is largely based on dubious recovery histories and is difficult to accept because of that region's close proximity to Boston. During the seventeenth and early eighteenth century, southeastern New Hampshire did not have an urban upholstery trade capable of competing with Boston's powerful network of artisans and merchants. The inhabitants of the Piscataqua region were relatively dispersed; many of those who owned leather chairs purchased them in Boston or through a branch of that city's commercial network. The Piscataqua leather chair "thesis" has not received support in recent publications on the early New Hampshire furniture industry (see Brock Jobe, ed., *Portsmouth Furniture: Masterworks from the New Hampshire Seacoast* [Hanover, N.H.: University Press of New England, 1992]; Gerald W. R. Ward, "Three Centuries of Life Along the Piscataqua River," *Antiques* 142, no. 1 [July 1992]: 60–65; and Gerald W. R. Ward and Karin E. Cullity, "The Furniture," *Antiques* 142, no. 1 [July 1992]: 94–103).

32. I. N. Phelps Stokes, *The Iconography of Manhattan Island, 1498–1909* 6 vols. (New York: H. R. Dodd, 1915–28), 4:422. Historian Charles W. Baird argued that Jean was probably born in St. Lo, Normandy, because that was the ancestral seat of the family name Chevalier (Charles W. Baird, *History of the Huguenot Emigration to America*, 2 vols. [New York: Dodd, Mead, 1885], 2:280). However, I discovered many Chevaliers in the archives for Saintonge, where it was a common Huguenot name. Like many Huguenots from the northwestern coast of France, Jean's branch of the Le Chevalier family may have moved to the southwest during the civil wars. Strong evidence of a Saintongeais origin for the Le Chevaliers of New Amsterdam–New York is in the "Réceuil de Manuscrits sur les Églises Réformées de France reunie par les soins de Mr. Alexandre Crottet, ancien Pasteur des Église Réformées de Pons, Gemozac et Mortagne en Saintonge," Charleston Library Society, Charleston, South Carolina (SCHS-51-31-1). There were also numerous Jean Chevaliers recorded in the birth, marriage, death, and burial registers of Aunis in the seventeenth century, where they were located predominantly on the coast, particularly on Île de Ré and in La Rochelle. See "Table des Baptêmes faits à St. Martin îsle de Ré par M. Barbault, le père, ministre en 1685, jusques et compris le mois de Septembre. Copiée sur le Registre de la dite Égise de 1685," in Notes et Collections d'Érudits, Archives Préfectures de La Rochelle, files J. 102 and 103, handwritten manuscripts by J. Pandin de Lussaudiere, n.p.; and Edward Elbridge Salisbury, *Family Memorials: A Series of Genealogical and Biographical Monographs*, 2 vols. (New York: privately printed, 1885), 2:540–44. Salisbury argues, on the basis of the unique Chevalier coat-of-arms, that Jean Le Chevalier Sr. probably came from Brittany rather than Normandy, however, Salisbury also states that the family was fragmented early into separate branches that moved to other areas of France. All of this evidence suggests that the Le Chevaliers of New York originated in Normandy and that a branch moved to Saintonge. After the Revocation, Jean Le Chevalier's family moved to London. On April 9, 1687, they appeared on a list of refugees who received a warrant for naturalization at Whitehall. Jean Jr., the eldest child, would then have been about seventeen years of age. There may have been a branch of this family in Charleston, South Carolina, during the late seventeenth and early eighteenth centuries as well. Joiner Pierre Le Chevalier's property is listed on *A Compleat Description of the Province of Carolina*, published by Edward Crisp and printed ca. 1711 (The author thanks Luke Beckerdite for this information).

33. Baird, *History of the Huguenot Emigration*, 2:212. *New York Historical Manuscripts Dutch: The Register of Salomon Lachaire Notary Public of New Amsterdam, 1661, 1662*, translated by E.B. O'Callachan, edited and introduction by Kenneth Scott and Kenneth Stryker-Rodda (Baltimore: Genealogical Publishing Company, 1978), xii, xvi. Salomon La Chaire was baptised in Amsterdam's Walloon Church on January 30, 1628. For Jean Chevalier's City Hall contract, see I. N. Phelps Stokes, *The Iconography of Manhattan Island*, 4:305.

34. *New York Genealogical and Biographical Record* 15, no. 1 (January 1884): 36. Valenciennes entered the maelstrom of Reformation confessional conflict as early as 1560, when public singing of Marot's psalms and other "impious songs" was deemed threatening enough to warrant an official interdiction of similar heretical activities. See Donald R. Kelley, *The Beginning of Ideology: Consciousness and Society in the French Reformation* (Cambridge: Cambridge University Press, 1981), p. 99.

35. See Baird, *History of the Huguenot Emigration*, 2:80. For Le Chevalier's involvement in

the L'Eglise Francais, see *Collections of the Huguenot Society of America* (New York, 1886). For a longer discussion of the significance of Le Chevalier's dual church allegiances, see Neil Duff Kamil, "Of American Kasten," p. 278. For more on Joshua Delaplaine's artisanal activity, see J. Steward Johnson, "New York Cabinetmaking Prior to the Revolution" (M.A. thesis, University of Delaware, 1964), pp. 23–24.

36. *New York State Calendar: English, 1664–1776* 15 (Albany: Office of the Secretary of State, N.Y. 1865–66), p. 247. *New York Historical Society Collections* (New York: Printed for the Society, 1886): 58. John Chevalier vs. Duie Hungerford, Mayor's Court, June 11, 1700; and Albany I, fol. 1-11, QC, KL, HDC. In an indenture dated June 1, 1700, New York joiner Edward Burling agreed to "Give to his Said Apprentice [Thomas Sutton] a good Sett of Carpenters Tools & Shall learn him to write Read & Cypher" (*New York Historical Society Collections* [New York: Printed for the Society, 1886]: 585). On Jean Bouyer (Bouhier), see Morgan H. Seacord, *Biographical Sketches and Index of the Huguenot Settlers of New Rochelle, 1687–1776* (New Rochelle, N.Y., 1941), p. 15.

37. See account of payments made by Thomas Weaver, Customs House, June 25, 1701, to September 25, 1701, in *An Account of Her Majesty's Revenue in the Province of New York, 1701–1709: The Customs Records of Early Colonial New York*, edited by Julius Block, Leo Hershkowitz, Kenneth Scott, and Constance D. Sherman (Ridgewood, N.J.: Gregg Press, 1966), p. 34.

38. A communicant in New York's first Trinity Church, the wealthiest and most politically powerful Anglican congregation in the city, Ellison's status was assured when he received the prestigious contract to build its first pulpit on October 5, 1696 (*First Recorded Minutes Regarding the Building of Trinity Church in the City of New York: 1696–1697*, Trinity Church, Office of the Parish Archives; and *Corporation of Trinity Church Minutes of the Vestry*, Trinity Church, Office of the Parish Archives, I: 1697–1791, 221–22, 229). As of November 16, 1725, Ellison's outstanding debts totaled £8165.1.1-1/2, and Jean Le Chevalier was among the debtors. See the inventory and "Book Debts from the ledger of John Ellison, in the hands of John Ellison, Jr." (also a joiner), Albany, I, fol. 2–94, QC, KL, HDC; and Inventory of John Ellison Jr., October 6, 1730, New York Historical Society Manuscript Division.

39. Fitch Letterbook. See also *New York Historical Society Collections* (1886): 87. Richard Lott "upholsterer" became a freeman on September 30, 1707. The Mayor's Court referred to him as a "chairmaker" in a suit for nonpayment of debts (Richard Lott vs. Johannes Cuyler and John Cruger, October 21, 1710, QC, KL, HDC).

40. Fitch Letterbooks. On the notion of "unintended performance," see J. G. A. Pocock, *The Languages of Political Theory in Early Modern Europe* (Cambridge: Cambridge University Press, 1987), p. 31; and Peter Sahlins, "Fictions of a Catholic France: The Naturalization of Foreigners, 1685–1787," *Representations* 47 (summer 1994): 97.

41. By 1720, New York hardware merchants began stocking British upholstery materials in response to their declining availability from Boston merchants. Abraham Brock, lately "merchant of Bristol," offered a tremendous quantity of textiles and yardgoods, woodworkers' tools, a variety of hinges, latches, and standard upholsterery materials including "7/8 of a gross of girth webb att 1.0.3," "41 bosses [probably boss-nails or metal studs] 0.3.5," and "3 Doz Tufting nails 0.3.5" (Inventory of Abraham Brock, May 4, 1720, QC, KL, HDC, folio 2–37).

42. A. V. Phillips, *The Lott Family in America* (Ann Arbor, Mich.: Edward Brothers, 1942), pp. 1–2; see also *Collections of the St. Nicholas Society of the City of New York: Genealogical Record* (New York: Printed for the Society, 1934), 4:185. On patterns of Huguenot migration, see Warren C. Scoville, *The Persecution of the Huguenots and French Economic Development, 1680–1720* (Berkeley and Los Angeles: University of California Press, 1960), p. 6. For example, George and Monwers Lott of New Utrecht were both carpenters, active in the 1750s.

43. Archives Départmentales de la Charente-Maritime, B 1325; 1350; 1417; 1492; 1568; and, E Supplt. 297; 317; 364; 800; 906; 907; 913. For evidence concerning members of the Suire family who were prone to conflict with both religious and secular authorities, see Archives Départmentales de la Charente Maritime (hereafter ADCM), E Supplt. 317 and 369, 1746–48.

44. On Suire's Saintongeais background, see Morgan H. Seacord, *Biographical Sketches and Index of the Huguenot Settlers of New Rochelle,* p. 50. Inventory of John Swear, March 12, 1715, QC, KL, HDC, Albany II, fol. 2–256.

45. Although the tools, materials, and skills involved in saddlery, leather upholstery, and shoemaking are related, Suire is unusual in having worked as a joiner and shoemaker. However, as we have seen, the Suires of La Rochelle ran an ordinary that shoemakers frequented with enough regularity to merit the attention of local police.

46. Some early Louisiana furniture was undoubtedly made by creole slaves and freedmen working in distinctive French regional idioms (see Jessie J. Poesch, *Early Furniture of Louisiana, 1750–1830* [New Orleans: Louisiana State Museum, 1972], pp. 18–19, 33). New York artisans also exploited slave labor, a fact evidenced by Jean Suire's "1 Negro about 8 yeares. . . 12:0:0" (Inventory of John Swear). On African American artisans in early New York, see Shane White, *Somewhat More Independent: The End of Slavery in New York City, 1770–1810* (Athens, Ga.: University of Georgia Press, 1991). On the church of St. Étienne, see Ministère de la Culture et de la Communication, *Inventaire Général des Monuments et des Richesses Artistiques de la France: Commission Regionale de Poitou-Charentes, Charente-Maritime, Cantons Île de Ré* (Paris: Imprimerie Nationale, 1979), pp. 153, 184–85.

47. Given this regional association, it is not surprising that the carved crest and front stretchers of the chair also recall Italianate architectural models and designs carried into southwestern France from northern Italy during the late sixteenth century. Elite elements of southwestern Reformed culture—including local Saintongeais nobility and such churchmen as the young Jean Calvin—made the pilgrimage south to places such as Milan in Lombardy, a city and region with strong historic ties to the French church and monarchy. Some varieties of London cane chairs also evidence this turning sequence.

48. In 1685, John Thomas of Hempstead, Queens County, owned "6 Cane Chars 3/0/0 [and] 6 Black Chars 1/4/0" (inventoried in order to signify a full set of 12) but no leather chairs (Inventory of John Thomas, 1685, Albany I: 1–124, QC, KL, HDC).

49. Variants of the screen's carved floral panels also relate to coastal Connecticut carved and painted furniture. Compare particularly with carved work on case furniture associated with Huguenot joiner Peter Blin of Wethersfield, Connecticut, and certain examples of painted furniture associated with the Connecticut shore, including two painted chests in Winterthur Museum. For illustration of the latter, see Dean A. Fales Jr., *American Painted Furniture 1660–1880* (New York: Bonanza Books, 1986), pp. 26–27 (figs. 24–25). For evidence of other important Huguenot woodworking networks dispersed to the Long Island Sound region, see Robert F. Trent, "A Channel Islands Parallel for the Early Eighteenth-Century Connecticut Chests Attributed to Charles Guillam," *Studies in the Decorative Arts* 2, no. 1 (Fall 1994): 75–91; and Susan Prendergast Schoelwer, "Connecticut Sunflower Furniture: A Familiar Form Reconsidered," *Yale University Art Gallery Bulletin* (Spring 1989): 21–38. On Ezekial Carré, see Forman, *American Seating Furniture,* p. 226.

50. For the southwestern French backgrounds of the Durand and Coutant families, see Baird, *History of the Huguenot Emigration*, 2:21, 61, 332; 1:306. See also Jacqueline Calder, "Westchester County, New York Furniture," *Antiques* 121, no. 5 (May 1982): 1195–98; Benno M. Forman, "The Crown and York Chairs of Coastal Connecticut and the Work of the Durands of Milford," in *Pilgrim Century Furniture: An Historical Survey*, edited by Robert F. Trent (New York: Main Street/Universe Books, 1976), pp. 158–65; Robert F. Trent, *Hearts and Crowns*, pp. 29–59; and Kathleen Eagen Johnson, "The Fiddleback Chair," in *Early American Furniture from Settlement to City: Aspects of Form, Style, and Regional Design from 1620 to 1830*, edited by Mary Jean Madigan and Susan Colgan (New York: Billboard Publications, 1983), pp. 92–97. See also Trent, "A Channel Islands Parallel," and Schoelwer, "Connecticut Sunflower Furniture."

51. What I call creolization is well documented as an art historical process in England and the Low Countries in Peter Thornton, *Seventeenth-Century Interior Decoration*.

52. Forman, "The Crown and York Chairs," p. 158, fig. 1. On Pierre Durand, see Baird, *History of the Huguenot Emigration*, 2:332.

53. The term "life of form" is borrowed from Henri Focillion's seminal essay of the same name, *Vie des Formes* (Paris, 1934). Benno M. Forman, *American Seating Furniture*, pp. 292–94.

54. Forman, *American Seating Furniture,* pp. 292–94. In different examples using the same artifactual language, truncated columns, vases, twists, and other lapidary forms stacked symmetrically between and above the balusters are also commonly found. The Van Cortlandt leather armchair is exceptional in that it does not have a slit under the crest rail. The term "French hollow" was never acknowledged by Forman, although he did carefully note this formal idiosyncracy in relation to Boston models.

55. Ibid., pp. 293–94.

56. Ibid., p. 293, caption for fig. 162. See in particular the London cane armchair illustrated in Peter M. Kenny, "Flat Gates, Draw Bars, Twists, and Urns: New York's Distinctive, Early Baroque Oval Tables with Falling Leaves," in *American Furniture*, edited by Luke Beckerdite

(Hanover, N.H.: University Press of New England, 1994), p. 120, fig. 25. The posts of this chair are nearly the same as the leather armchair illustrated in figure 27. In a recent discussion of the London high-back turkeywork chair illustrated in figure 38, Margaret Swain argued that the slit in the chair's crest rail may have been to accommodate varying, pre-cut sizes of turkeywork upholstery exclusively, and that "many" of the surviving New York chairs now covered in leather were probably originally upholstered in turkeywork (Margaret Swain, "The Turkeywork Chairs of Holyroodhouse," in Cooke, ed., *Upholstery in America and Europe,* pp. 56–57). This theory is undermined by several chairs with this construction technique and original leather upholstery, including the "European" leather chair and a New York leather chair at the Van Alen house in Kinderhook, New York (Collections of the Columbia County Historical Society), as well as by evidence that leather panels may also have been pre-cut. More likely, the slit was simply a sturdy, efficient, and economical way to upholster both turkeywork and leather chairs. Two similar, carved, "barley twist" London cane chairs descended in the Wright family of Oyster Bay, Long Island, and the Smith family of New York City and Setauket, Long Island. Both are illustrated in Dean F. Failey, *Long Island is My Nation, The Decorative Arts and Craftsmen: 1640–1830* (Setauket, N.Y.: Society for the Preservation of Long Island Antiquities, 1976), p. 24, figs. 19, 20.

57. Forman, *American Seating Furniture,* p. 293, fig. 162. Daniel Marot's contribution to the Anglo-French and Dutch court style is discussed at length in Thornton, *Seventeenth-Century Interior Decoration*, pp. 40–96.

58. *Inventaire Général*, p. 153. There is a local tradition that the choir screen may have originally been made for the Jesuit chapel in Saintes, the principal Gallo-Roman city in Saintonge, but there is no evidence to support this assertion. It probably dates from 1629, but its present overall form is the result of restoration campaigns undertaken in 1845 and 1891 when the screen, which had been separated into three distinct sections during the eighteenth century, was reassembled.

59. Forman, *American Seating Furniture,* pp. 152–3. This great chair may have been made by Jean Le Chevalier's paternal grandfather, "Jan Cavelier," who framed and repaired the royal arms on New York's city hall in 1675 or by a contemporary New York joiner and carver. Most significantly, as the subject of diffusion of motifs, a cherub with goat feet appears as a central motif in the recently discovered design book of John Berger (fl. ca. 1718–32), a Boston Huguenot painter-stainer whose family originated in La Rochelle. See Robert A. Leath, "Jean Berger's Design Book: Huguenot Tradesmen and the Dissemination of French Baroque Style," in *American Furniture,* edited by Luke Beckerdite (Hanover, N.H.: University Press of New England, 1994), pp. 137, 145.

60. As quoted in Peter Sahlins, "Fictions of a Catholic France," p. 85. State-sponsored suppression of heresy did not end officially in France until the Edict of Toleration in November 1787.

61. For a fuller development of my argument concerning animate materialism in southwestern France, see Neil D. Kamil, *Fortresses of the Soul: Metaphysics and Artisanal Experience in a New World* (Baltimore, Md.: Johns Hopkins University Press, forthcoming). The use of this method and language is exemplified by Jon Butler in *The Huguenots in America: A Refugee People in New World Society* (Cambridge, Mass.: Harvard University Press, 1983), esp. Part II, "The Disappearance of the Huguenots in America," pp. 69–198. For Butler's argument that "no significant stylistic differences separate the work of Huguenot from non-Huguenot silversmiths in the colonies," see ibid., pp. 178–81. As quoted in Arthur Herman, "The Saumur Assembly, 1611: Huguenot Political Belief and Action in the Age of Marie de Medici" (Ph. D. diss., Johns Hopkins University, 1985), p. 36.

62. For a good discussion of the interaction in social history methodology of folklore, linguistics, creolization, and pluralistic cultural convergence, see Charles Joyner, "A Single Southern Culture: Cultural Interaction in the Old South," in *Black and White Cultural Interaction in the Antebellum South*, edited by Ted Ownby (Jackson, Miss.: University Press of Mississippi, 1993), pp. 11–17. For the two classic formulations of this methodology, see Dell Hymes, *Foundations in Sociolinguistics: An Ethnographic Approach* (Philadelphia: University of Pennsylvania Press, 1974), and William Labov, *The Social Stratification of English in New York City* (New York: Center for Applied Linguistics, 1966), see esp. pp. 7–15.

63. Jack P. Greene, *Imperatives, Behaviors, and Identities: Essays in Early American Cultural History* (Charlottesville, Va.: University Press of Virginia, 1992), pp. 9–11. See also Neil D. Kamil, *Discursive Things*.

64. The term "French turned," which occasionally occurs in English accounts and inventories of the seventeenth century, refers to the inward spiral shaping brought to London by Huguenot turners. Spiral turning, when reduced to two dimensions, appears as a series of concentric circles. See R. W. Symonds, "Charles II Couches, Chairs and Stools, 1660–1670," *Connoisseur* 93, no. 389 (January 1934): 19–20. Anthropologist Edward T. Hall suggests that, in general, French handling of public and private space is "sociopetal," whereas the English is "sociofugal" (Edward T. Hall, *The Hidden Dimension* [New York: Anchor Books, 1969], pp. 146–48).

65. Quentin Skinner, "Meaning and Understanding in the History of Ideas," *History and Theory* 8, no. 1 (1969): 48.

66. Christian Norberg-Schulz, *Intentions in Architecture* (Cambridge, Mass.: M.I.T. Press, 1965), p. 29. Alfred Schutz, *Collected Papers I: The Problem of Social Reality*, edited by Maurice Natanson (The Hague: Martinus Nijhoff, 1962), pp. 229–30. On cultural theory and the control of knowledge, see Mary Douglas, *Risk and Blame: Essays in Cultural Theory* (London: Routledge, 1992), esp. p. 19: "In cognitive theory . . . the psyche is . . . primarily social. The social preoccupations of the person, infant or adult, would be like control gates through which all information has to pass. . . . News that is going to be accepted as true information has to be wearing a badge of loyalty to the particular political regime which the person supports; the rest is suspect, deliberately censored or unconsciously ignored."

67. Quotations are taken from the title page (Paris: Pierre Billaine, 1638). I am grateful to Orest Ranum for bringing this important reference to my attention.

68. See the epigraph that heads this essay.

69. In this context, perhaps the best evidence of the instability of convergence was the inability of New York's artisans to respond effectively to the more complex symbolic language that accompanied Boston's new fashioned "crook'd back" chair with "horsebone feet"—the artifact that finally supplanted the Boston and New York plain leather chair after it first appeared in the city around 1722. This chair was defined by both its upholstery and its frame. For more on the Boston "crook'd back" chair, see Forman, *American Seating Furniture*, pp. 296–356. For the classic text on the mechanically reproduced artifact, see Walter Benjamin, "The Work of Art in the Age of Mechanical Reproduction," in *Illuminations*, edited by Hannah Arendt (New York: Schocken Books, 1969), pp. 217–52. See also Fredric Jameson, *Postmodernism, or, The Cultural Logic of Late Capitalism* (Durham, N.C.: Duke University Press, 1991), pp. ix–xxii.

Book Reviews

James M. Gaynor and Nancy L. Hagedorn. *Tools: Working Wood in Eighteenth–Century America.* Charlottesville: University Press of Virginia, 1994. xiv + 140 pp.; 26 color and 142 bw illustrations, glossary, bibliography, index. $19.95.

In the words of the authors, this book is not meant to be a detailed technical discussion of eighteenth-century woodworking tools "but rather a summary overview of how these tools came to be, how their users acquired and learned to use them, and how they influenced the working lives and products of woodworking artisans" (p. ix). Within this framework, James Gaynor and Nancy Hagedorn have made a significant contribution to our understanding of tools and their impact on the life and work of early American woodworkers. They have also added to an increasing body of literature on the question of tool ownership and its meaning for artisans in a host of trades. Much of their information is relevant to the experiences of other producing craftsmen. Silversmiths, for instance, encountered many of the same obstacles when attempting to amass shop tools, and their working tools defined their products in much the same way as did the tools of woodworkers. What is perhaps most impressive about this book is the extent to which the authors have based their analysis on well-documented examples of eighteenth-century tools. Most collections include few tools that can be dated with any precision, and by bringing together the best documented examples, Gaynor and Hagedorn have provided curators of such collections with valuable information for dating and cataloguing the objects in their care. They have also proffered ample data for scholars attempting to put those tools into a wider historical context. The emphasis of the book and the exhibition that it accompanied is on the experience of artisans working in Virginia. Although many of the tools included in the book were owned by Virginia woodworkers, the authors flesh out their treatment with tools owned elsewhere in America. Most of the mass-manufactured tools treated here are of English origin, but the authors have also included as many American-made tools as possible, as well as some intriguing examples of tools made by the artisans who owned them.

The book is divided into two sections. The first section, lavishly illustrated with tools, period prints and paintings, and advertisements and documents, puts tools and the artisans who owned them into broader perspective and clearly demonstrates the symbiotic relationship between tradesmen and their tools. Covering sixty-two pages, this section of the book includes chapters on "English and American Toolmaking," "Tools for Sale," "Tools and Work," and "Tools and Products."

The first of these chapters, "English and American Toolmaking," explains the development of the English toolmaking industry during the eighteenth and early nineteenth centuries, with particular attention to the specialties of the principal manufacturing centers. The authors discuss the difficulties facing American toolmakers who attempted to compete with these inexpensive and well-made imports and explain that many Americans made tools or modified imported tools for their own use. The products of a few notable

American artisans who worked principally as toolmakers—including Francis Nicholson of Wrentham, Massachusetts (began working 1728), Samuel Caruthers of Philadelphia (beginning in the 1760s), and Thomas Napier of Philadelphia (beginning 1774)—are pictured here, and the authors draw extensively on surviving documents regarding American tool manufacture.

"Tools for Sale" explores the sources of tools for American cabinetmakers, joiners, coopers, and instrument makers and illustrates several well-known and well-documented chests of cabinetmakers' tools, including the Benjamin Seaton chest (English, 1797); the George William Cartwright II chest (Ossining, N.Y., 1819); the Thomas and Warren Nixon chest (Framingham, Mass., late eighteenth to early nineteenth century); the Duncan Phyfe chest (New York, ca. 1800–1830); and a chest of tools owned by an anonymous upstate New York craftsman, now at the Farmers' Museum in Cooperstown. The authors' primary focus, however, is on the sources from which Virginia woodworkers obtained their tools. Although Gaynor and Hagedorn comment that there is little documentation of this process in Virginia, they proceed to provide an exhaustive treatment of what information does exist—advertising, bills, and so on. They also make excellent use of available documents on such often-forgotten issues as how apprentices obtained tools and the process (and price) of importing tools directly from England. They include an excellent description of merchant factors in Virginia and their business dealings with agents in England.

"Tools and Work" deals with all aspects of the topic, beginning with the process by which apprentices learned to use common tools and developed design skills. Gaynor and Hagedorn use extant tool kits to explore how the availability of certain tools controlled variations in the work carried out by different types of woodworkers, from the general purpose woodworkers of rural areas to the highly specialized artisans of the seacoast towns. They find that specialized tools allowed artisans to create complex objects with ease, giving them a competitive edge over their fellow artisans, and that these tools standardized production in ways that allowed apprentices to assist masters in making complex items.

"Tools and Products" takes this discussion further by examining how specific objects were made by using particular assortments of tools and how the technical preferences of individual workers affected their choice of materials as well as the look of the objects they made. The authors suggest that "the practical capabilities of tools also influenced consumers' expectations regarding other product characteristics such as the uniformity of details" (p. 52). They further demonstrate how understanding the process by which an object was made helps us understand the decisions artisans made in allocating their labor. Finishing furniture, for instance, involved the use of a succession of planes, and cabinetmakers made decisions on how much to finish surfaces according to how visible the surfaces would be to the eventual customer. Such economies have been used by scholars to identify works from certain shops and regions, and here the study of tools helps us understand the decisions these artisans made.

The second section of the book is devoted to a detailed treatment of the design and evolution of several groups of tools—layout tools, chisels and gouges, saws, boring tools, and planes. The authors suggest that readers not familiar with basic tools and their uses consult this portion of the book first, a recommendation that even those fairly well acquainted with woodworking tools would do well to heed. In general, these discussions are clear and straightforward, with helpful illustrations that occasionally serve to explain the use or construction of a specific tool and that give helpful technical information to assist readers in dating tools themselves. These sections of the catalogue are extremely useful because they serve to elucidate the process by which these tools evolved and because they clearly demonstrate differences in homemade versus manufactured tools, English versus American tools, and early-eighteenth-century tools versus early-nineteenth-century tools. At times, however, it is possible for the reader to become confused because most "entries" attempt to describe tools that are grouped together in single composite photographs. The descriptors used to identify individual tools are not always consistent within a single discussion, and items grouped together in the same photograph are not necessarily treated in a consistent order (e.g., right to left, top to bottom). The authors undoubtedly believed that marks or other distinguishing features that would help readers understand the text would be visible in the final printed halftones. Unfortunately, sometimes these marks just do not show up well, either because the pictures are dark or because they are smaller than the authors anticipated. More clarity might have been achieved if each photograph in this section had been given a caption to accompany the narrative paragraphs.

I found only this one minor flaw in an otherwise important achievement, however. *Tools: Working Wood in Eighteenth-Century America* is a book that everyone interested in early American artisans from all producing trades—not just woodworking—will find fascinating. Those with a special interest in woodworkers and their tools will find it indispensable.

Barbara McLean Ward
University of New Hampshire

Katherine S. Howe, Alice Cooney Frelinghuysen, Catherine Hoover Voorsanger, Simon Jervis, Hans Ottomeyer, Mark Bascou, Ann Claggett Wood, and Sophia Riefstahl. *Herter Brothers: Furniture and Interiors for a Gilded Age*. New York: Harry N. Abrams in association with the Museum of Fine Arts, Houston, 1994. 272 pp.; 133 color and 167 bw illustrations, appendixes, chronology, bibliography, index. $60.00.

The furniture of the New York City cabinetmaking firm Herter Brothers first gained public attention in the 1970 Metropolitan Museum exhibition "Nineteenth-Century America" and its accompanying catalogue. Featured prominently in that landmark show were an ebonized and inlaid wardrobe and an ebonized and inlaid bedroom suite, all 1969 gifts to the Metropolitan, and part of a blond maple bedroom suite from Jay Gould's mansion,

Lyndhurst.[1] After that 1970 debut, Herter Brothers quickly assumed a widespread reputation as the quintessential maker of American aesthetic movement furniture during the 1870s and 1880s. Although the work of Herter Brothers remains the benchmark against which all other artistic furniture of this period is judged, no detailed study of the firm existed prior to *Herter Brothers: Furniture and Interiors for a Gilded Age,* written to accompany an exhibition that originated at the Museum of Fine Arts, Houston, and traveled to the High Museum of Art in Atlanta and the Metropolitan Museum of Art.[2]

As the first substantive examination of Herter Brothers, the catalogue seeks to place the Herters within a larger international context, discuss the firm within the New York furniture-making and interior design trade, and examine a "highly select and refined" body of about fifty Herter objects made between 1858 and 1883 (p. 6). The focus throughout is upon the lives and influence of Gustave Herter (1830–1898) and Christian Herter (1839–1883), who were personally involved with a cabinetmaking business in New York during that twenty-five year period. The book begins with three essays by European scholars who seek to link the work of the Stuttgart-born and -trained Herters to contemporary developments in the European furniture trade. Unfortunately, these essays are uneven: Simon Jervis's description of England's pivotal role in furniture design in the 1860s and 1870s and Marc Bascou's review of the French styles of the period—what Christian Herter could have seen in Paris in the late 1860s and early 1870s—shed little new light on the Herters' careers and are, in fact, summarized well at various points within the text and catalogue entries. Much of the current literature, such as Henry Hawley's article on a chair in the Cleveland Museum of Art, already talks about these various stylistic influences.[3] The authors of the catalogue under review thus could have simply incorporated the stylistic discussion into the body of their text and into the entries on the individual objects.

Hans Ottomeyer's essay on the context of German furniture-making shops after guild and trade restrictions were relaxed around 1830 sheds new and important light on American furniture, and on other decorative arts, of the third quarter of the nineteenth century. In Germany during the second quarter of the century, the development of large shops, staffed by highly skilled specialists trained under the old guild-enforced, small-shop tradition and working for a competitive national market, led to a distinctive design philosophy that stressed the combination of different decorative techniques such as carving, inlay, marquetry, and metal or ceramic mounts. As a result, artistic success was not judged by stylistic unity but by explicit celebration of lavish materials, exquisite craftsmanship, and extraordinary detail. Bombast reigned over stylistic coherence or restraint. Ottomeyer's essay thus offers valuable insight into the approaches and values of skilled craftsmen such as the Herters and Anton Kimbel. When economic and political disruptions provided the catalyst for their emigration in 1848, these German furniture makers brought highly developed skills and a specific craft-based sense of design with them to New York City.

Katherine Howe's introductory chapter on the Herters builds upon Ottomeyer's essay, tracking down the brothers' early careers in Württemberg before emigration and then demonstrating how they used their specific German artisan heritage in New York City. Drawing upon the brothers' biographies and the stylistic development of documented Herter objects, Howe lays out four distinct periods in Herter Brothers history: (1) 1848–1858, when Gustave was working with several other cabinetmakers (for example, Erastus Buckley and Thomas Brooks) on monumental pieces of furniture in historically derivative styles popular in France; (2) 1858–1864, when Gustave established his own firm, specializing in the production of baroque and Louis XIV furniture with heavily carved ornament and the supervision of lavishly ornamented interior furnishings; (3) 1864–1870, when Christian joined the business and became the chief designer, with a particular bent for Second Empire forms embellished with a variety of decoration such as carving, marquetry, porcelain plaques, and gilded mounts; and (4) 1870–1883, when Gustave returned to Germany and Christian ran the firm, turning away from French styles to English and Anglo interpretations of Japanese styles and making extensive use of marquetry and ebonizing. By noting the changes in the firm's leadership in conjunction with the changing appearances and styles of its products, Howe draws upon the discussion in Jervis's and Bascou's essays on the internationalism of design during this period, but she grounds her discussion within the work of the Herter firm; for example, she points out the importance of Christian's visit to London, Manchester, and Birmingham in the early 1870s. Her discussion, therefore, supersedes the two earlier essays.

Howe's introduction to the Herter firm is followed by two essays that discuss the actual Herter business in terms of the shop floor and the salesroom. Drawing upon a wide variety of sources including city directories, insurance maps, Dun & Bradstreet credit records, and census data, Catherine Voorsanger provides a richly textured depiction of the furniture trade in New York City and identifies the Herter firm as one of the small number of first-class cabinetmakers in New York, distinct from either mid-level furnishers or wholesale "slaughter" shops. The latter category, by far the majority of furniture firms in New York City, was centered in a lower East Side district called "Kleindeutschland" and relied extensively on German craftsmen. Solidly and meticulously researched and rich in comparative material, Voorsanger's essay discusses Herter business practices within the context of the economic cycles of the period, the widespread availability of relatively cheap skilled labor, and the increased interest in upscale merchandising along Broadway's "Ladies Mile." She deftly combines an eye for shop-floor detail with an awareness of the larger economic context. This thorough study of the furniture trade nicely complements Charles Venable's study of the silver business and should facilitate the further study of other New York firms such as Leon Marcotte, Alexander Roux, and Pottier & Stymus.[4]

In contrast to Voorsanger's tightly focused essay, Alice Frelinghuysen takes on two large topics—patronage and the business of interior decoration—in a more diffuse, more descriptive, and less analytical essay. Each of these topics deserves specific focus and investigation in a separate essay. The discussion of the interior furnishing aspect of the Herter business more logically should follow the Voorsanger essay and should go beyond the mere cataloguing of commissions and variety of wares offered by Herter. Establishing the types of interior decorators working in New York City at this time and comparing Herter with Alexander Roux and Leon Marcotte, as well as with the upholsterers and furnishers of the next level, would have shed more light on Herter's role in the city's decorating trades. Fuller exploration of the setup of the different decorative trades within the Herter shop and how the internal operation might have changed over time, patterns of hiring outside specialists such as Giuseppe Guidicini and Pierre-Victor Galland, influential relationships with different architects, and interaction with other interior decoration firms and importers would all help to provide a better sense of the company's changing business strategy. Was the Herter interest in total interior decoration part of their German artisan heritage, or did the firm market their decoration services more aggressively in the 1870s, just after they had moved their showroom to the Ladies Mile of Broadway? Was their interest in *Artistic Houses,* published in 1883, part of this promotional strategy? Was there any relationship between the richness of the 1870s work and the weak position of skilled craftsmen in the deflationary economy of the 1870s? Comparison with other decoration firms and a better analysis of the firm's strategies and operations would result in a much richer essay that would resonate well with Voorsanger's contribution.

The role of patronage also deserves more sophisticated and sustained analysis in its own essay. Frelinghuysen briefly speculates about the identity and aspirations of the Herter clients on pages 81 and 93 but does not systematically explore all clients in this one paper in order to probe the values and motives of the self-made, self-conscious railroad and hotel men. Were they excluded by, or did they feel inferior to, those established elites who possessed taste? Did they turn to the elaborate work of Herter to create their own distinct form of cultural property, a form of capitalist trophy? Greater comparison with other new monied capitalists and established New Yorkers such as John Taylor Johnston or Robert W. de Forest (both of whom served as president of the Metropolitan Museum of Art and both of whom patronized Leon Marcotte) would have made Frelinghuysen's essay less hagiographic and provided a more realistic context.

The catalogue of the forty-two major pieces of furniture in the exhibition begins with a helpful introduction that serves as a connoisseur's guide to Herter furniture: a discussion of woods is followed by a brief explication of the cabinetmaking techniques found on the furniture and a useful discussion of the chronological evolution of the firm's carving, marquetry, inlay, mounts and hardware, painting, and gilding. The entries provide extensive documentation of the objects and their stylistic influences and include good color photographs of the objects, sometimes accompanied by color or black-and-white details. When several objects from one commission are discussed (for example, the Ruggles Morse house in Portland, Maine, of 1858–1860; the LeGrand Lockwood house in Norwalk, Connecticut, of 1868–1870; the James Goodwin house in Hartford, Connecticut, 1871–1874; the Mark Hopkins house in San Francisco, 1875–1880; and the William H. Vanderbilt residence in New York City, 1879–1882), the authors have included a discussion of the commission accompanied by period photographs of the house and its appropriate interiors. Most of these important photographs are given at least a half page, but unfortunately, some of the most evocative interior photographs, such as the Ruggles drawing room or the Lockwood drawing room, are reproduced as only one-quarter-page illustrations.

Following the entries are several pictorial appendices that present photographic details of the characteristic types of marquetry, carving, hardware, and marks found on Herter furniture. Although these images testify to the beauty of Herter work, they are not really linked to the body of the catalogue. Instead of merely providing a simple encyclopedia of some of the elaborate decorations, it might have been more effective to use the details to support arguments in the text. For example, the technique of cutting out marquetry, discussed on page 178, allowed for different light and dark contrasts of the same design. It might have been helpful to show details that demonstrated such an effective practice. Following the pictorial appendixes, Sophia Riefstahl's chronology of the Herters and their firm provides a good succinct timeline for the firm's evolution and activity and follows the story up to 1907, the last time the firm is listed in the city directories.

Although no personal or business papers relating to the Herter firm in the 1858–1883 period have survived, the authors of this catalogue have produced a helpful history of the business by mining a variety of other source material—papers of patrons; public documents such as census and credit records, insurance maps, directories, and period literature; and the artifacts themselves. The time necessary to conduct such widespread research and the cost of assembling and traveling the accompanying exhibition make the possibility of another major Herter exhibition unlikely for some time. It is therefore important to examine some of the weaknesses of the catalogue.

One troubling aspect of the publication is the emphasis upon the uniqueness of the Herter furniture. Throughout the book, the products of the Herter shop are extolled for their creative individuality, the result of an American environment that encouraged the highest form of creativity away from the guild restrictions of Europe. Such an approach seems to be somewhat heavy-handed, American exceptionalist chauvinism, for Ottomeyer's essay underscores how closely the Herters' attitudes related to the German practices and aesthetics of the period. Howe and Voorsanger also suggest that Marcotte and the firm of Pottier & Stymus offered products of comparable quality and embellishment but packaged in a different style. The point is not so much that the Herters' work is the best or most exceptional but that the quantity of surviving works and the documentation of their commissions offer the best window into the first-class New York cabinetmaking practices of this period. The concern for American uniqueness also seems to have prevented the authors from making intriguing comparisons and interpretations, particularly in regard to patronage. For example, Howe's depiction of Christian Herter as an aggressive hunter of design trophies could have been better integrated with Frelinghuysen's brief characterization of the self-made, but culturally insecure, patron and discussed within the growing literature of post-processural material culture.[5]

The emphasis upon the objects with greatest artistic merit, that is, the showiest, also distorts the picture of the Herter firm as a business. The work lacks an example and discussion of one of the many plainer bedroom suites of bird's-eye maple that come up frequently at auction and appear to be one of the firm's bread-and-butter works. Why did the firm produce so many bedroom suites? Did the ebony suites retain their fashionable, modern, European association after 1876? Were there changing notions of bedrooms during this period, or did the Herters concentrate on that genre because it offered the opportunity to maximize the profitability of good design and skilled ornamentation since the same form could be executed in maple or ebonized cherry, dressed up with milled ornament such as moldings and turnings, and given distinctive marquetry whose negative image could embellish another suite? The Herter firm always delicately balanced custom and stock forms and decoration, oftentimes using the custom example as a prototype. The focus on the grandest individual commissions also skews the understanding of the overall Herter business. In addition to large-scale private commissions, the Herters worked on institutional projects such as the Seventh Regiment Armory and on commercial work such as bank interiors and the Reed & Barton display at the 1876 Centennial, as well as offering individual pieces of furniture for sale at their store; yet, the discussion of these elements is divided up among Howe, Voorsanger, and Frelinghuysen. Such a separation precludes a discussion of interconnections, such as the role of bank interiors in attracting new-monied clients, the role between commissions and store sales, or the motive behind Herter working on the armory.

Such dispersion of central themes and the duplication of others, such as the spread of international design—a common shortcoming of multi-authored volumes—weaken the overall scholarly impact of the catalogue. The catalogue lacks a central thesis, other than the exceptional beauty of the Herter products, to which each part can contribute in a clear and consistent fashion. There is considerable overlap between a number of the essays and between the Howe and Frelinghuysen essays and the catalogue entries. The broad topics of Frelinghuysen's essay and her discussion of the Herter firm in the post-1883 period especially underscore the need for a stronger editorial hand in the production of this volume. Careful, coordinated shaping and modeling of the individual essays would have produced a more effective, interpretive volume that would document the objects in the exhibition and provide invaluable information on the firm that made them.

Finally, I was intrigued that the Herter project had its genesis in the 1980s, another period during which both a new group of wealthy and powerful art patrons rose and sought to assert themselves and a class of furniture designers such as Michael Graves and Wendell Castle began to produce furniture distinguished by the use of lavish materials, an emphasis on exquisite craftsmanship as a form of artistic expression, the layering of extraordinary detail, and an exploitation of historical references. As Castle succinctly put his design philosophy, "More is more." One does not have to harp on the parallels between the 1980s and 1870s, but it might be helpful to draw ideas from the consumerism literature of the 1980s to shed light on the earlier period. Newly wealthy individuals like the Hopkins, Goulds, Lockwoods, and other Herter clients certainly viewed their patronage of Herter goods and services as an instrument of economic growth and cultural coup that gave them a group identity and confirmed their rise to elite status. Apparently they had found it difficult to crack the establishment of taste, personified by men such as William Shepard Wetmore and John Taylor Johnston, who favored antique furniture or the showy but more restrained work of Leon Marcotte.[6]

Although *Herter Brothers: Furniture and Interiors for a Gilded Age* contains some interpretive shortcomings, the landmark monograph does provide an accurate, helpful overview of one of the major American cabinetmaking firms. It documents several important domestic commissions such as the Ruggles, Hopkins, and Vanderbilt houses and provides the foundation and the departure point for subsequent analyses of the other leading New York firms of the period. Future studies of Marcotte, Pottier & Stymus, Roux, and other firms and research into the business practices of interior decoration should draw upon the important work of Howe, Voorsanger, and Frelinghuysen.

Edward S. Cooke Jr.
Yale University

1. *19th-Century America: Furniture and Other Decorative Arts* (New York: Metropolitan Museum of Art, 1970), cat. nos. 209–12.

2. Several articles have appeared on specific aspects of Herter Brothers, but the two most complete sources for the firm prior to this publication under review remain a small exhibition pamphlet by David Hanks and references within a larger exhibition catalogue for an exhibition on the aesthetic movement: *Christian Herter and the Aesthetic Movement in America* (New York: Washburn Gallery, 1980); and Doreen Bolger Burke et al., *In Pursuit of Beauty: Americans and the Aesthetic Movement* (New York: Metropolitan Museum of Art, 1986).

3. Henry Hawley, "Four Pieces of American Furniture: An 'Aesthetic' Sidechair," *Bulletin of the Cleveland Museum of Art* 69, no. 10 (December 1982): 330–32, 338–39.

4. Charles Venable, *Silver in America, 1840–1940: A Century of Splendor* (New York: Harry N. Abrams, 1994).

5. For example, see Pierre Bourdieu, *Distinction: A Social Critique of the Judgement of Taste* (Cambridge, Mass.: Harvard University Press, 1984); and Ian Hodder, ed., *The Meaning of Things: Material Culture and Symbolic Expression* (London: Unwin Hyman, 1989).

6. For example, see Deborah Silverman, *Selling Culture: Bloomingdale's, Diana Vreeland, and the New Aristocracy of Taste in Reagan's America* (New York: Pantheon Books, 1986); Stuart Ewen, *All Consuming Images: The Politics of Style in Contemporary Culture* (New York: Basic Books, 1988); and Davira Taragin, Edward Cooke, Jr., and Joseph Giovannini, *Furniture by Wendell Castle* (New York: Hudson Hills, 1989), esp. pp. 60–94.

Michael L. James. *Drama in Design: The Life and Craft of Charles Rohlfs.* Buffalo, N.Y.: Burchfield Art Center, Buffalo College Foundation, 1994. 104 pp.; 85 color and bw illustrations, appendixes, bibliography, checklist of exhibition. $30.

Drama in Design: The Life and Craft of Charles Rohlfs is the first comprehensive study of the personal life and creative career of Charles Rohlfs (1853–1936) and is the culmination of over a decade of interest in Rohlfs by author Michael L. James, an independent scholar in Buffalo, New York. This richly illustrated book, published in conjunction with the 1994 exhibition "The Craftsmanship of Charles Rohlfs" at the Burchfield Art Center, Buffalo, will prove to be an important reference work, even if some of its assertions about Rohlfs's place in the arts and crafts movement and the influences on his work are questioned.

In a 1900 address to an arts and crafts conference, Rohlfs explained that "the things produced in the glow of enthusiasm are the things that have stood the test of time because they have been natural to the producer" (p. 93). His quotation aptly describes his own idiosyncratic furniture. It received wide recognition in his lifetime, but it was then left unexplored until the 1970s when scholars became interested in the American arts and crafts movement.[1] James contends that lack of information about Rohlfs has caused his principles and motivations to be poorly understood and has consequently left him unrecognized by the general public. James states in his introduction that his goal is to elevate Rohlfs's status as an artistic furniture designer (p. 9)—a reputation once accorded him and still, the author asserts, entirely deserved.

Drama in Design presents a great deal of new information on Rohlfs.[2] Each succinct chapter reveals previously unknown details of his life and knits a fascinating tale that well reflects his "glow of enthusiasm" for all his endeavors. The text follows a biographical format—the opening chapters detail Rohlfs's early life and career, the text then explores his creative nature as manifested in furniture, and it closes by outlining his personal and civic efforts.

James fully recounts Rohlfs's acting career and his collaboration with his wife, novelist Anna Katharine Green, topics only briefly mentioned in earlier published information. Rohlfs began his artistic career as a cast-iron stove and furnace designer in New York City while attending night classes at Cooper Union and pursuing his first true passion, acting. Rohlfs's 1877 stage debut was followed by a brief tenure with the Boston Theater Company. Unable to attain significant roles, however, Rohlfs retreated to a design career and continued his self-study in acting—a pattern that continued throughout his early career. By 1880, Rohlfs garnered some respectable reviews and consequently attained roles in traveling performances and held the lead role in several of his own productions. Critics responded equivocally to his later performances, citing his "peculiar interpretation" and display of "real dramatic power" (p. 29). The same assessment might be made of his furniture, which suggests the intimate and heretofore undocumented association between Rohlfs's theatrical and furniture-making careers; drama was essential to both.

James chronicles Rohlfs's cabinetmaking career from the earliest indications of his interest in furniture in 1887 through the development and growth of his company. Rohlfs initially made furniture for his own apartment, but interest in his creations resulted in numerous commissions. Rohlfs soon outgrew his modest attic work area and opened his first shop in Buffalo, where he and his family had settled in the late 1880s.

"The Sign of the Saw," the most extensive chapter in the book, explores the production of Rohlfs's furniture, its distinguishing characteristics, and the international recognition it achieved. When Rohlfs's business expanded, he no longer constructed the works but limited his role to designing furniture. He continued, however, to assert his artistic philosophy in the production process. He referred to his workmen as "fellow-laborers" and believed their sentiments were integral to the manufacture of the work: "to produce artistic furniture," he said, "they 'must be in sympathy and work with the feeling that they are part of the plan'" (p. 57). Unlike his contemporaries, Rohlfs maintained a close relationship with the fabrication of the object. After he completed the initial design, a scale model of the object was presented to Rohlfs for approval. The manufacturing process included hand and machine labor and resulted in aesthetically unusual, even whimsical, forms, distinguished by Rohlfs's sinuous motifs. Similar processes and enthusiasm were part of the production scheme for other wares by Rohlfs, such as lamps and chafing dishes.

Rohlfs's work found increasing favor among an international audience, as James's account documents. Rohlfs participated in numerous national and international expositions. His acclaim was so far-reaching that he received accolades from European royalty and numerous commissions for entire room suites. The most well-documented Rohlfs interior is the house he and his wife constructed in 1912. *Drama in Design* contains outstanding images of the house. They depict a diverse group of Rohlfs's objects in the setting for which they were intended—he also designed the interior of the home including wood and plaster work and light fixtures.

The book concludes with two chapters that summarize Rohlfs's participation in various arts-related organizations, the patents he developed during his lifetime, and the last decades of his personal life. These chapters are visually rich, and the images, combined with the wealth of details, lend insight into the personality of a designer who was, and is, often considered eccentric. The final section of *Drama in Design* reprints five speeches and interviews, including "True and False in Furniture" (an address given to a 1900 arts and crafts conference in Buffalo) and a 1902 speech given to an arts and crafts conference in Chautauqua, New York. These selections illuminate Rohlfs's beliefs and document that he never lost his flair for dramatic presentation. The closing pages contain a bibliography and a checklist of the exhibition at the Burchfield Art Center.

A closer look at some of the key assertions in *Drama in Design* reveals its limitations. The chapter "Sources of Rohlfs' Style" presents information on the stylistic influences on Rohlfs, a topic that has surfaced but has not been developed in prior publications. James suggests apparent "concessions to derivation" in Rohlfs's work, including assimilation of Moorish, medieval English, and Oriental motifs. He also acknowledges previously made connections between Rohlfs's work and that of architect Louis Sullivan and designer Edward Colonna but asserts them to have been unlikely; rather, James argues, Rohlfs drew on "ideas absorbed over a lifetime," which manifested themselves in a fresh and unique manner in his work. James also refutes the connection of the furniture to the mission (or arts and crafts) style; Rohlfs himself claimed to prefer "my own style (not 'Mission')" (p. 44). James contends that "'the product of natural ideas' aptly summarizes Rohlfs' work, as nature was the primary inspiration for his craft." He supports this assertion with a thorough discussion of Rohlfs's "reverence for wood grain" as manifested in the arresting carved embellishment found on the furniture.

Although Rohlfs's work illustrates a persuasive naturalistic inspiration, combined with some of the aforementioned aesthetics, James too readily accepts Rohlfs's assertion that "natural ideas" and his own creative genius were the sources of his designs. James easily dismisses other potential effects, noting that "it is tempting to speculate on the possible influences and connections among the multitude of artists and craftsmen . . . [but] it is difficult to distinguish casual threads from a collective exchange and merging of ideas" (p. 44). Yet with such a great quantity of artistic activity in upstate New York, combined with Rohlfs's design training, New York City upbringing, and extensive European travels a decade earlier, it seems implausible that he could have worked so free of other influences.

In the introduction, James expresses his intent to place Rohlfs in the context of the arts and crafts movement, but by arguing so persuasively that Rohlfs's work is difficult to categorize, he undermines this goal. James maintains, "Although some of Rohlfs' work does resemble the Mission style, the majority of his furniture speaks for itself in disputing that connection" (p. 44). He contends that Rohlfs's work may be more appropriately "cited as an American expression of *L'Art Nouveau*, or . . . a hybrid of that style and American Arts and Crafts" (p. 44). He offers no support for these claims by references to individual works, however, and although the entire book is well illustrated with photographs of the period and the furniture, at no time does the text cite specific images. It leaves the interpretation of the works solely to the reader. References to Rohlfs's house are in the text, for example, but James does not discuss the specific images.

James claims in the introduction that Rohlfs's furniture relates to "the art furniture of today" and that he hopes greater understanding of Rohlfs's life and craft "will establish his place in the Arts and Crafts Movement." Unfortunately, the book leaves both tasks undone. James discusses Rohlfs's philosophy in the context of the arts and crafts movement, noting, for example, that Rohlfs "identified himself with the arts and crafts philosophy of the time" and that "his ideas strongly parallel those of John Ruskin." Readers would have been given a deeper understanding of Rohlfs's position in the movement, however, if James had incorporated this discussion into the text and had compared Rohlfs's work and philosophy with that of his arts and crafts colleagues integral to the thesis. Further, Rohlfs explained that he was not a reformer, yet his speeches to arts and crafts societies included in the appendixes strongly promote the rhetoric of the movement. He also adamantly distinguished his work from the mission style, yet later we learn that he drew on the aesthetics of the arts and crafts movement for the interior design of his own home. According to the introduction of the book, Rohlfs's "ideas, closely aligned with English Arts and Crafts principles, evolved over time" (p.10). To what extent Rohlfs influenced other reformers or designers, and to what degree he was influenced by the English or American stylistic vocabulary of the movement (in the use, for example, of natural materials and exposed joinery), are not completely addressed.

Despite these limitations, *Drama in Design* offers ample new information on the art and life of Charles Rohlfs. It is well presented, thoroughly researched, and abundantly illustrated. James's efforts represent the advancing scholarship initiated by earlier ground-breaking exhibitions and catalogues. This study should certainly help bring to light additional examples of Rohlfs's work. More importantly, however, James's text makes an enigmatic character, his arts, and his philosophy more accessible to a general audience through a judicious balance of personal information and art historical research.

Anna Tobin D'Ambrosio
Munson-Williams-Proctor Institute

1. Previously published information on Rohlfs includes: Robert Judson Clark, ed., *The Arts and Crafts Movement in America, 1876–1916* (Princeton, N.J.: Princeton University Press, 1972), pp. 28–31; Wendy Kaplan, *"The Art that is Life": The Arts and Crafts Movement in America, 1875–1920* (Boston: Little, Brown and Co., 1987); Coy Ludwig, *The Arts and Crafts Movement in New York State: 1890–1920s* (Hamilton, N.Y.: Gallery Association of New York State, 1983). See also Michael L. James, "The Philosophy of Charles Rohlfs: An Introduction," *Arts and Crafts Quarterly* 1, no. 3 (April 1987): 14–18; Michael L. James, "Charles Rohlfs and the 'Dignity of Labor,'" in *The Substance of Style: New Perspectives on the American Arts and Crafts Movement* (Winterthur, Del.: Winterthur Museum, forthcoming).

2. James attained access to the collection of Rosamond Rohlfs Zetterholm, Charles Rohlfs's granddaughter, which contains archival papers and photographs. This collection was James's primary source.

John R. Porter, editor. *Living in Style: Fine Furniture in Victorian Quebec.* Montreal: Montreal Museum of Fine Arts, 1993. 527 pages; 60 color and 490 bw illustrations, bibliography, index. $95.00.

Victorian Quebec—what potential for cultural collision in those words. On the one hand, the adjectival term (defining, modifying, possessing?) evokes the long-lived queen whose name is synonymous with a weighty package of cultural and design values exported around the world by Britain at the height of its power. The other term, however, defines Canada's separatist province, ancient heartland of New France, where French has long been the dominant language and where license plates still bear the evocative slogan, "Je me souviens."

The juxtaposition of these words, nevertheless, is not hypothetical. French Quebec has been part of British Canada for over two centuries. Like other places dominated by Britain, it, too, underwent the process of Victorianization. The evidence of this process is still clearly visible on its urban landscapes. This book now tells us that corroborating evidence can be found inside the buildings as well. Editor John Porter and his associates demonstrate convincingly that there really is Victorian furniture in Quebec; furthermore, some of it is pretty remarkable.

Neither of these messages will be universally welcome, for Quebec's accepted design history has, at least in some quarters, long been dominated by emphasis on early French traditions. Porter explicitly states that one of the purposes of *Living in Style* is to counteract common stereotypes about Quebec as a land of *habitants,* of rural descendants of the early French settlers, somehow living outside of time, adhering to venerable French ways, and free from the corrupting influences of British imperialism and, later, the invasive cultural expressions of the industrialized United States. As attractive and ideologically functional as these stereotypes may be, they misrepresent or ignore much of Quebec's material culture of the nineteenth century and later. There can be no doubt that traditional French-inspired design continued into the nineteenth century, as Jean Palardy (*Les meubles anciens du Canada français,* 1963) and others have demonstrated. Still, there can also be no doubt that the style of international capitalism, which is another way of describing Victorianism, became increasingly prominent in nineteenth-century Quebec. A major accomplishment of *Living in Style* may well be its willingness to speak the obvious truth about cultural and design change in culturally conflicted Quebec.

Living in Style reveals that the story of furniture in nineteenth-century Quebec is in many ways like the story of furniture in the eastern United States. We see gradual transitions from hand to machine production, from small shops to large factories, from local production and consumption to national and even international networks of exchange. There is, though, an important difference as well, for Quebec had a caste system of sorts that finds no exact parallel in the States. There, the upper reaches of society and commerce were dominated by an English-speaking, Protestant minority, while the French-speaking, Catholic majority constituted something of an underclass. The most wealthy patrons and the most prestigious furniture manufacturers were thus, with some exceptions, English-speaking. What impact this situation may have had on furniture production or preference, however, is never directly addressed in this volume, and that omission strikes me as somewhat odd.

The ideological barriers to frank examinations of British imperialistic culture in Quebec may explain much that is odd about this book, for I have to admit that I find *Living in Style* a rather difficult book to assess. If I were more fully versed in Quebec political discourse, I might have a better understanding of the conditions that spawned and shaped this ambitious production. From my distance in the States, I can only describe the freely commingled strengths and weaknesses of this volume with the hope that my commentary will be helpful to others seeking some evaluation of this work. Frankly, I wish I liked it more.

Living in Style is an elegant, massive, and very heavy volume—over seven pounds, in fact. Design, printing, and paper are all of the highest quality; this book must have been very expensive to produce. Leafing through the pages of the book is most enjoyable, for they are richly adorned with hundreds of well-printed images, both in color and black and white. Reading it from cover to cover is another matter, however. As I made my way through the hundreds of pages, I wondered if this book might be the product of yet a different kind of cultural conflict than the one described in its text.

Living in Style is the outcome of a joint venture, with prominent parts played by the Montreal Museum of Fine Arts, the Museé de la civilisation in Quebec City, and the Université Laval. Editor John Porter was joined by fourteen other contributors, including conservators, curators, historians, and art historians, several of them graduate students at Laval when the book was written. In the preface to the book, ranking officers of the three collaborating institutions speak proudly of supporting "scholarly research on a subject situated at the point where art and material culture meet."

"Where art and material culture meet"—the phrase not only has a nice ring to it but also seems generous and open-minded. What it reveals, of course, are the different stances and intellectual orientations of the two museums involved. Although the phrase suggests parity of the two perspectives, it also points to a confusion of purpose that seems to plague the entire volume. Is this the catalogue of an art exhibition? Is it an essay on material culture? Curiously enough, while it is nominally both, it turns out to be neither. Although we are treated to vast masses of data and seemingly countless essays and papers, the furniture itself seems largely ignored, given neither the customary celebratory treatment of the art museum nor the more contextualized examination and analysis of a material culture study. Since the authors may be surprised by this assessment, I will describe the organization and contents of this volume at some length and then comment in detail on what seems to be missing from this aggressively lavish production.

The text of *Living in Style* is arranged into four major sections: The Context, The Users, The Furniture Makers, and The Furniture. Each of these major sections contains between eight and fifteen separate entries, including survey essays newly written for this publication; brief studies of particular figures, buildings, furnishings, or phenomena; and reprints of period texts of several sorts. The more sweeping or survey essays are printed on white paper; the more focused, on gray. Like a good exhibition, the book is color coded. So far so good.

The quality of the essays, however, varies considerably, as does their relevance. The first section begins with a history of Quebec society in the nineteenth century, sketching the broad contours of a century of domination, conflict, and social and cultural conservatism. This essay on white paper is followed immediately by four short works on gray paper, each describing the contexts for which extravagantly expensive pieces of Victorian furniture were produced. We get a glimpse of the furniture made for Hugh Allen, the richest man in Canada in the 1860s and 1870s. From a reprint of an article published in 1866 we learn about a lavish mirror frame created for the steamship *Quebec* but now lost. Other entries tell us about a bedroom suite constructed for the visit of the Prince of Wales to Montreal in 1860 and a large settee installed in a reception room at Université Laval in 1859. We nevertheless learn little beyond the fact that these objects exist or existed. There is little analysis, little interpretation.

The next white-paper essay, on the arts in nineteenth-century Quebec, begins to reveal some of the structural and intellectual problems that hobble this book. In the first place, the relevance of a chapter dealing primarily with painting and sculpture to a book on furniture is not immediately apparent. The final sentence of this essay notes that "home interiors and furniture naturally evolved along the same lines" (p. 78), but that case is not made here or elsewhere. This essay, like many others in the book, suffers from a lack of explicit integration into a central thesis or even a dominant story line. Essays follow one another like letters in the alphabet, but linkages between them are slight at best. We might surmise that they possess relevance to the alleged subject through association or proximity, but the burden remains on readers to puzzle out how one chapter relates to the others and how, together, they illuminate the topic of "fine furniture in Victorian Quebec."

I suspect that the art chapter was included because one of the sponsoring institutions is an art museum, which brings us to another unresolved, even unacknowledged problem with this book. The subtitle of *Living in Style* includes the ambiguous term, "fine furniture." The term is never clearly defined. I understand it as meaning expensive furniture that art museums are willing to exhibit. How, then, can the authors claim to reconcile a material culture approach to the study of furniture with the cultural biases of contemporary art museums? If the work specified that the study was of furniture of Victorian Quebec's ruling elites such a reconciliation would have been possible, and the study could have had real merit; but no such candor or sophistication informs these pages. Instead, we struggle along under the delusion that art and material culture are happily married and that this study rests on an objectively selected sample of cultural production. Not so. We never learn the ideology behind the determination of which objects to include and which to exclude. We have no idea how many well-documented objects were passed over because they were not considered "fine." We do not know which documents, catalogues, photographs, or inventories were brushed aside because they helped us understand furniture inappropriate to this book.

I mentioned candor and sophistication. Lack of candor may be less a problem with this publication than lack of sophistication. Although there are some exceptions I will discuss shortly, a good deal of this book strikes me as naive and out of touch. Parts of it could have been written thirty years ago. Texts typically generalize from secondary sources instead of particularizing from data at hand. Authors often seem uncomfortable with their material and unfamiliar with other writing on related subjects. Few if any of the essays acknowledge studies of the furniture of other regions or address ongoing discussions or problems within the history of furniture. In short, this book seems to have been written in a vacuum. As such, it does little to sweep away stereotypes of isolated *Québécois,* and that is unfortunate.

Too much of this book is blandly descriptive and derivative. As such it adds only minor details to our understanding of cultural change in nineteenth-century North America. Some of the essays, however, have real merit. The most original and useful part of the book, at least as I see it, is the section on the furniture makers. John Porter provides a helpful overview of transformations in the furniture business in nineteenth-century Quebec. Rénald Lessard uses census data from 1871 to reconstruct a cross-section of the furniture trade. His essay deals not only with the large metropolitan firms that dominated the trade but also with the more than three hundred smaller operations scattered around the province employing one, two, or three people. Although these little firms were abundant, their share of the market was slight. Quebec's three largest firms were responsible for one-third of all production in the province.

Even in this valuable essay problems emerge, however. A full picture of the furniture industry includes both ends of the spectrum. Here we get a verbal description of the entire phenomenon but no images of the products of these smaller shops. In this curious and unequal meeting of art and material culture, material culture may get an essay or two, but art gets most of the images.

In the same section, Jean-François Caron's account of William Drum and the advent of industrialization provides exactly the kind of particularized data missing in other sections of the book. Although its focus is on a single manufacturer, and Caron makes little attempt to compare Drum to other manufacturers in Canada or the States, the essay is informed, capable, and mature, and it generates a real sense of confidence in its author.

I wish I could say the same about the final section of the book, the one that alleges to deal with the furniture. After four hundred pages of other material, I was more than ready to enter into deep and meaningful communion with the furniture itself, but, alas, disappointment was to be my lot. This book turned out to be a furniture version of *Waiting for Godot.*

What do readers actually encounter in the furniture section? A short essay explains that Quebec furniture is based in large part on design ideas generated elsewhere, including France, England, Germany, and the United States; another essay describes patented furniture and novel materials; there is commentary on woods, veneers, and finishes, on construction techniques, and on metal furniture; a highly derivative essay speaks of styles; and a discussion exists on decorative motifs. Little of this narrative directly confronts the abundant and excellent images, which decorate the pages like so much wallpaper. Even the caption data accompanying the images is not particularly reassuring or rewarding. An upholstered armchair with carved caryatid arm supports in the style of Jelliff is represented as the work of

Marius Barbeau, born in 1883. If so, this attribution is noteworthy. A Gothic-style chair with upholstered seat, made of an unidentified wood, is ascribed the date of 1900 but is virtually identical to chairs made in this country in the 1840s. Is this date accurate? A pedestal table, apparently ebonized and gilt with a marquetry top, would date from the 1870s on this side of the border. Can it really have been made between 1880 and 1900 in Quebec? Dates in general seem on the late side. Perhaps they are accurate, but because the authors do not share their documentation with us, we have no way of knowing. Perhaps they are not aware that dates are themselves cultural data. Elsewhere, a laminated rosewood chair of the sort associated with Meeks is reported to be by Belter. Other captions are unsatisfying in various ways.

The discussion of comfort and innovative materials gives ample evidence of American and foreign penetration of the Quebec market. The text mentions the plywood furniture of Gardner & Co. and illustrates a Hunzinger chair. We encounter papier-mâché furniture from England, bentwood goods from Thonet and Kohn of Vienna, and wicker or rattan chairs, many of which, I suspect, came from Heywood-Wakefield in this country. We are left to speculate, however, on how rare or common any of these goods were.

This book is, then, strangely unsatisfying. Its grand scale and glorious production led me, at the outset, to anticipate something mature and interpretive, but form seems to have triumphed over content here. Art and material culture may have met, but, keeping alive an old Quebec tradition, that meeting has not been on an equal footing. Material culture has come off badly. One of the basic tenets of material culture inquiry has been ignored here, for although material culture study may involve contextualization of goods, it also typically relies on a close analysis of those goods. Context we have plenty of here, at least in a general way, but object analysis is almost totally lacking. Consequently, after more than five hundred pages, the furniture still remains elusive, beyond my understanding. I really do not feel that I know much about Quebec furniture, only a lot about this book, which is not the same thing. Perhaps the fault is entirely mine, but I suspect that much of the responsibility can be attributed to the derivative and diffuse character of this luxurious but undisciplined book.

Still trying to figure out why I learned so little, I finally recognized that, although there is a more or less logical order to the various episodes of the text, there is none whatsoever to the images. They are scattered over the five hundred plus pages of the book without regard to date, style, form, or any other organizing principle that I could discern. I am probably not the only one who will therefore find it difficult to get a cognitive grip on the material. To make sense of the random data, it must be organized in some way. Without order, as arbitrary as it may be, comprehension is difficult. Here we find hundreds of pieces of a picture puzzle, randomly paraded before us. Some of the individual pieces are surely fascinating, but it is extremely difficult to figure out from these pieces what the assembled picture might look like. At the end of this book, I still had little idea how Quebec furniture changed over time, how it varied according to region, social class, or taste culture, when and how the most prominent forms developed and changed, or much of anything at all concrete. A very basic understanding of how learning takes place has been ignored in organizing this book. Actually, art and material culture people tend to be visually oriented. Logically, then, the images should have formed the core of the book, and the text arranged to conform. This book was apparently put together backwards.

For me, the best thing about *Living in Style* is the inclusion of some sixty wonderful period photographs from the Notman Studio of Montreal. Notman images have been published before, but their full potential as documents of domestic life has not yet, as far as I know, been fully exploited. Including them here was a good idea, but more can be done. I offer, then, a modest proposal to our friends in Montreal. Seek funds from agencies in Canada and the United States interested in supporting comparative cultural studies. With those funds, bring together a circle of knowledgeable people from Canada, the States, France, and England to examine and analyze the content of the most detailed and best documented of the Notman photographs of furniture and domestic interiors. Turn the cumulative insights of this group into an exhibition and a book. Both will be worthy successors to *Living in Style*.

Perhaps it is best to think about this book as a beginning exploration of relatively unknown material. If the package seems too lavish for the contents and we learn too little about too much, we can attribute both to the enthusiasm of discovering new terrain. If future products emerge, whether they take the shape I have suggested or some other form, we will know that this book has had the impact that I think its creators hoped for. This work is, after all, a first attempt. Creative and inquiring minds looking through this book will be able to frame a host of questions that will require further exploration, and that is exactly as it should be. Sometimes the greatest accomplishment of introductory studies is their offspring. From that perspective, the profusion of topics, references, objects, and images included in this book will be beneficial, for the suggested lines of exploration are abundant and alluring.

Kenneth L. Ames
New York State Museum

Timothy D. Rieman and Jean M. Burks. *The Complete Book of Shaker Furniture*. New York: Harry N. Abrams, 1993. 400 pp.; 117 color and 283 bw illustrations, bibliography, glossary, index. $75.00

Just when you thought it was safe to go back to Barnes and Noble, another book on Shaker furniture has appeared in the shop window. It's not as though the world has been lacking for literature on the subject: over the years we have seen a stream of books on the furniture of this communal sect, including, for example, *Shaker Furniture, Religion in Wood: A Book of Shaker Furniture, The American Shakers and Their Furniture, Illustrated Guide to Shaker Furniture, Drawings of Shaker Furniture, The Book of Shaker Furniture,*

The Shaker Chair, and *Shaker Furniture Makers,* to say nothing of the scores of magazine articles, dozens of exhibition catalogues, and hundredweights of volumes of color plates, all about the Shakers but dwelling chiefly on their furniture. Could there possibly be anything more to say? Could anyone possibly come up with one more original title?

Yes, and yes. At 400 pages and 5.2 pounds, *The Complete Book of Shaker Furniture* is the best (and biggest) book on the subject. Authors Timothy D. Rieman (woodworker, historian of craft technology, and coauthor of *The Shaker Chair)* and Jean M. Burks (adjunct professor at the Bard Graduate Center for Studies in the Decorative Arts, and author of *Documented Furniture* at Canterbury Shaker Village and of *Birmingham Brass Candlesticks*) have created a comprehensive regional and chronological study of the furniture produced by members of America's oldest communal society. Theirs is the first book to embrace the full range of Shaker furniture made in communities from Maine to Kentucky, from the late eighteenth through the early twentieth centuries.

What has taken furniture historians so long to come to terms with Shaker furniture? How hard could this task be? The Shakers' communities numbered fewer than twenty, populated by a membership of probably no more than 20,000 souls over the course of 220 years. What could be so elusive about country furniture made and used in self-contained communities that the task of distinguishing its regional characteristics and identifying its makers could have sustained a minor industry of book production?

Plenty, it seems. The Shakers had the gift to be simple, and the stylistic analysis of furniture can be tough going when the subject's most distinctive feature is its lack of ornament. A comparative analysis of construction techniques can be just as hard when the makers of this furniture espoused uniformity as a virtue. Even the role of documentary evidence is limited in supporting field research in Shaker materials. Although the Shakers wrote extensively about their spiritual lives, they showed an annoying lack of interest in the material world, and their records yield relatively little mention of their furniture and the men and women who made it. What is more, the provenance of Shaker furniture is not always what it seems at first look. As the authors of this new book repeatedly demonstrate, not all furniture in Shaker villages was of Shaker manufacture. Some was brought along by converts when they joined a community, and some the Shakers went out and purchased. Of the furniture actually made by the Shakers, some migrated from one community to the next as needs dictated, confounding collectors who assumed that tracing an object to a specific community also determined its place of origin. These complexities and subtleties of Shaker material life often eluded early writers (my favorite example being the recent conclusion that, in Shaker parlance, the term "clothes pins" probably refers to the ubiquitous pegs mounted on the walls of their rooms, thus laying to rest the canard about Shakers inventing laundry clothespins). In comparison with those earlier books, however, *The Complete Book of Shaker Furniture* is characterized by a sophisticated methodology of furniture scholarship, informed by unprecedented access to research materials in Shaker collections.

In the course of this study the authors examined well over a thousand pieces of furniture. On page after page of their handsome book are excellent illustrations and knowledgeable descriptions of an encyclopedic variety of chairs, tables, beds, clocks, counters, chests, cupboards, and cases, many published here for the first time. Throughout, the authors support their findings with impressive written and pictorial evidence from virtually every archival source imaginable. Over the ten years it took them to conduct their research, they also drew upon a wave of important new scholarship in the field. Their comprehensive book synthesizes authoritative information from such diverse sources as June Sprigg's observations on original finishes, Jerry Grant's biographical study of Shaker cabinetmakers, Priscilla Brewer's work on the historical demography of Shakerism, Steven Stein's examination of the philosophical underpinnings of the Shaker experience, and the research of the late Br. Theodore E. Johnson and of the late Edward F. Nickels, whose community-based studies of the furniture of the Maine Shakers and the furniture of the Kentucky Shakers were presented at the ground-breaking symposium on Shaker furniture held at the Metropolitan Museum of Art in 1982.

The Complete Book of Shaker Furniture is divided into two parts. In the first section, the authors set the stage by describing the Shaker experience in America. The Shakers' origins and their daily life, the cultural context of Shakerism, Shaker design, and the tools and technology of nineteenth-century America are all discussed here and all extensively documented by historical references. Those readers familiar with Rieman's article on Shaker built-in furniture in the spring 1995 issue of *Home Furniture* or with Burks's article on the evolution of design in Shaker furniture in the May 1994 issue of *Antiques* will recognize the individual contributions of the authors to this book. Rieman the woodworker interprets historical process through the toolmarks Shaker cabinetmakers left on their work. His precise mechanical drawings of case pieces illustrate his analysis of the patterns and proportions that characterize Shaker furniture, and in words recorded in the journals of the nineteenth-century Shaker cabinetmaker Freegift Wells, he takes us step by step through the construction of a single piece of furniture from green lumber to finished bookcase.

Burks the historian relates specific pieces of Shaker furniture to designs in commercial furniture pattern books and to comparable furniture produced by the Shakers' contemporaries in nineteenth-century America. The concept that the Shakers were influenced by their surrounding cultural environment is illustrated in side-by-side comparisons of Shaker furniture with its non-Shaker counterparts. Though these comparisons occur inconsistently and are lamentably few, they do effectively refute the simplistic perception of the Shakers as unique beings existing in a cultural vacuum.

In their second section, the authors tighten their focus to identify the actual furniture made and used by the Shakers. Wisely, they have organized this part not primarily by form but by form within a geographical region, demonstrating how the furniture within a bishopric (the Shakers' term for individual villages linked by geography and administered under a central authority) shares common characteristics. Following the model of furniture study developed in the 1970s, they start by identifying specific elements of architectural woodwork extant in original Shaker buildings. Having recognized the local vocabulary of furniture making, the idiosyncrasies of joinery, turning, and molding and of woods, finish, and hardware, the authors proceed to identify related features in a variety of forms and styles of freestanding furniture, which can then be ascribed to each community. In the course of their research, the authors also encountered numerous pieces signed or otherwise marked by their makers (in apparent violation of Shaker law), strengthening the attributions to specific craftsmen and expanding the list of known Shaker furniture makers to more than 250 names.

The authors make an important contribution in identifying furniture from outside the Shakers' "classic" period of from 1820 to 1840. Anyone who hasn't read a Shaker furniture book since the late Robert F. W. Meader concluded his 1972 *Illustrated Guide to Shaker Furniture* with a discussion of "the horrors of Victorianism" is in for a big surprise here. Starting with the frontispiece, where a plain, painted washstand made ca. 1840 in Enfield, New Hampshire, is paired with a ca. 1890 Grand Rapids–inspired desk made by Br. Delmer Wilson at Sabbathday Lake, the authors make clear their intention to encompass the entire range of Shaker furniture—the good, the bad, and the ugly. Along with superstars in the league of the celebrated $200,000 work counter purchased at auction in 1990 by Oprah Winfrey, they also document some of the rare early and stylistically undeveloped Shaker furniture as well as the fancier furniture inspired by changing tastes in Shaker communities after the Civil War. The authors are also to be commended for eschewing some old standards in favor of illustrating previously unpublished examples (though I do wonder about the fairly weird tripod stand with a "possibly unique" birdcage [fig. 127, p. 188], which, despite its unlikely appearance and the apparent absence of any provenance, is attributed to the Enfield, Connecticut, community, presumably on the basis of lathe turnings alone). From village to village, the authors are so conscientious about documenting even the wallflowers of Shaker furniture that one can forgive their occasional excursion into such airy captions as, "Beautifully constructed of heavily figured curly maple, this is one of the finest Western Shaker case pieces extant (p. 291)."

Rieman's excellent photographs of Shaker furniture are augmented by his detailed drawings. Among my favorites is a diagram clearly explaining the workings of a wonderfully complicated mechanism for locking simultaneously the five drawers of a sewing case (p. 180). This book is also richly illustrated with historical images—period photographs, wood engravings, and watercolor renderings from the *Index of American Design*. When these pictures are integrated with the text, they enrich the authors' presentation by serving as the visual evidence of Shaker history. When the authors illustrate historic photographs or a Shaker "spirit" drawing without any accompanying explanation, however, as they sometimes do in the introductory section, these images are left stranded outside the interpretive structure with their potential as historical evidence unrealized. Because historical images are employed so effectively elsewhere in the book, certain sections suffer by comparison when these images are used as decoration.

This book is by and large of a descriptive nature. Though several times it crosses the threshold into interpretation, using furniture as a means of revealing Shaker history, it generally adheres to the authors' stated goal "to develop useful criteria to help identify Shaker furniture and, when possible, to determine the community of origin, the construction date, and the name of the maker (p. 11)." The authors accomplish this task splendidly. Not only do they decipher Abner Allen's signature on the back of a drawer, thereby finally setting the record straight and expunging the apocryphal "Abner Alley" from the list of Shaker furniture makers, but they make a creditable attribution of a whole group of furniture based on the characteristics of this one signed chest (pp. 190–91).

Authors Rieman and Burks have done an exemplary job of factoring the complicated and elusive corpus of Shaker furniture down to its primary elements. It's all here: the cabinetmakers, the woods, the construction techniques, the signatures, the finishes, and the communities of origin. This book is a storehouse of the information that has eluded generations of students of Shaker furniture since Edward Deming Andrews and Faith Andrews published their pioneering article on the subject in 1928. With such an enormous amount of facts firmly in hand, one would expect *The Complete Book of Shaker Furniture* to be the last word on the subject; but this book reveals just enough about the Shakers themselves, their yearning for perfection, their ambivalence about conformity, to open the window to larger questions about the place of material objects in Shaker life. For the Shakers, furniture was never an end in itself, of course, and the social historians among us await a study of what meaning their furniture held for them. Such abstractions, however, were never the purpose of this book. *The Complete Book of Shaker Furniture* delivers on its promise to serve up the facts, and in that regard, it is hard to imagine how it can be surpassed.

Robert P. Emlen
Brown University

Philip Zea and Donald Dunlap with measured drawings by John Nelson. *The Dunlap Cabinetmakers: A Tradition in Craftsmanship.* Mechanicsburg, Pa.: Stackpole Books, 1994. 210 pp.; 24 color and 68 bw illustrations, numerous line drawings, index. $49.95.

In the rarefied, often fastidious, and sometimes arcane world of eighteenth-century furniture, the work of John and Samuel Dunlap, and other cabinetmakers they trained and inspired, continues to delight the eye and refresh the spirit. Lively, bold, and unpretentious, this furniture of south-central New Hampshire survives in great numbers and attracts deserving appreciation and study.

Dunlap furniture had been recognized and associated with the Dunlap name long before Charles S. Parsons, a retired textile manufacturer turned decorative arts researcher, authored the seminal exhibition catalogue *The Dunlaps and Their Furniture* in 1970.[1] That catalogue unlocked the potential for broad and diverse study of Dunlap furniture by illustrating and discussing some one hundred objects and summarizing the Dunlap cabinetmakers' lives and community. More importantly, Parsons reprinted John Dunlap's account book (entries dating from 1768 to 1789), his estate inventory, indentures, and plans for pulpits, and he provided information on tools and templates still in the family's possession along with several tables, tabulations, and graphs. Parsons's thoroughness, exceeded only by the expanded personal archive he bequeathed to the New Hampshire Historical Society upon his death in 1988, has served subsequent scholars well as they return to the Dunlap material to investigate subject areas that Parsons never developed fully nor perhaps imagined.

The other key publication on the Dunlaps is Donna-Belle Garvin's "Two High Chests of the Dunlap School." This careful and systematic documentation of two objects establishes most of the fascinating historical circumstances now associated with the Dunlap school and its furniture: relationships between and among masters, apprentices, and journeymen, including account-book payments to one individual on behalf of another; furniture sales to women; terminology (much of which is based on Parsons's work); use of mahoganizing stains for maple and of colorful paint and gilding to highlight pediment details; and specific construction details and anomalies and their association with individual makers.[2]

The most recent entrée is a fully illustrated work by two authors of markedly different backgrounds: Philip Zea is a curator, and Donald Dunlap, a descendent of the Dunlap family of woodworkers, is a contemporary furniture maker. Combinations of such different perspectives are too rare in current scholarship. Granted, any collaboration requires nurture and compromise to bring the project to closure, but such efforts offer great promise for creativity and synergy. How much better, for example, are works that balance perspectives of curators and conservators, specialists and populists, inventive and conventional outlooks?

The authors, who speak with a single voice, introduce their work as a study of the Scotch-Irish through their furniture. They emphasize the importance of "place" as "the most telling component of cultural history" (p. 3). Author Donald Dunlap (hereafter called Donald to distinguish him from his several Dunlap forebears) is woven into the study as a modern representative of the region. The book is divided into three parts: a description of Scotch-Irish (whom the authors call "Scots-Irish") settlers in eighteenth-century New Hampshire, an account of the furniture from that time, and a "catalogue" of fourteen contemporary recreations by Donald, accompanied by brief comments on the history of the form. The first part adequately summarizes secondary works addressing regional Scotch-Irish habitation and more general settlement patterns. The section on the furniture discusses Dunlap products on their own merits and in relation to other groups of furniture from the region. The third section, consuming three-quarters of the book, provides details, instruction, measured drawings, and sprinklings of folksy observations and preferences that personalize Donald and his work for practicing furniture makers and clients. The last section seems to be written for a *Fine Woodworking* audience, in contrast to the conventional furniture history readership of the first two sections.

To fathom the depths of New Hampshire English-speaking culture, and thereby to gain better understanding of its material culture, it is necessary to look below the surface of apparent uniformity to find a Scotch-Irish subculture. One of the few readily apparent differences between the Scotch-Irish and their Anglican counterparts is that the Scotch-Irish worshipped in Presbyterian rather than Congregational churches. The vitality of their religious community is firmly demonstrated with the First Parish in Londonderry (now East Derry), which regularly attracted 500 to 600 communicants, high numbers indeed in rural New Hampshire, to biannual celebrations of the Lord's Supper throughout the 1720s and 1730s.[3] To ask whether Scotch-Irish cultural ties and traditions influenced the material culture of this region, a very inviting assumption, is a deserving question and is one that the authors raise, at least implicitly.

Zea and Dunlap track with a broad brush the New Hampshire Scotch-Irish subculture through town names and settlement patterns predating 1740. To extend their subject into the time of the furniture they discuss, they follow Parsons and Garvin in their use of primary references from Dunlap accounts and from the rich *Diary of Matthew Patten of Bedford, N.H., 1754–1788*. The degree to which the Scotch-Irish assimilated into a broader English-speaking culture is not resolved (p. 14). As this reviewer observed previously with specific reference to Dunlap furniture, definition of any Scotch-Irish subculture may rest almost entirely on material culture analysis.[4]

Zea and Dunlap open their analysis of the Dunlap brothers' Scotch-Irish origins and resulting implications for furniture study by reaffirming visual relationships already published between Dunlap furniture and the 1695 joined chair by Robert Rhea, a Scotch immigrant to New Jersey. These visual relationships, although separated by two generations of cabinetmaking and representing strikingly different regions, nevertheless suggest that the imaginative Dunlaps may have drawn on design traditions from their Scottish homeland at the time of their parents' migration.[5] The authors then introduce other examples of late-eighteenth- and early-nineteenth-century American furniture that has or might have Scotch-Irish origins, one of which is a desk-and-bookcase by John Shearer of Martinsburg, West Virginia. Its heavy pediment, supported by a bold egg-and-dart molding, recalls contemporary Dunlap pediments. Regrettably, visual analysis yields no further linkages, and the authors fall back on the crutch of speculation, noting that these inadequately understood yet fascinating objects "may prove Scottish rather than simply bizarre" (p. 40).

Questions regarding the Scotch-Irish qualities of Dunlap and other furniture remain unanswered. Immigration statistics confirm the formidable presence of the Scotch-Irish throughout the colonies, with New England concentrations in southern New Hampshire and central Massachusetts.

Furniture historians continue to catalogue eighteenth-century furniture of Scotland, Ireland, and northern England. Stronger historical ties must be established between these objects and the furniture of the Dunlaps, Shearer, William Sprats, and others before design features such as paired small drawers flanking a central one can be accepted as Scotch-Irish motifs (pp. 24, 154).[6] Discovering who in America trained the Dunlaps would not only help bridge the hiatus between late-seventeenth-century Scottish design sources and late-eighteenth-century Dunlap products but might also reveal some of the motives that sustain cultural identity or inspire assimilation.

The ranging essay on the furniture ends abruptly with the statement that, by 1810, "the visual heritage of the old generation had passed away" (p. 45). What happened in rural New Hampshire that could cast away such strong expressions of tradition and cultural identity? This question becomes all the more problematic in light of the many woodworking Dunlap brothers, cousins, and nephews of John and Samuel that populate historical records during the 1810s and 1820s; moreover, chests bearing flowered ogee molding and cabriole legs might be dated in the mid-1810s (p. 95, n. 165). Furniture historians might thus expect several Dunlap features to remain in use for years to come.

Donald Dunlap finds inspiration for his modern creations by recalling the generations of Dunlap woodworkers who settled in his hometown of Antrim after 1812. He conjures an image of rural craftsmen who, having found a design solution that works, are loath to change, no matter what others might produce. There may be nothing fanciful or romantic about this image. The Maskell Ware family of chairmakers in southern New Jersey, for example, suggests the possibility of an intriguing and instructive parallel. They did little to change their product from the 1790s until well into the twentieth century, although George Sloan Ware (1853–1940) did substitute a motor for foot power to operate his lathe.[7]

Donald's modern work does not attempt to reproduce exactly Dunlap, or even eighteenth-century, furniture. In addition to using modern tools to rough out the work, which is then finished with hand tools, Donald introduces different internal framing structures, uses different fasteners, cuts mortises differently, and takes whatever other steps he thinks useful to speed his work. He is outspoken about the use of modern tools, saying pointedly that Major John would have plugged in his table saw if he could have (p. 47). He shares freely many technical aspects of construction and design, as well as assorted tips and observations that have come from his furniture-making career.

Unlike the twentieth-century Ware chairmakers, Donald appears not to belong to an unbroken woodworking tradition. He and Zea remain remarkably unaware of, or at least silent on, the subject of Donald's own sensibilities as a cabinetmaker participating in a recreated tradition of handwork, nor do the authors reflect on Donald's own aesthetic experiences, reactions, and means of expression. An interview might have disclosed meanings and values that he has discovered by participating in what appears to be a genuine revival. More specific to his craft and his artistic intentions, what does it mean to him to create, through adaptation, forms such as dressing tables and basket-weave china tables that the Dunlap's never produced? Why does he emphasize further the "exaggeration [that] is the heart and soul of Dunlap furniture" (p. 79)? Readers might recall the new insights into craft processes that came from Michael Owen Jones's detailed study of contemporary furniture makers in *The Hand Made Object and Its Maker* (Los Angeles and Berkeley: University of California Press, 1975).

The text is heavily footnoted, with all of the notes appearing at the end, making inconvenient the lack of a bibliography or short-title index. The book would also have benefited from better editing for diction and style, especially the propensity for alliteration that is ineffective, intrusive, and irritating. Nonetheless, readers should come away from *The Dunlap Cabinetmakers* with increased awareness of the Scotch-Irish and their contributions to furniture making as well as a heightened sense of opportunity for further research into a deserving area of study.

Philip D. Zimmerman
Lancaster, Pennsylvania

1. Manchester, N.H.: Currier Gallery of Art, 1970.

2. *Historical New Hampshire* 35, no. 2 (summer 1980): 163–85. Another article of note is Ann W. Dibble, "Major John Dunlap: The Craftsman and His Community," *Old-Time New England* 68, nos. 3–4 (winter-spring 1978): 50–58.

3. Philip D. Zimmerman, "Ecclesiastical Architecture in the Reformed Tradition in Rockingham County, New Hampshire, 1790–1860" (Ph.D. diss., Boston University, 1985), p. 86, n. 60. Records of the First Church in Derry, N.H. (1726–1808). Major John Dunlap designed and built a pulpit for one of the Londonderry congregations in 1783 (Parsons, p. 45ff.).

4. Published by the town, 1903. Philip D. Zimmerman, "Regionalism in American Furniture Studies," in *Perspectives on American Furniture,* edited by Gerald W. R. Ward (New York: W. W. Norton & Co., 1988), p. 36.

5. The visual relationships and hypothesis first appear in ibid., pp. 33–38.

6. Interestingly, this distinctive drawer configuration, which is common in New Hampshire but appears throughout Massachusetts and Connecticut, is rarely encountered in Dunlap furniture.

7. Deborah D. Waters, "Wares and Chairs: A Reappraisal of the Documents," in *American Furniture and Its Makers: Winterthur Portfolio 13,* edited by Ian M. G. Quimby (Chicago: University of Chicago Press, 1979), p. 167.

Compiled by Gerald W. R. Ward

Recent Writing on American Furniture: A Bibliography

▼ THE FOLLOWING lists have been compiled in the same manner as the bibliographies included in the first two volumes of *American Furniture*. Additional titles for 1993 and 1994 are listed first, followed by 1995 titles that had been noted by the time this issue went into production in early May 1995.

Once again, staff members of several libraries have been helpful in compiling this material. Neville Thompson of the Winterthur Museum Library, in particular, has provided invaluable help. Errors and omissions are my responsibility.

I would be glad to receive citations for books and articles, especially those in museum journals and bulletins, that should be included in these annual lists. Review copies of pertinent works would also be welcome. Please send information and materials to:

Gerald W. R. Ward
Carolyn and Peter Lynch Associate Curator of American Decorative Arts and Sculpture
Museum of Fine Arts, Boston
465 Huntington Avenue
Boston, Massachusetts 02115

ADDITIONS TO 1993 AND 1994 TITLES

Abercrombie, Stanley. *George Nelson: The Design of Modern Design.* Cambridge, Mass.: MIT Press, 1994. xx + 353 pp.; 58 color and 112 bw illus., bibliography, index.

Adelman, Everett Mayo. "The Thrones and Chairs Leroy Person Made." *Folk Art* 19, no. 3 (Fall 1994): 48–50. 4 color illus.

Aldrich, Megan. *Gothic Revival.* London: Phaidon Press, 1994. 240 pp.; 150+ color and 100 bw illus., glossary, bibliography, appendixes, index. Distributed by Chronicle Books, San Francisco.

Antique Wicker from the Heywood-Wakefield Catalogue with Price Guide. Atglen, Pa.: Schiffer Publishing, 1994. 160 pp.; illus. (Reprint of 1929 catalogue.)

Atterbury, Paul. "A. W. N. Pugin, an Inspirational Designer." *Antiques* 145, no. 6 (June 1994): 858–67. 17 color and 2 bw illus.

Atterbury, Paul, and Lars Tharp, eds. *The Bulfinch Illustrated Encyclopedia of Antiques.* Boston: Little, Brown and Company, a Bulfinch Press Book, 1994. 332 pp.; 1,100+ color illus., glossary, index. (See Tim Forrest, "Furniture," pp. 158–259.)

Atterbury, Paul, and Clive Wainwright, eds. *Pugin: A Gothic Passion.* New Haven: Yale University Press in association with the Victoria and Albert Museum, 1994. 310 pp.; 300 color and 100 bw illus., glossary, index.

Austin, Bruce A., Frederick R. Brandt, Laurene Buckley, Charles F. Hamilton, Rixford Jennings, Jack Quinan, Robert Rust, Kitty Turgeon-Rust, Marjorie B. Searl, Tran Turner, Marie Via, and Jean Francois Vilain. *Head, Heart, and Hand: Elbert Hubbard and the Roycrofters.* Rochester, N.Y.: Memorial Art Gallery, University of Rochester, and the American Federation of Arts, 1994. 192 pp.; 171 color and 94 bw illus.

Barnet, Peter, and MaryAnn Wilkinson. *Decorative Arts 1900: Highlights from Private Collections in Detroit.* Detroit: Detroit Institute of Arts, 1993. 132 pp.; 61 color and 83 bw illus., biographies, bibliographies, index. Distributed by University of Washington Press, Seattle.

Barquist, David L. "'The Honours of a Court' or 'the Severity of Virtue': Household Furnishings and Cultural Aspirations in Philadelphia." In *Shaping a National Culture: The Philadelphia Experience, 1750–1800,* ed. Catherine E. Hutchins, pp. 313–33. Winterthur, Del.: Winterthur Museum, 1994. 8 bw illus.

Barquist, David L. Review of *Portsmouth Furniture,* ed. Brock Jobe. In *American Furniture 1994,* ed. Luke Beckerdite, pp. 234–38. Milwaukee, Wis.: Chipstone Foundation, 1994. Distributed by University Press of New England, Hanover, N.H.

Beard, Geoffrey. "Some Eighteenth-Century English Seats and Covers Re-Examined." *Antiques* 145, no. 6 (June 1994): 842–49. 11 color and 2 bw illus.

Beckerdite, Luke. "Architect-Designed Furniture in Eighteenth-Century Virginia: The Work of William Buckland and William Bernard Sears." In *American Furniture 1994,* ed. Luke Beckerdite, pp. 28–48. Milwaukee, Wis.: Chipstone Foundation, 1994. 35 color and bw illus. Distributed by University Press of New England, Hanover, N.H.

Beckerdite, Luke. "An Identity Crisis: Philadelphia and Baltimore Furniture Styles of the Mid Eighteenth Century." In *Shaping a National Culture: The Philadelphia Experience, 1750–1800,* ed. Catherine E. Hutchins, pp. 243–81. Winterthur, Del.: Winterthur Museum, 1994. 42 bw illus.

Beckerdite, Luke, ed. *American Furniture 1994.* Milwaukee, Wis.: Chipstone Foundation, 1994. xi + 264 pp.; numerous color and bw illus., bibliography, index. Distributed by University Press of New England, Hanover, N.H.

Beylerian, George M., with text by David Revere McFadden. *Chairmania: Fantastic Miniatures.* New York: Harry N. Abrams, 1994. 144 pp.; color illus.

Bivins, John. *Authenticating Antique Furniture.* Charleston, S.C.: Pilaster Productions, Inc., 1994. Two VHS videotapes.

Brettell, Richard. *The Museum of the Americas: Dallas Museum of Art.* London: Apollo Magazine, 1993. 83 pp.; color and bw illus. (Includes some furniture.)

Brown, Charlotte Vestal, and Nina Strizler-Levine. *Bob Trotman: A Retrospective of Furniture and Sculpture.* Raleigh: Visual Arts Center, North Carolina State University, 1994. 48 pp.; 43 color and 1 bw illus., exhibition checklist, chronology.

Brown, Michael K., and Chris A. Shelton. "Bayou Bend's Latest Acquisition: Old World Inspiration for a New World Masterpiece." In *The Forty-Second Annual Theta Charity Antiques Show,* pp. 22–23, 26–27, 30. Houston: Theta Charity Antiques Show, 1994. 4 bw illus. (Re acquisition of white and gilt armchair, Philadelphia, ca. 1790–1810.)

Buck, Susan. "A Masonic Master's Chair Revealed." In *American Furniture 1994,* ed. Luke Beckerdite, pp. 162–71. Milwaukee, Wis.: Chipstone Foundation, 1994. 13 color and bw illus. Distributed by University Press of New England, Hanover, N.H.

Burks, Jean M. "Living with Antiques: A Folk Art Collection in Pennsylvania." *Antiques* 146, no. 4 (October 1994): 506–15. 12 color illus. (Re Shaker furniture.)

Burns, Charles J. "Hunter House Highboy." *Newport Gazette,* no. 133 (Winter 1994): 2–3. 1 bw illus. (Re Newport high chest, ca. 1760, on display in the Hunter House, Newport, R.I.)

Burrows, Linda. "Props in the Play of Life: Peter Danko." *American Craft* 53, no. 2 (April/May 1993): 54–57. 1 bw and 3 color illus.

Busch, Akiko. "Judy McKie: Connecting to the World." *American Craft* 54, no. 6 (December 1994/January 1995): 32–35. 4 color illus.

Byars, Mel. *The Design Encyclopedia.* New York: John Wiley and Sons, 1994. 612 pp.; 118 bw illus.

Calloway, Stephen. *Baroque Baroque: The*

Culture of Excess. London: Phaidon Press, 1994. 239 pp.; numerous color and bw illus., index. (Includes some furniture.)

Carson, Cary, Ronald Hoffman, and Peter J. Albert, eds. *Of Consuming Interests: The Style of Life in the Eighteenth Century*. Charlottesville: University Press of Virginia for the United States Capitol Historical Society, 1994. 721 pp.; bw illus., tables, line drawings, index. (See esp. essay by Kevin M. Sweeney.)

Chairs. Ed. George Nelson. Reprint. New York: Acanthus Press, 1994. 184 pp.; 350 illus.

Clark, Michael E., and Jill Thomas-Clark, eds. *J. M. Young Arts and Crafts Furniture: 181 Photographs: J. M. Young Furniture Catalogue*. Camden, N.Y., 1904. Reprint. New York: Dover Publications, 1994. 99 pp.; 170 bw illus., 11 line drawings.

Clowes, Jody. "Romancing the Surface." *American Craft* 54, no. 4 (August/September 1994): 54–57, 68. 4 color illus.

Conforti, Michael, ed., with essays by Marcia G. Anderson, Michael Conforti and Jennifer Komar, Mark Hammons, Alan K. Lathrop, Louise Lincoln and Paulette Fairbanks Mohn, and Thomas O'Sullivan. *Minnesota 1900: Art and Life on the Upper Mississippi, 1890–1915*. Minneapolis: Minneapolis Institute of Arts, 1994. Newark, Del.: University of Delaware Press; London and Toronto: Associated University Presses in association with The Minneapolis Institute of Arts, 1994. 333 pp.; numerous color and bw illus., exhibition checklists, bibliographies, appendixes.

Connors, Kathleen A. "Southern Comfort: The Art Chairs of Richard Dial." *Folk Art* 19, no. 3 (Fall 1994): 50–52. 4 color illus.

Coutts, Howard. "Formal Dining in Europe." *Antiques* 146, no. 2 (August 1994): 186–97. 10 color and 13 bw illus.

Crom, Theodore R. *An Eighteenth Century English Brass Hardware Catalogue*. Hawthorne, Fla.: T. R. Crom, 1994. iv + 15 pp.; 128 plates, illus., bibliography, index.

Cullity, Brian. *"A Cubberd, Four Joyne Stools & Other Small Thinges": The Material Culture of Plymouth Colony, and Silver and Silversmiths of Plymouth, Cape Cod, and Nantucket*. Sandwich, Mass.: Heritage Plantation of Sandwich, 1994. 183 pp.; numerous bw illus., appendixes, glossary, bibliography. (See Rob Tarule and Ted Curtin, "On the Reproduction of the Original Pieces on Exhibit," pp. 18–20.)

Deschamps, Madeleine. *Empire*. New York: Abbeville Press, 1994. 256 pp.; 150 color and 55 bw illus., bibliography, index.

Dilnot, Clive. "The Enigma of Things." *Harvard University Art Museums Bulletin* 2, no. 2 (Winter 1993–94): 55–68. 4 bw illus., 1 line drawing. (Prepared as commentary on the exhibition, "What, if Anything, Is an Object," organized by the author at the Fogg. Of at least theoretical interest to furniture historians.)

Doares, Robert F. "'That They May Long Remember Me . . .': Henry Lamond, Cabinetmaker from Edinburgh, North Britten." *Journal of Early Southern Decorative Arts* 20, no. 1 (May 1994): 1–44. 25 bw illus.

The Earthly Paradise: Arts and Crafts by William Morris and His Circle from Canadian Collections. Toronto: Art Gallery of Ontario and Key Porter Books, 1993. 294 pp.; numerous color and bw illus., bibliography, index.

Edwards, Clive. *Twentieth-Century Furniture: Materials, Manufacture, and Markets*. Manchester, England: Manchester University Press, 1994. 228 pp.; 40 bw illus., glossary, bibliography, index. Distributed by St. Martin's Press, New York.

Eickhoff, Hajo. *Himmelsthron und Schaukelstuhl: die Geschichte des Sitzens*. Munich: Hanser, 1993. 255 pp.; illus., bibliography.

Eidelberg, Martin. "The Arts and Crafts American Style." *American Craft* 54, no. 2 (April/May 1994): 46–53. Color and bw illus.

Evans, Nancy Goyne. "Identifying and Understanding Repairs and Structural Problems in Windsor Furniture." In *American Furniture 1994*, ed. Luke Beckerdite, pp. 2–27. Milwaukee, Wis.: Chipstone Foundation, 1994. 31 bw illus. Distributed by University Press of New England, Hanover, N.H.

Evans, Nancy Goyne. "The Philadelphia Windsor Chair: A Commercial and Design Success Story." In *Shaping a National Culture: The Philadelphia Experience, 1750–1800*, ed. Catherine E. Hutchins, pp. 335–62. Winterthur, Del.: Winterthur Museum, 1994. 21 bw illus.

Federhen, Deborah Anne. "Politics and Style: An Analysis of the Patrons and Products of Jonathan Gostelowe and Thomas Affleck." In *Shaping a National Culture: The Philadelphia Experience, 1750–1800*, ed. Catherine E. Hutchins, pp. 283–311. Winterthur, Del.: Winterthur Museum, 1994. 13 bw illus., 4 tables.

Fennimore, Donald L., Amanda E. Lange, et al. *Eye for Excellence: Masterworks from Winterthur*. Wilmington, Del.: Winterthur Museum, 1994. 144 pp.; 90 color and 5 bw illus. (See Robert F. Trent, "Furniture," pp. 65–86.)

Fleming, John A. *The Painted Furniture of French Canada, 1700–1840*. Camden East, Ontario: Camden House Publishing and Canadian Museum of Civilization, 1994. 179 pp.; numerous color and bw illus., appendixes, bibliography, index. Distributed by Firefly Books, Buffalo, N.Y..

Foy, Jessica H., and Karal Ann Marling, eds. *The Arts and the American Home, 1890–1930*. Knoxville: University of Tennessee Press, 1994. xxiv + 194 pp.; illus., bibliography, index.

Frakes, Mary. "Alphonse Mattia and Rosanne Somerson." *American Craft* 53, no. 6 (December 1993/January 1994): 38–43, 64. 4 color and 3 bw illus.

Furniture History 29 (1993). v + 216 pp.; numerous bw illus. (This issue, dedicated to Helena Hayward, contains twenty-one articles on English and European furniture.)

Furniture History 30 (1994). v + 182 pp.;

numerous bw illus. (This issue of the annual journal contains eleven articles on English eighteenth-century furniture. See esp. Adam Bowett on commercial introduction of mahogany and John Cross on the timber industry in London.)

Gavin, Robin Farwell. *Traditional Arts of Spanish New Mexico: The Hispanic Heritage Wing at the Museum of International Folk Art.* Sante Fe: Museum of New Mexico Press, 1994. 96 pp.; numerous color illus., bibliography. (Includes some furniture.)

Gordon, Glenn. "The Bowback Chair of Dennis Young." *American Craft* 53, no. 4 (August/September 1993): 26–31, 53–55. Color and bw illus.

Gordon, Robert B., and Patrick M. Malone. *The Texture of Industry: An Archaeological View of the Industrialization of North America.* New York and London: Oxford University Press, 1994. xi + 442 pp.; numerous bw illus., bibliography, index. (Some references to woodworking.)

Graham, Clare. *Ceremonial and Commemorative Chairs in Great Britain.* London: Victoria and Albert Museum, 1994. 134 pp.; illus., bibliography, index.

Gray, Nina. "Leon Marcotte: Cabinetmaker and Interior Decorator." In *American Furniture 1994,* ed. Luke Beckerdite, pp. 49–72. Milwaukee, Wis.: Chipstone Foundation, 1994. 36 color and bw illus. Distributed by University Press of New England, Hanover, N.H.

Greenhalgh, Paul, comp. and ed. *Quotations and Sources on Design and the Decorative Arts.* Manchester, England: Manchester University Press, 1993. 246 pp.; bibliography. Distributed by St. Martin's Press, New York.

Gruber, Alain, ed. *The History of Decorative Arts: The Renaissance and Mannerism in Europe.* Trans. John Goodman. New York: Abbeville, 1994. 495 pp.; 829 color and bw illus., appendixes, glossary, bibliography, index.

Gustafson, Eleanor H. "Museum Accessions." *Antiques* 146, no. 6 (December 1994): 744. 3 color illus. (Re high-style Boston rococo side chairs, 1760–80, from the De Wolf family set, acquired by the Museum of Art, Rhode Island School of Design, Providence.)

Hamilton, John D. *Material Culture of the American Freemasons.* Lexington, Mass.: Museum of Our National Heritage, 1994. xii + 308 pp.; 34 color and 225 bw illus., line drawings, appendixes, index. Distributed by University Press of New England, Hanover, N.H. (See esp. chapter 3 on lodge furnishings.)

Hammel, Lisa. "Wendy's World." *American Craft* 53, no. 1 (February/March 1993): 28–31. 7 color illus. (Re Wendy Maruyama.)

Harwood, Barry R. "Two Early Thonet Imitators in the United States: The Henry L. Seymour Chair Manufactory and the American Chair-Seat Company." *Studies in the Decorative Arts* 2, no. 1 (Fall 1994): 92–113. 23 bw illus.

Hawley, Henry. "An Indo-American Tall Clock." *Bulletin of the Cleveland Museum of Art* 80, no. 4 (April 1993): 170–73. 3 bw illus.

Hays, John. Review of David L. Barquist, *American Tables and Looking Glasses in the Mabel Brady Garvan and Other Collections at Yale University.* In *American Furniture 1994,* ed. Luke Beckerdite, pp. 238–40. Milwaukee, Wis.: Chipstone Foundation, 1994. Distributed by University Press of New England, Hanover, N.H.

Heckscher, Morrison H. "English Furniture Pattern Books in Eighteenth-Century America." In *American Furniture 1994,* ed. Luke Beckerdite, pp. 172–205. Milwaukee, Wis.: Chipstone Foundation, 1994. 23 color and bw illus., checklist and catalogue of English furniture pattern books. Distributed by University Press of New England, Hanover, N.H.

Hodges, Theodore B. *Erastus Hodges, 1781–1847: Connecticut Manufacturer, Merchant, Entrepreneur.* West Kennebunk, Maine: Phoenix Publishers, 1994. 359 pp.; 170+ bw illus., index.

Howe, Katherine S. "Gustave and Christian Herter: The European Connection." *Antiques* 146, no. 3 (September 1994): 340–49. 9 color and 7 bw illus.

Howe, Katherine S., Alice Cooney Frelinghuysen, Catherine Hoover Voorsanger, Simon Jervis, Hans Ottomeyer, Marc Bascou, Ann Claggett Wood, and Sophia Riefstahl. *Herter Brothers: Furniture and Interiors for a Gilded Age.* New York: Harry N. Abrams in association with the Museum of Fine Arts, Houston, 1994. 272 pp.; 133 color and 167 bw illus., appendixes, chronology, bibliography, index.

Humbert, Jean-Marcel, Michael Pantazzi, and Christine Ziegler. *Egyptomania: Egypt in Western Art, 1730–1930.* Paris: Réunion des musées nationaux; Ottawa: National Gallery of Canada, 1994. 607 pp.; numerous color and bw illus., bibliography.

Hunting, Mary Anne. "The Reform Club in London: A Nineteenth-Century Collaboration." *Antiques* 145, no. 6 (June 1994): 878–85. 7 color and 6 bw illus.

Hutchins, Catherine E., ed. *Everyday Life in the Early Republic.* Winterthur, Del.: Winterthur Museum, 1994. 369 pp.; numerous bw illus., tables, line drawings. (See esp. the article by Barbara McLean Ward cited elsewhere.)

Hutchins, Catherine E., ed. *Shaping a National Culture: The Philadelphia Experience, 1750–1800.* Winterthur, Del.: Winterthur Museum, 1994. x + 375 pp.; numerous bw illus. (See esp. the articles by Luke Beckerdite, Deborah Anne Federhen, David L. Barquist, and Nancy Goyne Evans cited elsewhere individually.)

Jackson, Lesley. *"Contemporary": Architecture and Interiors of the 1950s.* London: Phaidon Press, 1994. 240 pp.; numerous color and bw illus., glossary, appendix, bibliography, index.

James, Michael L. *Drama in Design: The Life and Craft of Charles Rohlfs.* Buffalo: Burchfield Art Center, Buffalo State College, 1994. 104 pp.; 85 color and bw illus., appendixes, bibliography, checklist of exhibition.

Kardon, Janet, ed. *Revivals! Diverse Traditions: The History of Twentieth-Cen-*

tury American Craft, 1920–1945. New York: Harry N. Abrams in association with the American Craft Museum, 1994. 304 pp.; 275 color and bw illus., resource list, bibliography, index. (Includes some colonial revival and other furniture.)

Kaye, Myrna. "Addendum: Discovering Portsmouth's Finials." *Maine Antique Digest* 22, no. 9 (September 1994): 11B. 6 bw illus.

Kaye, Myrna. "Discovering Portsmouth, New Hampshire's Premier Cabinetmaker." *Maine Antique Digest* 22, no. 7 (July 1994): 1B–4B. 21 bw illus. (Re Robert Harrold, working 1765–92.)

Kenny, Peter M. "Flat Gates, Draw Bars, Twists, and Urns: New York's Distinctive, Early Baroque Oval Tables with Falling Leaves." In *American Furniture 1994,* ed. Luke Beckerdite, pp. 106–35. Milwaukee, Wis.: Chipstone Foundation, 1994. 34 color and bw illus. Distributed by University Press of New England, Hanover, N.H.

King, Carol Soucek. *Furniture: Architects' and Designers' Originals.* Glen Cove, N.Y.: PBC International, 1994. 208 pp.; 350 color illus., appendixes, index.

Knell, David. *English Country Furniture: The Vernacular Tradition.* Princes Risborough, England: Shire Publications, 1993. 104 pp.; color and bw illus., bibliography, index.

Lahikainen, Dean. *In the American Spirit: Folk Art from the Collections.* Salem, Mass.: Peabody Essex Museum, 1994. 161 pp.; numerous color and bw illus., checklist. Also published as *Peabody Essex Museum Collections* 130, nos. 2/3 (April/July 1994): 1–161. (Contains two or three pieces of furniture and some wood carvings of interest to students of furniture.)

Lears, Jackson. *Fables of Abundance: A Cultural History of Advertising in America.* New York: Basic Books, 1994. xiv + 492 pp.; illus., bibliography, index.

Leath, Robert A. "Jean Berger's Design Book: Huguenot Tradesmen and the Dissemination of French Baroque Style." In *American Furniture 1994,* ed. Luke Beckerdite, pp. 136–61. Milwaukee, Wis.: Chipstone Foundation, 1994. 6 bw illus., and 18-page color and bw facsimile reprint of design book of Jean Berger (w. ca. 1718-32). Distributed by University Press of New England, Hanover, N.H.

Lesko, Diane, ed. *Catalogue of the Collection: Museum of Fine Arts, St. Petersburg, Florida.* St. Petersburg, Fla.: By the Museum, 1994. 338 pp.; numerous color and bw illus., index. (Includes a few pieces of furniture.)

Lindquist, David P., and Caroline C. Warren. *English and Continental Furniture with Prices.* Radnor, Pa.: Wallace-Homestead Book Co., 1994. viii + 232 pp.; 400+ color and bw illus., bibliography, index.

Lindsey, Jack L. "Cedar Grove: A Quaker Farmhouse near Philadelphia." *Antiques* 146, no. 6 (December 1994): 776–85. 16 color illus.

Ly, Tran Duy. *Long Case Clocks and Standing Regulators.* Part 1, *Machine Made Clocks.* Fairfax, Va.: By the author, 1994. 504 pp.; 1,150+ bw illus., index.

Lyons, Mary. *Master of Mahogany: Tom Day, Free Black Cabinetmaker.* New York: Charles Scribner's Sons, 1994. 42 pp.; color and bw illus. (For young readers.)

McBrien, Johanna. "The Cabinetmakers of Portsmouth, New Hampshire, 1798–1837." In *Emerging Scholars in American Art: Proceedings from the First Annual Symposium,* ed. Edward S. Cooke, Jr., pp. 71–108. Boston: Department of American Decorative Arts and Sculpture, Museum of Fine Arts, Boston, 1994. 11 xerographic illus.

McCauley, Daniel J., III. "The Paintings of Henry and Elizabeth Lapp." *Folk Art* 19, no. 3 (Fall 1994): 53–61. 7 color illus.

McGaw, Judith A., ed. *Early American Technology: Making and Doing Things from the Colonial Era to 1850.* Chapel Hill: University of North Carolina Press, 1994. x + 482 pp.; illus., maps, bibliography, index.

McNeil, Peter. "Designing Women: Gender, Sexuality and the Interior Decorator, c. 1890–1940." *Art History* 17, no. 4 (December 1994): 631–57. 13 bw illus.

Marling, Karal Ann. *As Seen on TV: The Visual Culture of Everyday Life in the 1950s.* Cambridge, Mass.: Harvard University Press, 1994. 328 pp.; illus., bibliography, index.

Maxwell, James, and Shirley Massey. *Gothic Revival.* New York: Abbeville, 1994. 95 pp.; color and bw illus., bibliography.

[Metropolitan Museum of Art.] "Recent Acquisitions: A Selection, 1993-1994." *Metropolitan Museum of Art Bulletin* 52, no. 2 (Fall 1994): 54, 56–57, 61. 3 color illus. (Re side chair designed by Benjamin Latrobe, ca. 1808; Alexander Roux sideboard, ca. 1853–54; Herter Bros. chair, 1879–82.)

Michie, Thomas S. Review of Philip Zea and Robert C. Cheney, *Clock Making in New England, 1725–1825.* In *American Furniture 1994,* ed. Luke Beckerdite, pp. 240–44. Milwaukee, Wis.: Chipstone Foundation, 1994. Distributed by University Press of New England, Hanover, N.H.

Miller, Paul F. "The Gothic Room in Marble House, Newport, Rhode Island." *Antiques* 146, no. 2 (August 1994): 176–85. 9 color and 9 bw illus.

Mills, Angie. "Hosea Hayden: Homilies to Sit Upon." *Folk Art* 19, no. 3 (Fall 1994): 44–47. 1 color and 6 bw illus.

[Milwaukee Art Museum.] "Acquisitions." In *Annual Report 1993,* p. 19. Milwaukee, Wis.: By the Museum, 1994. 1 color illus. (Re cabinet, ca. 1904, by Byrdcliffe Colony.)

Montgomery, Susan J. "A Material Culture Time Capsule: The Field-Hodges House in North Andover, Massachusetts." *Nineteenth Century* 14, no. 2 (1994): 10–15. 6 bw illus. (Includes some discussion of furniture.)

Moore, William D. "Selling the Sacred: Masonic Lodge Rooms, Their Furnishings, and Business, 1870–1930." In *Emerging Scholars in American Art: Proceedings from the First Annual Symposium,* ed. Edward S. Cooke, Jr., pp.

137–79. Boston: Department of American Decorative Arts and Sculpture, Museum of Fine Arts, Boston, 1994. 20 xerographic illus.

Moss, Roger W., ed. *Paint in America: The Colors of Historic Buildings.* Washington, D.C.: The Preservation Press, National Trust for Historic Preservation, 1994. 318 pp.; 90 color and 25 bw illus., bibliography, index. Papers from "Paint in America: A Symposium on Architectural and Decorative Paints," held in 1989.

[Museum of Fine Arts, Boston.] "Curatorial Departments: Acquisitions." In *The Museum Year, 1991–92: The One Hundred Sixteenth Annual Report of the Museum of Fine Arts, Boston,* p. 23. Boston: By the Museum, 1993. 1 bw illus. (Re Kimbel and Cabus desk, ca. 1876.)

[Museum of Fine Arts, Boston.] "Curatorial Departments: Acquisitions." In *The Museum Year, 1992–93: The One Hundred Seventeenth Annual Report of the Museum of Fine Arts, Boston,* p. 19. Boston: By the Museum, 1993. 1 bw illus. (Re Essex County high chest, ca. 1740–80.)

[Museum of Fine Arts, Boston.] "Curatorial Departments: Acquisitions." In *The Museum Year, 1993–94: The One Hundred Eighteenth Annual Report of the Museum of Fine Arts, Boston,* p. 19. Boston: By the Museum, 1994. 1 bw illus. (Re kast attributed to Roelof D. Demarest, ca. 1790–1810.)

Mussey, Robert, and Anne Rogers Haley. "John Cogswell and Boston Bombé Furniture: Thirty-Five Years of Revolution in Politics and Design." In *American Furniture 1994,* ed. Luke Beckerdite, pp. 73–105. Milwaukee, Wis.: Chipstone Foundation, 1994. 43 color and bw illus., appendix. Distributed by University Press of New England, Hanover, N.H.

Naeve, Milo M. "Craft and Art: A Review Essay." *Newsletter of the Decorative Arts Society* 3, nos. 1/2 (Winter/Spring 1994): 4–8. (A review of six books and seven exhibitions of arts and crafts objects, including shows on Charles Rohlfs and Joseph P. McHugh.)

National Association of Watch and Clock Collectors. *The Watch and Clock Museum of the National Association of Watch and Clock Collectors.* Columbia, Pa.: By the Association, 1993. Videotape.

Nicolle, George. *The Woodworking Trades: A Select Bibliography.* Plymouth, England: Twybill, 1993. 150 pp.; index. (English emphasis.)

Olmert, Michael. "Tools at an Exhibition." *Colonial Williamsburg* 17, no. 2 (Winter 1994/95): 45–54. Color illus.

Ottomeyer, Hans. *Mobel des Neoklassizimus und der Neuen Sachlichkeit: Katalog der Mobelsammlung des Munchner Stadtmuseums.* Munich and New York: Prestel, 1993. 234 pp.; numerous color and bw illus., bibliography, index.

Parissien, Steven. *Palladian Style.* London: Phaidon Press, 1994. 240 pp.; numerous color and bw illus., directory of designers, glossary, appendixes, bibliography, index. Distributed by Chronicle Books, San Francisco.

"Period Furniture Added to Moffatt-Ladd House's Collection." *Antiques and the Arts Weekly* (September 16, 1994): 107. 2 bw illus. (Re federal furniture and other objects acquired by an historic house in Portsmouth, New Hampshire.)

Pile, John. "Conservation by Design." *American Craft* 54, no. 2 (April/May 1994): 32–37, 76. Color illus.

Powell, Richard E., Jr. "Coachmaking in Philadelphia: George and William Hunter's Factory of the Early Federal Period." *Winterthur Portfolio* 28, no. 4 (Winter 1993): 247–78. 16 bw illus.

Priddy, Sumpter T., III, and Martha C. Vick. "The Work of Clotworthy Stephenson, William Hodgson, and Henry Ingle in Richmond, Virginia, 1787–1806." In *American Furniture 1994,* ed. Luke Beckerdite, pp. 206–33. Milwaukee, Wis.: Chipstone Foundation, 1994. 37 color and bw illus. Distributed by University Press of New England, Hanover, N.H.

Rauschenberg, Bradford L. Review of Luke Beckerdite, ed., *American Furniture.* In *Journal of Early Southern Decorative Arts* 20, no. 1 (May 1994): 91–95.

Regional Furniture 8 (1994): 1–92. Numerous bw illus. (Ten articles on English furniture.)

Roberts, Kenneth D., and Snowden Taylor. *Eli Terry and the Connecticut Shelf Clock.* 2d rev. ed. Fitzwilliam, N.H.: Ken Roberts Pub. Co., 1994. 384 pp.; 59 color and 500+ bw illus., 75 tables.

Rouland, Steve, and Roger Rouland. *Heywood-Wakefield Modern Furniture.* Paducah, Ky.: Collector Books, 1994. 352 pp.; illus.

Roycrofters, The. *Roycroft Furniture Catalog, 1906.* East Aurora, N.Y., 1906. Reprint. New York: Dover Publications, 1994. 64 pp.; 96 bw illus., 48 line drawings. (Reprint of *A Catalog of Roycroft Furniture and Other Things.*)

Ruhling, Nancy, and John Crosby Freeman. *The Illustrated Encyclopedia of Victoriana: A Comprehensive Guide to the Designs, Customs, and Inventions of the Victorian Era.* Philadelphia: Running Press, 1994. 208 pp.; 210+ color illus., bibliography, index.

Schorsch, David A. *Masterpieces from Two Distinguished Private Collections: American Folk Art and Furniture.* New York: David A. Schorsch Company, 1994. 65 pp.; color illus.

Smith, Terry. *Making the Modern: Industry, Art, and Design in America.* Chicago: University of Chicago Press, 1993. xvi + 512 pp.; 156 bw illus.

Sweet Dreams: Bedcovers and Bed Clothes. Text by Marianne Carlano. Boston: Museum of Fine Arts, Boston, 1994. Pamphlet. Illus.

Trent, Robert F. "A Channel Islands Parallel for the Early Eighteenth-Century Connecticut Chests Attributed to Charles Guillam." *Studies in the Decorative Arts* 2, no. 1 (Fall 1994): 75–91. 8 bw illus., appendix.

"Viceregal Cabinet Acquired." *Decorative Arts Guild of North Texas* (Newsletter) 3/4, nos. 3/1 (Summer/Fall 1993): 4–5. 2 bw illus. (Re cabinet made in the colonial Phillipines, ca. 1680–1700, of mahogany, mother of-pearl, and tortoiseshell, acquired by the Dallas Museum of Art for their Museum of the Americas.)

Ward, Barbara McLean. "Marketing and Competitive Innovation: Brands, Marks, and Labels Found in Federal-Period Furniture." In *Everyday Life in the Early Republic,* ed. Catherine E. Hutchins, pp. 201–18. Winterthur, Del.: Winterthur Museum, 1994. 8 bw illus.

Ward, Barbara McLean , ed. *Produce and Conserve, Share and Play Square: The Grocer and the Consumer on the Home-Front Battlefield during World War II.* Portsmouth, N.H. : Strawbery Banke Museum, 1994. 240 pp.; numerous color and bw illus., index. Distributed by University Press of New England, Hanover, N.H. (Includes some vernacular furniture.)

Ward, Gerald W. R. Review of Sheila Conner, *New England Natives: A Celebration of People and Trees.* In *American Furniture 1994,* ed. Luke Beckerdite, pp. 245–46. Milwaukee, Wis.: Chipstone Foundation, 1994. Distributed by University Press of New England, Hanover, N.H.

Ward, Gerald W. R., comp. "Recent Writing on American Furniture: A Bibliography." In *American Furniture 1994,* ed. Luke Beckerdite, pp. 247–56. Milwaukee, Wis.: Chipstone Foundation, 1994. Distributed by University Press of New England, Hanover, N.H.

Ward, Roger, and Patricia J. Fidler, comps. and eds. *The Nelson–Atkins Museum of Art: A Handbook of the Collection.* New York: Hudson Hills Press in association with the Museum, 1993. 414 pp.; numerous color and bw illus., index. (Includes a few examples of American furniture.)

Wilson, Eva. *Ornament: 8,000 Years: An Illustrated Handbook of Motifs.* New York: Harry N. Abrams, 1994. 208 pp.; 620 illus., bibliography, index.

Wooden Artifacts Group. *Abstracts of Papers Presented at "Painted Wood: History and Conservation," Williamsburg, Virginia, November 11th–14th, 1994.* Washington, D.C.: Wooden Artifacts Group of the American Institute for Conservation of Historic and Artistic Works, 1994. 65 pp. (Papers to be published later.)

Woods, Marianne B. "Viewing Colonial America through the Lens of Wallace Nutting." *American Art* 8, no. 2 (Spring 1994): 67–86. 25 color and bw illus.

Wright, John H. *Vernacular Visions: Folk Art of Old Newbury.* Newburyport, Mass.: Historical Society of Old Newbury, 1994. 119 pp.; 103 color and bw illus., bibliography, index. (Includes some furniture.)

Young, Anne Mortimer. *Antique Medicine Chests, or Glyster, Blister, and Purge.* Brighton, England: Vernier Press, 1994. 92 pp.; 12 color and 43 bw illus.

Zea, Philip, and Donald Dunlap, with measured drawings by John Nelson. *The Dunlap Cabinetmakers: A Tradition in Craftsmanship.* Mechanicsburg, Pa.: Stackpole Books, 1994. 210 pp.; 24 color and 68 bw illus., numerous line drawings, index.

1995 TITLES

"Be Seated." *American Craft* 55, no. 2 (April/May 1995): 56–59. 14 color illus.

Brander, Sue M. "Thomas Seymour's Chair: A Silent Witness to History." *Antiques and the Arts Weekly* (February 24, 1995): 48. 1 bw illus. (Re corner chair, ca. 1760–90, in collection of Hartford Steam Boiler Inspection and Insurance Co., said to have been used by distinguished personages in early America.)

Breed, Allan. "Remaking a Masterpiece." *Home Furniture,* no. 2 (Spring 1995): 18–23. 8 color illus. (Re reproduction of Newport desk and bookcase.)

Buchanan, Richard, and Victor Margolin, eds. *Discovering Design: Explorations in Design Studies.* Chicago: University of Chicago Press, 1995. 288 pp.; illus.

Burns, Charles J. "Newport in the Nineteenth Century." *Antiques* 147, no. 4 (April 1995): 564–69. 10 color illus. (Includes some furniture.)

Byars, Mel, with an introduction by Robert A. M. Stern. *The Chairs of Frank Lloyd Wright: Seven Decades of Design.* Washington, D.C.: The Preservation Press, National Trust for Historic Preservation, 1995. 168 pp.; 90 color and 110 bw illus.

Cantor, Jay. "The Nicholson Collection." *Christie's International Magazine* 12, no. 1 (January/February 1995): 18–21. 6 color illus.

Carpenter, Ralph E. "Newport: A Center of Colonial Cabinetmaking." *Antiques* 147, no. 4 (April 1995): 550–57. 12 color illus.

Christie's. *The Collection of Mr. and Mrs. Eddy Nicholson.* Sale 8082, New York, January 27–28, 1995. New York: Christie's, 1995. 392 pp.; numerous color illus. (Contains some furniture.)

D'Ambrosio, Anna T., with Stacy Pomeroy Draper. *Artistry in Rosewood: The Work of Elijah Galusha.* Utica, N.Y.: Munson–Williams–Proctor Institute, 1995. 6 pp.; 3 color and 6 bw illus. (A brochure accompanying exhibition of twenty pieces of furniture by Galusha [d. 1871] of Troy, N.Y., and his contemporaries.)

Ehninger, Jillian. "Furniture Hardware from the Boston Workshop of Henry K. Hancock." *Antiques* 147, no. 5 (May 1995): 732–39. 8 color and 6 bw illus.

Frelinghuysen, Alice Cooney. "The Aesthetic Movement in Newport." *Antiques* 147, no. 4 (April 1995): 570–77. 13 color illus. (Includes some furniture.)

Frelinghuysen, Alice Cooney. "Christian Herter's Decoration of the William H. Vanderbilt House in New York City." *Antiques* 147, no. 3 (March 1995): 408–17. 11 color and 7 bw illus.

George, Jennifer. *Collector's Guide to Oak Furniture: Identification and Values.* Paducah, Ky.: Collector Books, 1995. 126 pp.; 140 color illus.

Gustafson, Eleanor H. "Museum Accessions." *Antiques* 147, no. 5 (May 1995): 656, 658, 660. 3 color and 3 bw illus. (Re acquisitions of federal furniture by the Art Institute of Chicago; rococo furniture by the Los Angeles County Museum of Art; and a corpse preserver, ca. 1871, by the Connecticut Historical Society.)

Heckscher, Morrison H. "Copley's Picture Frames." In *John Singleton Copley in America,* by Carrie Rebora et al., pp. 143–59. New York: Metropolitan Museum of Art, 1995. Distributed by Harry N. Abrams. Color and bw illus.

Humphrey, Samuel A. *Thomas Elfe, Cabinetmaker.* Charleston, S.C.: Wyrick, 1995. xi + 116 pp.; color and bw illus., bibliography.

Hurst, Ronald L. "Prestwould Furnishings." *Antiques* 147, no. 1 (January 1995): 162–67. 11 color illus. (Re contents of historic house, built ca. 1794–95, near Clarksville, Virginia.)

Johnson, Bruce. *The Pegged Joint: Restoring Arts and Crafts Furniture and Finishes.* Asheville, N.C.: Knock on Wood Publications, 1995. 96 pp.; illus.

Johnson, Kathryn C., ed., with essays by Henry Adams, Richard Armstrong, Louise Lincoln, Evan M. Maurer, and Sarah Nichols. *Made in America: Ten Centuries of American Art.* New York: Hudson Hills Press, 1995. 192 pp.; numerous color and bw illus., index. (Includes some furniture.)

King, Thomas. *Neo-classical Furniture Designs: A Reprint of Thomas King's "Modern Style of Cabinet Work Exemplified," 1829.* Intro. by Thomas Gordon Smith. New York: Dover Publications, 1995. 128 pp.; illus.

Lewis, Johanna Miller. *Artisans in the North Carolina Backcountry.* Lexington, Ky.: University Press of Kentucky, 1995. xii + 200 pp.; illus., bibliography, index.

Lindsey, Jack L. Review of David L. Barquist, *American Tables and Looking Glasses in the Mabel Brady Garvan and Other Collections at Yale University.* In *Studies in the Decorative Arts* 2, no. 2 (Spring 1995): 102–3.

McClelland, Nancy A. "The Bayoud Collection of Works by Thomas Molesworth." *Christie's International Magazine* (May/June 1995): 26. 1 color illus.

Mahoney, Kathleen. *Gothic Style: Architecture and Interiors from the Eighteenth Century to the Present.* New York: Harry N. Abrams, 1995. 264 pp.; 258 color and 31 bw illus., bibliography, glossary.

Massey, James, and Shirley Maxwell. *Arts and Crafts.* New York: Abbeville, 1995. 96 pp.; 55 illus., bibliography.

"New-Grec Table at Brooklyn Museum." *Antiques and the Arts Weekly* (March 10, 1995): 101. 1 bw illus. (Re Neo-Grec white and gilt table attributed to Allen Brothers of Philadelphia, ca. 1875, acquired by the Museum.)

Olmert, Michael. "Tools at an Exhibition." *Colonial Williamsburg* 17, no. 2 (Winter 1994/95): 45–54. Color illus.

Raynes, Walter. "Choosing Brass Hardware for Period Furniture." *Home Furniture,* no. 2 (Spring 1995): 88–91. 6 color illus.

Rees, Jane, and Mark Rees, eds. *The Tool Chest of Benjamin Seaton: 1797.* n.p.: Tools and Trades History Society, 1995. 72 pp.; illus. Distributed by Astragal Press, Mendham, N.J.

Rieman, Timothy D. *Shaker: The Art of Craftsmanship, The Mount Lebanon Collection.* Alexandria, Va.: Art Services International, 1995. 178 pp.; numerous color and bw illus., line drawings, bibliography.

Rieman, Timothy D. "Shaker Built-In Furniture." *Home Furniture,* no. 2 (Spring 1995): 30–35. 9 color illus.

Robertson, Cheryl. Review of Wendy A. Cooper, *Classical Taste in America, 1800–1840.* In *Studies in the Decorative Arts* 2, no. 2 (Spring 1995): 98–102.

Robinson, Charles A., with an intro. by Philip Zea. *Vermont Cabinetmakers and Chairmakers Before 1855: A Checklist.* Shelburne, Vt.: Shelburne Museum, 1995. 126 pp.; 14 color and bw illus., index.

Sack, Israel, Inc. *Israel Sack Newsletter* 1, no. 1 (April 1995): 1–16. Color and bw illus.

Sanders, Barry. *A Complex Fate: Gustav Stickley and the Craftsman Movement.* Washington, D.C.: The Preservation Press, National Trust for Historic Preservation, 1995. 256 pp.; 35 color illus.

Solis-Cohen, Lita. "Magdalena Leininger's Dower Chest." *Maine Antique Digest* 23, no. 4 (April 1995): 10-A. 1 bw illus. (Re 1788 Berks County, Pennsylvania, chest sold at auction in England.)

Solis-Cohen, Lita. "A Video for Beginner and Expert Alike." Review of John Bivins, *Authenticating Antique Furniture,* videotapes. *Maine Antique Digest* 23, no. 4 (April 1995): 6-B. 1 bw illus.

Stayton, Kevin L., and Martha Deese. "The Patented Folding Mirrors of Peter Wiederer's Firm, New York City, 1880s–1905: Technology, Style, and Marketing." *Studies in the Decorative Arts* 2, no. 2 (Spring 1995): 29–47. 10 bw illus.

Sullivan, Edward J., Ruth Krueger Meyer, et al., eds. *The Taft Museum: Its History and Collections.* 2 vols. in hardcover, or 4 vols. in paperback. New York: Hudson Hills Press, 1995. 724 pp.; 630 color and 387 bw illus., index. (Includes some American furniture in vol. 1. See "Furniture and Interior Decoration at the Taft Museum," by Lisa Krieger [pp. 73–87] and "American Furniture" by Lisa Krieger [pp. 88–116.])

Talbott, Page. "Classical Furniture in Savannah, Georgia." *Antiques* 147, no. 5 (May 1995): 720–31. 19 color and 2 bw illus.

"Three Centuries of High-Style Furniture in L.A. Exhibition." *Antiques and the Arts Weekly* (April 21, 1995): 75. 4 bw illus. (Re exhibition entitled "Common Forms, High Art: Three Centuries of American Art," at Los Angeles County Museum of Art, composed of two hundred objects from the Museum's permanent collection. Partial tour of the exhibition available from LACMA on CD-ROM.)

Venable, Charles. "Herter Brothers: A Golden Age of Furniture." (Exhibition review.) *Apollo* 140, no. 395 (January 1995): 49–50. 1 bw illus.

Voorsanger, Catherine Hoover. "Gustave Herter, Cabinetmaker and Decorator." *Antiques* 147, no. 5 (May 1995): 740–51. 18 color and 1 bw illus.

Webster, Donald Blake. "The Furniture of New France." *Antiques* 147, no. 2 (February 1995): 298–307. 16 bw illus.

West, James T. "Vermont Clockmaker Jeremiah Dewey." *NAWCC Bulletin* 37, no. 2 (April 1995): 219–24. bw illus.

Whisker, James B. *Pennsylvania Clockmakers and Watchmakers, 1660–1900.* Lewiston, N.Y.: Mellen Press, 1995. 372 pp.

Willard, William L. "Thomas Harland: Clockmaker, Watchmaker, and Entrepreneur." *NAWCC Bulletin* 37, no. 2 (April 1995): 185–96. bw illus., figures.

Witt-Dorring, Christian. "Drawing Instruction for Viennese Cabinetmakers." *Antiques* no. 1 (January 1995): 174–83. 16 color illus.

Wittkopp, Gregory. "Saarinen House, Bloomfield Hills, Michigan." *Antiques* 147, no. 5 (May 1995): 752–61. 12 color illus.

Wittkopp, Gregory, ed., with intro. by Roy Slade and essays by Gregory Wittkopp and Diana Balmori. *Saarinen House and Garden: A Total Work of Art.* New York: Harry N. Abrams, 1995. 176 pp.; 150 color and 58 bw illus., bibliography, index.

Zimmerman, Philip D., and Frank M. Levy. "An Important Block-Front Desk by Richard Walker of Boston." *Antiques* 147, no. 3 (March 1995): 436–41. 5 color and 3 bw illus.

Zogry, Kenneth Joel. *"The Best the Country Affords": Vermont Furniture, 1765–1850.* Bennington, Vt.: Bennington Museum, 1995. 176 pp.; 56 color and 145 bw illus., bibliography, index.

Zogry, Kenneth Joel. "Urban Precedents for Vermont Furniture." *Antiques* 147, no. 5 (May 1995): 762–71. 16 color and 1 bw illus.

Zygas, K. Paul, and Linda Nelson Johnson, eds. *Frank Lloyd Wright: The Phoenix Papers.* Vol. 2, *The Natural Pattern of Structure.* Tucson: University of Arizona Press, 1995. 159 pp.; 30 color and 57 bw illus.

Index